P9-EEL-403

Tracing Literary Theory

Tracing Literary Theory

Edited by
Joseph Natoli

University of Illinois Press
Urbana and Chicago

Manufactured in the United States of America
1 2 3 4 5 C P 5 4 3 2 1

This book is printed on acid-free paper.

Library of Congress Cataloging-in-Publication Data

Tracing literary theory.

Includes bibliographies and index.
Contents: Tracing a beginning through past theory voices / Joseph Natoli—Structuralism and critical history in the moment of Bakhtin / A.C. Goodson—Tracing hermeneutics / Albert Divver—[etc.]
1. Criticism—History—20th century. I. Natoli, Joseph P., 1943– .
PN94.T73 1987 801'.95 86-24982
ISBN 0-252-01383-2 (cloth)
ISBN 0-252-01384-0 (paper)

I imagine the whole to be something like an immense novel, multi-generic, multi-styled, mercilessly critical, soberly mocking, reflecting in all its fullness the heteroglossia and multiple voices of a given culture, people and epoch.

—Mikhail Bakhtin,
The Dialogic Imagination

Contents

Preface

LITERARY THEORY EMERGES from two conditions or modes at the heart of Mikhail Bakhtin's theorizing: heteroglossia and dialogism. Heteroglossia describes a "basic condition governing the operation of meaning in any utterance. . . . At any given time, in any given place, there will be a set of conditions—social, historical, meteorological, physiological—that will insure that a word uttered in that place and at that time will have a meaning different than it would have under any other conditions; all utterances are heteroglot in that they are functions of a matrix of forces practically impossible to recoup, and therefore impossible to resolve."[1] A world dominated by heteroglossia expresses itself in the epistemological mode of dialogism. "Everything means, is understood, as a part of a greater whole—there is a constant interaction between meanings, all of which have the potential of conditioning others."[2] This "dialogic heteroglossia" creates a universe of voices or perspectives with which we interweave our own voice, our word with the alien word. Theory is therefore in a state of being "always already," so that to enter it is really to be already into it and therefore "beginnings" have a suspect validity. To achieve an "ending," a sense of closure, is an equally suspect task. And in the very midst of saying something about theory we are equally in the midst of a still-operant theorizing. Thus theory itself inevitably discloses a fissure, an opening in any attempt to create a smooth, polished narrative surface for theory, one with an unproblematic origin, middle, and ending.

The state of theory at this moment is like a crucial moment in a well-publicized, perhaps extremely delicate operation. All the surgeons are at their posts, everything they need is in the room, and the body—theory—is being handled with great care. What is the next step to be taken? The operation has gone on for so long, the records show such an exhaustive series of exploratory probings, counterindications, silences, anxieties, timidities, rhetorical extravagances, deferments that we have reached the stage where a summary, a "history" of the encounter, is needed. But histories of theory also fall within the province of theorizing itself and are rendered suspect. Intentions and the identities which spawn them are problematic, as they are themselves always already shot through with the voices of others, always already mixed within an internalized dialogic. The clarity of single, wholly self-possessed, distinct voices meeting other such voices in a traditional dialogue can no longer be offered.

This collection cannot detour around or fly over this moment in theorizing. It is simply not possible to extricate this "history" from within the carnival of theory itself, to remain un-self-reflexive and un-self-critical under a white flag of an "objective, historical review," a "state-of-the-art summary." "This is a moment for scrupulous clarity," A. C. Goodson wrote to me in the last stages of preparing the collection, "after a time of *engouement* with critical terminology." Perhaps our fascination at this moment for critical theory is also a fascination which threatens us. It chokes us but at the same time fascinates us, draws us further and further into it. But it is part and parcel of this fascination of which we are dangerously filled to the brim to yet remain self-reflexive, to remain scrupulously observant within the carnival while yet adding our own voices to it.

In the face of all this, it must yet be said that *Tracing Literary Theory* undoubtedly has a beginning, which it at once attempts to displace; goes on for hundred of pages; and ends, although it attempts to end without imposing closure; and presents voices which attempt to reveal the theory body which it comprises. That revelation involves leaving the theory body circumscribed and yet open, leaving it a shape both delineated in itself and yet diffused in its interaction with the world. This attempt at tracing a shape to theory within a suspect history by means of suspect intentions generates a certain fear and trembling, an angst, at the threshold, at the portals of preface. To rush into this operating room bearing all the accoutrements of a theoretically unselfconscious age (when?) is like entering with muddy boots and all the instruments no longer fit for the job. To rush in and to be expecting to be standing on something. Or outside something. "There is no way," Jay Martin writes, "to find an Archimedean point outside the hermeneutic circle."[3]

This collection forms a first-order narrative—a narrative which, according to Jean-François Lyotard, gives up all claim to a metanarrative or higher order of knowledge—of contemporary literary theory in its interrelationship with other discourses, discourses which have interpenetrated literature and established a dialogue with it. The "tracing" of this body thus involves a number of narratives, none of which eschew facts or meaning. Jane Tompkins has pointed out that "facts and meanings have not disappeared with the advent of poststructuralism, it is just that we no longer regard them as absolute but as dependent upon the interpretative codes that fill our consciousness."[4] And John Searle has argued that we do indeed proceed in the absence of firm metaphysical foundations. Especially in the case of this present historical survey of theory, we proceed in the absence of firm external points of reference in both history and source. "The only foundation," Searle writes, "that language has or needs is that people are biologically, psychologically, and socially constituted so that they succeed in using it to state truths, to give and obey orders, to express their feelings and attitudes, to thank, apologize, warn, congratulate."[5]

Thus the reader's consideration of these first-order narratives inevitably involves the kind of rational critique—the power of reflective understanding which Jürgen Habermas argues for—a critique which the intertextuality of the essays demands. But it also inevitably involves an attending to each essay with a certain pragmatism, a pragmatism "where knowledge is conceived as the ongoing process of reflective adjustment between various cultural needs and interests."[6] Deconstruction stands at the pinnacle of this collection, overshadowing and tempering a move toward both metanarrative and theory-as-first-order narrative. Deconstruction, in the words of Christopher Norris, "is most importantly a textual activity that works to undermine the kinds of consoling self-image given back by a dominant cultural tradition."[7] It can operate, in short, against a "pragmatic" reading. But it is also undeniably a "handy ruse for dismantling the truth-claims of philosophers from Plato to Heidegger"—for dismantling, in short, metanarratives which privilege a "power of reflective understanding."[8]

Within the intertextual domain of these essays, deconstruction's voice modulates the reader's move toward metanarrative *and* toward theory-as-narrative. The Derridean sense of "trace" also modulates the traditional voice of historical survey, as there is in each of these essays a referring back to what is absent—a trace of what has come before in the chain of signification—as well as a referring forward to what is also absent—a trace of what ensues, of the future. There is a tendency to erase the present or, in an often-used word, to make it "indeterminate." The essays, then, are divided by past and future yet in themselves are not privileged constructions in the chain of signification which is literary theory. Thus by tracing literary theory we are not so much deconstructing that effort but placing it within the unprivileged ranks of rhetorical temporality. To some extent this is commensurate with Terry Eagleton's view of rhetorical discourse and the structural implications involved. These essays attempt, similarly, to see how the interrelationship of different discourses has been structured and organized, and, variously, to examine such effects.

However, the essential function here is dialogic—grounded in the openings of the theory body—and not structural—grounded in the regular surface of binary opposition. Language itself is the site of this dialogized heteroglossia. "The word, directed toward its object, enters a dialogically agitated and tension filled environment of alien words, value judgments and accents, weaves in and out of complex interrelationships, merges with some, recoils from others, intersects with yet a third group."[9] Our words make up a carnivalization of critical discourse, one which balances a continual dialogizing of one's own word and the alien word, a continual effort to reveal "ever new ways to mean" and discourse's "power to mean in real ideological life."[10] Our words are always already laden with a pluralism of contending discourses, a heteroglossia, which seeks to reveal meaning "with dialogic vigor and a deeper penetration into discourse itself."[11] Just as our own personal ideological development is "an intense struggle within us for hegemony among various available verbal and ideological points of view, approaches, directions and values," so too does each contributor in this collection seek to overcome heteroglossia, seek to achieve "a real although relative unity."[12]

A reader's desire for ideological hegemony, for unity, parallels that of each contributor, but in the situation of each such closure is denied, is subverted by a carnivalesque interpenetration of voices. The awareness of a continual interplay of intertextuality ultimately exposes—traces—the lineaments of the theory body. Every text, according to Julia Kristeva, forms a mosaic of quotations, every text involves assimilation and alteration of another text. Because every "text echoes another text unto infinity, weaving the fabric of culture itself," a text of culture inevitably constrained by language, no one text has a "pure" being, in Bakhtin's terms, a voice that does not already partake, interact, emerge from other voices.[13] In Derridean terms, each text—each essay, for instance, in this collection—holds a trace of another text, another essay. Derrida's notion of *différance*—of deferment (tying text to text, past and future texts) and difference (tying the existence of one text to its distinction from another text)—renders any text itself a trace of another text, a trace of a presence and absence only perceived within a never-ending chain of texts, of signifiers, of language.

Each essay here then serves as a context for every other essay, thus placing the "meaning" one derives from any one essay within a dynamic back-and-forth reading of the whole, a reading in which similarities and identities may give way to differences and differences may collapse into identities. What is present in any one essay is present in terms of its interpenetrations with what is absent in itself and in other essays; what is absent in any one essay emerges from a context of what is present in itself and in other essays. Presence and absence alter within the same essay as the force of intertextuality recreates both after-the-fact, so that the last essay here, on semiotics, may serve as the precursor to a reading of the first essay, on structuralism, and reveal what was always present but not perceived, what was always absent but not perceived. Just as the context of one essay serves as a frame for the reading of another essay, and vice-versa, so too does the reader, each reader of this collection, inevitably read through his or her own lens so that the reader's own history is a text which interpenetrates the texts of these essays. Within this wide-ranging, shifting universe of intertextuality, the reader attempts to shape interpretation, meaning, understanding, even against the force of a polyphony of voices interpenetrating the reader and the force of an inescapable *différance*. Therefore both presence and absence in any one essay are modulated, strung out in an intertextual fashion over the entire collection and begin to "wiggle" the reader toward a dilemma in reading, a dilemma with which the substance of the collection is engaged.

This intertextuality of voices is not grounded here in this prefactory "point of origin," but the preface is itself somewhere in the interweaving, and intertextuality itself becomes subject to intertextuality. In his essay on history, Daniel Stempel writes that a "program of a temporal intertextuality which reads backward in order to read forward is only another variant of the history founded on the reading of sacred texts; it transforms history into prophecy and reduces each rhetorical innovation to mere prolepsis" (96). Fredric Jameson, in Eva Corredor's estimation, presents a view of history as providing "the unity of all collective narrative, of all texts and cultural manifestations. Lacan's psychoanalysis, stylistics, semiotics, ethical and structuralist criticism fall into the same all-encompassing cultural category. Jameson views literature, and we could say any *text*, as a 'socially Symbolic Act'" (108). And Corredor's text resonates in the context of Carolyn Allen's words on feminist literary criticism, which, "with its emphasis on canon reformation and women's literary tradition, is for some feminists becoming cultural criticism, which integrates a revisionist postmodern discourse with feminist social and political theory. . . . Seen from one angle feminism, with its commitment to material change, has nothing in common with postmodernism and its preoccupation with language and the free play of signifiers" (278–79).

A context for both Corredor's and Allen's texts may be Barney's: "Marxism provides deconstruction a needed socio-political context for its operation, and it gives feminism a much more effective means for analyzing the social and economic position of women. Deconstruction brings to both its collaborating perspectives a set of powerful strategies for locating the philosophical and metaphysical assumptions that undergird the phenomena of social organization" (202). According to Barrie Straus, the rewritings of deconstruction "also pointed out the main problem with speech-act theory: its model of textuality as a human voice" (244–45). But it is feminist criticism that Straus sees as generating a countertext to this: "Speech-act theory needs to take into account what difference the presence or absence of women's voices or women as speaking subjects makes in literary and other discourses" (245). The "anthropomorphism" of Straus's speech-act theory is itself read in terms of the phenomenology described by Herman Rapaport, a phenomenology which is also intertwined with deconstruction. "Unfortunately," Rapaport writes, "Merleau-Ponty died in the early 1960s, and there is good cause to believe that, had he lived, the Derridean analysis which followed *Signs* would have influenced Merleau-Ponty to develop his phenomenological investigations in ways that would have allowed us to follow a deconstructive path less hostile to the notions of consciousness and more open to epistemological researches" (174).

And Rapaport's contention "that phenomenology itself is the basis out of which the newer languages of criticism and theory rise" reads back to the first essay of the collection, on structuralism, and A. C. Goodson's contention that "Eagleton's projected revival of rhetoric is only the visible tip of a real structural legacy to Anglo-American critical practice. It is not just a terminology that has been propagated, but a sense of language as an institution within which literature performs" (49). Both provide an intertextual relationship with Corredor's text: "By continuously challenging itself and other existing discourses, [Marxism] has contributed to the modification and 'correction' of extreme structuralism, modernism, deconstruction, and reader-response. Its dialogue with its own past and the other theoretical present curtailed the arrogance and possible monopoly of any one of them" (123). This self-critical, continually questioning aspect is what Albert Divver claims for Gadamer's hermeneutical philosophy which questions "dogmatic adherence to systems of explanation that claim to have grounded their applications in first principles. For Gadamer, first principles are precisely those aspects of thinking which demand the crucial perspective of self-reflective historical understanding" (76).

Stempel's text on a hermeneutic historical understanding interacts here, and the intertextual dialogue between his text and that of Divver is indeed rich. "The limitations," Stempel writes, "of Bloom's hermeneutic history, and perhaps of all hermeneutic histories, are inherent in the model of perspective, which is so fundamental to Husserl's phenomenology. The horizon of the reading, which is ideally fused with the horizon of the text, is only one element of this model: the fine adjustments of focus in close reading are important, but so is the breadth of the field of vision. The critic who peers into history by using a magnifying glass on texts may see further but see less than the critic on a mountain top using his own unaided vision" (100). "Gadamer," Divver writes, "offers the example of translation from a foreign language as evidence that the act of interpretation is always a translation and that understanding is always an interpretation. Understanding is an interpretation of the tradition, which is itself preserved primarily in texts" (76). "The hermeneutic critic," Stempel writes, "chooses a set of texts to form a canon then goes on to argue that tradition is nothing more than a linking of the texts and their readings in some sort of diachronic or pseudodiachronic order" (96). And we hear Rapaport tell us that his "essay will outline four important position papers written by major phenomenologists in order to demonstrate how phenomenology has been crucial for much contemporary theory. . . . This survey is largely historical in outlook" (148).

But neither history, historical outlook, nor interpretation is presented as an univocal text in this collection. "The basic problem of placing the work of art in a historical context has not changed," Stempel writes, "but the analysis of the problem has been recast in terms of a new approach to textual analysis and interpretation. It is worthwhile, I think, to take a second look at deconstruction and its complex relation to history which is epitomized in the confrontation of Derrida and Foucault, grammatology versus archaeology" (81–82). Confrontation in the Derridean view generates a context which redescribes a traditional notion of confrontation. "First," Irene Harvey writes, "it is clear that univocity, unity, coherence, and systematic totality are not the aims of interpretation for [Derrida]. Indeed, the nature of textuality radically excludes these possibilities a priori. This nature entails at least two levels—one controlled by the author, one not; one declared by the author, one described; one metaphysical, one not; one entailing form, one content; one entailing a principle, one a practice, and so on. However, these levels are not related in an oppositional manner, nor in an hierarchical one. Instead, they are disjunctive with respect to their presentation to the 'reader'/interpreter" (142).

And this text of reader/interpreter itself must be read intertextually. "The transactional model," Gregory Colomb writes, "assumes that to practice a particular way of reading is to adopt a specific, though not necessarily well-defined, set of reading codes and that to adopt this or that way of reading is a matter not of literary necessity but of value-governed choice" (314). "A chapter on reading," Temma Berg writes/reads, "is, necessarily, concerned with difference. And certainly, as my calculated use of that over-determined term *différence* might indicate, my essay, as a whole, is meant to suggest that deconstruction has affected and continues to affect the course of reader-response theory" (248).

Thus the deconstructive voice continues to sound a strong intertextual note. Deconstruction "goes further than structuralist theories by claiming that language is also divided against itself. The rules that govern its structure are inconsistent, thus creating a text that at the simplest level states the impossibility of its own unity" (179). Barney's words here reverberate through the course of one's entire reading of these essays. But not monologically. "Again we engage the network of unlimited semiosis," Colomb declares, "although we should not conclude that unlimited semiosis leads us either to the domain of free play or to a prison house of language. In practice, the infinite chain of interpretants is broken by the demands of particular situations and the interests of the participants; and the multiplication of interpretants is precisely what makes meaning public, accessible, and so richly connected to our world" (337). "Finally," Harvey writes, "we wish to insist that this analysis is itself far from a so-called 'deconstruction of deconstruction.' Such a project seems to us nothing less than naive if one has not clarified in advance more precisely *what* the 'strategy of deconstruction' is and what notions of meaning, language, textuality, and understanding it entails as such" (139).

The dialogic context of intertextuality underlines the fact that any attempt at tracing literary theory in its present polyphonic, open form, tracing its present irregular surface, imposes an image of theory which in turn is constructed/deconstructed by its own voices. The image of the theory body which *Tracing Literary Theory* presents is a Rabelaisian one, one which Bakhtin has called the grotesque body:

> The grotesque body . . . is a body in the act of becoming. It is never finished, never completed; it is continually built, created, and builds and creates another body. Moreover, the body swallows the world and is itself swallowed by the world. . . . Next to the bowels and the genital organs is the mouth, through which enters the world to be swallowed up. And next is the anus. All these convexities and orifices have a common characteristic; it is within them that the confines between bodies and between the body and the world are overcome: there is an interchange and an interorientation.[14]

This grotesque body, this theory body, is traced within this collection in a carnivalesque fashion, one diametrically opposed to the smooth surface of what Bakhtin has called the "classic" mode.[15] The continuity and closure of the "entirely finished, completed, strictly limited body, which is shown from the outside as something individual" is replaced with that which "protrudes, bulges, sprouts, or branches off (when a body transgresses its limits and a new one begins)."[16] Continuity and closure are replaced with disruption-eruption and openness. Interpenetration here is between the grotesque body and the world in its carnivalesque guise; the world of carnival itself is a world of openings, of holes and tears in the fabric of the social order. The polyphony of the grotesque theory body attends to the voices of the carnivalesque world.

It is in this spirit, within this image, that the many voices of theory are sounded, each voice sounding its own monologic note, each becoming the voice of the "other." The heteroglossia of carnival becomes a ground for the heteroglossia of theory, and the Rabelaisian grotesque body becomes a ground for the theory body. Within carnival there is no notion of origin, of roots emerging from that origin, of history as firm ground, of success in establishing a position outside what we interpret, of, finally, tracing a firm Platonic order, a polished surface, which the tracing of literary theory reflects. To be without any of these, however, does not affect the impetus, the presentation, or the impact in a rhetorical setting of these essays. Indeed, *Tracing Literary Theory* follows in the wake of Frank Lentricchia's notion of an "after the new criticism," a debate, actually, which is both concerned and unconcerned with undecidable beginnings and ends as the subverters of historical referentiality. In this debate, literary history is viewed either as undecidable text endlessly rewriting itself or as part of "a thick reality of discourse" in which "literary, philosophical, scientific, and religious modes of writing find point of contact."[17] Yet another view might see literary history as a record of our consciousness of standing within a still-operant history of interpretation.

This presentation of theory emerges from a discursive context and contributes to it, but it is a presentation which is not intended to be itself theoretically ground breaking. Neither does it intend to engage in a one-upmanship in which the use of yesterday's terminology is indicted as a retrogressive act, nor does it attempt to contort itself ingeniously in an effort to shake off the anxiety of too-observable influences. It intends to present what has gone on in theory already, to go over old ground, to see and hear voices which make up the heteroglossia of theory—to do all this not only for those always already in theory but also for those who believe they are contemplating the theory body from a distance, from undergraduates to those teaching literature courses in a state of theoretical aporia or Johnsonian refutation and, finally, to those in other "disciplines" who feel, as Dominick LaCapra does, that "literary criticism and philosophy are in many ways the 'heavy sectors' of self-reflexive and self-critical theory at the present time."[18]

The theory carnival then is loud with many voices, but each voice, each chapter, in this collection is tempted, if you will, by monologism. Each tracing promises the closure which all monologism promises, its own monologism ultimately subverted by the heteroglossia of the collection as a carnival whole. Tracing does not circumscribe but leaves openings; the past interpenetrates both the present and the future. Time itself—a continuity of past, present, and future, so necessary to the discursive tracing of each theory voice—is subverted by a carnivalesque interpenetration. Thus, both the Derridean sense of absence and the Bakhtinian sense of opening modulate through their own voices the traditional voice of historical survey. The smooth, polished plane of linear time becomes the irregularity of temporal hills and valleys, of the inside of the past and the outside of the future, fashioning the surface plane of the present. A tracing in the present is thus an interpenetration of the past, an exchange leading to a reorientation.

NOTES

1. Michael Holquist, "Glossary," in M. M. Bakhtin, *The Dialogic Imagination: Four Essays,* ed. Michael Holquist, trans. Caryl Emerson (Austin: University of Texas Press, 1981), p. 428.
2. Ibid., p. 426.
3. Jay Martin, "Should Intellectual History Take a Linguistic Turn? Reflections on the Habermas-Gadamer Debate," in *Modern European Intellectual History*, ed. Dominick LaCapra (Ithaca: Cornell University Press, 1982), p. 102.
4. Jane Tompkins, "Graff Against Himself," *Modern Language Notes* 96 (1981), 1095.
5. John Searle, "The World Turned Upside Down," *New York Review of Books* 30 (October 27, 1983), 78.
6. Christopher Norris, *The Contest of Faculties* (London: Methuen, 1985), p. 148.
7. Ibid., p. 165.
8. Ibid.
9. Bakhtin, *The Dialogic Imagination*, p. 276.
10. Ibid., pp. 346, 352.
11. Ibid., p. 352.
12. Ibid., pp. 346, 270.
13. Jeanine Parisier Plottel, "Introduction" to *Intertextuality: New Perspectives in Criticism*, vol 2, ed. J. P. Plottel and Hanna Charney (New York: New York Literary Forum, 1978), p. xv.
14. Mikhail Bakhtin, *Rabelais and His World* (Bloomington: Indiana University Press, 1984), p. 317.
15. Ibid. The grotesque and classic canons are contrasted in chapter 5, "The Grotesque Image of the Body and Its Sources."
16. Ibid., p. 320.
17. Frank Lentricchia, *After the New Criticism* (Chicago: University of Chicago Press, 1980), p. 205.
18. Dominick LaCapra, "Introduction" to *Rethinking Intellectual History: Texts, Contexts, Language* (Ithaca: Cornell University Press, 1983), p. 15.

Acknowledgments

SINCE THIS COLLECTION has bibliographic intentions and emerges from my own bibliographic "monitoring" of theory, it is appropriate that I first acknowledge a debt to the unpublished structuralism bibliography of Eddie Yeghiayan, to Richard Barney's Society for Critical Exchange deconstruction bibliography and to Michael Clark's Michel Foucault bibliography as well as to the bibliographic assistance of my colleagues Michael Unsworth, Leena Siegelbaum, Anita Evans, and Mary Ann Tyrrell. Conversations with Alan Bewell amid the Irvine environment put an exclamation mark and a question mark next to the word "theory" in my mind, and in response to my ensuing questions Robert Newsom, Paul Armstrong, Gary Lee Stonum, Ellie Ragland-Sullivan, William Tyrrell, A. C. Goodson, Herman Rapaport, William Johnsen, and Eddie Yeghiayan wrote or spoke the kind of words that helped me cut up the theory pie. I am grateful to Alex Gelley, Jonathan Arac, Steven Mailloux, Wallace Martin, David Hoy, Marc E. Blanchard, Jane Tompkins, Elaine Showalter, Rodolophe Gasché, Sydney Janet Kaplan, and William Johnsen for helping me find contributors to this collection. James Sosnoski publicized the project in the Society for Critical Exchange Newsletter, and the response from Society members encouraged the project just at the right moment. At the writing stage, collaboration assumed center stage and to the contributors I express at once my gratitude for their industry and endurance and my hope that the collection as a whole meets their expectations. At the reading stage, I am of course grateful to the University of Illinois Press readers for their comments and to those who read portions of the whole: Joyce Ladenson, William Johnsen, A. C. Goodson, Temma Berg, Richard Barney, Herman Rapaport and all those others who read at the request of individual contributors. I am especially grateful to Lawrence Farese for a reading which worked simultaneously on the level of concrete particulars and abstract universals. At the publishing stage I am indebted to Ann Lowry Weir, senior editor at the University of Illinois Press for all those qualities which good editors display—an expeditious, intelligent efficiency as well as enthusiasm and concern—and to Cynthia Mitchell for her copyediting efforts. The time and attention I gave to this volume were taken from my personal life, from Elaine and my daughters, Amelia and Brenda. There is no way of repaying this debt, but I feel I must acknowledge it nonetheless.

Tracing Literary Theory

JOSEPH NATOLI

Tracing a Beginning through Past Theory Voices

> Fear can only enter a part that has been separated from the whole, the dying link torn from the link that is born. The whole of the people and of the world is triumphantly gay and fearless. This whole speaks in all carnival images; it reigns in the very atmosphere of this feast, making everyone participate in this awareness.
>
> —Mikhail Bakhtin, *Rabelais and His World*

In *The Crisis in Criticism* William Cain expresses an intention to delineate major trends and issues in theory in order to help "the general reader get his or her bearings."[1] Jonathan Culler in *On Deconstruction* expresses a similar intention. That book is directed to those "who, without reliable guides, find themselves at a modern Bartholomew Fair, contemplating what seems to them a 'blank confusion' of 'differences' that have no law, no meaning, and no end."[2] Cain is not concerned with somehow tying theory together, pursuing an argument from within theory itself, but rather he wishes to find a niche for theory within English studies: "We need to use and draw upon theory to specify the aims of work in English, the purposes of teaching, the skills and values that we seek to transmit in pedagogy and research."[3] Instead of slanting theory toward "close reading" as advocated by J. Hillis Miller, for example, we should slant it toward "questions of pedagogy, education, social and cultural practice."[4] And whereas English studies should be restructured, neither departments nor disciplines should be abolished. To seek their abolition would be to "indulge in an unreal and irrelevant gesture."[5] However, as intellectual workers, literary critics should "draw on many disciplines, contest the opposition between the canonical and non-canonical, and exhibit skills in a variety of culturally oriented ways."[6]

In Cain's view, over-zealous readers of Michel Foucault have espoused a kind of "institutional determinism," one which Cain counters with a traditional view of individuals and groups as "definers of reality." But I am not concerned here with either the placing of Foucault or the quick dismissal of both the structuralist and poststructuralist view of this issue. I believe that Frank Lentricchia's suggestion that Culler merited the MLA's imprimatur for making structuralism safe for us can apply to what Cain is doing here for all of literary theory.[7] That charge is inevitable, but it really doesn't affect the lurking presence beneath Cain's concerns. This presence can be first expressed as questions: Is literary theory a privileged discourse? Is it possible to say what its purposes and limitations are without already ascribing to a view which privileges it? Is it possible to consider theory in a pragmatic light, bring it into the institutional fold, recommend a course of assimilation without in some way establishing an image of theory, without drawing upon such a ground?

Cain's focus is on the crisis in criticism and its remedies. The theory body, rather than being presented as a whole, is got at piecemeal, through a number of texts. The intention is to remain pragmatic, untheoretical. Thus it is a matter not of absent texts but of treating the crisis in theory untheoretically, something we all know at this point cannot be done. Pointing out that Cain has less affiliation with the structuralists and Foucault than with Edward Said, less with Jacques Derrida than with the hermeneuticists, is probably less true than saying the ground for our trip through this book's Bartholomew Fair is yet another Bartholomew Fair that is uncharted.

Nevertheless, Cain's book commands a strategic timeliness on the literary scene. Undoubtedly both theory and literature, not to speak of pedagogy, practice, departments, and disciplines, are experiencing a "crisis." But the root of the crisis is "criticism," and the root of that criticism is theory—not just one theory but a myriad of theories. Howard Felperin has most recently pointed a finger at the deconstructionists as the cause of a widespread crisis in the house of literary studies: "They envision a carnivalization of the institution in which the old divisions between departments of national literature, between departments generally, disappears, and a new free play reigns, where students are given high marks for making puns and dispensing with footnotes."[8] Any overall consideration of theory, whether it be a collection of various essays or a monograph, involves, implicitly or explicitly, some image theoretically grounded on the theory body. If we are to "relate theory and practice, resist compartmentalization of work, and see theory as a source of new terms and tools for teaching as well as for research," we must first have that theory and practice, those terms and tools, within our grasp, and that can only occur once we are able to portray theory as a world, perceive some unity beyond all diversity, some harmony in contrariety.[9] I am not saying that a "correct" relationship between theory and practice is grounded in some prior romantic ground—a groundless theory—but that an image of how theory has its "being," how theories interweave and on what scale, must be necessarily grounded in a theory or theories.

This collection presents a heterogeneous image of theory in which the theory body of interconnected and interrelated discourses draw upon each other in differing fashions and with differing, often contrary, results. Thus in this collection the quest for unity and harmony is not for a monolithic, monologic unity and harmony but for a harmony which supports a Rabelaisian carnival image in which a cultural heteroglossia reigns—a new vision of reality created and opened, in Bakhtin's view, by the Russian Revolution and then closed and securely locked by Stalin. Not only is Bakhtin's view of reality as a carnival of heteroglossia the ground for *Tracing Literary Theory*, but also Bakhtin's apprehension of what is crisis and what is not, what is harmony and what is not, provides instructive analogies to our "crisis in criticism." This collection then is a cultural carnival in the sense of Bakhtin, a textual acknowledgment of the necessity of a cultural-discursive heteroglossia confronting the heteroglossia of literature without reducing either to "an impenetrable facade."[10] It replaces the classic canon of a neat-and-tidy, homogeneous reality with a vision of reality as carnivalesque, grotesque, and baroque.

Any attempt to unify interconnections of theory univocally

would be an obtuse transgression of the carnivalesque conception of reality. The entire collection is multivoiced in order to meet the multivoiced nature of a theory body in the present whose form emulates a carnivalesque reality. Issues and dilemmas and crises in the theory body are simultaneously issues and dilemmas and crises in carnival—all of which become the subject matter of *Tracing Literary Theory* and determine its form. In every respect then this collection is not merely a convenience apparatus but is a response in itself, in its own form, to the nature of a theory body grounded in carnival. And from within carnival there is an equal necessity to hear each voice in its own right.

Issues—pertinent to crucial—in any presentation of theory include dichotomies of theory and praxis, departments/disciplines and cultural heteroglossia, a privileged textuality and a theory heteroglossia. There are a variety of voices which attempt to drown out or subvert all other theory voices—a crucial issue in itself. But the force of the whole is against the erection of any "monologic" horizon. An equally crucial issue is the reduction of both theory and literature to a question of the determinacy or indeterminacy of meaning. All these issues are placed on carnival ground, a ground that is this collection's own ground and that is traced here, not directly, but by working through voices already sounded.

Behind crucial issues are voices, some equanimous, some strident. It is possible to look upon the diversity of people involved in theory from a political perspective, one which cannot be confined to the advocacy of particular theories but extends to the whole gamut which we associate with the political, rational, as well as so-called irrational factors. One can say that we have a diversity beyond *langue* and *parole,* a diversity that is ripe for a Foucauldian archaeological treatment. A Foucauldian "archaeology" does not restrain discourse within a "sign-thing" relationship as present in Ferdinand de Saussure's sense of both language and speech but attempts to reveal and describe underlying assumptions, gestures, rules, procedures. Such an archaeology of contemporary literary theory goes beyond the scope of this collection since it involves the "conditions of reality" behind each theory voice, "a set of 'positivities' that reveal discourse as a 'practice' and show that 'to speak is to do something—something other than to express what one thinks.'"[11] But one doesn't have to dig too deeply into the current polemics of theory to find that we have a Yale mafia and its ephebes (this same mafia has established tyranny at Yale!), deconstructive angels, cultural barbarians, weak textualists, canny and uncanny critics, hard- and soft-core deconstructivists, perennial positivists, charismocrats, hermeneuts for hire, purveyors of antihistorical viruses, and so on. In other words, there is a whole level of the colloquial carnival attached to the literary theory enterprise which has both more and less to do with determinate or indeterminate readings of what Derrida or Foucault or Bakhtin or anyone else has written. While Cain, among others, has pointed out the congruence of New Criticism and the Anglo-American mind-set, the continental theorists have experienced no such accommodation. Theory is seen as the alien Other, as in essence disruptive, intrusive, a transgression, a subversion—quite like literature itself both as an obvious transgression of a fixed, unified, and monologic order and as an exhibitor in its multivoiced guise of a heteroglossia which the carnival spirit reflects.

The diversity of theory after the New Criticism contributes to this cold reception, since profusion and lack of agreement seem to indicate that here chaos reigns because too many moorings have been unleashed, too many systematic mappings of the literary order have been violated. But this image is not apt in regard to the reality connection; it is not a matter of theory having more or less connections to reality in New Criticism and after-the-New Criticism. Certainly the romantic notion that whatever the imagination perceives is necessarily true cuts loose all moorings except the subject, and neither New Criticism nor what comes after is free and tied in precisely this way. While Derrida comes closest to this state—of not obstructing any word by attaching it to "reality"—Foucault attaches the word to the thickest, richest layers of "World." Both, however, annihilate the romantic notion of a subject. There are other images which would doubtlessly reverse polarities here—the tied would be untied, the untied would be tied. What we have on this level of theory discussion, and this is the level Cain wishes to affect, are not ideas and proponents but signs which cannot be separated from their settings, signs of varied settings and varied significance.

But Cain's intentions of bringing theory into the fold ascribes to a certain image, a certain semiology, in which literature is here, theory is there, pedagogy is someplace else, close readings are in yet another place. In Cain's view, literary theory is presented as reaching out to other discourses, reaching toward classroom practice, cutting itself off clearly and cleanly from New Criticism, putting neither all nor none of its eggs in the praxis basket, and, finally, tempering its excesses with the rod of pedagogy. The carnival image I propose for the present work is different. Theory is wrapped inextricably around and through and in other discourses, is both a product of them and a creator of them. This world of interaction between literary theory and other discourses is unamenable to pedagogy in the present because it challenges the very foundations of traditional conceptions of learning, of pedagogy, disciplines and departments—all of which Cain wishes to preserve. What Felperin has to say regarding deconstruction's influence on the Institution of Literature can reasonably be expanded to include all of present theory's influence: "We are dealing, after all, with recent institutional history to which most of us have borne witness, and it does not take a Michel Foucault to remind us of the will-to-power that inheres in any will-to-knowledge and its institutional discourse. Suffice it to say that considerable power was and still is at stake, nothing less than that latent in the pedagogical discourse and practice of literary study at all levels . . . so the anxiety has run high in proportion to the stakes at risk."[12]

Now a carnivalesque view of theory necessarily engenders a new kind of pedagogy, one that does not remain constrained by departmental and disciplinary boundaries. "While carnival lasts," Bakhtin writes in *Rabelais and His World,* "there is no other life outside. During carnival time life is subject only to its laws."[13] The crisis that Cain describes is thus carnival, the carnival of lost boundaries. The high anxiety that Felperin describes is also carnival, the carnival of lost continuity, a severance from the unity of the Western tradition, its "core values of reason and freedom," and its "preference for non-contradiction and for the ideality of the text."[14]

Culler also clearly knows what a carnival of theory implies and the difficulties of reducing heteroglossia to a monologic discourse. In his preface to *On Deconstruction,* he not only points out the existence of a lively and confusing debate about theory but intends to "undertake an exposition of issues that often seem poorly understood."[15] This exposition is not restricted to deconstruction but confronts "the confusing and confused notion of post-structuralism, or more specifically, the relation of deconstruction to other critical movements."[16] But Culler indicates where his poststructuralist focus fails to encompass all of theory—the voices not heard: Harold Bloom and René Girard remain outside this net, and feminist criticism does also. Culler does make an attempt to bring feminist approaches into the fold in his chapter on reading, but he admits that in "mapping contemporary criticism as a struggle between New Critics, structuralists and post-structuralists, one would find it hard to do justice to feminist criticism."[17] It would be hard indeed to place within the Bartholomew Fair of theory—what I have retraced positively as a Bakhtinian carnival—feminist discourse, which is as heterogeneous, as multivoiced as theory. In a heteroglossia of all worldly voices, theory and feminist discourse hear each other but do not strike the same note.

In describing works of theory, Culler states that though they may rely on familiar techniques of demonstration and argument their force comes "not from the accepted procedures of a particular discipline but from the persuasive novelty of their redescriptions."[18] In other words, when literary theory or feminist theory interconnect with other discourses, they affect them and are affected by them so that what was once a distinct and "pure" voice now becomes altered. Or, polyphony ultimately coheres into a dominant chord. In spite of Culler's expressed approval of the interdisciplinary fruitfulness of theoretical approaches, his obvious preference seems to be for harmony by means of the modulation of discordant notes. The antiritual doesn't receive a ritualized status; the ritualized redescribes it as ritual. The ritual of department and discipline are clear-cut entities to Culler as well as to Cain; they are real reference points, signifiers which one hesitates to suggest signify anything.

Unlike Cain, Culler is not in a rush to shore up the dam or resolve the conflict. Instead, he presents a confidence that department, discipline, pedagogy, practice, and theory all finally revolve centripetally around an unexpressed core—Literary Studies? Centrifugal forces only return, are eventually drawn back, to the center. But the crisis is more imminent elsewhere.

Reducing theory, as Steven Knapp and Walter Michaels do in "Against Theory," to "nothing else but the attempt to escape practice," which they argue no one can succeed in doing, would terminate not only literary theory but all theory connected with any discourse.[19] Such a result would be as meaningless as they suggest separating meaning from intention, language from speech acts, knowledge from true belief would be. Theory is not a search for a preeminent ground upon which to "govern interpretations of a particular text"—govern practice—but rather a discourse interpenetrating other discourses. This interpenetration, by virtue of its own dialogic existence, questions the isolation, integrity, telos, origin of established practices. Rather than seeking a preeminent ground for interpretation, its mode involves self-reflexiveness, difference, a questioning of limits—all of which result in a disruptiveness and intransitiveness in the face of traditional pedagogy and practice. Without such "theorizing," literary discourse would return to the fold which Daniel O'Hara calls "native American, fly-by-the-seat-of-one's-pants critical pragmatists and know-nothings."[20] But the ritual does not simply involve one discursive account deconstructing another discursive account, native American pragmatism being countered by a Rabelaisian license of theory.

My discursive account of the theory-praxis-department-pedagogy crisis is yet another chess move preceded by theory's discursive attempt to become a privileged ground for all and by Knapp and Michaels' discursive attempt to "unground" theory. If a Foucauldian *pouvoir-savoir* relationship exists here—a connection which infers a causal reciprocity between power and knowledge—then what prevails does so not because of a seemingly discursive inevitability but because it is an institutionalized discourse, one that fits within a cultural episteme and in turn lends its support to that episteme. A parallel with Bakhtin persists: how very little hope he must really have had to replace the centripetal forces of Stalinism with the centrifugal forces of carnival simply by describing the possibility of heteroglossia manifested in carnival. The Stalinesque outcome of October 1917 resolved, not sounded, a note of crisis. Quite obviously, to Bakhtin the moment of revolution was the carnival, a pre-text to heteroglossia. Carnival only becomes a crisis to be resolved once all forces are drawn inward, all notes return to scale.

In sounding *his* note of crisis, Robert Scholes in *Textual Power* sees the need of a "major rebuilding" by "repositioning or redefining literary study."[21] He doesn't redefine literary discourse in any earth-shattering way (his is a practice which draws upon theory, structural-semiotic preferred) but does indeed redefine literature itself. The theory-based practices that we employ to study literature should not be restricted to our literary canon but must extend to all texts. This is certainly a dramatic "crisis" move, one which Scholes does not attempt to establish within a survey of theory as Terry Eagleton does. But it is really not possible to trace theory's relation with practice without engaging, as Scholes does, the nature of literature itself. How theory serves practice and vice versa is a theoretical question about theory's relationship with literature. By maintaining that literature as well as all discursive disciplines and other nondiscursive disciplines stand beneath the umbrella of "textuality," Scholes is accepting a particular theoretical focus which enables him to resolve "crisis" by putting both theory and literature at the disposal of this "textuality." But it is the discursive text which has the power to draw all centripetal forces inward, to turn carnival into order on every level. Power lies with the text that promises a monologic unity; power lies with the critic of that text. Thus, much power is gained by such a simple redefining of "literature." Crisis is no longer carnival. Crisis is converted to triumph. Theory and practice and pedagogy remain untouched within formalized systems, those systems themselves unrestructured (perhaps expanded and renamed), as the voice of literature joins the chorus of text. There are, however, theory narratives which tell a story in which literature is not equatable with any discursive discourse, say, theory itself.

Frank Lentricchia in *After the New Criticism* locates a crisis in theory precisely in its own interrelationships and in its relationship with literature: "The crisis is generated . . . by, on the one hand, a continuing urge to essentialize literary discourse by making it a unique kind of language—a vast, enclosed textual and semantic preserve—and, on the other hand, by an urge to make literary language 'relevant' by locating it in larger contexts of discourse and history."[22] But it is Lentricchia himself who turns this apparent division, this confrontation, into a displacement. He argues for "an intertextual mingling among contemporary theorists . . . that the differences among contemporary theories are not clean discontinuities."[23] In his Afterword, he comments that this very intertextuality necessarily points out the "historicity of literature . . . its fundamental entanglement with all discourses."[24] Clean discontinuities do not exist in the theory carnival although they are in demand if a monologism is to be preserved. The historicity of literature is part and parcel of literature's entanglement with both a cultural heteroglossia and the entire theory body. Entanglement is carnival; enclosed, textual preserves enact monologic rituals.

When the dialogic entanglement between theory and literature, literature and heteroglossia is reduced to monologue—theory's voice sounding without literature and literature's voice sounding without its environment—then there is a need for this monologism to be resisted in order to save both theory and literature. In *The Subject in Question,* David Carroll argues for an interpenetrating relationship between theory and literature. In his view, literature, like theory, possesses a multiple nature penetrated by discourses "which are not strictly speaking original to it and whose history and implications it cannot totally make its own."[25]

Literature attracts very diverse considerations because it inhabits as diverse a terrain as theory. Literature's terrain is a refuge from the discourse of power. It is a polysemic discourse which transgresses the constraints and limitations of other discourses, a polysemic discourse which violates the rules which govern and limit the production of meaning. But literature's very transgression exists in an inevitable dialogic relationship with a cultural heteroglossia which is ultimately its ground. The many voices of literature—only a few of which may be culturally privileged—are voices which can be heard in the world. "We may call this world," Bakhtin writes, "the world that *creates* the text, for all its aspects . . . participate equally in the creation of the represented world in the text. Out of the actual chronotopes of our world (which serve as the source of representation) emerge the reflected and *created* chronotopes of the world represented in the work (in the text)."[26] Katerina Clark and Michael Holquist point out the historical nature of the nonliterary chronotope: "At different times, differing combinations of space and time have been used to model exterior reality. The most paradigmatic expression of past chronotopes is to be found in literary texts. Since authors model whole worlds, they are ineluctably forced to employ the organizing categories of the worlds that they themselves inhabit."[27]

Rabelais struck a note which the chronotope of his own age left unplayed, a note which ripped through that chronotope, a carnival note. He struck in fact many such notes, and Bakhtin declared himself a speaker of those previously "unheard" notes. What first emerges from a cultural heteroglossia—the myriad of voices both sanctioned and unsanctioned, said and unsaid, within any particular chronotope—and becomes literature is capable of being heard because heteroglossia is the ground for, is prior to, any particular chronotope. But it is the chronotope which is the bridge between real and represented worlds. Rabelais works through it, transgresses it, uses its words to speak the words of the Other, and ultimately leaves it torn open. Within and through and against the chronotope of Stalin, Bakhtin celebrates the carnival, epitomized in the work of Rabelais, work which was created within and through and against the chronotope of the Roman Catholic Church and the Holy Roman Empire. But Bakhtin's discursive text conceals its own transgression of the chronotope while pointing to the yet-unheard voices of Rabelais's world, a literary world which is not dependent on discursive concealment but whose very nature remakes a monologic chronotope into a carnival of heteroglossia.

Within the carnival, the social order is restructured and defiled. The chronotope of the social order remains the bridge between a literary world and a cultural heteroglossia. It becomes the mental lens, similar in function to the Kantian categories of time and space, by which and through which and against which other chronotopes are formed in literary worlds. World and represented world are "indissolubly tied up with each other and find themselves in continual interaction. . . . The work and the world represented in it," Bakhtin writes, "enter the real world and enrich it, and the real world enters the work and its world as part of the process of its creation, as well as part of its subsequent life, in a continual renewing of the work through the creative perception of listeners and readers. Of course this process of exchange is itself chronotopic: it occurs first and foremost in the historically developing social world, but without ever losing contact with changing historical space."[28]

If theory in its heterogeneous form draws upon literature, sets its camp so to speak in literature, it does so both to replenish itself and grow and to bring literature itself into the world. In this view, literature expresses what cannot be said discursively in the world, becomes a refuge site for "other" signifying practices, which can only be heard in a literary life-world. Theory, in turn, is a self-reflexive amalgam of discursive practices whose very diversity emulates literature itself. Theory subverts its own discursiveness by entering the literary life-world, an act which paradoxically extends its discursive nature by incorporating a voice or voices given to it by literature. Without doubt, Bakhtin's discursive eclecticism, one which exceeds the Stalinesque chronotope, enables him to hear Rabelais's carnival and is itself extended by such an encounter.

Rabelais's *Gargantua and Pantagruel* does not, however, become Bakhtin's *Rabelais and His World*. Bakhtin may enable us to hear the carnival voices in Rabelais's work but the voices themselves are sounded in Rabelais. We are led to the conclusion that, had literature and theory no relationship, no dialogic entanglement, literature would become inaudible, and all discursive practices would necessarily sound the note—often a monologism—of the prevailing chronotope. All this is somewhat more intricate than the theory-praxis connection maintains. The fear that Jeremy Hawthorn mentions in *Criticism and Critical Theory*—theory cutting us off from texts—is replaced in my view with the fear that without theory literature itself and its purposes and functions are cut off from us: the present and future Rabelais texts would remain unheard.[29] As the multivoices which ground all chronotopes and find expression in literature are not brought to us via literature, the need for the carnival text grows greater while simultaneously our capacity to hear such a text lessens. A one-fold tradition of encountering the polyphonic transgression that is literature serves the monologism of the prevailing chronotope but not literature or the cultural heteroglossia which is its true interlocutor.

Ultimately, any privileging of one voice above all voices is a Blakean, one-fold vision. Texts which privilege texts and textuality, the structural thread, human needs and interests, a "rhetoric-Marxism" are sounding one note. In such cases a privileged monologic voice sounding within theory rises above the carnival of theory itself. In some fashion, of course, all texts which seek the dominant chord are "crisis" texts, texts which attempt to subdue the discordant notes of theory by ignoring the disruption and openness of the postmodern and replacing it with an attempt at continuity and closure. Continuity and closure promise meaning and that issue shall be the last traced here. But first the monologic texts must be heard.

Like Cain and Culler, Ira Konisberg in his *American Criticism in the Poststructuralist Age* views the multivoiced nature of theory as not generating a new kind of practice, one compatible with carnivalesque reality, but as producing a temporary cacophony which an indefatigable literary study can assimilate within its own order, its own ritual.[30] And this order, according to Culler's *On Deconstruction,* Josué Harari's *Textual Strategies,* and John Fekete's *The Structural Allegory,* has its roots intertwined around one voice: poststructuralism is intertwined with structuralism from the start and is neither a replacement for structuralism nor a refutation of it.[31] The structural allegory becomes the mediator between encounters of theory and literature. Structuralism is the privileged thread that can be traced all through theory. But John Sturrock in his introduction to *Structuralism and Since* has difficulty in finding a common thread in the structuralism of Lévi-Strauss, Barthes, Foucault, Lacan, and Derrida. In his view the five coincide at some points and "at others they do not."[32]

Laurence Lerner's *Reconstructing Literature* faces the heterogeneity of theory with as firm a purpose in mind as Cain's. But while similar to Cain, who places theory under the restraint of worldliness and practice—"It is the duty of the intellectual worker . . . to resist theory when theory loses touch with the reality of 'human needs and interests' "—Lerner is more specific and sees us as "refusing to abandon our belief in reason, in the possibility of meaning, in the conception of literature and in the need for value-judgments."[33] Both Cain and Lerner subject theory to the very set of relations which theory questions, relationships supposedly grounded in a unified experience of order and its modes of being. Apparently, then, only a certain kind of theory, one which supports Cain's conception of human needs and interests, should be unresisted. Perhaps human needs and interests may be what Lerner defines them to be—our need to believe in reason, in the possibility of meaning, in the conception of literature, and in the need for value judgments. But perhaps even this is too limited for carnival.

In the Cain-Lerner view, when *la nouvelle critique*—that criticism which, according to Lerner, ascribes to both structuralism and political radicalism—transgresses these human interests and needs, it, *la nouvelle critique*, should be resisted. Of course one could define the criticism of the last two decades as no more than a transgression of what has been defined as "human interests and needs." In attempting to redefine the future of intellectual history according to Foucault, Mark Poster defines the same traditional grounds in the Western tradition in which literary studies are situated. But present questioning makes these grounds problematic: "It is legitimate to question the basis of this discipline, to ask if its project is defensible, to investigate its role in the cultural totality and to propose alternatives to it."[34] Again, the fact that theory in its diversity sets out to explore and question the foundations of these beliefs, these constructions (these are notes sounded within the carnival of theory), and place those foundations in question, place them in a setting in which they appear not so much intrinsic to what is human but as fashioned and reinforced by our very efforts to define our humanity, our world—all this precludes the possibility of restraining theory within such beliefs. When we sanction theory only so long as it remains answerable to that which it questions, theory inevitably has only one recourse—to become the stuff from which literature is made, to fight through the ritual of accepted discursive practices and find a voice in the carnival of literature. In some way centrifugal forces find place; the monologism of the authoritarian word–though it be a note sounded on behalf of what is perceived to be human interests and needs—is subverted, is countered by "other" words. An attempt to resolve the "crisis" in theory by measuring it with the rod of a prevailing rhetoric implicitly defines crisis as carnival. The many voices of theory are restrained, and an encounter with literature is similarly restrained. What is preserved intact is the integrity of a certain "order of discourse" which extends to the "Institution of Literature."

In a review of Terry Eagleton's *Literary Theory,* Jonathan Culler points out that Eagleton's perspective, his arguing "throughout a particular case"—a Marxist case—has an advantage over other histories of theory because it has a story to tell.[35] The Marxist story basically connects literature within the world, within specific social ideologies grounded in the model of base and superstructure, and thus resolves a dilemma which, in Eagleton's view, other perspectives have been flying from. The perspective organizes the book masterfully and gives Eagleton ample occasion to apply the rod of a Marxist story to anaesthetic, ahistorical perspectives in theory. Culler's review, while acknowledging the efficiency of the work, indicates where and how Eagleton has set his theory in "an oblivion of its own." Thus, if "one purpose of [*Literary Theory*] is to lift that repression and allow us to remember," one purpose of Culler's review is to lift what Eagleton has repressed and allow us to remember. It is interesting to note that Culler wishes to supplant Eagleton's Marxist ground with his own structuralist one and, in fact, argues that Eagleton's Marxism, which Eagleton calls a reinvented rhetoric or discourse theory or cultural studies or "whatever," is really called "Structuralism" or "Semiotics." "I am countering," Eagleton writes, "the theories set out in this book not with a *literary* theory, but with a different kind of discourse . . . which would include the objects ('literature') with which these other theories deal, but which would transform them by setting them in a wider context."[36] Thus a perspective is privileged throughout but, chameleon-like, alters its identity at the end and becomes "or whatever," which conveniently has the power to elude the criticism which terms like "Marxist" and "structuralist" bear with them, self-deconstruct upon utterance. However, by bringing all of theory into the political arena, Eagleton acknowledges theory's inextricable being-in-the-world and its antagonism to views which tolerate it only within traditional boundaries of pedagogy, practice, and profession.

Theory's "full impact on the student of literature and the general reader," if pursued to its logical end, could in a variety of ways affect pedagogy, practice, and profession. Eagleton feels that, as it stands now, if the canon is questioned the offenders are "blasted out of the literary arena."[37] But the canon should not be set in stone because in Eagleton's view literature itself is a "name which people give from time to time for different reasons to certain kinds of writing within a whole field of what Foucault has called 'discursive practices,' and . . . if anything is to be an object of study, it is this whole field of practices rather than just those sometimes rather obscurely labelled 'literature.' "[38] Some discursive practices, Eagleton feels, wind up being "literature" and others do not, and since all literature so declared is in a determined causal relationship with prevailing discursive practices, as all discourse is, there is absolutely no ground for a privileged entity called "literature."

I have countered the view of literature as a direct product of discursive practices with a basically Bakhtinian dialogic view, one in which such practices make up a prevailing chronotope through which literature's voices reach us—voices not privileged but capable of being sounded and heard, voices from which any chronotope is formed. Thus, literature is inevitably grounded in the world, in the environment, but it achieves its nondiscursive status by transgressing the chronotope and reaching a world of heteroglossia, a carnival world. Within this world, literature finds and sounds words that exist unfound and unsounded in the social order. Discursive practices which determine discourse therefore alter the nature of discourse, but this change only affects the way in which literature employs the new chronotope to reach carnival. It also seems apparent that the literature of this carnival of heteroglossia does not necessarily become canon, that the literary canon is a product of the prevailing chronotope. In terms of theory, a particular theory is privileged and a canon is endorsed. Of course Eagleton privileges a particular theory and is as anxious as Leavis to establish a canon. The erection of a canon of carnival within, inevitably within, a prevailing chronotope could only take place if that chronotope was synonymous with a cultural heteroglossia. Rabelais enters the canon truly when theory—in the form of Bakhtin's work—enables us to hear what has been unheard.

The problematic of all relationships—theory, literature, the world—gives way to the problematic of meaning. The intertextuality of a heterogeneous discourse possesses an openness and disruption which make determinacy of meaning problematic. Ultimately, the carnival of heteroglossia must be seen as threatening what Bakhtin calls "the space-time of the official world," a world of restraints which themselves insure determinate meaning. And it is in regard to this crisis of meaning that this collection must finally add its voices.

Timothy Reiss in *The Discourse of Modernism* considers that literature and literary criticism are not only discourse-specific—that is, tied to a social, historical, and ideological context—but are also connected to postmodern discourse's display of arbitrariness as a way in which power is demystified.[39] Thus this arbitrariness is not a deficit within an empirical-positivist scheme but a basic attribute of postmodern discourse. To reveal power in all its arbitrariness is actually to show that "disruption and openness" prevail in postmodern discourse/postmodern art in contrast "to the general modernist tendency toward continuity and closure." This dichotomy of determinate and indeterminate meaning rivals the textuality versus discourse dichotomy and relates to it when we consider it is Derridean free play which has given us the notion of textual indeterminacy and that free play stands in opposition to representation, to language representing a world and the world as representing itself in language. By asserting that indeterminacy exposes a sense of arbitrariness in power, Reiss makes discourse—a worldly text—out of Derridean free play.

On a broader scale, Reiss's opposing disruption and openness to continuity and closure is a Derridean trembling which leads to a "non-regional opening," which itself destroys the limits of history, politics, economics, sexuality, etc. In other words, the openness and disruption which leads to indeterminacy is a feature not only of the text but of the theory body as a whole, of discourse in its heterogeneous guise. And continuity and closure in turn reinforce the possibility of distinct, privileged disciplines—Derrida's "forms of reality" which can enclose their domains of language and pursue determinate meanings within those enclosures, Lentricchia's enclosed textual and semantic preserves.

This view of the heterogeneity of discourse as a basic quality of postmodern theory and literature contrasts then with the view of closed disciplines and with the view of literature as a privileged and difficult, but still determinate, discourse—a modern discourse. In this modernist view, literary discourse possesses the wherewithal to ascend beyond the first-order narrative of literature to its true core of meaning. Both literary discourse and literature, thus, seem to have metadimensions upon whose planes determinate meaning is revealed by a metascheme of explanation. Jean-François Lyotard's *The Postmodern Condition* describes the move to postmodernism as a move down from such metanarrative levels and a recognition that all discourse is a first-order narrative, and what we extract from the first-order narrative of literature is not a higher, more determinate core but another first-order narrative.[40]

If we draw back from this larger picture and focus upon the

theory body, we perceive that we have a determinate-indeterminate opposition—a question of the possibility of finding meaning in a text, meaning which itself can be privileged above all other suggested meaning. While Reiss sees indeterminacy of meaning as the ground for a positive relation with the world—a critique of power—Lyotard finds first-order narratives and the possibility of determinate meaning incompatible and replaces privileged meaning with a pragmatics of meaning. Whether or not interpretation is possible is a dilemma that runs through theory as a whole, but the ways in which it is viewed as occurring or not occurring, the ways in which it is handled, defined, mapped, and evaluated, are so varied that we really are not getting a thematic grip on theory. Is determinate or indeterminate meaning the product of interpretation? What qualities of the text are relevant to interpretation? Are the author, the reader, the world, the language, or the text factors in interpretation and in what ways, to what degree, and in what interrelationship? These are the questions Ann Jefferson and David Robey have raised in organizing their collection, *Modern Literary Theory,* but to consider these questions is to translate theory into an interrogative mode, not to find a theme within it.[41]

Nevertheless, interpretation/attendant meaning is a major dilemma within theory and has become the focus, the impetus to considerations of theory. It has also become that issue which contemporary critics feel they must resolve in order to go about the close reading of texts. And, of course, assuming a commonsensical approach and/or ignoring the problematics of interpretation as conceived by theory are also theoretical positions. On the evidence of an issue of *New Literary History* devoted to "Problems of Literary Theory," Catherine Belsey describes the central problem as the problem of meaning: "What divides empiricist criticism from formalism, and both from poststructuralism, is centrally a debate about meaning; and this debate cannot be resolved because what is at stake is a contest between the different theoretical frameworks within which each group conceptualizes language, subjectivity, and the world."[42] In her view, the crisis in criticism is theory's inability "to justify itself as a knowledge of texts and their meanings."[43]

In *Interpreting Interpreting,* Susan Horton wishes to construct an "interpretive ladder" for us—historical-biographical, local stylistics, structural stylistics, poetics, semiotics—but must first deal with the ways multiple meanings prevent her from constructing that ladder, from interpreting.[44] She responds to the view that interpretation should be redirected from meaning to searching for "the conditions under which meaning becomes possible" by affirming that it would "be very difficult to discuss the conditions under which a particular meaning became possible if we are unable or unwilling to venture a statement of meaning in the first place."[45]

Charles Altieri in "The Hermeneutics of Literary Indeterminacy" similarly must face the arguments of indeterminacy before he can present a performance model of interpretation, one which enables "us to retain confidence in traditional assumptions that competent readings can distinguish between more and less adequate critical interpretations."[46] In his essay "The Infinitude of Pluralism," Morse Peckham, at the tail end of the Miller-Abrams debate regarding Abrams's *Natural Supernaturalism,* displaces this conflict between determinate and indeterminate meaning with the problem of building limits into any theory of interpretation.[47] How can we have a plurality of interpretive methodologies and not an undiscriminated plurality of meanings? And a carnivalesque theory body may be viewed as a step further into chaos, a step beyond interpretive plurality which at least promises consensus or some final amalgamation of parts into a harmonious whole. Within this "true" interpretive plurality of consensus, strategies and methods are different but restrictions and limitations manage to affect a delimiting of the meaning-universe, manage to restrict that meaning-universe to something in which this interpretive pluralism can range. In this view, if we can restrict the questions we ask to those sanctioned by a privileged literary discourse, we can at least have some hope of creating this fenced-in meaning-range. If we persevere in extricating the thread of literary discourse from its present entanglements with other discourses, we can yet find our own domain and consider literature within it. Neither of these possibilities is advocated by this collection.

A determinate, univoiced meaning is not the undertaking of either literature or theory. Achieving some sense of literature's varied significance, in its particular and varied relationships with the world, is an accomplishment defined, conducted, and necessarily affected by the heterogeneity of discourse itself. The existence of such heterogeneity does not lead to determinate meaning but rather compels the scrutiny, the self-reflexiveness, of all claims to such. If New Criticism achieved determinate meaning by setting up high barriers to keep out false gods of extra-literary discourses, including non–New Critical theories, it was doing no more than—in the words of James Kincaid—"pretending that a busy whorehouse is a monastic cell."[48] The pedagogical implications of acknowledging what has really always been so—determinate meaning was what the institution determined it to be—are a part of those implications mentioned as resulting from an acceptance of the heterogeneity of theory itself.

Once again the voice of Bakhtin offers a dialogic encounter between centrifugal and centripetal forces as the creator of meaning. The theory carnival is like the heteroglot novel in that this carnival's heteroglossia exposes a privileged monologism of the monoglot novel. The heteroglot novel acts as a corrective rod on the monoglot novel, that novel in which centripetal forces turn flux into a single language, a single style, and, thus, a single assured meaning. A carnival of theory aspires to a context of heteroglossia in which and through which literature is capable of finding meaning, meaning comprised of those voices which create difference and those which create coherence. Those centripetal and centrifugal forces exist both in theory and in literature within the context of heteroglossia. It is through theory that the voice of the Other within every text is sounded, thus displacing a monologic determinate meaning with polyphony and difference.

Theory's quest is to hear the unheard voices of literature, to go beyond meaning that is heard only within and through a prevailing chronotope. The context of literature is the context of heteroglossia—multivoices which do not achieve harmony through reducing this polyphony to unity but which achieve an understanding of carnivalesque reality in the variety and constant interaction between all voices. To hear the voices of Rabelais—to find meaning in his words—involves an interaction by the reader not only with the chronotope of his or her age but also with the heteroglossia of Rabelais. The theory carnival enables that interaction, that encounter, to take place. Meaning is thus reached through many voices. Monologism speaks one voice with one meaning; heteroglossia speaks many voices with many meanings.

But since the theory carnival itself is filtered through the chronotope, meanings ultimately become contextualized within a specific social and historical situation. Only the continual counterpoint, counter harmony provided by each voice within this theory carnival offers us any hope of reaching the voices of literature. The chronotope is not only the lens through and against which literature itself is realized, but it is also the lens through which it is interpreted. Literature expands theory and theory in turn enables us to hear more of what has been unheard in literature. Bakhtin's entanglement with Rabelais is an example of this. Bakhtin's influence on the theory carnival leads not only to new meaning but also to a new meaning of meaning. Heteroglossia and carnival are not regressions into chaos—centrifugal moves away from a cohesive center, a fixed social order—but the ground from which privileged meanings, generated by privileged theories, have emerged. The carnival of theory as well as the carnival of literature are composed of voices which cannot be sounded in monologue. Their expression or creation confronts a monologic culture just as Bakhtin's Rabelais was meant to be a confrontation with a Stalinesque monologism. Bakhtin's "examination of Rabelaisian license," Clark and Holquist write, "is a dialogic meditation on freedom."[49]

Literary theory is part of a multiple discourse in which, according to Michel Serres, "polymorphism remains irreducible," a multiple discourse in the world and for the world, a discourse whose polymorphism subsumes all monologic voices.[50] Not only discourse is irreducibly polymorphic; we—as readers and interpreters—are also "constituted in polyphony." "Human consciousness," Bakhtin writes, "does not come into contact with existence directly, but through the medium of the surrounding ideological world. . . . In fact, the individual consciousness can only become a consciousness by being realized in the forms of the ideological environment proper to it: in language, in conventionalized gesture, in artistic image, in myth, and so on."[51] The open discourses of theory fashion the open selves of the interpreter encountering the heteroglossia of literature itself. In *Tracing Liter-*

ary Theory our image of this polyphonous consciousness is a body image—the grotesque, Rabelaisian theory body interpenetrating literature, world, and interpreter.

NOTES

1. William Cain, *The Crisis in Criticism* (Baltimore: Johns Hopkins University Press, 1984), p. xii.
2. Jonathan Culler, *On Deconstruction: Theory and Criticism after Structuralism* (Ithaca: Cornell University Press, 1982), pp. 17–18.
3. Cain, *The Crisis in Criticism,* p. xiii.
4. Ibid., p. 249.
5. Ibid., p. 277.
6. Ibid., p. xvii.
7. Frank Lentricchia, *After the New Criticism* (Chicago: University of Chicago Press, 1980), p. 104.
8. Howard Felperin, *Beyond Deconstruction* (London: Oxford University Press, 1985), p. 138.
9. Cain, *The Crisis in Criticism,* p. xviii.
10. Mikhail Bakhtin, *Rabelais and His World* (Bloomington: Indiana University Press, 1984), p. 320.
11. Michael Clark, *Michel Foucault An Annotated Bibliography: Tool Kit for a New Age* (New York: Garland, 1983), p. xxxi.
12. Felperin, *Beyond Deconstruction,* p. 111.
13. Bakhtin, *Rabelais and His World,* p. 7.
14. Mark Poster, "The Future According to Foucault: *The Archaeology of Knowledge* and Intellectual History," in *Modern European Intellectual History*, ed. Dominick LaCapra (Ithaca: Cornell University Press, 1982), p. 139.
15. Culler, *On Deconstruction,* p. 7.
16. Ibid., p. 12.
17. Ibid., p. 30.
18. Ibid., p. 9.
19. Steven Knapp and Walter Michaels, "Against Theory," *Critical Inquiry,* 8 (Summer 1982), 742.
20. Daniel O'Hara, "Revisionary Madness: The Prospects of American Literary Theory at the Present Time," *Critical Inquiry,* 9 (Summer 1983), 732.
21. Robert Scholes, *Textual Power* (New Haven: Yale University Press, 1985), pp. 10–11.

22. Lentricchia, *After the New Criticism*, p. xiii.
23. Ibid.
24. Ibid., p. 351.
25. David Carroll, *The Subject in Question: The Languages of Theory and the Strategies of Fiction* (Chicago: University of Chicago Press, 1982), p. 3.
26. M. M. Bakhtin, *The Dialogic Imagination: Four Essays*, ed. Michael Holquist, trans. Caryl Emerson (Austin: University of Texas Press, 1981), p. 253.
27. Katerina Clark and Michael Holquist, *Mikhail Bakhtin* (Cambridge: Harvard University Press, 1984), p. 278.
28. Bakhtin, *The Dialogic Imagination*, p. 254.
29. Jeremy Hawthorn, *Criticism and Critical Theory* (London: Edward Arnold, 1984), p. xii.
30. Ira Konisberg, *American Criticism in the Poststructuralist Age* (Ann Arbor: University of Michigan Press, 1981).
31. Josué Harari, *Textual Strategies* (Ithaca: Cornell University Press, 1979); John Fekete, *The Structural Allegory* (Minneapolis: University of Minnesota Press, 1984).
32. John Sturrock, *Structuralism and Since* (Oxford: Oxford University Press, 1979), p. 5.
33. Cain, *The Crisis in Criticism*, p. 10; Laurence Lerner, *Reconstructing Literature* (Oxford: Blackwell, 1983), p. 9.
34. Poster, p. 139.
35. Jonathan Culler, rev. of *Literary Theory: An Introduction*, by Terry Eagleton, *Poetics Today*, 5 (1984), 149–56.
36. Terry Eagleton, *Literary Theory: An Introduction* (Minneapolis: University of Minnesota Press, 1983), p. 205.
37. Ibid., p. 214.
38. Ibid., p. 205.
39. Timothy Reiss, *The Discourse of Modernism* (Ithaca: Cornell University Press, 1982).
40. Jean-François Lyotard, *The Postmodern Condition* (Minneapolis: University of Minnesota Press, 1984).
41. Ann Jefferson and David Robey, *Modern Literary Theory* (London: Batsford, 1982).
42. Catherine Belsey, "Problems of Literary Theory: The Problem of Meaning," *New Literary History*, 14 (1982), 175.
43. Ibid., 180.
44. Susan Horton, *Interpreting Interpreting* (Baltimore: Johns Hopkins University Press, 1979).

45. Ibid., p. 10.
46. Charles Altieri, "The Hermeneutics of Literary Indeterminacy," *New Literary History*, 10 (1978), 71.
47. Morse Peckham, "The Infinitude of Pluralism," *Critical Inquiry*, 3 (1977), 803–16.
48. James Kincaid, "Coherent Readers, Incoherent Texts," *Critical Inquiry*, 3 (1977), 802.
49. Clark and Holquist, *Mikhail Bakhtin*, p. 298.
50. Michel Serres, *Hermes* (Baltimore: Johns Hopkins University Press, 1982).
51. Pavel Medvedev and Mikhail Bakhtin, *The Formal Method in Literary Scholarship* (Baltimore: Johns Hopkins University Press, 1978), p. 14.

A. C. GOODSON

Structuralism and Critical History in the Moment of Bakhtin

In a recent apologia, Tzvetan Todorov recounts his role as spokesman for the structuralism of the seventies. "A Dialogic Criticism?" tells the story of a conversion of sorts, from the modern promotion of reading as verbal processing to an older sense of literature as social engagement.[1] The revisionist tone confirms the demise of the structuralist revival, while the title looks forward to its sublation in other forms. Todorov is a representative figure for this development, his career exemplary of the fate of structuralism in the West. Trained in Bulgaria, active in Paris from the sixties, Todorov was an emissary of Slavic formalism at a propitious moment. Roland Barthes, who would sponsor his assimilation to the French school, had been applying the linguistic hypotheses of Ferdinand de Saussure to the reading of literary texts and, for popular consumption, to advertisements, automobiles, and fashion. Todorov was to provide Barthes's method with a past and a future. His *Dictionnaire encyclopédique des sciences de langage* (1972, with Oswald Ducrot) codified the ascendant understanding of language as the formal matrix of literature. *Poétique,* the journal he was instrumental in founding, began appearing in 1970. It was committed to Roman Jakobson's rehabilitation of poetics as the ground of an invigorated critical discourse—not an interpretive discourse, a scientistic one rather, concerned with the conditions of the poetic as object of investigation. Critics would have to become poeticians before they could presume to interpret, much less to pass judgment.

Jakobson's structural poetics, spawned some fifty years before, thus gave rise to a late progeny. It became the point of departure for influential work by literary professionals, mostly writing in French, whose names would become as familiar to academic readers in the seventies as those of the New Critics had once been. Their domesticated structuralism recurred to the terminology of classical rhetoric, but their understanding was governed by a homemade cognitive psychology. Jakobson had appropriated "metaphor" and "metonymy" as names for the mental operations of substitution and combination. These were no longer grasped as tropes of language but as tropes of thought—a distinction elided in his exposition. In the first issues of *Poétique,* such cardinal terms were accepted at face value, for the most part. They were there to be recovered and put to use. Mikhail Bakhtin's work, among others', was part of the ore of a Slavic mine which the journal set out to quarry.

The promoter of dialogic understanding, in a special sense of the word, Bakhtin stands in the title of Todorov's apologia as the personification of what happened when the new poetics took the high road to academic orthodoxy. The pursuit of the chimera of structure derailed under circumstances which are still hardly appreciated. To some extent these were indigenous to the enterprise, a matter of inherent limits as well as of the deconstructive pressure which built up within the elaboration of the method. What was a crisis for structuralism as a movement of methodological renovation would thus prove, in the practice of its second-generation adherents, an advanced stage of a developing understanding. But larger forces, too, worked against the new structuralism—forces which can be called historical. In "A Dialogic Criticism?" the crisis is recognized under personal auspices. Political helplessness, withdrawal—familiar responses to Cold War gridlock in the East Bloc as in the West—had insulated the poetician from the realities. A sense of engagement came over him gradually. The circumstances are sketchy; they do not matter much. But his account is leading, and his recovery of appetence indicative of what became of the structuralism he was responsible for transmitting. A dialogic criticism would entertain that open and provocative relation with its object which Bakhtin had identified in Dostoevsky's novelistic polyphony. The literary deployment of the forms and formulae of contemporary social experience would become the model for an engaged critical activity.[2] A dialogic criticism would abandon that discourse of the master (that structuralist point-of-view on high) which strives to control what it cannot engage directly. It would go public, as it were, instead of confining itself to a merely institutional future. A dialogic criticism would be alert to historical situation, the larger contexts of verbal utterance, and the moral imperative.

Will Bakhtin bear this load? Todorov's detailed exposition of his career suggests that he will.[3] For Bakhtin is of the generation of Jakobson and Viktor Shklovsky—of the Russian milieu in its moment of political cataclysm, subject to the same disruption but distinguished by his reaction against formalist reductions of literary experience. Dynamic Russia—arch-modern in the arts, scientistic in aspiration—was the original setting of the formalism which underwrote the structural method. Returning to it through Bakhtin meant, for Todorov, turning on it. For recent thinking about literature, it has meant recurring to the modernist source to find something different from the solidarity of formalist understanding.

In the beginning, before the October revolution, there was the Moscow Linguistic Circle, Jakobson at its center, preoccupied with the new poetry, but also with folklore, and with language as their common mainspring.[4] Language was understood in this moment in a way inspired by the dreams of the dominant philology, without its historical insistences: as the *materia prima* of cognition, irreducible matrix of culture in general. Such a sense of Language—abstract, hypothetical, deracinated—is perhaps best grasped by reference to its circumstances. Traditional arrangements were collapsing in a social free-fall. F. R. Leavis's reification of English in the thirties was different in elaboration, certainly, yet he too sought security in what was left of the ancestral bond. The language, as repository of cultural value, became the last refuge of a historical consciousness under siege.[5] Jakobson's adoption of an antiseptic version of Language is commonly regarded as antihistorical, by analogy to the contemporaneous formation of Cambridge English under I. A. Richards. I shall be expanding on their real differences shortly, but it is worth entertaining the comparison long enough to appreciate the commonality of situation, if not of purpose. In the wake of war and revolution, new ideas of language responded to a dramatically altered sense of the past. For Jakobson, Language became the field of an all-consuming cognition, a mathematical map of consciousness articulated by coordinate axes and representing a sort of graph of mental process.

The dialogic criticism which Todorov raises as a possibility supposes such a sense of Language even as it would surpass it. Bakhtin now appears as the original critic of the structuralist position, the one who was there all along. His reception casts him as a negative voice, suppressing all that was wrong with *langue* (as de Saussure had called it) and its formalist mediations. Yet Bakhtin's dialogical understanding attained to authority with this massive idealization of Language in place, perhaps because it retains the linguistic fundamentalism of Jakobson's enterprise even as it escapes the limiting conception: "The human sciences are the sciences of man in his specificity, and not the sciences of a *voiceless* thing and a natural phenomenon. Man, in his human specificity, is always expressing himself (speaking), that is always creating a text (though it may remain *in potentia*). Where human being is studied outside of the text and independently of it, we are no longer dealing with the human sciences."[6] To put his affiliations in current context: without the structuralism of the seventies, there would have been no Bakhtin reception of the scope we are witness to. For why, in that case, would his work have spoken with such effect to the institutional condition? His Dostoevsky book was written of as "ingenious" by René Wellek in 1962.[7] The formalist moment is in no way excluded in Bakhtin's writing; rather, it is contested from within. The structuralist position was essential preparation for his mature critical practice. It remains essential for the current appreciation of what is involved in it.

Dismissed by deconstruction, reviled by the neo-Marxists, the structuralist revival remains the formative event of the critical history of the past twenty years, not for what it brought to the understanding of texts (though it brought more than is now admitted) but for what it revealed of the state of criticism on location and for the alternative ideas to which it gave rise. Its reception on the Anglo-American front was tormented from the beginning, at once anxious and obsessive. The encounter might be described in terms of a series of negations, with Bakhtin emerging at the end to save the show. This is how I propose to treat its brief history here. Comparatively little critical work in English was inspired by Jakobson's structuralist poetics in its new incarnation despite the currency of his ideas and terminology. The revival failed to take, but the threat posed by its sense of purpose shook the critical institution from a deep isolation.

Modernism and Language

The modernist milieu from which structuralism emerged in the twenties gave rise, in England, to the new Cambridge English of I. A. Richards, with its emphasis on poetry as language and on language as coded meaning. The unremitting rationalism of his idea was true to the moment, but its particularism distinguishes it from more evolved accounts of language in the period, including Jakobson's. In *The Meaning of Meaning* (1923), with C. K. Ogden, Richards had set his own course, dispatching Saussure at the outset. *Langue,* the Swiss linguist's reification of language as a complete grammatical system, was too hypothetical for English understanding. More to the point, perhaps, the social insistence of such a conception was temperamentally averse to his own psycholinguistic preoccupations. Language in the individual mind was better suited to the taste for poetry. The relation of linguistics to poetics, as he conceived it, was casual if not quite accidental.[8] Richards went to the rescue of poetry without resolving basic questions of language, though he raised them constantly.

When the New Critics in England and America looked to Richards for an orienting sense of language, they found his linguistic base threadbare, a tissue of fabrication. The New Criticism which shaped the reading of two generations would be confronted, in the structuralism of the seventies, with versions of language it could hardly imagine. Yet its roots lay in the modernism which had been so hospitable to thinking about language elsewhere. And its reputation was made on close reading—on an attention to language which presumed a larger sense of the matter than had been customary in the belletristic practice against which it reacted. The New Criticism in its inspired moments made much of the peculiar difficulties of poetic language. What it seldom displayed was a sense of the social vocation of poetic language—of the relation of poetry to language in general. The insularity of its idiom might be posed as a failure to think in terms larger than those raised by local problems of poetic language.[9]

Roman Jakobson had been active in America for years by the time the linguistic base of critical practice came to be seen as an issue of the first magnitude. It had been raised in the forties by John Crowe Ransom and Allen Tate in response to Charles Morris on symbolic and iconic signs, but to no great effect, perhaps because Richards's abortive "semasiology" had clouded the waters. Jakobson's coordinate commitments to language and poetry went back to Moscow and 1915. He was still urging professional linguists to take poetry seriously as recently as 1978. What had been an inconsequent and even confusing relation in Richards's work was a matter of rigorous reciprocity for Jakobson's structuralism. He was not a man of letters out of his depth in the science of language (as Richards himself conceived it) but a linguist for whom poetry mattered fundamentally. He realized, in short, the marriage of concerns which had eluded Richards, with long-term consequences for critical practice in English.

Colleagues at Harvard, Richards and Jakobson occupied the same stage at the Indiana conference on style in language in 1958.[10] The contrast was jarring. Richards's putative science of meaning, doubtfully derived from Coleridge on language, had boiled down by this date to disjointed remarks on word selection in a poem of his own. His large claim was not for the forms of language in the study of literature but for an approach to poetry which was not biographical. Meaning was to be regarded as intratextual. Context was reduced, meanwhile, to "the lives of poets." His reply to a question about sound and sequence in the title of his poem showed him to be fighting this battle within himself (*SL*, 9–24). Jakobson's astute follow-up relied on expectation in English metric to explain why phrase sequence could not be reversed in Richards's title. The Russian linguist's Indiana paper, a closing statement on linguistics and poetics, lays down premises he had established some forty years before:

> Poetics deals primarily with the question, *What makes a verbal message a work of art?* Because the main subject of poetics is the *differentia specifica* of verbal art in relation to other kinds of verbal

> behavior, poetics is entitled to the leading place in literary studies. Poetics deals with problems of verbal structure, just as the analysis of painting is concerned with pictorial structure. Since linguistics is the global science of verbal structure, poetics may be regarded as an integral part of linguistics. (*SL*, 350)

John Hollander's response to this, in a related paper, objected to the forbidding generality of Jakobson's "designation of a poem as a text in which the coding was of greater interest than the message." The poem lost its personal qualities in so abstract an understanding (*SL*, 398).

This preliminary skirmish is significant because it is indicative. A clash of cultural styles was evident in the reception of structuralism among an English profession unsure it wanted anything to do with method, though it had honored the idea in one way or another since Richards. Jakobson's detailed discussions of individual poems are nothing if not methodical, even if the method is not always very productive. Few English professionals have worked through one of them, on the evidence of citation, perhaps because Jakobson ordinarily writes about Slavic texts. Best known, mainly by French readers, is his collaboration with Lévi-Strauss on Baudelaire's sonnet "Les Chats."[11] This piece gave rise to reactions which epitomize a first negation of the structuralist position by Anglo-American readers. The convergence of the anthropological and the linguistic points of view on an indifferent sonnet looked like a serious challenge. It set the stage for confrontations about the relation of sound and sense in poetry, and about the relation of linguistic description and literary interpretation in general. The realized consensus was that "no grammatical analysis of a poem can give us more than the grammar of the poem."[12]

The paper on "Les Chats" broke the text down to conventional stanzaic units and these to propositional units, whose purely formal internal relations (thematized, characteristically, as oppositions) were correlated with sound patterns and substantive content—a rigorous, yet hardly revolutionary, exercise so far. But incidental correlations were made to assume a sort of necessity after the fact, as though the sonnet had been contrived for effects which remain subliminal—if that—in reading. The poem as artifact is a truism of English studies, but the tedious screening performed by the authors produced a system of signification which did not signify. Their interpretation of the poem failed to follow their analytic and came to exemplify the difference between analyzing and reading.

What did the linguist's account of the language of the text have to do, then, with signification and with meaning? Michael Riffaterre attempted to pick up some of the pieces. An essay on "Yew-Trees," the Wordsworth poem, and Geoffrey Hartman's response to it recall the pressure exerted by Jakobsonian structuralism and the countervailing resistance to its hypostasis of poetic language as textuality.[13] For Riffaterre, the issue was reference; the textuality he was defending had something in common with ambient assumptions of the sufficiency of the text in the New Criticism. The terms in which he mounted his argument were, however, resonant of a newer idiom: "History, and referentiality, are thus all at the verbal level. Names anchor the description solidly in time because of their metonymic function, their ability to stand for a whole complex of representations. Suggestiveness is circular: the descriptive sentence finds its reference in a name whose referent need only be the preceding part of the sentence leading up to it" (*IDP,* 133). To this Hartman rejoined with concerns of voice and intention, defending a sense of the poem as someone speaking, with locus, moment, and context as primordial values. The structural method was granted a provisional claim on the collation of linguistic features indissociable from good reading, but its programmatic claims were dismissed as "impersonal."

Now this word is replete with situational irony, recasting the encounter against the background of the dominant Anglo-American criticism within which structuralism would be naturalized. Eliot's "impersonality" made the poet a ventriloquist; its effect was conspicuous in *The Waste Land,* where the question "Who's speaking?" could only be answered evasively. (Tiresias is not the poet, nor does it add much to observe that the voices are to be regarded as speaking through him, as Eliot would have it.) Bakhtin's "heteroglossia" lies down this line, but we are a world removed from such a conception with Hartman's insistence on personality against structuralist "impersonality." It is a romantic insistence, of course, true to the assumptions of Wordsworth's poetry and responsive to "Yew-Trees" in this way. The censorious charge of impersonality reminds us where we are, all the same. A tenacious defense of the particularity of voice and place characterizes English critical tradition at its best. Resistance to the displacement of these cardinal commitments was fierce.

"The poetic function projects the principle of equivalence from the axis of selection into the axis of combination."[14] Jakobson's ambitious formula, reposing on his study of aphasic speech, made poetry a calculus of similitude—not semantic or propositional similitude (scholars are like lovers since they both keep cats) so much as syntactic and aural similitude. Still it is striking that a poem such as "Les Chats," which is distinctive mainly for its analogic content, should have been presented as a case study. The meaning often appeared to shadow the grammatical categories employed by Jakobson and even his a priori sense of what was poetic.

His claim on interpretive power was severely qualified by his new audience. On Jonathan Culler's calculation,

> It is as a theory of the operations which grammatical figures can induce readers to perform that Jakobson's account of poetic language is most usefully considered. To say that there is a great deal of parallelism and repetition in literary texts is of little interest in itself and of less explanatory value. The crucial question is what effects patterning can have, and one cannot approach an answer unless one incorporates within one's theory an account of how readers take up and structure elements of a text.[15]

Such an act of adaptation made Jakobson over as an improved specimen of Richards—an inspired practitioner of the code. The first contribution of the structuralism of the seventies to professional readers in the West was this sense of a code—of language as an institution, distinct from whatever message it might be made to convey. The simple system of code and message formalized "meaning" in a way that seemed clear where the native critical idiom was uncertain. It pointed to problems of ground but also of purpose. Structuralism in the Anglo-American setting was an infatuation which told of doubt in the critical institution.

Linguistics and Its Antagonists

Jakobson was a marginal presence at the Johns Hopkins symposium of 1966, "The Languages of Criticism and the Sciences of

Man."[16] This event, an American launching pad for the *sciences humaines* and its literary camp, was cast as a challenge to humanistic thinking and critical anomie. "Man" was in question: it was the year of Michel Foucault's *Les Mots et les choses,* with its demolition of all positivity, including that social positivity in which the *sciences humaines* were grounded.[17] If Man did not exist, what was anthropology but one more dismal science, exposed for the idealist fraud it was? Structuralism was introduced at the conference as a new broom which would sweep clean the cobwebs of disciplinary habit. Yet it was on trial from the start, and what would stick in the minds of readers of the proceedings was Jacques Derrida's bald attack on the premises of the *sciences humaines,* which had adopted structuralist methods via Lévi-Strauss. Without Jakobson to make the case, the most powerful voices in literary structuralism would sound thin against this corrosive *bruit de fond.* Structuralism was on its way to poststructuralism before it had recovered from jet lag.

Derrida showed structural anthropology to be steeped in the ethos and terminology of the *logos.* Nature and culture, *phusis* and *nomos,* were exhausted remnants of a collapsed understanding. Nothing new could come of anything so old. Yet Derrida himself had come of it, orienting his enterprise by the light he would despise as *mythologie blanche.*[18] Structuralism he saw as its modern inheritor, and he made a place for himself denouncing it. *Jarndyce vs. Jarndyce* was hardly more parasitic than Derrida *contra* Lévi-Strauss.[19] His case against structuralism was important, but hardly as devastating as its Anglo-American audience assumed. Lévi-Strauss became the scapegoat of a quarrel with philosophic language—a quarrel luminously developed in Derrida's subsequent work, which would dominate theoretical discourse in the seventies. Paralinguistic argumentation was familiar to professional philosophers. Wittgenstein had made an erratic career of it, Heidegger a cultural politics. But these were little more than names to English and French professionals. Derrida's radical skepticism played well to the restlessness of the period, when the breakup of New Critical orthodoxy left readers with an uncertain sense of purpose. He was instrumental in turning the languages of criticism against the critical institution.

Was a discourse of literature—a critical discourse—possible at all? Derrida's piece would convince readers that they did not know their words, much less their minds. An inquisition of the languages of criticism would have to precede anything which might meaningfully be said about literature. Meanwhile, other participants in the conference proved to have leading things to say about it. Much of this could be called structuralist insofar as it pursued the analogy of literature to language—literature as "a kind of extension and application of certain properties of Language," in the words of Paul Valéry, an analogy full of imaginative possibility and no less full of snares (*LCSM*, 125).

The most imaginative deployments of it are the ones which stand out in retrospect—extravagant gestures of a structural revolution which hardly got off the ground. They were fiercely resisted from the moment they were delivered. Barthes's "To Write: An Intransitive Verb?" played fast and loose with the voices of verb systems (active, middle, passive) in order to define the distinctive timbre of modern voicing:

> In the modern verb of middle voice *to write*, however, the subject is immediately contemporary with the writing, being effected and affected by it. The case of the Proustian narrator is exemplary: he exists only in writing. These remarks suggest that the central problem of modern writing exactly coincides with what we could call the problematic of the verb in linguistics; just as temporality, person, and diathesis define the positional field of the subject, so modern literature is trying, through various experiments, to establish a new status in writing for the agent of writing . . . to substitute the instance of discourse for the instance of reality (or of the referent), which has been, and still is, a mythical "alibi" dominating the idea of literature. The field of the writer is nothing but writing itself. (*LCSM*, 133–34)

It was not only the "coincidence" of grammatical structure and authorial situation which came under attack in this tableau. Paul de Man convincingly disputed the view of literary history it entailed, while Jean-Pierre Vernant dispatched its grammatical simplifications on philological grounds, stranding Barthes "at the level of pure metaphor" (*LCSM*, 150–52).

Literature could not convincingly be defined as a second-order code reposing on the primary code of language, *pace* Lévi-Strauss on myth—not in this way.[20] Yet something else was at stake here. What comes through Barthes's paper, as through much of his published work, is a horror of writing adrift in the miasma of mass culture. A commitment to the survival of modern literature was the moral edge of his critical activity. Why write? A semblance of this question had haunted Lévi-Strauss in his celebrated autobiography, *Tristes Tropiques* (1955), where the idea of "referring" to his Amazonian exploits in a travel narrative provoked nausea on page 1.[21] To write for the sake of writing, not as a virtuoso exercise of *l'art pour l'art* but as an extension of self in a way that recurred to Montaigne: such was the vocation that Barthes would defend by insisting on literature as language.

For language was more than a convenience, the prefabricated discourse of the world. It constituted a system, complex beyond the dreams of cybernetics, a world of its own. Recourse to this other was not a form of escape but engagement on another level. Barthes's plea for a return to rhetoric as the basis of critical discourse was compromised by lapses of attention, but its goal was a revival of a sense of the literary, which was under siege. Writing was an endangered act, the author a vanishing species. Institutional criticism might at least call attention to the fact. Barthes's arch-modernity is nowhere more clearly indicated than in his defense of modern writing—of Gide, his mentor of choice, in his first published piece and later of Sollers, his friend and contemporary. His career had this in common with the careers of American critics who operated outside the academy at first, becoming institutions in their own right as the new literature for which they spoke attained to academic caste.

Barthes's case is complicated by his attachment to the mass culture about which he wrote for *Réalités* and *Le Nouvel Observateur*, among others—to give some idea of the range of his audience. But then Mallarmé had once published a fashion magazine under a pseudonym. Barthes went public from the beginning, enlisting the literate media in his crusade. His cultural analytic would aspire to "the construction of the intelligibility of our time."[22] The moral critic took linguistics as his means, and if the methods he elaborated turned out to be private, not readily transferred to other hands, they can still be said to have performed the task he set himself. What posed as method (and he often took it for that) turned out to be a way of writing personally for institutional consumption.

The doubts of de Man and Vernant point up what his academic

readers had recognized from the publication of *Sur Racine* (1963)—that Barthes saw older literature in a rear-view mirror, collapsing literary history for his own purposes. The modern critic would read the writing of the past as protomodern or he would not read it at all. His insight made him blind or, rather, one-eyed (*borgne*). Yet structural methods were peculiarly adapted to reconstructing the intelligibility of texts far away in time or space, as Gérard Genette had argued early on in *Figures*.[23] So long as structuralism was seen as a critical outpost of modernism and associated with Barthes's considerable presence, it would be viewed nevertheless as an instrument of modernist domination. This association proved unfortunate for the future of structural methods in the Anglo-American setting.

The brilliant work of Vernant and of Marcel Detienne, his student, showed what these might bring to the study of earlier literature.[24] A classical scholar concerned with the social formation of the early Greek mind, Vernant employed binary opposition to break an intractable problem child of Greek mythology, Hesiod's myth of the races. The solution consisted in resolving a diachronic series (the races of man presented as a succession) into a synchronic set based on a cluster of related oppositions operating through a mass of detail. His essays on Oedipus are perhaps more suggestive for current work. Taking the name to incorporate a peculiar but apposite opposition, "I know/foot," he showed how the Sophoclean plays work out a logic of reversal based on the transformation of one term into the other and back again. These reversals are not disembodied mental operations; they are full of social history and cultural implication. René Girard plundered Vernant's essay for his own discussion of Oedipus, a cornerstone of the argument of *La Violence et le sacré*. A book of great originality, it drew important evidence from Vernant's analytic despite Girard's hostility to the method.[25] The Hopkins conference, where both gave papers, thus proved catalytic in promoting secondary growth on the main branches of an established structuralist agenda.

In the politics of postmodern theory, structuralism is identified with an ingenious linguistic determinism. Yet the conception of the relations of language and literature entertained by its best practitioners proved productive, and not only in reading texts. The sense of the matter developed in the work of Barthes, in particular, opened a horizon he did little to explore, that of critique. In his later work he recognized language as the infrastructure of ideology—as the institution *par excellence* of social order, of relations of power in general. It is hardly surprising that Foucault should have taken the lead in securing a chair of literary semiology for him at the Collège de France. In his inaugural lecture Barthes spoke of

> power as the parasite of a trans-social organism, linked to the whole history of man, and not only to the political story—to the historical. This object in which power is inscribed from time immemorial is language. Or to be more precise, its necessary means of expression: the tongue we speak. Language is a sort of legislation, the tongue we speak a legal code based on it. We do not observe the power contained in our tongue, because we forget that any tongue is a form of ordering, and that ordering is oppressive. *Ordo* means both division into parts and condemnation. Jakobson showed that an idiom is defined less by what it allows one to say than by what it obliges one to say . . . for us it remains only to play tricks with the tongue, to trick the tongue. This salutary trickery, this dodge, this magnificent lure, which permits us to understand the tongue outside power, in the glory of a permanent revolution of language, I shall call literature.[26]

The stance of the *sciences humaines,* with their approach to Man instead of men, dictates the limits of this view. Critique would remain for Barthes above the level of real social engagement. As some of his last "Chroniques" show, he had little faith in his idiom outside the academy. Faced with the ubiquity of power, he could only imagine a retreat into the particularity of his condition.

Not so ignominious a retreat, perhaps: not more than Adorno's, nor even Bakhtin's. Yet the particularity of Barthes's condition, of his voice, marginalizes critical discourse in a way that they do not. For Barthes's recourse to the trans-social evades engaged historical understanding. The dialogic relation which Bakhtin entertains with the past has, to put a point to it, altogether more vitality. The past lives for him not as a pretext for the modern but as an active participant in the construction of its intelligibility. The carnival, a conspicuous instance, enters literature as it passes out of collective practice. It becomes a residual form of social affirmation, telling on the poverty of modern experience—a quiet act of defiance in Stalin's emergent State, full of historical resonance.[27] Bakhtin's version of language is not at all trans-social, as Barthes's aspired to be. Here is no transcendent *langue,* no Language imagined as the lair where Power lurks.

Bakhtin reacted to the formalist hypostasis of language much as American criticism of the same period reacted to Richards's psycholinguistic fabrications—with an adherence to the specificity of literary utterance, divorced from a larger sense of the matter. Todorov assimilates his position to Wilhelm Dilthey's, in which a rigorous separation of the scientific from the interpretive point of view is instituted (*MB,* 27–28). When poststructural criticism takes Bakhtin as a model for discourse analysis, it may only be recurring, circuitously, to the habits of its critical past, camouflaging its instinctive particularism in a theoretical smokescreen. Using Bakhtin in this way, against the formalism to which he responded, is problematic, for reasons I have suggested. It is the example of his tenaciously historical imagination which ought to count for the criticism now in formation.

Narratology Monologic and Dialogic

Fifteen years after the conference which launched structuralism in America with a mutiny in progress, another conference, this one on postmodernism, attempted to come to terms with what had happened in criticism and the arts.[28] It was something of a morning-after exercise, as it turned out. A sense of excess, and of lost bearings, weighs on many of the papers. Structuralism was now the past, Bakhtin a new voice unconnected with all that. Hartman linked his polyphony with Adorno's "intransigence of theory," with the poem as artifact of the New Criticism and with Barthes's refusal to debase the text to any fixed schemata (*I/R,* 101)—an oddly sorted regiment, mustered to fight for the autonomy of the work of art against the hegemonists of theory. The theoretical was now consuming itself in an effort to save the organism it fed on. This development, familiar in consciously retrograde forms as the "refusal of theory," made a program of Dominick LaCapra's dry observation, on site, that "actual dialogue in certain circumstances may itself be among the least dialogical of phenomena" (*I/R,* 57).

Deconstruction had led, in an entirely logical way, to a resignation of the aspiration to principle which motivates theoretic discussion. If nothing came of nothing, it was only the moment that mattered. The devaluation of history in high modernism had found a respondent in postmodern criticism. Valéry's thesis of the uselessness of history was thus raised to a critical principle of sorts, in the absence of anything else that might serve. The example of Bakhtin's resistance to such nihilism, in the original stage of the process, is worth considering in counterpoint. Bakhtin endured not as a conscript of structuralism but not as a drop-out from principle, either. His defense of the novel as the great modern form depends on a simple but efficacious distinction between the monologic and the dialogic. The former was the voice of the author in the old sense; the latter, a polyphonic montage in which the author acted as ventriloquist for the contesting voices of others. In modern English poetry, the difference might be exemplified by "The Wreck of the *Deutschland*" on the one hand, *The Waste Land* on the other. But the novel was the classic venue of the dialogic for its originator.

So long as narrative was conceived as monophonic, the voice of the narrator writing, the study of narrative was bound to monologic notions of textuality. The monologic agenda promoted concepts of unity, continuity, and structure conceived as agents of the author in language. Genette's programmatic study of Proust shows how such an agenda was expressed in structuralist versions of narrative in the seventies.[29] Beginning from the hypallage, a stylistic feature of little apparent consequence, Genette demonstrated that Proust often proceeds from relations of contiguity to relations of similarity in his descriptive imagery. The role of metonymy in the formation of metaphor is the mark of the novelist, for whom authentication by reference to a real world is of cardinal importance. The analogy seems natural because it arises out of the material proximity of its terms. Thus, Proust would describe a church spire seen over a field of grain as a spike of wheat, with everything that could be extracted from the comparison.

Metonymy begot metaphor within the language of Proust's narrative, but their relation was reversed in *mémoire involontaire,* Bergson's term for subliminal recall, which Proust identified as the principle of his narrative. The "miracle of analogy" gave rise to a flood of related detail, as though in substantiation of the premise.

Such was the structure of Proust's narrative as Genette presented it. The intergenerative relations of metonymy and metaphor took Proust's novel to the bounds of poetry and prose. It is within a settled sense of Language as a cognitive field animated by the perpendicular axes of the metonymic and metaphoric poles (the syntagmatic axis of combination, the paradigmatic axis of substitution) that such an account proves illuminating. The advantages of the structuralist approach to narrative stem directly from this settled sense. Jakobson's terminology is clear enough and congruent with important contemporary developments, notably Bergson's attention to association. Both have roots in the association psychology of the eighteenth century. Proust lends himself to such treatment in part because he is of this milieu. Historical understanding proceeds on secure ground, without hermeneutic contortion. Structuralism and modernism go hand in glove in this way, but only so long as the modern voice is grasped in terms of projection from the speaking subject.

The critical legacy of the new structuralism is generally identified with bourgeois narrative despite Jakobson's commitment to poetry. Barthes on Balzac, in *S/Z* (1970, trans. 1974), was a crux.[30] It not only exhibited Barthes's narratology at its best, it represented his definitive account of the conditions of bourgeois narrative—conditions which are not only, or not initially, "formal." By responding to the desire of his reader-consumer, Balzac kept him reading to the end, obliging him to buy another book. Bourgeois narrative must be readable (*lisible*) to sell; it must be writable (*scriptible*) to become literature. The classic literary text would be accessible as a "galaxy of signifiers," not only as a commercially available structure of signifieds. It was monophonic but plural—polysemous, modestly plural—in signification. That was the sign of its literariness.

Barthes's reading of bourgeois narrative meant to be subversive. He set out to break with the philological *and* the semiotic identification of denotation as the meaning of the text. Against the univocal (*univoque*) sense of narrative promoted by an interpretive idiom devoted to ideals of unity and structure, Barthes would propose a plural (*pluriel*) text in which the smooth delivery of denotation was rived, line by line, by five codes of connotation, in an expanded sense of the word. This emphasis was characteristic.

As Genette had observed of Barthes's deviant semiotic, "The systems which interest him are always 'semiologies which dare not speak their name,' codes shameful or unconscious, always marked by a certain bad faith":[31] connotation at war with denotation, innuendo with plain meaning—a very Gallic conception of discourse, conversational or literary, from a certain point of view. Anglo-Saxon irony appeared forthright by comparison.

Not so gratuitous a point, if we step back for a moment to measure this plural text, and literature as *cacographie,* against Bakhtin's sense of polyphonic narrative and his heteroglossia. Without resorting to an extended comparison, it is perhaps worth risking the claim that what Bakhtin found interesting in the cacophonous text of Dostoevsky Barthes described in other forms in classic French narrative. The novel discloses the tensions lurking beneath the veneer of social order (whatever order) within the structures of its discourse. The superiority of novelistic discourse, for Barthes as for Bakhtin, stems from its disruptive engagement with the forms of order, beginning with the forms of literary order—with meaning as univocal, with the text as a unified field. Classical rhetoric had proved an inadequate resource for response to the novel, though both Barthes and Bakhtin drew on it. (The figure of antithesis loomed large in the symbolic code which Barthes elaborated in *S/Z.*) Both forged what might be described as pararhetorical alternatives to irony in their versions of the novel—unrelated versions, certainly, yet the community of interest is real.

For the Anglo-American reader of the seventies, however, *S/Z* appeared unlike anything that was familiar—forbiddingly systematic, a sort of narrative scanner. Barthes's exhaustive analysis of an obscure story looked both scientistic and perverse. Yet the book's aspiration was to liberate the signifier (in words resonant of the period) from the tyranny of the signified—to open a space for writing outside the arcades of commodity culture. *S/Z* was tenacious in its insistence on the difference between writing and consuming. Writing was freedom, *l'infini du langage,* and the world was its prison. To informed readers Barthes looked defiantly antistructuralist, or perhaps counterstructuralist, in dramatically refusing to accept Language as the irreducible ground of interpretation and in dismissing reductive versions of narrative. Northrop Frye must have come to many minds in connection with the latter.

Barthes was evidently reacting to the narrative grammar proposed by Todorov in *Grammaire du Décameron* (1969) and perhaps to Julia Kristeva's *Sèmiotikè* (1969) and other early work. These took formalist positions to limits that were bound to meet with resistance from so private a critical intelligence.

A high-profile instance was Todorov's *Introduction à la littérature fantastique* (1970, trans. 1973; *F*), a book which attracted considerable attention abroad, eliciting responses that figured in their own right in the critical history of the period. *The Fantastic,* as it was called in translation, represented a microcosm of the formalist position on narrative.[32] It was so conspicuous in part on account of the new currency of structuralism. Its opening chapter, a broadly argued résumé of genre theory, became a touchstone. Like Derrida's paper of 1967, it was brief enough to be attended to, comprehensive enough to be argued with. Moreover, it had one eye on the Anglo-American audience, something unprecedented. Frye figured prominently in Todorov's quarrel with Western conceptions of genre, and this drew most of the attention. It is worth recalling that he was also answering Benedetto Croce's bald rejection of genre, Maurice Blanchot's dismissal of anything of the kind, and the general drift of modernist critical practice away from a vital sense of the relation of modern literature to its antecedents.

Frye's anatomy provided Todorov an ideal entry to the theoretical calculations of the Anglo-American school. Through it he would make the case not just for genre but for a specifically formalist conception of it, with Language as constitutive ground. Frye was exposed as ethically entrenched, something he would have admitted in any case. His generic categories were discarded as purely theoretic. Yet what Todorov arrived at was only another taxonomy. The fantastic as a literary type was now as thoroughly subsumed by Language as it had been, in Frye, by Literature:

> If the fantastic constantly makes use of rhetorical figures, it is because it originates in them. The supernatural is born of language, it is both its consequence and its proof: not only do the devil and vampires exist only in words, but language alone enables us to conceive what is always absent: the supernatural. The supernatural thereby becomes a symbol of language, just as the figures of rhetoric do, and the figure is, as we have seen, the purest form of literality. (*F,* 82)

Here, the fantastic became paradigmatic of literature in general—of a Literature conceived allegorically as the Figure of Language. What had begun as a study of a limited literary type ended in this way as a formalist vision on a grand scale.

The Fantastic became in its turn the Figure of Formalism, a sketch of a comprehensive position. It remains interesting in the perspective which Todorov opens in "A Dialogic Criticism?" mainly for the way it converts literature into history via its vision of Language: "The nineteenth century transpired, it is true, in a metaphysics of the real and the imaginary, and the literature of the fantastic is nothing but the bad conscience of this positivist era. But today, we can no longer believe in an immutable, external reality, nor in a literature which is merely the transcription of such a reality. Words have gained an autonomy which things have lost" (*F*, 168). The historical comes into view in the end as a way of establishing relation to a larger world. But the "history" here imagined is utterly desiccated, formulaic beyond recognition. The categorical separation of "now" and "then" isolates the past as a place of contamination. Its relation to the present is mechanical—positivism as a prior stage, since surpassed. History was thus worn down to one more version of Language, that *beau idéal* of the modernist imagination.

The 1969–70 season can be seen in hindsight to have been a turning point of sorts for structuralism in the West. The preoccupation with Language which rose to a crescendo at the time forced the matter not to resolution, certainly, but to confrontation with other ways of seeing. The reaction was already advanced in the work of Barthes, for whom the discourse of Language would remain important all the same. Genette and Todorov continued to pursue it, in different ways, well into the seventies, with a mounting following at home and abroad. But the seventies would soon be in the thrall of Derrida's counter-realization of Language as Script. The culture of criticism across the Channel and over the Ocean, already under siege from within, was driven by these developments to consider its condition. The formalist legacy was not entirely alien to Anglo-Saxon pragmatics: its modernism made it attractive, even if its rigor seemed manic. The question of language could hardly be put off any longer. The very idea of language as a question was offensive to some, a sign that the comfortable autonomy of literature had been resigned. English was sufficient, understanding a matter of common sense improved. A habitual Francophobia mingled with the suspicion of anything East Bloc to secure this party in its settled track. The larger, European view descending from Arnold and Eliot devolved meanwhile on a fractious cadre which felt at odds with institutional criticism and its literary commitments. For this alternative party, literature often meant modernism, and history began from the Great War.

After the New Pyrrhonism

By 1983 it was possible for a veteran of these lines of argument to observe that "structuralism has already more or less vanished into the literary museum."[33] The ferocious negativity of deconstruction had debased the word to a stereotype. Had anyone ever really believed in structure? Derrida continued to work it up into terminological quiddities designed to collapse on order in the next sentence. The persistence of "structure" was most pronounced just where it was most abused. The paradox was only apparent. Deconstruction could in fact be accounted for within the generative model of Saussurean linguistics. Its name told the truth; it enjoyed the inside connection with the method it despised.

The quest for structure had disclosed only doubt. Structural method now appeared futile, a shot in the dark. It rapidly gave way to celebrations of uncertainty and to that metaphysics of absence described by a cunning observer as "ironic structuralism." What Barthes had confronted by working out the implications of semiotic, Derrida was turning into cat's cradles. One commentator situated this blackout in a long rationalist perspective:

> Structural thought understands its object as if that object were a deduction from language. But unlike Descartes, who undertook to deduce the existence of the physical world from the apodictic certitude invested in the Cogito, Barthes—and more radically, Derrida—would show how the primacy of the linguistic model uncovers a structure of uncertainty at the very root of meaning. One is never "outside" language, in a "privileged" position to decide, to judge, whether meaning is or is not initially verbal.[34]

Uncertainty about the basis of meaning, so glaring in the New Criticism, had not been dispelled by the coming of Language.

Instead, it was formalized, spun out in a critical metalanguage which propagated like virus *in vitro*. With the acrobatics of deconstruction, critical discourse contemplated with a vertiginous plunge.

The way through the interpretive maze was now thought to lie in a radical critique of Language. Deconstruction made its strongest appeal to those who had invested in the metaphysics of presence in its modernist versions—the inheritors of phenomenology and hermeneutics, and of a distinguished tradition of philosophical aesthetics. Hans-Georg Gadamer's *Truth and Method* (1960) had codified the problematics of method for them, and Derrida's cursory critique of structuralism made him a kindred spirit.[35] Outside the hermeneutic circle, meanwhile, deconstruction appeared either as the new French wave, with all that implied, or as the last stand of the suburban ideology of liberal humanism.

The latter is Terry Eagleton's version of events. It shows the survival instinct developed by observers abroad who kept reading through the fine Gallic frenzy: when one of these movements is finished, it's on to the next. Eagleton's forthright survey, *Literary Theory: An Introduction,* exemplifies the "movement" view of recent critical history which is now pervasive. Yet his conclusion is deeply indebted to the past he devotes himself to burying. His call for a "theory of discourse" concerned with "the kinds of *effects* which discourse produce, and how they produce them" (*LT,* 207) is so plainly a product of the structuralism which he has just consigned to the museum that it is perhaps worth asking how else he might have arrived at this point. Is it really a fossil, or do these bones live? In *The Function of Criticism* (1984) Eagleton works out his idea in the arena of Habermas's "public sphere."[36] But his call for a return to rhetoric, applied to "the field of discursive practices in society as a whole," grounds his project squarely in the Paris of the sixties, when Barthes was still interested in the old rhetoric, and in cultural formations of every kind. Eagleton's program is retrospective in this way and limited in advance by the burden of the French experience. For his aspiration to a general semiotic is just what Barthes was about in *Mythologies* (1957), some of his *Essais critiques* (1964), and *Système de la mode* (1967). Barthes's quandaries are well-known. Why should things fare differently in the English reenactment? The evidence of recent critical history compels recognition that rhetoric is a formidable propagator of rhetoric. It is self-regarding and self-consuming.

Which is not to say that the structuralist revival came to nothing—far from it. Much has been opened up to productive reconsideration along the way—narrative in particular. Eagleton's projected revival of rhetoric is only the visible tip of a real structural legacy in Anglo-American critical practice. It is not just a terminology that has been propagated but a sense of language as an institution within which literature performs. Ambient assumptions, especially about reference, have been worked through in a leading way. The cardinal matter of representation is under consideration everywhere as a result. Formalist (and structuralist) thinking about literature battened on the naive mimeticism of academic criticism. Suspicion of representation ran deep in the sixties, but this was no more than a phase. In the long run the doubts have served to invigorate, not to undermine, the concept. The reactive indictment of structure as autotelic, the natural enemy of anything more inclusive, is a consequence of early excesses. Such polarized positions tell on underlying tensions within the critical institution—between text and world, language as self-fulfilling, and language as symbolic action.

This is the ground on which any critical "movement" will have to play. Real understanding of what happened to structuralism in the Anglo-American setting must begin from a sense of the institution and of the way it naturalizes what is alien to it. If structuralism appears, then, to have gone the way of the New Criticism, it should remind us that it was precisely in terms of the New Criticism that it was grasped here, as an antidote to uncertainty in the linguistic base and, in the end, as another method of close reading.

NOTES

Bibliographical notes in the text cite date of original publication, date of translation where appropriate, and abbreviation in subsequent citations.

1. Tzvetan Todorov, "A Dialogic Criticism?" *Raritan*, 4 (1984), 64–76.
2. M. M. Bakhtin, "Discourse in the Novel," in *The Dialogic Imagination: Four Essays*, ed. Michael Holquist, trans. Caryl Emerson (Austin: University of Texas Press, 1981), esp. pp. 313, 349.
3. Tzvetan Todorov, *Mikhail Bakhtin: The Dialogical Principle* (Paris:

Editions du Seuil, 1981; English translation, Minneapolis: University of Minnesota Press, 1984), cited hereafter as *MB*.

4. See Elmar Holenstein, *Jakobson, ou le structuralisme phénoménologique* (Paris: Seghers, 1974), pp. 15ff. For a broader account of the origins of formalism, including developments in St. Petersburg, see Victor Erlich, *Russian Formalism: History—Doctrine* (The Hague: Mouton, 1955; 4th ed., 1980), pp. 63ff. On the relation of formalism to Prague structuralism, see Peter Steiner, "The Roots of Structuralist Aesthetics," in *The Prague School,* ed. Peter Steiner (Austin: University of Texas Press, 1982), pp. 174–219. Steiner dwells on the differences, but Jakobson was instrumental in the formation of both. His considerable figure links structuralism to the origins of formalism and (through Lévi-Strauss) to the French *sciences humaines.* The turn against structuralism in the wake of its revival in the West implicated the formalist position at the theoretical base and so, evidently, did Bakhtin, working close to the original stage. See Fredric Jameson, *The Prison-House of Language: A Critical Account of Structuralism and Russian Formalism* (Princeton: Princeton University Press, 1972); and Todorov, *MB,* pp. 20–21. For purposes of exposition, I assume a theoretical convergence in the linguistic base without presuming on practical consequences.
5. For discussion, see Francis Mulhern, *The Moment of "Scrutiny"* (London: Verso, 1981), pp. 36–37.
6. Following Todorov, I take Bakhtin's role in the formation of P. N. Medvedev's *The Formal Method in Literary Scholarship* (Leningrad: Priboĭ 1928; English translation, Baltimore: Johns Hopkins University Press, 1978) to be essential to its conception. His Dostoevsky book of the following year, revised from a text of 1922, inaugurates the search for a dialogical principle. Chronology confirms the supposition that the latter arises within the critique of the formalist position. See Todorov, *MB,* p. 17, citing the revised edition of 1934 as Bakhtin.
7. René Wellek, "A Sketch of the History of Dostoevsky Criticism," reprinted in *Discriminations: Further Concepts of Criticism* (New Haven: Yale University Press, 1970), p. 310.
8. Writing in 1970, George Steiner subordinated Richards and his inheritors to "Petersburg and Prague half a century ago," while tracing a native line of paralinguistic critical inquiry through William Empson and John Crowe Ransom. The local developments ignored in such a reckoning deserve broader treatment. Cambridge brought its own emphases to language, and however limited by comparison, these responded in their way to the conditions of modern reading. See

"Linguistics and Poetics," in *Extraterritorial* (1971; rpt. Harmondsworth: Penguin, 1975), p. 147.

9. See R. K. Meiners, "Marginal Men and Centers of Learning: New Critical Rhetoric and Critical Politics," *New Literary History*, 18 (1986): "The New Critics pressed their implacably sceptical intelligences toward the subtle and intimate behavior of words, but they did so without the benefit of any systematic understanding of linguistics and, indeed, fended off possible alliances with linguistics as more unwelcome intrusions of 'science'; their scepticism and their knowledge of words was thus turned toward the preservation of a mysterious presence, an 'experience' or 'unity' beyond the reach of mere language or the systematic study of language. This should have led not only to linguistics but to a critique of politics and/or theology: but the New Critics chose to remain in the sceptical scrutiny of languages."
10. Proceedings printed as *Style in Language*, ed. Thomas A. Sebeok (Cambridge, Mass.: M.I.T. Press, 1960), hereafter cited as *SL*.
11. Roman Jakobson and Claude Lévi-Strauss, "'Les Chats' de Charles Baudelaire," *L'Homme*, 2 (1962), 5–21, translated as "Charles Baudelaire's 'Les Chats,'" in *Introduction to Structuralism*, ed. Michael Lane (New York: Basic, 1972), pp. 202–21. For context and commentary, see Robert Scholes, *Structuralism in Literature* (New Haven: Yale University Press, 1974), pp. 31–40.
12. Michael Riffaterre, "Describing Poetic Structures: Two Approaches to Baudelaire's 'Les Chats,'" *Yale French Studies*, 36–37 (1966), 213.
13. Michael Riffaterre, "Interpretation and Descriptive Poetry," *New Literary History*, 4 (1973), 229–57, hereafter cited as *IDP*; Geoffrey Hartman, "The Use and Abuse of Structural Analysis: Riffaterre's Interpretation of Wordsworth's 'Yew-Trees,'" *New Literary History*, 6 (1975), 165–89.
14. *SL*, 158. See "Two Aspects of Language and Two Types of Aphasic Disturbances," in Roman Jakobson and Morris Halle, *Fundamentals of Language* (The Hague: Mouton, 1956), pp. 55–82.
15. Jonathan Culler, *Structuralist Poetics* (Ithaca: Cornell University Press, 1975), p. 71.
16. Proceedings published as *The Languages of Criticism and the Sciences of Man: The Structuralist Controversy*, ed. Richard Macksey and Eugenio Donato (Baltimore: Johns Hopkins University Press, 1970), hereafter cited as *LCSM*.
17. Michel Foucault, *Les Mots et les choses*, translated as *The Order of Things* (New York: Pantheon, 1971).
18. Jacques Derrida, "La Mythologie blanche," *Poétique*, 5 (1971), 1–52;

published as "La Mythologie blanche: la métaphore dans le texte philosophique," in *Marges de la philosophie* (Paris: Minuit, 1972), pp. 247–324, and in *Margins of Philosophy,* trans. Alan Bass (University of Chicago Press, 1982).

19. For discussion, see A. C. Goodson, "Oedipus Anthropologicus," *MLN*, 94 (1979), 688–701.
20. For discussion of the premise, see Albert Cook, *Myth and Language* (Bloomington: Indiana University Press, 1980), pp. 13–36.
21. For discussion, see Jeffrey Mehlman, *A Structural Study of Autobiography* (Ithaca: Cornell University Press, 1974), pp. 187ff.
22. Roland Barthes, *Essais critiques* (Paris: Seuil, 1964), p. 257, translated as *Critical Essays* (Evanston: Northwestern University Press, 1972), p. 260.
23. Gérard Genette, *Figures* (Paris: Seuil, 1966), p. 159.
24. Jean-Pierre Vernant, "Le Mythe hésiodique des races: essai d'analyse structurale," in *Mythe et pensée chez les grecs* (Paris: Maspero, 1969), pp. 19–47; "Ambigüité et renversement. Sur la structure énigmatique d'*Oedipe-Roi*," in *Mythe et tragédie en grèce ancienne* (Paris: Maspero, 1973), pp. 99–131. See also Marcel Detienne's books, *Les Maîtres de vérité dans la grèce archaique* (Paris: Maspero, 1967); and *Les Jardins d'Adonis* (Paris: Gallimard, 1972).
25. René Girard, *La Violence et le sacré* (Paris: Grasset, 1972), pp. 102–29, translated as *Violence and the Sacred* (Baltimore: Johns Hopkins University Press, 1977), pp. 68–88.
26. Roland Barthes, "Leçon inaugurale" (Paris: Collège de France, 1977), pp. 8, 9, 11.
27. For discussion, see Dominick LaCapra, *Rethinking Intellectual History: Texts, Contexts, Language* (Ithaca: Cornell University Press, 1983), pp. 304–6.
28. See *Innovation/Renovation,* ed. Ihab Hassan and Sally Hassan (Madison: University of Wisconsin Press, 1983), hereafter cited as *I/R*.
29. Gerard Genette, "Métonymie chez Proust ou la naissance du Récit," *Poetique,* 2 (1970), 156–73.
30. Roland Barthes, *S/Z* (Paris: Seuil, 1970); English translation (New York: Hill and Wang, 1974).
31. Genette, *Figures,* p. 195.
32. Tzvetan Todorov, *Introduction à la littérature fantastique* (Paris: Seuil, 1970).
33. Terry Eagleton, *Literary Theory: An Introduction* (Minneapolis: University of Minnesota Press, 1983), p. 199, hereafter cited as *LT*.

34. Evan Watkins, *The Critical Act* (New Haven: Yale University Press, 1978), p. 75.
35. Hans-Georg Gadamer, *Wahrheit und Methode* (Tübingen: T. C. B. Mohr, 1972); English translation, *Truth and Method* (London: Sheed and Ward, 1975).
36. Terry Eagleton, *The Function of Criticism: From "The Spectator" to Post-Structuralism* (London: Verso, 1984), p. 102.

ALBERT DIVVER

Tracing Hermeneutics

MODERN DEFINITIONS OF HERMENEUTICS, while unexceptionable as *modern* definitions, do not immediately shed light on the nature and function of hermeneutic thought or mark it off as a distinctive intellectual endeavor. Paul Ricoeur, for example, writes that "hermeneutics is the theory of operations of understanding in their relations to the interpretation of texts."[1] Richard Palmer, in his fine survey of hermeneutics, uses similar terms, though without the functional emphasis. "Hermeneutics," he says, "is the study of understanding, especially the understanding of texts."[2] To the reader innocent of the historical context of these definitions, it might seem that hermeneutical inquiry merely does what any theoretically grounded literary criticism must do: inquire into the conditions which govern textual interpretation. As such, hermeneutics would only be another name for literary theory, or at least for that part of literary theory pertaining to interpretation. It is only when the terms of these definitions, "understanding," "interpretation," and "texts," reveal themselves to be problematic—as occurring within a particular historical context and, indeed, within a mode of thinking that takes historical context as the inescapable limiting condition of all human inquiry—that hermeneutics makes its claim on the attention of literary critics, especially in the United States, where "literary history" has been received largely as a precursor to New Criticism and to the more recent structuralist and poststructuralist movements, which favor synchronic perspectives. Hermeneutics' contribution to contemporary literary discussion is particularly valuable because it alerts an interpretive community to the historical contingencies which impinge upon any systematic engagement with texts. At the same time, it reflects upon its own historically contingent understanding of "method" in interpretation, whether that method be Marxist, psychoanalytical, or structuralist/poststructuralist.

Hermeneutics itself is an ancient discipline which has made its way into contemporary literary discourse largely through nineteenth- and twentieth-century German philosophy. In the nineteenth century, positivist theories of knowledge and inquiry which accompanied the explosion of scientific achievements had the effect of either relegating humanistic pursuits to the status of unverifiable speculation or subsuming them under the straitening criteria of empirical science. The first way of regarding humanistic studies, if acceded to by humanists, would have meant seeing historical and literary pursuits as a kind of grand entertainment, like puzzle solving or charades. Adopting the second way would have required that scholars and critics subscribe to a strict neutrality of observation, the formulation of hypotheses that proceed from general laws of causal explanation that could be "tested," and the accumulation of results that have predictive power. Such a dismissal of the personal, the intentional, and the introspective or intuitive aspects of inquiry would have eliminated almost everything that traditionally defined historical and philological study of texts. Hermeneutics in its modern form, then, emerged as a result of a crisis in the human sciences, which in turn elicited a nineteenth-century controversy as yet unresolved, and unresolvable by the criteria of empirical science which engendered it.

Although hermeneutics has attracted the interest of some American philosophers, it has largely escaped the attention of literary critics in this country, perhaps because the man who most influenced American academic critics in this regard introduced them to the field by writing a polemical rejection of much hermeneutical philosophy. E. D. Hirsch's *Validity in Interpretation* appeared amid a controversy about relativism in interpretation which tended to polarize American critics into "objectivists" and "relativists."[3] In attempting to rescue American criticism from what he saw as its theoretical confusion and at the same time to stem the tide of imported "relativism," Hirsch ranged thinkers like Heidegger and his student Hans-Georg Gadamer with the "relativists" and so seemed to damn them by simple categorization. In so doing he applied principles and distinctions to their thinking that their thinking itself had brought into question.

The result of the orientation Hirsch brought to discussions of hermeneutics was that categories such as "subjective" and "objective," which denoted distinctions between "relativistic" and "nonrelativistic" approaches to interpretation, came to serve as foundational categories for the discussion of the "ontological" hermeneutic philosophy of Heidegger and Gadamer. In other words, an orientation that accepts the epistemological premises of a Cartesian methodology applies its own assumptions to a way of thinking that challenges those assumptions in its own point of departure. This essay will sketch the context which brings together the "epistemological" hermeneutics of Hirsch and his German predecessors with the "ontological" hermeneutics of Heidegger, Gadamer, and their followers. It makes no claim to comprehensiveness. In fact, it will proceed through illustrative example, a juxtaposition of thinkers which follows a rough chronology but which aims chiefly to lead the reader to the central issues of hermeneutic thought. My own bias allies me more closely with Gadamer and Heidegger than with Hirsch and "positivist" theories of interpretation. However, my understanding of "historicity," Heidegger's conception of the inescapable condition of all human understanding, makes me aware of the limitations inherent in all such controversies. The adoption of a "point of view," necessary to any exposition, will shape my arguments and partly determine my conclusions, which represent the best understanding of the subject that I have at this time. But the language of this initial section, bristling with the terms which thinkers use to reveal the process of understanding texts (e.g., "understanding," "historicity," "epistemological," "ontological," "subjective," "objective") itself needs disclosure. This inquiry into hermeneutic thought, then, will be as much an exploration of the way this essay understands its own language as it is an exploration of the subject, "hermeneutics."

In the third book of his *Essays* Montaigne adopts a radically antihermeneutic stance. He complains that "it is more of a job to interpret the interpretations than to interpret the things, and there are more books about books than about any other subject: we do nothing but write glosses about each other. The world is swarming with commentaries; of authors there is a great scarcity."[4] Montaigne's complaint does not oppose a modern sense of creativity to imitation, but rather the delight in the study of "things" to the study of books. Experience becomes the standard of inquiry and so of writing. The "essay" contrives to follow the mutating mind in its exploration of the changing world. "Knowledge" for Montaigne is thus the result of an activity or even an activity itself, provisional, changing, and always alive. If the process of acquiring knowledge is inseparable from what is thereby known, then knowledge itself is an activity, for the mind "does nothing but ferret and quest, and keeps incessantly whirling around, building up and becoming entangled in its own work."[5] Tangled up, bewildered, lost, the truth seeker may give in to weakness and rest, either by leaving off the inquiry or by adopting another's ideas. But the adoption of another person's ideas is always a "dilution" of them, a process intrinsic to interpretation.

According to Montaigne, even Aristotle failed to make himself understood, and Luther, who aimed to bring clarity to scriptural interpretation, left more difficulties than he began with. Rather than end dispute, commentary inevitable breeds more disagreement. Montaigne's antihermeneuticism occurred at the time of Reformation, when commentary on the Bible was more than an academic pastime. Theological disputes were weapons in the arsenal of bloody religious warfare.

Montaigne's radical rejection of antecedent texts as referents takes aim at one tendency in traditional hermeneutics—the desire to be "correct," the desire to align oneself with an authority, a guarantor of "truth." Luther attempted to solve the problem by bypassing the mediation of tradition as promulgated by the Roman church. By substituting "spirituality" for the collective principle of tradition, or "teachings" of the church, Luther hoped to establish an incontrovertible personal access to truth and to separate the process from institutional power. As Gerald Bruns points out, spirituality has to do with how one reads, not just with the text itself, and is thereby a "hermeneutic category."[6] It is a hermeneutic category, however, only in that it supplements the "literal text" with an extra-textual, i.e., interpretive, principle. Luther's "spirituality" does not really serve the needs of a fully hermeneutic approach to reading because it confines itself to a private transaction between the reader and God. The problem of communication with other human beings remains. To be inspirited in reading is one thing. To participate in the social act of discourse is quite another. It is here that Montaigne's criticism must be met, for lurking within Luther's spiritualism is a kind of objectivism to be met again in the relatively demystified phenomenology of Husserl. As long as reading is a private act with a divine guarantor of truth, it claims objective knowledge that can neither be supported nor refuted in discourse. As soon as reading becomes a subject of discourse, it must lose the perfection of unmediated understanding, even within the community of the faithful.

If Luther's doctrine depended upon a suffusion of divine grace, Augustine, speaking for a church still struggling to establish an orthodoxy, offered, in his *On Christian Doctrine,* a principle of interpretation designed to overcome embarrassing obscurities met in Scripture: "Whatever appears in the divine Word that does not literally pertain to virtuous behavior or to the truth of faith you must take to be figurative. Virtuous behavior pertains to the love of God and of one's neighbor; the truth of faith pertains to a knowledge of God and of one's neighbor."[7] Augustine's principle, unlike Luther's, is communicable and social. It recognizes a relationship between interpretation and action and posits a "teachable" approach to Scripture. At the same time it allows that the "literal" meaning of certain passages does not convey their "full" meaning and may even mislead the uninitiated.

Augustine thus sets himself against tendencies in the writings of early Christians (exemplified in the works of Origen) to conceive of Scripture as a hermetic text, secret doctrines accessible only to those granted special grace. He accepts "knowledge" of "virtuous behavior" as an objective principle of interpretation which places the sacred text in the context of a living tradition. The tradition itself, however, forms the guarantor of truth—a mediated, as opposed to Luther's socially unmediated, form of understanding. Both Luther and Augustine work from the assumption that the text of the Bible contains truth and that what remains at issue is the means of obtaining it in a fallen world. Both assume that the reception of biblical truth involves the salvation of the receiver. In other words, there is an existential aspect of interpretation that transcends any single "method" of interpretation. The success of an interpretative method would depend upon a prior stage of receptivity within the soul of the interpreter.

Although Augustine and Luther emphasize different "hermeneutic" principles (Augustine would hardly deny the importance of grace, and Luther had his own limited notion of social hermeneutic, which he called "grammaticality"), they shared a concern central to modern hermeneutics. They aimed to provide a foundation for interpretation, a principle of understanding prior to any method of interpretation. Their answers to the problem were confined to a special text (or a single tradition) and so do not meet Montaigne's skepticism head on. Nor do they help the modern secular theorist, who looks back on a hermeneutical tradition which, in the last several centuries, has been concerned to "demystify" the conception of textual interpretation and to question all such foundational assumptions. Nevertheless, by placing the problem of interpretation in the general context of understanding rather than in the principles of interpretive methods, Luther and Augustine foreshadow a movement that animated hermeneutic thought in the nineteenth century.

Modern Hermeneutics

Hermeneutics in the nineteenth century seems to play itself out in a dance of binary oppositions: understanding/explanation, absolute/relative, reason/experience, and, not least of all, historicism/historicism. Although the term "historicism" occurs early in the nineteenth century, it achieved general use only late in the century.[8] As the opposition of "historicism" to itself indicates, however, the chief importance of historicism for hermeneutics is in the contradictions which led to the dilemmas surrounding the conception of understanding itself. The opposition between understanding and explanation, upon which Dilthey attempted to build his defense of the human sciences, emerges from the scientistic and relativistic assumptions of historicism, which ended by discrediting the study of history itself.

The prestige which historical study attained in the nineteenth century is often thought to have been at the expense of an ahistorical ethos associated with the Enlightenment. Though this is a simplification, nineteenth-century historicists certainly believed that they were reacting against Enlightenment rationalism. The historical irony which befell these proponents of "history" lay in the fact that they used the rationalistic categories of "man" and "reason" to effect their intellectual revolt and so left themselves open to the charge of emptying "history" of its normative force.

A rationalist philosophy holds that human reason is unchangeable and universal, a standard whose operations guarantee that knowledge will also be universal and immutable. Since reason is the defining characteristic of human nature and since the study of history is the study of human actions, then the study of history (and historical texts) reveals manifestations of human nature. Historical knowledge deals therefore with essences. But, as Herbert Schnädelbach shows, the Enlightenment enlightened itself—that is, arguments within Enlightenment philosophy turned to criticism of Enlightenment conceptions of reason, history, and human nature themselves.[9] The result was that "Reason" declared the concept of reason to be historically situated and therefore historically bounded. Since Enlightenment foundational terms became bracketed in this way, they could no longer serve as guarantors of immutable truth or universal understanding. The secularizing Enlightenment, having undermined scriptural authority, performed the same operation on its own governing categories.

If the reduction of Enlightenment universals to historical categories "deconstructed" its absolutes by revealing their implication in contingency, the submission of "history" to the criteria of positivist science destroyed, or at least deflated, history itself. The apparent defeat of "Reason," which became a less crucial norm as the Enlightenment waned, had left its self-generated successor, historicism, free of rationalist "essences." The growing influence of positivist scientific theory, however, introduced a different form of absolutism into historical studies, the notion of universal scientific laws. The study of history, which had obvious implications for Enlightenment doctrine because both took human action as the norm and object of inquiry, had no such obvious connection with the scientific study of the nonhuman world, except in the Cartesian or La Mettrian formulation of man as machine. Nevertheless, it is in terms of the scientific formulation of method that the hermeneutics of Dilthey appeared, with its distinction between explanation and understanding. And it is in terms of scientific doctrine that historicism divided against itself into "objectivist" and "relativistic" modes.

Historicism in the nineteenth century owes its peculiar character to its attempt to make historical study conform to positivist science, thus setting up a specious opposition between objective and subjective (i.e., nonscientific) approaches to historical study. Historicism in this guise privileges the first term because it appears to link the human sciences with the prestigious methods of scientific inquiry. It rejects all normative elements of historical investigation and all inferences that do not follow from the reconstruction of "facts."

Among the hidden assumptions of such positivist theories of knowledge is the assumption that facts are primitives—that is, facts stand out immediately against the knowing mind. This questionable assumption masks the interpretive activity that determines what is to be considered a "fact" and, moreover, what is to be considered a "significant" fact. In turn, "significance," which belongs to the domain of meaning rather than to that of logic or empirical method, suggests the other important presupposition of positivism (which Dilthey reacted against)—that the study of historical events (or texts) is the study of objects. Objectivism needs "objects" of study. The hermeneutical stance regards this ascription as a "category mistake." The study of human activities and works involves the study of meaning and requires "understanding" rather than explanation. The human sciences address themselves to the problem of understanding other people, which requires an approach distinct from the scientific investigation of the physical world. Thus, the hermeneutic theory of understanding need not situate itself within the epistemological and methodological contexts of either rationalist or positivist method.

Historicism in the second sense, historical relativism, curiously enough receives its plausibility from the opposed, positivist formulation. Historical relativists accepted both the positivist definition of knowledge and the antirationalist doctrine that all human activity is historically bound (even Dilthey could not think through the resulting contradictions). In this view no method can attain certainty, because, as Schnädelbach puts it, "the phenomena themselves lack the factual status which explanation presupposes." Historicism as a theory "thus faces us with the alternatives of being either barbarians with convictions or refined relativists. Culture on this view rests on the only thing which the scientific approach to history in a scientific age can furnish: historical facts and connections which, for the sake of scientific objectivity, may only be stated."[10] What this amounts to is a science without scientific inference, since the human or cultural element does not provide phenomena suitable to scientific inquiry and so does not provide a base of "facts" upon which to construct the edifice of scientific generalizations.

Friedrich Schleiermacher usually receives credit for articulating the first general hermeneutics (i.e., one which comprehends interpretation of any text, as opposed to the traditional distinction between legal, scriptural, etc., methods of interpretation). More important, Schleiermacher is the first to locate hermeneutics in the problem of understanding itself. Describing how, in conversation, he often attempts to go beyond "ordinary" understanding and to trace the ways in which his respondent makes the transition "from one thought to another" or how it is that he expresses himself in one way and not another on the subject he is discussing, Schleiermacher concludes that "the same facts, which every attentive person will have to give evidence of from his own case, manifest . . . clearly enough that the solution of the problem for which we are seeking the theory in no way depends on those situations of discourse which are fixed for the eyes by means of writing, but that it is to be found wherever we have to understand thoughts or sequences of thought by means of words."[11]

The hermeneutical situation, then, arises whenever the listener, or reader, must relate discourse to understanding. Moreover, hermeneutics is an art, "the art of relating discourse [*Reden*] and understanding [*Verstehen*] to one another: discourse, however, being on the outer sphere of thought, requires that one must think of hermeneutics as an art, and thus as philosophical"[12]—that is, the study of discourse is to be distinguished from the study of rhetoric, which has to do with exposition (*Darlegens*) in the external or technical sense. Hence discourse is the obverse side of understanding, which is the proper subject of philosophy. The hermeneutic situation emerges from dialogue, but dialogue as such is external to the proper scope of hermeneutics, a principle emphasized by an early formulation, which distinguishes between *subtilitas intelligendi* (acuteness of understanding) and *subtilitas explicandi* (acuteness of explication). As soon as explication is more than the outside of understanding ("sobald sie mehr ist als die äussere Seite des Verstehens"), it belongs to the art of presentation ("zur Kunst des Darstellens").[13] The relationship between the articulation of thoughts in language and the understanding of thoughts so formulated seems to prepare the way for a hermeneutics based on a linguistic model and so to anticipate the "linguistic turn" that has animated so much twentieth-century thought, including the thought of Gadamer.

Schleiermacher's emphasis upon the dialogic context of the hermeneutic situation and his reference to discourse as the "mediation of shareable thought" place the actual work of hermeneutics "on the outer sphere of thought" where discourse takes place. He considers the possibility that discourse is no more than "manifested thought" because "thought becomes complete only through interior discourse" but immediately rejects it since "where the thinker thinks original thoughts, he himself requires the art of discourse to transform them into expressions that afterwards require exposition"(*Auslegung*).[14]

Auslegung refers to "discursive" understanding, part of the hermeneutic process which follows upon *Verstehen*, or immediate understanding—a preliminary grasp of the whole. But the preliminary grasp (much like the "pre-understanding" of later hermeneuticists) turns out normally to be a *misunderstanding*, which is the starting point of "strict interpretation." What Schleiermacher calls "careless interpretation" never modifies its own preassumptions but bends the text to conform to them. Strict interpretation, on the other hand, begins with misunderstanding and through continual modifications strives for a "precise" understanding. The assumption that "misunderstanding" is the usual situation of the interpreter distinguishes Schleiermacher's hermeneutics from earlier "arts of interpretation," where difficulties were seen as local problems in otherwise transparent texts. In Schleiermacher's view there can be no such thing as a local difficulty because each part of a text depends for its understanding on a grasp of the whole, and the whole is understood only through a grasp of each of its parts. This, of course, is the hermeneutic circle, which Schleiermacher expounded within the context of attaining "complete knowledge."[15] This totalizing tendency, characteristic of German philosophical and historical writing, will lead Schleiermacher to identify "scientific" knowledge with "complete" knowledge, an aspiration that seems to contradict his dialogic model of understanding.

Turning against Hegelian teleology, Schleiermacher allied himself with the "historical school," which interpreted works as "products of their age." He included the crucial work—Scripture as well as secular works—under this rubric, but he departed from the historicists in that he also allowed that creative works altered the language and presuppositions of the age even as they drew upon them. Besides, then, the movement of understanding between the parts and wholes of a text, Schleiermacher posits a similar movement between the work and the works of the age, from the viewpoint of both language and conceptual analysis. This is not a reductive historical analysis but a dialectical process whereby interpretation moves between the "whole language" and individual expression, the whole age and the individual author's mind. With all his openness toward development (Schleiermacher implicitly criticizes the historicists for offering no explanation of historical change), Schleiermacher's goal seems to have been a "complete" knowledge of the author's mind. As such he seems to recommend that the interpreter engage in an endless process and at the same time suggests that the process leads to understanding superior to that which the author himself had. Dilthey adopted a version of this principle, which Gadamer calls "a formula that has been respected ever since and in the changing interpretation of which the whole history of modern hermeneutics can be read."[16]

Hans-Georg Gadamer argues that Schleiermacher's passage from an apparently dialogic model of understanding to the idealistic psychologism implicit in his goal of "complete" knowledge exemplifies what he calls "the questionableness of romantic hermeneutics."[17] Romantic hermeneutics assumes that by making explicit the ideas implicit in a text the interpreter can come to know the author's "intentions" even where they have been obscure to the author himself. Intentionality, of course, forms the foundation of E. D. Hirsch's hermeneutics, though in Hirsch's work it does not bear the burden of providing the interpreter with understanding superior to that of the original author's self-understanding. It also provides the basis for Emilio Betti's magisterial work in legal hermeneutics, where the issue of intention is crucial. As a philosophical concept, however, intention remains a vexed issue, often asserted rather than demonstrated by the objective canons that intentionalists hold as necessary to any rational argument.

Dilthey, according to Gadamer, was the first to notice the epistemological problem. His insight led him to attempt a way out of the idealist/empiricist dichotomies, which neither Schleiermacher nor the positivist, Rankean historicists had thought through. Dilthey's great contribution to their resolution is his argument that the human sciences deal with experience, not with facts. The German word, *Erleben,* which Dilthey uses, has an active sense much stronger than the English "experience." It connotes lived experience, not merely experience as a series of facts for analysis or commentary. Such an orientation emphasizes experience as a living process intrinsic to history itself and as such part of the fabric which unites text as the record of experience with interpreters who share the bond of lived human experience. This orientation doesn't resolve the contradictions of historicism, but it offers a potentially fruitful perspective. Where Schleiermacher's hermeneutics focuses on the object of inquiry as the chief element in the problem of understanding, Dilthey directs attention to the subject interpreting. Understanding is possible because the subject experiences "life," which shapes his assumptions about the "Other," whose texts he wishes to interpret. The historical gap between an author and his interpreter can be overcome because both share "lived experience," which Dilthey offers as a category bridging rationalist notions of "human nature" and positivist conceptions of "historical facts."

Leaving for now the difficulties which Dilthey's formulation encounters, we will look at a specimen of Hirsch's inquiry into the "intentions" of an author, an argument which introduces the notion of "willed" meaning into the hermeneutic process. In an appendix to *Validity in Interpretation* Hirsch argues against the twin dangers of "subjectivism and relativism," which he sees as the inevitable result of assuming "that the meaning of a word sequence is directly imposed by the public norms of language, that the text as a 'piece of language' is defined by public norms." Since norms of language change, according to Hirsch it would follow, if textual meanings were determined solely by their role in language, that meanings would change too. Against this assumption Hirsch opposes a reciprocal image: "Just as language constitutes and colors subjectivity, so does subjectivity color language. The author's subjective act is formally necessary to verbal meaning, and any theory which tries to dispense with the author as specifier of meaning by asserting that textual meaning is purely objectively determined finds itself chasing will-o'-the-wisps."[18]

Few would quarrel with Hirsch's assertion that language as a system and language as utterance are mutually defined. More questionable are the inferences he draws from his observation. First of all, having granted that system and utterance "color" one another, Hirsch jumps to the conclusion that the author (subjective term) specifies the meaning, which Hirsch takes to be objective, determinate, self-identical, reproducible, universal, unchanging.[19] This seems a bit peculiar because he locates the determinant of objective meaning in the subjective realm, while he finds relativism in the public systematic domain of language. This relativism he attributes to changing norms within the language system. If he really means that the norms of language are unstable, however, it is difficult to see how any individual linguistic expression, which is itself subject to these changes, can offer a stable determinant of meaning. Nor is it clear how an author can "will" this determination.[20] First of all, one would have to decide what "norm of language" existed at the moment of the work's appearance, before determining what the meaning of the utterance was (or is now and will ever continue to be, in Hirsch's view). Second, if the work itself has the power to "color" language, then it very likely is tinted by the system it colors.

Determination of the changing "norms of language" depends on inferences made about particular utterances, while the understanding of particular utterances is impossible without recourse to "norms of language." If an author *specifies* or wills a meaning, the meaning he "wills", insofar as it must be construed from a linguistic expression, would seem to be subject to the constraints of a hermeneutic circle, operating between the determination of the individual work's "meaning" and the "norms of language" applicable at that time. Only by assuming a *stable* language system, as in the Saussurian mold, can one develop a theory of *meaning* as a foundation for the analysis of particular utterances, so that the public norms of language would seem the only possible starting place for the process of understanding. But this starting place brings hermeneutics into a semiotic disposition which Hirsch cannot accept, because whatever the heuristic value of such a model, it cannot reveal an author's intention and so, in Hirsch's view, leads to relativism.

The question remains, then, whether there is any way to stabilize the realm of the willing or intending subject in Hirsch's hermeneutic. Hirsch attempts to solve this problem by staging an end run that turns out to be a reverse play. He first tries to get around the apparent circularity of the linguistic model by developing his dictum that "meaning is an affair of consciousness, not of words."[21] Referring directly to Dilthey's concept of *Sichhineinfühlen* (an empathic projection of oneself back into the mind and situation of an author, which is possible because interpreter and author share *Erlebnis*), Hirsch argues for a goal of reconstructing the author's intention. Reconstruction of the author's meaning, i.e., intention, must employ both intra-and extra-textual information, although the text remains the primary source, because it "is the safest source of clues to the author's outlook." But even if the text is the "final authority, the interpreter should make an effort to go beyond his text wherever possible, since this is the only way he can avoid a vicious circularity." Because inferences about a text are extrinsic to it, there is no point in limiting oneself solely to the text in an effort to reconstruct its meaning. Hirsch cautions that one must not confuse the result of reconstruction with the process of reconstruction. While the final understanding of the text must be limited by the text, it does not follow that the making of this understanding should be so constrained, especially since an incorrect initial stance toward the text becomes more persuasive the more one concentrates on the text alone.[22]

What this amounts to is a new version of psychologism. Reacting against what he saw as American New Criticism's text-bound formalism, Hirsch posited a new version of "intentionalism." He argued that "The interpreter's primary task is to reproduce in himself the author's 'logic,' his attitudes, his cultural givens, in short, his world. Even though the process of verification is highly complex and difficult, the ultimate verificative principle is very simple—the imaginative reconstruction of the speaking subject."[23] Hirsch's argument, which draws on Husserlian phenomenology, is too lengthy to review here, but it has not convinced many that he escapes the textualism that he decries.[24] First of all, Hirsch puts his doctrine in the service of a positivist aim, a scientific goal abandoned even by contemporary philosophers of science: an exact and objective knowledge of another mind, as though it were an object in the world. This treatment of meaning and intention, which Hirsch claims to distinguish from physical phenomena, in fact violates Dilthey's crucial distinction. Second, Hirsch confuses "imaginative reconstruction" with verification. The first is an abiding and, on the whole, unobjectionable part of the hermeneutic process. The operative word, however, is "imaginative," which suggests something other than verifiable knowledge or even validation.

What Hirsch has run up against, as did Schleiermacher and Dilthey before him, is the gap between the desire to ground interpretation in a certain epistemological foundation and the limitations of human understanding. In the service of restoring "historicity" to literary studies, Hirsch has in fact argued for aversion of positivist historicism, which conflates "fact" and interpretation.

The problems encountered in Hirsch's hermeneutical thought, then, might be characterized as foundational and epistemological. Hirsch and his predecessors in the tradition of Schleiermacher assume that the fundamental problem of hermeneutics is the establishment of a foundation which secures a rational basis for explaining how it is that human beings can know the original meanings of texts produced in historical periods other than their own. They conceive this problem as a special case of the epistemological inquiry into the way human beings come to know anything at all. Hirsch is correct in looking to Husserl as the great modern exemplar of this sort of foundationalism, though Husserl found his primary data in an "intentional consciousness," which left the problem of communication with other consciousnesses difficult to establish. Thus their attempt to distinguish understanding from explanation in the empirical sciences tends to collapse back into the metaphysical presuppositions of positivism, while maintaining a largely ceremonial distinction between "meaning" and the "objects" of physical science. It is the epistemological stance itself which produces the binary opposition between object and subject, mental and physical, process and product, which it must then overcome. This is so because epistemology begins by setting mental operations against external stimuli, *res cogitae* (thinking substance) against *res extensae* (physical substance). The strategy of objectivist hermeneutics is to grant the mental objects properties analogous to those of physical objects, so that subjective data might constitute evidence in the determination of authorial meaning and so that verbal signs might serve as what Emilio Betti calls "objectivations of mind."[25]

From Hirsch's own objectivist stance, the influence of Martin Heidegger looked like the most insidious sort of apostasy from the values of reason and what he has more recently come to term the "ethics" of interpretation.[26] According to this doctrine, interpreters *ought* to aim at discovering the original meaning of a text, whether or not they can actually reach that goal. Hirsch's ethical stance assumes that human beings are free agents who have the ability to make free choices. Choosing to pursue the author's meaning is thus a moral choice, the violation of which is tantamount to offending against truth and to trespassing on the private property of the author. Heidegger, Gadamer, and others, whom Hirsch calls "cognitive atheists," do not merely challenge epistemological presuppositions. They violate an ethical norm as well. Hirsch's use of religious imagery here is probably not accidental. Its theological overtones suggest that the theory of objective meaning is an orthodoxy beset by the heresies of relativism.

Heidegger articulated a version of the hermeneutic circle which undermined theories of objective interpretation. He did this by shifting the focus of hermeneutic philosophy from epistemology, a move foreshadowed by Dilthey's unsuccessful attempt to transcend positivism through his introduction of *Leben* and *Sichhineinfühlung*. Dilthey's attempt to establish a passage from "life" to "life" as a means of empathic understanding failed because it remained within the epistemological context of transcendental philosophy. Heidegger, on the other hand, radicalized the concept of historicity itself by criticizing Dilthey's acceptance of the "self-givenness of experience," which was to secure the return to "life" in the achievement of understanding.

Heidegger's critique of historicist and phenomenological foundationalism once again brought history to the foreground, but in a way different from Dilthey's life-philosophy. For Dilthey human acts and works were expressions (*Ausdrücke*) of life and so were to be understood not through rationalistic assumptions about human nature or positivistic conceptions of facticity but rather through lived experience. Lived experience enables the interpreter to bring self-understanding that emerges from the facticity of experience, and the consequent preunderstanding of the object of inquiry, to bear on interpretation. Since the object of inquiry is itself the result of (the expression of) the lived experience of another human being, the interpreter's route passes from lived experience through a reconstructive process to the expressed lived experience achieved in a work, whether written or otherwise. In other words, interpretation is linked to its object by the bond of lived experience, which somehow transcends the differences of time and place. Heidegger rejected the appeal to lived experience as a ground for interpretation. Rather, he argued that all such "foundational" categories are in fact posterior to the ontological question of Being itself.

One result of Heidegger's "ontological turn" is the theory that understanding does not proceed from the subjectivity of a consciousness that must reach out toward the world. "Subjectivity," rather, occurs as a conceptualization (a mistaken assessment of the situation) by Dasein, already characterized by its ontological understanding and its standing "toward" the world. This standing further characterizes Dasein's mode of being as temporal—not an epistemological temporality of consciousness but an ontological status through which subjectivity itself is conceived. It is here that Gadamer finds the key to his own hermeneutics, for temporality so viewed becomes for him not a source of distance and puzzlement, either between a consciousness and the world (human or physical) or between one age and another, but a positive concept, a continuum which makes possible the understanding of the other.

Heidegger's hermeneutic circle differs profoundly, then, from the version Schleiermacher adapted from traditional interpretation theory. It does not depict a state of misunderstanding which is to be overcome through ever-widening contexts of investigation. It neither sharply distinguishes procedures in the natural sciences from those in the human sciences (Dilthey's emphasis) nor attempts to "raise" interpretation to the level of objectivity. Rather, it regards scientific inquiry as a special case of understanding's turning to objects in the world. It is neither an epistemological nor a logical circle. It states an ontological condition from which epistemological theories follow and as such is vicious only from the mistaken epistemological stance that "forgets" the question of Being. In Heidegger's classic formulation,

> *But if we see this circle as a vicious one and look out for ways of avoiding it, even if we just "sense" it as an inevitable imperfection, then the act of understanding has been misunderstood from the ground up.* The assimilation of understanding and interpretation to a definite ideal of knowledge is not at issue here. Such an ideal of knowledge is itself only a subspecies of understanding—a subspecies which has strayed into the legitimate task of grasping the present-at-hand in its essential unintelligibility. If the basic conditions which make interpretation possible are to be fulfilled, this must rather be done by not failing to recognize beforehand the essential conditions under which it can be performed. What is decisive is not to get out of the circle but to come into it in the right way.[27]

Heidegger traces what he sees as the cultural and intellectual confusions of the technological age to "the forgetting of Being," which began with Greek metaphysics, and its replacement by an imperialist instrumentalism. His later writings are a long journey of discovery, a quest to uncover Being hidden under the accretions of Western metaphysics. Although Gadamer adopted Heidegger's conception of historicity as the limiting condition of all understanding, he did not follow Heidegger in the pursuit of Being. It may be that Gadamer perceived a different sort of foundationalism lurking within this radical assertion of historicity, or it may be that Heidegger's sense of the heroic task of the philosopher did not appeal to him. What he did take from Heidegger's example was his own adaptation of the "tradition" of interpretation. What Heidegger saw as a profound misrepresentation of Being Gadamer perceived as the necessary enabling condition for understanding. What Heidegger portrayed as a chasm Gadamer depicted as a bridge. The history (and historicity) of a work's effects (*Wirkungsgeschichte*), i.e., interpretations, commentaries, vilifications, displacement by other works, and whatever else of it survives in the historical space that separates it from its would-be interpreter, constitutes an ongoing process of reception and transformation. No interpreter stands outside the tradition, the *Wirkungsgeschichte*, when he engages a work. Rather, from the beginning he participates in the historicity of the interpretive process.

Gadamer's location of understanding within the context of historicity does away with a distinction central to Hirsch's theory of meaning. For Hirsch meaning is always the author's meaning. This he distinguishes from significance, which names a relationship between that meaning and a person, or a conception, or a situation, or indeed anything imaginable."[28] "Significance" delineates a context in which meaning is first understood and then applied to a concern of the interpreter's. In Gadamer's view there can be no separation of interpretation from understanding or of "meaning" from "significance." Understanding is already situated in a context which requires "self-reflection." Any movement toward the understanding of a work is also (if it is to be a *hermeneutic* act) a movement toward self-understanding. Hermeneutics, then, cannot be a "method" of interpretation, or even simply a study of method. It does not arbitrate among interpretive strategies. Hermeneutics is an inquiry into understanding itself: "not what we do or what we ought to do, but what happens to us over and above our wanting and doing." If understanding, because of its existential situation, is always a reflexive process, then there is no ground either in a transcendental ego or in a world of "facts" that can remove the interpreter from his own act of understanding. As Gadamer states often in *Truth and Method,* "All understanding is interpretation."[29]

Gadamer's existential situating of interpretation argues against what he calls the Enlightenment "prejudice" of assuming that historical inquiry can provide a prejudice-free analysis of texts, and thus it promotes "prejudice" or "pre-understanding" as the productive component of all interpretation. The aim of interpretation is to open oneself to the possibility of "truth" in historical texts and so to attain a fusion (and concomitant enlargement) of one's personal "horizons" with the "horizon" of the text. Gadamer's rejection of "objectivity" aims to restore the "authority" of "tradition," which shapes the interpreter even as he enters into a dialogue with it. Entrance into a dialogue with ancient texts (dialogue here is a model, an analogue, not to be taken as having all the elements of an actual conversation) requires that the dialoguist attempt to orient himself toward "the subject matter." Like a participant in a productive conversation, the interpreter must see the process as a cooperative effort, in which he solicits the help of the text to enlarge his understanding.

It may be, as many of Gadamer's critics have claimed, that he relies too much on the wisdom of tradition, as one steeped in a German classical education might tend to do, but it is probably more helpful to see Gadamer's work as emphasizing the existential condition of all interpretation. Interpreters begin with texts they presume to have some authority, which alone accounts for the fact that they turn to the text at all. The text appears in the context of its historical survival, in the distanced perspective that makes of it a historical succession of texts and the cultural changes which have inevitably "changed" them. It is change itself, the historicity of the text, that makes approach to it possible at all. The historical fate of a work, as well as the historical condition of the interpreter, is part of a process that cannot be "overcome" through the application of a method.

It is historical distance, according to Gadamer, that allows what he calls the "real nature" of the works to emerge, "so that the understanding of what is said in them can claim to be authoritative and universal."[30] Here "real" and "universal" must also be subsumed under "historicity," for in the movement of time that constantly changes the relationship of understanding between the past and present, such absolutes are only so in a *context*. There are no context-free universals. "Real nature" must therefore be entailed in "historicity." Art as well as interpretation is "historical" insofar as an art work can be considered merely as an object devoid of existential contingencies: i.e., as an object of empirical, scientific inquiry, it is no longer productive of hermeneutic understanding. A work of art, according to Heidegger, is precisely that toward which one *cannot* take a neutral stance.[31] It elicits an involvement. To "objectify" a work of art, to make it a source of "information," is to empty it of its possibilities for dialogue. While it might be possible to assign a "meaning" to an art work and indeed to range it among neatly categorized "meanings" in a chronological or critical taxonomy, to do so would be to subject it to the instrumentality and manipulation that empirical science commands over the objects of its inquiries. Objectification, then, is a form of alienation, a reduction of an I-thou relationship to an I-it relationship. It amounts to an assertion of dominance over the "other." The task of hermeneutics, far from *denying* the reality of objective science, however, "is to reconnect the objective world of technology, which the sciences place at our disposal and discretion, with those fundamental orders of our being that are neither arbitrary nor manipulable by us, but rather simply demand our respect."[32]

Gadamer finds the basis for his dialogic conception of hermeneutics in his reading of Aristotle and Plato. In the *Nichomachean Ethics* Aristotle develops the concept of practical reason, or *phronesis*. Practical reason links theory and practice—that is, an understanding of principles of right action is not separable from their application. To understand in a principled way the ethical context of any action is to understand concrete situations that cannot be already understood by an ethical theory. David Hoy sets out Gadamer's use of *phronesis* very well:

> Gadamer's concept of application is very similar to the notion of *phronesis,* since it too does not mean applying something to something, as a craftsman applies his mental conception to the physical material, but is rather a question of perceiving what is at stake in a given situation. Unlike *techne,* the craftsman's art, which possesses a teachable knowledge, practical wisdom cannot be taught. Nor is practical wisdom purely a reasoned state for "a state of that sort may be forgotten, but practical wisdom cannot." For Gadamer understanding is like *phronesis* in that it is a matter not only of reflection but also of perception and experience.[33]

Just as Gadamer takes his model of hermeneutic understanding from Aristotle, he finds his model of the hermeneutic process in Plato. For Gadamer the dialogue is the form most like hermeneutic activity because it engages people as partners in a common endeavor. The structure of question and answer in dialogue is properly aimed at orienting the participants toward the subject matter which engages them, not at establishing the mastery of one over the other.[34] What engages people most intensely are those questions most basic to living the examined life—those questions which probe the "tradition" to reveal what others have to teach in these matters. This engagement has something of the intensity of a game, a combination of free play within a structure that is needed to confer form and significance to the play. The play of dialogic inquiry, however, acts not to effect closure but to "open" up possibilities of further understanding. Since the inquiring dialogician begins with his "prejudices," the limited "horizons" resulting from his irreducible historicity, he questions tradition with the goal of coming to recognize his own prejudices and thereby enlarging his horizons. Gadamer uses the metaphor of the "fusion of horizons" (*Horizontverschmelzung*) to convey both the movement into the tradition and the change of tradition itself in history. The historicity of dialogue insures that hermeneutics puts issues in play but does not play them out.

Clearly Gadamer's thinking moves far from the rather arid discussions about single or multiple "meanings" in a text, engendered by disputes that assume an inevitable opposition between objectivism and relativism. Since any subject manifests itself within history, so any interpretation must itself be part of a historical process. The results of interpretive inquiry constitute what someone can understand at a particular historical moment. The process of interpretation, however, remains open, in the sense that the truth of the subject matter is never finally disposed of in such a way that future commentators will have only to get right what some authoritative author has already concluded.

Gadamer's hermeneutics links him with the concerns that have preoccupied classical and Christian thinkers of the "tradition." The subject matter which engaged Plato and Aristotle, Augustine and Luther made up the "questions" they found essential to the conduct of human life. Their way of understanding assumed a vital connection between the thinking being and human agency in the world. If Christian apologists were consumed with what we in our own historical situation find to be dogmatic theological bias, they at least did not imagine themselves analytic engines for reconstructing meanings. In fact, the dangers as well as the virtues of their practice we come to understand from the example of their own struggles with the "truth" of these issues. There are always dangers in thinking, but the modern analytic separation of "meaning" from "application," interpretation from action, surely presents its own dangers by denying the implication of all thought in a historical and pragmatic context. The objectivist bias is the product of a theory and, like any theory of fundamental principles, is consequent upon an often-unacknowledged preunderstanding of what it is to be a thinking being in the world.

Since the manifestation of any subject matter is "given in language," in Gadamer's terms, the distinction between past and present is itself made in and by language. Gadamer offers the example of translation from a foreign language as evidence that the act of interpretation is always a translation and that understanding is always an interpretation. Understanding is an interpretation of the tradition, which is in itself preserved primarily in texts.[35] If a text is to be understood (i.e., if it is to "speak"), it must speak to the person it reaches, whether through the translation called "interpretation" or through the interpretation called "translation" from a foreign language. The "historical life" of a tradition "depends on constantly new assimilation and interpretation." Understanding and language are inseparable, but they are not objects to be studied. "Neither is to be grasped simply as a fact that can be empirically investigated. Neither is ever simply an object, but comprises everything that can ever be an object."[36]

The task of hermeneutics, then, is not explicitly to form a literary theory or even a theory of interpretation. It offers no heuristic. Its implications for literary study are therefore not "practical," a fact which may make Americans, especially, impatient with its claims upon their own understanding. As a philosophical stance, however, it has much to offer in the perspective it gives on the theoretical wars that rage about the American academies. It offers a habit of mind that is reflexive, perspectival, and insistent on the value of cooperation rather than combat in intellectual endeavors.

Gadamer's own hermeneutic philosophy investigates what happens in understanding, whether in interpretive theory or in revolutionary theory. His rehabilitation of tradition does not advocate either political quietism or revolutionary programs. It does, however, question dogmatic adherence to systems of explanation that claim to have grounded their applications in first principles. For Gadamer first principles are precisely those aspects of thinking which demand the critical perspective of self-reflexive historical understanding. His own adherence to openness does not of course deny that the "truth" of the subject matter may be found by responding to such texts and such claims. He maintains only that "truth" results from questioning and that it is a process which orients the questioner in a direction that itself is questionable. Since questions occur within a historical context, the answers they bring are themselves historically bound. This finitude, which Gadamer calls "perspectism," is relativism only in relation to an absolutism which seeks an end to questions and an application of answers already found. As a matter of historical experience it seems that the expounders of answers have left their successors only more questions. A view of understanding that holds to its questing should be assessed against one that theorizes its objectivity.

Gadamer's hermeneutic philosophy is itself a process, not a systematic assertion of doctrine. What is most valuable in it may not be any of the things usually cited: his reading of traditional hermeneutics, his dialogic model of understanding, his linguistic turn, with its claim that the hermeneutic situation is "universal," or his arguments for the historicity of interpretation. In the current context of critical theory, where Gadamer's work forms part of the controversies about all these issues, his most valuable contribution may be that he advocates listening, openness, the willingness to grant that there may be "truth of the subject matter" in the questioned as well as in the questioner. His attention to what should unite partners in dialogue, the search for what is true, may provide a stance more productive than the isolating confrontation of competing doctrines propounded by "schools of thought," a phrase which might then appear as an oxymoron.

NOTES

1. Paul Ricoeur, *Hermeneutics and the Human Sciences,* ed. John B. Thompson (Cambridge: Cambridge University Press, 1981), p. 43.
2. Richard Palmer, *Hermeneutics: Interpretation Theory in Schleiermacher, Dilthey, Heidegger and Gadamer* (Evanston: Northwestern University Press, 1969), p. 8.
3. E. D. Hirsch, *Validity in Interpretation* (New Haven: Yale University Press, 1967). Hirsch also collected a series of essays, many of which were responses to critics, in his *Aims of Interpretation* (Chicago: University of Chicago Press, 1976).
4. Michel de Montaigne, *The Complete Essays of Montaigne,* trans. Donald Frame (Stanford: Stanford University Press, 1958), p. 818.
5. Ibid., p. 817.
6. Gerald Bruns, *Hermeneutics: Questions and Prospects,* ed. Gary Shapiro and Alan Sica (Amherst: University of Massachusetts Press, 1984), p. 148.

7. St. Augustine, *On Christian Doctrine*, trans. with intro. by D. W. Robertson, Jr. (New York: Liberal Arts Press, 1958), p. 87.
8. A succinct account of the "historicisms" discussed here occurs in Herbert Schnädelbach, *Philosophy in Germany, 1831–1933*, trans. Eric Mathews (Cambridge: Cambridge University Press, 1984), pp. 34–65.
9. Ibid., pp. 37ff.
10. Ibid., p. 35.
11. Friedrich Schleiermacher, "*The Hermeneutics:* Outline of the 1819 Lectures," trans. in part by Jan Woijik and Roland Haas, in *New Literary History*, 10, no. 1 (Autumn 1978), 1–16.
12. Ibid., 1.
13. Friedrich Schleiermacher, *Hermeneutik,* ed. Heinz Kimmerle (Heidelberg: Carl Winter Universitätsverlag, 1959), p. 31.
14. Schleiermacher, *The Hermeneutics,* 10.
15. Ibid., 7.
16. Hans-Georg Gadamer, *Truth and Method,* 2nd ed. (New York: Crossroads, 1975), p. 169.
17. For Gadamer's discussion of the issues see ibid., pp. 155–92.
18. Hirsch, *Validity in Interpretation,* pp. 224–26.
19. Ibid. This is a formidable list, but justifiable. See chapter 1, where Hirsch argues against variability in meaning, and chapter 2, where he argues for the characteristics enumerated above. Appendix 1, from which the above quotations are taken, outlines the purest form of his argument, an exercise in positivism which calls for the "verification" of interpretation. His later modification of verification to "validation" suggests that Hirsch retreats to the logical category of coherence, but actually he does not consistently distinguish the two.
20. For a good discussion of intentionalism see David Hoy, *The Critical Circle: Literature, History and Philosophical Hermeneutics* (Berkeley: University of California Press, 1978), chapter 2.
21. Hirsch, *Validity in Interpretation,* p. 4.
22. Ibid., pp. 241ff.
23. Ibid., p. 242.
24. For other critical responses to Hirsch see, for example, Frank Lentricchia, *After the New Criticism* (Chicago: University of Chicago Press, 1980), and T. K. Seung, *Semiotics and Thematics in Hermeneutics* (New York: Columbia University Press, 1982).
25. Emilio Betti, "Hermeneutics as the General Methodology of the Geisteswissenschaften," in Joseph Bleicher, *Contemporary Hermeneutics* (London and Boston: Routledge and Kegan Paul, 1980), p.

52. Betti's work remains largely untranslated. He is the foremost exponent of objectivist legal hermeneutics in the twentieth century.
26. Hirsch, *The Aims of Interpretation,* chapter 5.
27. Martin Heidegger, *Being and Time,* trans. John Macquarrie and Edward Robinson (New York: Harper and Row, 1962), p. 194.
28. Hirsch, *Validity in Interpretation*, p. 8. More properly a maladaptation of Frege's distinction between *Sinn* (meaning) and *Bedeutung* (reference), as Hoy, *The Critical Circle,* pp. 22–24, has pointed out.
29. Gadamer, *Truth and Method,* pp. 349ff, xiv, 350.
30. Ibid., p. 265.
31. See "The Origin of the Work of Art" and "Letter on Humanism" in *Martin Heidegger: Basic Writings,* ed. David Farrell Krell (New York: Harper and Row, 1977).
32. Hans-Georg Gadamer, *Philosophical Hermeneutics,* trans. and ed. David E. Linge (Berkeley: University of California Press, 1976), pp. 3ff.
33. Hoy, *The Critical Circle,* pp. 58ff.
34. Gadamer, *Truth and Method,* p. 325.
35. Ibid., p. 351.
36. Ibid., pp. 358, 365. Gadamer uses the word *umgreifen,* which is a stronger word than "comprise." It is an action, a seizing and surrounding at the same time.

DANIEL STEMPEL

History and Postmodern Literary Theory

IN 1963 DOUGLAS BUSH OPENED an international congress on literary history and literary criticism with a disarming confession: "It is perhaps inauspicious to admit that every time I have looked through the program for this Congress I have been stricken with inarticulate paralysis. Almost every topic is a reminder of the infinite extent of literature and criticism and of one's own finite ignorance. While there may be polymaths among us who have no reason to be so troubled, it can probably be assumed that most scholars and critics have some acquaintance with despair, unless they early reconciled themselves to picking up pebbles on the shore or cultivating their own small garden."[1]

More than two decades later the task which struck this learned scholar with inarticulate paralysis has become far more complex. The relations of history, literary history, and literary theory are so problematical that literary criticism often appears to be the exclusive province of deeply troubled and desperate polymaths. One polymath who has preserved his equanimity is René Wellek, whose extensive view of the history of criticism makes him a useful guide in distinguishing what is really new from a rewriting of the old. As late as 1973, in an essay on "The Fall of Literary History," Wellek dismissed the first two numbers of *New Literary History* as "valuable articles, but no new ideas of literary history beyond the study of periods, genres, and influences are suggested" and gloomily predicted that "the new literary history promises only a return to the old one: the history of tradition, genres, reputations, less atomistically conceived as in older times, with greater awareness of the difficulties of such concepts as influence and periods but still the old one."[2]

Since the beginning of the seventies Geoffrey Hartman has been attempting to define an acceptable form of literary history, moving from limiting literary history to national cultures to a search for a method of canon formation which would produce another kind of limited literary history, not national but intertextual, based on the selection and reading of canonical texts. As his book on Derrida's *Glas, Saving the Text* (1981) demonstrates, Hartman has moved from the phenomenology of thematics as a basis for historical writing to the contemporary preoccupation with textuality.[3]

The path which Hartman has been following, from a national literary history to a textual literary history, is telescoped in two books by Wesley Morris. *Toward a New Historicism* attempts to redefine the theory and practice of American critics and historians, but in *Friday's Footprint: Structuralism and the Articulated Text,* the unsolved problem of the relation of history to critical theory and practice which was the legacy of the New Criticism is no longer the focus of his work.[4] Morris now turns his attention to the relation between history and textuality. In the earlier book there is no mention of Continental philosophers and critics; in the later, Heidegger is Morris's guide "Toward a Literary Hermeneutics" (part 4), leading him through the dark wood of textual theory. Examining and commenting on the linguistic interpretations of Derrida, Lacan, and Lévi-Strauss and the historical interpretation of Michel Foucault, Morris seeks a compromise: "The text, in its tensional revelation of the battle between the author's drive toward primal consciousness (being-there) and, in opposition, the systematicity of society, reveals the *possibility* of history and provides the foundation for communication."[5]

Morris's shift of ground from an Anglo-American view of literary history to the problems of Continental textuality is a sign of the spirit of the age. The basic problem of placing the work of art in a historical context has not changed, but the analysis of the problem has been recast in terms of a new approach to textual analysis and interpretation. It is worthwhile, I think, to take a second look at deconstruction and its complex relation to history, which is epitomized in the confrontation of Derrida and Foucault, grammatology versus archaeology.

That confrontation begins with Derrida's deconstruction of Foucault's discussion of Descartes's exclusion of madness from reason in *Madness and Civilization.* In his "Cogito and the History of Madness" Derrida denies that any boundary, historical or textual, can be drawn between reason and madness in Descartes's meditations.[6] Historically, Derrida argues, why should Foucault begin with the medieval treatment of insanity? Why not go back to the Greek *logos* and examine the hidden rupture at the center of Western metaphysics? For Derrida the classical expulsion of madness is merely another instance of a perennial contest within philosophy. Textually, Derrida adopts the tacit assumption that no text (and the cogito is a text) can divide itself into two texts. Indeed, if one looks at the metaphysical premises of Derrida's reading, a metaphysics which he seeks to exclude from his own methodology, we find him positing that all is text and admitting that his own text, despite his efforts, cannot break away into a text which is truly contrary to it, a counter-text. The hyperbolic figure (or hypothesis) of the *malin génie,* who supplies misinformation to the cogito, proves, Derrida claims, that madness is part of the cogito and that madness is not expelled by reason. Foucault's history is inauthentic because both the modern reader and the classical texts are trapped in the same metaphysics without being aware of it.

Foucault's contemptuous response points out that Derrida's rhetorical reading of a central figure, hyperbole, as the organizing principle of Descartes's text ignores the other function of rhetoric—persuasion, or to use Foucault's term, discourse.[7] Descartes's meditation, Foucault insists, demands a double reading: as a system of linked propositions and as an exercise. The word "exercise," as Foucault surely knows, would have meant for Descartes the great example of the *Spiritual Exercises* of Loyola. In these exercises the mind conceives its worst possibilities, faces them, and struggles to defeat them. One does not have to be an atheist to wrestle with the temptation of atheism nor does one have to be mad in order to conceive of a world which is a lie and an illusion. An exercise is an interior battle, a psychomachia between truth and error. Hyperbole is invoked in order to be defeated by reason; madness is expelled from reason as Satan is expelled from the presence of God.

This confrontation is founded on two totally opposed theories of the historic function of the text. For Derrida, following Husserl, history is an attempt to find a point of origin, not an origin, a beginning to which all subsequent sameness and difference can be referred. In his introduction to Husserl's *Origin of Geometry* Derrida defines the role of phenomenology as a means of establishing the possibility of an authentic history. For phenomenology, "*If there is any history,* then historicity can only be the passage of Speech [*Parole*], the pure tradition of a primordial Logos toward a polar Telos."[8] Intentionality, the sense of a direction, is the root of historicity. As Derrida says, "In all the significations of this term, historicity is *sense.*" ("*Sens*" has two definitions in French, "meaning" and "direction.") But Husserl's phenomenology refuses the question of the ground "Why?" It does not deal with problems of ontology, as Heidegger's does.

Derrida asks the questions which Husserl could not ask: How can a fact be exemplary, begin a historical direction, and, at the same time, be part of that direction? "In other words, knowing what sense is as historicity, I could clearly ask myself why there would be any history rather than nothing." What Derrida is seeking is a principle of sufficient reason for history: "The impossibility of resting in the simple maintenance [nowness] of a Living Present, the sole and absolute origin of the De Facto *and* the De Jure, of Being *and* Sense, but always other in its self-identity; the inability to live enclosed in the innocent undividedness [*indivision*] of the primordial Absolute, because the Absolute is *present* only in being deferred-delayed [*différant*] without respite, this impotence and this impossibility are given in a primordial and pure consciousness of Difference."[9]

It is clear that Derrida's "authentic history" grows out of a directed historicity which starts from a phenomenal, not an ontological, beginning yet can retain its authenticity only by reminding itself of an ontology which posits an origin and an end of which it can have no knowledge. History may be written and read as the sequence of sedimentary layers in time, inauthentic history, or as authentic history, constantly mindful that its beginning is not its origin, that since the forgetting of Being in the birth of Western metaphysics, all interpretation falls within the limits of a perspective shaped by forgotten metaphors. For Derrida, Foucault's historiography has no beginning because it ignores or forgets its origin. It does not ask how; more important, it does not ask why. Both grammatology and archaeology are geologies of the past, but Derrida's past is an absolute past, while Foucault's is a finite past; it can be charted, measured, and reconstructed in relation to the present. Derrida is a vulcanologist who probes in the extinct craters of etymology and metaphor for the subterranean movements of an invisible magma of meaning. Foucault is a geologist who maps the structures and layers of buried strata.

What would a Derridean or deconstructive literary history turn out to be, if one could be written? J. Hillis Miller, in "Tradition and Difference," a review of M. H. Abrams's *Natural Supernaturalism,* has outlined the requirements for just such a history. After taking Abrams to task for an uncritical attitude toward both language and history, Miller writes, "Nietzsche and the others I have cited do not so much reject this scheme (it cannot be rejected, for our languages repeat it to us interminably), as deconstruct it by turning it inside out, by reinterpreting it. They affirm that the situation of dispersal, separation, and unappeasable desire is the 'original' and perpetual human predicament. The dream of primal and final unity, always deferred, never present here and now, is generated by the original and originating differentiation. The beginning was diacritical." Miller concludes, "In place of the notion that history proceeds in stages from a beginning toward some preordained goal, Nietzsche puts the idea of an eternally repeated operation, without origin or end. If history has no origin and no goal, then it is not going anywhere, getting neither better nor worse, or sometimes better and sometimes worse, according to arbitrary principles of evaluation, and according to no externally operating power but by the momentary successes of ordering energy in one man or group or another. . . . This alternative scheme, with its various aspects or motifs, has always been present as a shadow or reversed mirror image within the Western tradition, even in the texts Abrams discusses, for example, in the Platonic dialogues or in *The Prelude*. His failure to recognize its pervasive presence in texts both traditional and modern is perhaps the chief limitation of *Natural Supernaturalism*."[10]

In another review Miller rejects the kind of periodization which Foucault has employed: "Each period is itself equivocal.

Periods differ from one another because there are different forms of heterogeneity, not because each period holds a single coherent 'view of the world.' There is literary history because texts are 'undecidable,' rather than the other way around, since one side of the aporia of deconstruction is always referential statements, that is, statements that point to time and to history. The question of the kind of literary history which would result from the application of a deconstructive rhetoric to the study of literature has hardly begun to be answered, though Harold Bloom and Geoffrey Hartman, in their different ways, have begun to write a revisionist literary history."[11]

Miller's characterization of a possible deconstructive literary history as a secret history of texts obscured by conventional readings places him squarely in opposition to Foucault's method and the historiography produced by that method. Foucault is a positivist: he has identified three periods on the basis of the discourse of three disciplines. Although he has stressed structural parallels in these disciplines, particularly in the classical period, which best lends itself to the binary symmetry of structuralism, he has never claimed that the episteme is more than a construct, a useful synchronicity. If it is true, as Miller claims, that deconstructive readings are always referential, their purpose appears to be the questioning of historical referentiality by references to undecidable quasi-ontological problems, topics with which Foucault is not concerned.

In practice, a history of deconstructive readings would be not a history but a counter-history. It would be a comparison of distances from an arbitrary beginning rather than a free genealogy of apparent repetition and actual novelty. Wayne Booth has called this kind of counter-history "parasitic," that is, dependent on the prior texts of historians like Abrams whose work can be reversed through deconstructive rhetoric. At the risk of adding to the complexity of Miller's etymological game in his reply to Booth, "The Critic as Host," I should like to point out that "parasite" also means "noise" or "static" in French and that Michel Serres in *The Parasite* and in his essays on information theory calls the parasite "the third man," who is excluded from the message between sender and receiver.[12] Paradoxically, however, the deconstructive third man can exploit the ambiguity of noise and information: what is noise in one context is information in another. A fire siren is noise to a concert goer but information to a driver.

Deconstructive readings convert noise into information. Metaphorical and etymological distortions that are subordinated to the text's rationality, its will to knowledge, are used to counter its message. White noise (*bruit de fond*) is the unfathomable depth of textuality from which the deconstructive analysis is dredged up. What appears to be a failure of sense, a blank in the text, is actually concealed information; it is an alternate message, an ambiguity, perhaps even a white mythology. If, as Rodolphe Gasché has argued, deconstruction is not merely a reversal of conventional interpretation but a reinscription of that reversal in the historical closure of metaphysics, the question remains: Can it be reinscribed without either destroying that history or simply remaining as a singularity, a black hole in the historical ordering of texts?[13] If we accept Derrida's reading of Descartes, Foucault's history vanishes; the incarceration of the insane in institutions and by institutions is not a novelty. It is merely the repetition of a false division rooted in the imperialism of the Logos.

Paul de Man was less hopeful than Miller of a rapprochement between deconstructive literary theory and literary history. In his essay "Literary History and Literary Modernity," he wrote, "We are more concerned at this point with the question of whether the history of an entity as self-contradictory as literature is conceivable. In the present state of literary studies this possibility is far from being clearly established. It is generally admitted that a positivistic history of literature, treating it as if it were a collection of empirical data, can only be a history of what literature is not. At best, it would be a preliminary classification opening the way for actual literary study, and at worst, an obstacle in the way of literary understanding. On the other hand, the intrinsic interpretation of literature claims to be anti- or a-historical, but often presupposes a notion of history of which the critic is not himself aware."[14] The entire essay appears to be an extrapolation of a sentence in Heidegger's *Sein und Zeit:* "The inauthentically historical existence [*Existenz*], burdened with the legacy of the 'past' which has become unrecognizable to it, seeks the modern."[15] If there is to be a proper literary history, de Man insisted, it must be an interpretation of texts, not events.

In an essay titled "Philosophy *Before* Literature: Deconstruction, Historicity, and the Work of Paul de Man," Suzanne Gearhart sums up de Man's determination to separate literature from all referentiality except its own self-reference: "De Man's work constitutes a radical theory of literature, one that rejects all traditional forms of totalization, whether formal, aesthetic, hermeneutic, or historical. But in spite of de Man's resistance to all attempts to close off literature and treat it as a discrete object, his work persistently reassures us that literature, literary language, and the text are there all along, deconstituting themselves in a process that only confirms their priority and their privilege. According to the logic of such a theory of literature, all forms of history or even of historicity are derived from language. However much literature may undercut itself in de Man's theory, it remains closed off from a historicity that can be reduced neither to an intra-worldly nor a transcendental connection and that, as such, figures the irruption of the non-linguistic 'within' language and literature themselves."[16] De Man's problem, then, is how a history of the interpretation of texts is possible, or, more accurately, how the interpretation of texts can become a historical text. The project, he admitted, was perhaps not impossible, but he had not turned his attention to the question of the temporality of rhetoric—and this was precisely what Foucault was doing.

In *Criticism and Social Change* Frank Lentricchia attacks de Man's contention that history is only texts and that it is therefore trapped in the fundamental aporia of all literary language.[17] Lentricchia charges that de Man, like Derrida, says nothing about the function of language in society, a use which does not necessarily depend on the adequacy of representation. His theory limits its praxis to the reading of certain canonical texts, philosophical and literary. Lentricchia is, in short, in agreement with the conclusion which can be drawn from Foucault's rebuttal of Derrida's reading of Descartes: there *is* a temporality of rhetoric. Descartes's meditation has a specific discursive context, not a general one. For Derrida his meditation is a variation on a perennial theme; for Foucault it is part of the classical transformation of Renaissance rhetoric.

While a deconstructive literary history still remains to be written, Foucault's historiography has already stimulated the production of studies such as Timothy Reiss's *The Discourse of Modernism,* in which the rhetoric of literary texts is analyzed as part of a general development of a specific kind of discourse: "analytico-referential" as opposed to the medieval patterning, the mythical correlations of sign and semblance.[18] Reiss is not simply working out Foucault's history of discourse. On the contrary, he finds continuities where Foucault finds discontinuities. Reiss urges that the privileged status of literature, which de Man insists on, be removed by the critic. Literary discourse is not a perpetually repetitive discourse that weaves its way in and out of the events of history, at times allying itself with the contemporary situation and at other times claiming a knowledge which transcends history. Reiss sees literature as one form of discourse among many. The kind of rereading which the critic applies to literary texts can be applied to any of these discourses. But, Reiss claims, literary criticism is actually an institutionalized, hidden evaluation of the social utility of other discourses. He calls for a "progressive discursive criticism" that "will be continually, so to speak, coming after itself, not effacing, but retracing and rereading its own footsteps."[19] It is worth noting that two of the three epigraphs which introduce *The Discourse of Modernism* are taken from the writings of Foucault and Michel Serres, both of whom have acknowledged their indebtedness to the great French historians of science. Derrida's history is not their history.

Unlike Derrida, Foucault writes history in order to delineate a succession of periods which are also problems: to define a period is to define a problem. He never assumes a total frame of logocentric metaphysics which compresses all of history into a single paradigm, that is, all of Western history, if by Western we mean those civilizations whose canonical documents are Indo-European. Would Derrida include Chinese and Tibetan translations of the Buddhist scriptures? Or medieval Arabic Aristoteleans? The Foucauldian episteme has aroused suspicion among those who can cheerfully teach a course in the romantic period or Victorian literature without having bad dreams. Again and again Foucault has insisted that the episteme is not a total history; it is a general history based on the examination of the discourse of selected disciplines, whose sole authority is its marshalling of documentary evidence and its selection of common elements and common structures.

The Order of Things, for example, is clearly most successful in its structured center, the classical period, where Foucault sets up a double binary pattern as a parallelogram of forces unifying the analysis of wealth, natural history, and general grammar. When that structure is fragmented in the nineteenth century, Foucault outlines the limits of its dispersal. Michel Serres, a critic trained in mathematics and the physical sciences, constructs models of history for the same periods which do not invalidate Foucault's models but simply extend the richness of general history into new areas. For Serres the rise to dominance of historical methodology in the early nineteenth century is epitomized in the heat engine, a device whose theory gives a new dimension to historical time as an entropic process. Of Turner's "Rain, Steam, and Speed: The Great Western Railway" Serres writes dramatically: "Fire, the new history, passes like a thunderclap over the green water where a boat rocks."[20]

Frank Lentricchia gives a generally favorable estimate of Foucault's historical method in *After the New Criticism*, but he prefers Foucault's definition of a genealogical analysis of history to his use of the episteme, which Lentricchia terms "the weakest component of Foucault's earlier work."[21] Nietzsche's genealogy, as interpreted by Foucault, can lead to a valid form of literary history, Lentricchia believes. It emphasizes *Herkunft,* descent, in the biological sense, by bringing in obscure and forgotten ancestors. Unlike Harold Bloom's patrilineal genealogy, which is more biblical than biological, it includes recessive as well as dominant traits. The possibility of novelty, of *Entstehung* or emergence, again in the biological sense, emphasizes the discontinuity of what appears to be the continuous flow of history; a hidden or recessive element suddenly becomes dominant and changes the cultural paradigm. Like Reiss, Lentricchia comes to the conclusion, on the basis of his study of Foucault, that the most adequate literary history is only one discourse among many and that it is constantly aware of its interaction with others as part of a general history: "So our hypothetical historian of American poetry will need to take stock of the poetic writing of other nations at some stage, and he will need to pinpoint areas of discursive intersection where literary, philosophical, scientific, and religious modes of writing find a point of contact."[22]

This historical method, as well as the concept of history that demands its use, contrasts strongly with the actual practice of the Yale critics, all of whom stress the importance of a limited canon for their readings, either genealogical or ahistorically intertextual. Their canon is fixed by two factors: a prior determination of the importance of the text by the institutionalized discourse of the academy and the responsiveness of the text to a deconstructive reading. Minor literary works or nonliterary sources are usually disregarded. But Foucault warns, "Genealogy . . . requires patience and a knowledge of details and it depends on a vast accumulation of source materials. Its 'cyclopean monuments' are constructed from 'discreet and apparently insignificant truths and according to a rigorous method'; they cannot be the product of 'large and well-meaning errors.' In short, genealogy demands relentless erudition. Genealogy does not oppose itself to history as the lofty and profound gaze of the philosopher might compare to the molelike perspective of the scholar; on the contrary, it rejects the meta-historical deployment of ideal significations and indefinite teleologies. It opposes itself to the search for 'origins.' "[23]

The function of genealogy, in short, is not merely to generate a history of a discipline, such as literary history, but to integrate it into general history. In the classical period, if Foucault is correct (and I am not sure he is!), there was a single dominant discourse and therefore there should be a broad range of discursive intersections between literary texts, scientific texts, and theological texts, such as Leibniz's *Theodicée* or Butler's *Analogy*. In the nineteenth century, particularly after the violent discontinuity of the period from 1790 to 1830, the search for intersections becomes much more difficult as the hegemony of a dying discourse is fragmented by new discourses which are themselves models of genealogy. Perhaps Lovejoy was right: there is no Romanticism, there are only romanticisms. If one were to criticize Abrams's literary history from Foucault's point of view, its weakness would appear to be that the strong influence of the history of ideas rules out the interaction of episteme and genealogy. Emergence springs from inheritance; it does not repeat it.

Before surveying some of the critical articles which have taken one side or the other in the clash between grammatology and archaeology or have attempted to mediate between them, I want to stress again that Nietzsche's genealogy is modeled on nineteenth-century biology, as his choice of terms demonstrates, and is fundamentally scientific in its approach. In contrast, the current mode of limiting literary history to a history of the interpretation of selected canonical texts, a practice employed by both deconstruction and hermeneutic criticism, is itself genealogically derived from the reading of sacred texts. In his conclusion to *The World, The Text, and*

The Critic Edward Said calls for a return to secular discourse in criticism: "Once an intellectual, the modern critic has become a cleric in the worst sense of the word."[24]

Said has both explained and defended Foucault's history in a series of books and articles dating back to the early seventies. His most concise and comprehensive defense of Foucault against Derrida is "The Problem of Textuality" (1978).[25] Most of the article is devoted to presenting the case for Derrida and deconstruction in the most favorable light. Said neither rebuts nor rejects deconstruction; he merely points out its limitations. Although Derrida juxtaposes texts, his method is really intratextual, not intertextual. As Said points out, his analysis is purely syntactical; it effaces the semantic or referential intention of language and concentrates on the tensions between logical argumentation (rhetoric as persuasion) and the abysses of meaning inherent in syntactical connectives (rhetoric as figural language). Said believes this analysis is detached from social reality, except insofar as it represents Derrida's own persuasive strategies for controlling power in academic circles. Foucault, in contrast, shows how discourse is not only formed by the praxis of a social discipline but possesses the intentionality of an unconscious will to knowledge which is also a will to power over the unknown and the excluded.

David Carroll has criticized Foucault for excluding the subject, as the center of consciousness, from discourse while granting the same role to the episteme.[26] But the episteme is not a transcendental ego; it is not a consciousness nor is it a subject. The episteme neither speaks nor dictates nor controls; it is nothing more than a map, a set of lines connecting points of congruence between selected disciplines. One could argue that Foucault himself is unaware of the congruence of physical science and his three disciplines, a congruence which is evident in his description of classical discourse as a Cartesian grid and modern discourse(s) as fields of force between polar opposites, on the model of electromagnetic fields. Foucault's attack on the atomism of structural linguistics (phonemes, morphemes, sememes, mythemes) reflects his own commitment to a concept of language which treats it as a field in which events, rather than units, can be isolated.

The broader topic of history and fictionality is discussed at length in Carroll's book *The Subject in Question: The Languages of*

Theory and the Strategies of Fiction. In chapter 5, "The Times of History and the Orders of Discourse," Carroll traces Foucault's antisubjectivism to the work of the *Annales* historians and notably to Fernand Braudel, whose theories of historical time are summarized. "The questions of the subject, of continuity, and of order in history, because they are no longer accepted as givens by the 'New History,' no longer given transcendent or metahistorical status above, outside, or at the origin of history, are precisely the questions with which history must deal, if it is not simply to repeat the limitations and restrictions of traditional history. If the arguments of Braudel and Foucault are to be taken seriously, it seems clear that there can be no truly critical history which does not in some form or another confront such questions—for both the form and the sense of history are at stake in the responses given to them."[27]

Joseph N. Riddel pairs Derrida's *Of Grammatology* and Foucault's *Language, Counter-Memory, Practice* in an article, "Redoubling the Commentary." He describes Foucault's contribution to literary criticism as "rewriting the place of a marginal, disruptive discourse in the history of discourses, or marking and remarking its significant madness. He would appropriate literature as the excluded or repressed voice that cannot be accounted for by history."[28] Yet Foucault makes exactly the opposite point. *Don Quixote* is the first modern literary work, Foucault writes, because it mirrors the division between science and analogy, identity/difference and resemblance, which marks the passage from the Renaissance to the classical. It is significant precisely because it can be accounted for by history and in turn it accounts for history. Similarly, he turns to a brief discussion of literature in the transition from the classical to nineteenth-century culture and asserts that, in opposition to that philology which Nietzsche both taught and destroyed, literature has locked itself up in its own transcendence, in a self-referential, eternal return to its own textuality, which, as in some of Mallarmé's experimental poetry, is not linguistic at all.[29]

Riddel argues for Derrida's method of rereading or opening texts and quotes a passage from *On Grammatology* in which Derrida points out that history must operate as a limit on readings, though it cannot open a text by itself. This is, of course, in keeping with Derrida's determination to keep all semantic reference out of deconstructive criticism. But why should not an excluded semantic frame, facts and events which contradict the overt intention of the text, also deconstruct a text? We have all read scholarly articles in which the explication of an unknown reference has changed the entire structure of the reading. The semantic level is not outside the text. This is the point made by György Lukács in his reading of Balzac's novels: despite Balzac's reactionary politics, his will to knowledge created an ironic reversal of his stated values.

Derrida, Riddel sums up, "who poses as an an-archist against the tradition, has shown us the limited future of an illusion, of a scientific criticism which might extract the referent beyond from that which in the text represents it, the text's privileged signs."[30] Yet Michel Serres, a historian of science, has written on Verne, Zola, and Michelet and has shown that their texts embody the objects and processes of their age, scientific models and actual machines. Serres calls his method "application," not explication: "It is not necessary to introduce methods to read this text: the method is *in* the text. The text is its own criticism, its own explication, its own application."[31]

This is much the same point as that made by Jonathan Morse in his article "History in the Text." Morse argues persuasively and logically that texts themselves are history, not merely as documents of a socially determined discourse, but as language with its own history. He allies himself with Foucault in opposition to Derrida and deconstruction, making the startling but justifiable claim that the literary history of twentieth-century American literature is already a totalized episteme: "Because it is becoming obvious that the literary history of the twentieth century is going to resemble that of the eighteenth, with most of the books appearing to have been written in the first half, we look for ghosts to keep us company. . . . That need of ours to be haunted is the pathognomonic sign of a fully periodized era of literary history. It indicates to us that our literary episteme has completely pervaded the world of sense data around us, so that our ways of perceiving are confined to modes of textual production."[32] Morse concludes that history in the text is not a key to interpretation but a resistance to interpretation that can be put to use by the reader.

In "Textual Politics: Foucault and Derrida" Michael Sprinker evaluates the influence of both on contemporary literary criticism as praxis, that is, in actual classroom applications as well as in publications. Sprinker points out that Derrida's readings not only repeat themselves but are shaped by a concealed ontology. Foucault has touched on Derrida's failure to develop a flexibility of response: "According to Foucault (and his reasoning seems almost irresistible on this point in the light of much of Derrida's other writing), for Derrida all thinkers are one thinker, the history of Western thought is but a series of permutations on a central theme (presence, God, logocentrism, the transcendental reduction, the *cogito*), and all differences can be collapsed (as Derrida collapses the Cartesian distinction between reason and madness) into a unitary concept of reason."[33]

But, Sprinker reminds the reader, Derrida is much more an analyst of textual differences than Foucault. Foucault's "methodology," as explained in *The Archaeology of Knowledge*, simply disappears in his later work. "In the end, Foucault is not, as Derrida clearly is, a theoretician of the text. Foucault's archaeologies and genealogies are not epistemological investigations but practical researches into the sites of modern knowledge and power that make our disciplinary society possible." Sprinker returns to his opening theme: Foucault's value for literary criticism and theory is his analysis of the role of the intellectuals in "advanced industrial societies." Derrida, in contrast, practices a deconstruction which turns out to be "nothing more than commentary," a commentary which is brilliant but lacks the historical context and is therefore isolated from the actual ways in which texts contend for dominance in society.[34]

E. M. Henning takes a very different position on the relation of Foucault and Derrida to history in "Foucault and Derrida: Archaeology and Deconstruction." Like Sprinker he contrasts the rigor of Derrida's deconstructive readings with the bricolage of Foucault's works, which subordinate theoretical consistency to the actualities of the development of institutions in a social context. Henning believes that Foucault has not broken free of Western metaphysics: "His theory of the archive and episteme, his idea of history as a discontinuous series of largely synchronic structures, his tendency to remain at the reversal stage of conventional dichotomies—all these are thoroughly traditional (if not metaphysical) aspects of his work. Derrida, by contrast, demonstrates a surer grasp of such problems and appears more consistently to avoid them. His desire for a general displacement and subsequent reinscription of traditional options, his perception of history as a relation of similarity and difference, of repetition with change over time—all these seem to give his work a far more radical appearance."[35] One might add that Foucault, like Spengler, believes that no thinker can break free of the discourses of his epoch; it is possible that Derrida is even more deeply enmeshed in the rhetoric of modern discourse than Foucault, a possibility to which, I suspect, Derrida would readily assent.

Gary F. Waller wrestles with the same problem but applies it to a different period, taking up the question of "Deconstruction and Renaissance Literature." Waller believes that deconstructive readings can revitalize the Renaissance canon by opening up the disjunctures of form, dislocations of meaning, and historical breaks in texts on which a false coherence has been imposed by traditional scholarship. Waller believes that American deconstructive practice has ignored historical contextuality, both Derridean and Foucauldian, focusing instead on reading autonomous texts in the style of the New Criticism. He argues correctly that Derrida has never claimed that texts are independent of history but bases his contention on what Derrida has said in interviews, not on Derrida's crucial critique of Husserl's phenomenological analysis of the history of geometry. He fails to see that Derrida and Foucault can be reconciled only by writing two different kinds of history simultaneously. Each would deny or undermine the premises of the other, but, after all, that is the function of deconstruction.[36]

Dominick LaCapra also recommends borrowing from deconstructive practice in order to rethink the significance of the canonical texts of intellectual history. LaCapra examines the relation of the authorial intention to the text, the relation of the author's life to the text, and the relation of society to the text. He argues that Derrida's criticism of Foucault's reading of Descartes is not a simple rejection: "Derrida's argument . . . must be seen in the broader context of his understanding of the long but tangled tradition constituting the history of metaphysics." The problem, as LaCapra sees it, is one of linking a long tradition, a specific period, and a specific text. History, he concludes, should not be merely a reconstruction of the past but a dialogue with the past, the reader interrogating the text and the text responding to the reader: "A good reader is also a patient and attentive listener."[37]

This is, of course, the aim of hermeneutic criticism, which in its modern theoretical form is largely the creation of Hans-Georg Gadamer. Under the broad rubric of hermeneutic criticism, however, one could assemble a group of critics who appear to have little in common with Gadamer and less with each other: Northrop Frye, Frank Kermode, Stanley Fish, and Harold Bloom. Without pointing an accusing finger at Gadamer, as Lentricchia does, and claiming that his historical bias is a cloak for a Nietzschean power play on behalf of the concept of tradition, a Foucauldian might pose some questions for hermeneutics in a nonaggressive manner. If, as Foucault has suggested, there are no authors who are real subjects but only texts designated by proper names, perhaps there are no readers, real, ideal, or elitist, but only readings. If this is so, then the posited continuity of a tradition must be traced through selected commentaries and interpretations, not through a line of critics; the history of criticism is not the history of critics.

Further, is it justifiable to expand the circular reasoning of the "hermeneutic circle" from the interpretation of texts to a procedure for constituting a history of texts? The hermeneutic critic chooses a set of texts to form a canon then goes on to argue that tradition is nothing more than a linking of the texts and their readings in some sort of diachronic or pseudo-diachronic order. One could fall back, I suppose, on Sainte-Beuve's argument that whatever survives is canonical, but literary survival is often more a matter of resurrection than immortality.

In *Toward an Aesthetic of Reception* Hans-Robert Jauss has suggested that a new literary history can be constructed on Gadamer's principles.[38] His theory of literary history is based on an aesthetics of reception which is used to define or redefine a Great Chain of Texts, a canon in which all works are aesthetically contemporary and historically successive. But this program of a temporal intertextuality which reads backward in order to read forward is only another variant of the history founded on the reading of sacred texts; it transforms history into prophecy and reduces each rhetorical innovation to mere prolepsis. As Gadamer himself has stressed, even where hermeneutics has been secularized in the service of the *Geisteswissenschaften*, it maintains a parallel and dynamic interchange with the theological tradition from which it has sprung.[39] In short, interpretation as typology continues to be the major concern of hermeneutic literary history, even when it is secularized as the history of narrative form, as recent works by Frye and Kermode on the Bible indicate.

What kind of history, then, can we expect from hermeneutic criticism, which claims to represent a mode of interpretation rooted in the historical consciousness of the critic? At best, it recognizes its limits. Its focus is on documents: an *Urtext* which is never exhausted by commentary, commentaries which produce further commentaries, and, ultimately, the selection of a canon of approved documents in order to define a tradition of either texts or commentary or both. At worst, it leads to the comforting dogma that there is no *Urtext,* just interpretation all the way back, or, to put it another way, unlimited semiosis invites unlimited interpretation. For this nihilistic regression Nietzsche's authority is usually invoked, but since he said a great many things, including some which appear to be self-contradictory, his invocation has questionable merit. Nietzsche played with antinomies; as Jean Granier has shown, he insisted on *both* unlimited interpretation and strict philological reading.[40] The *Urtext* of reality is available only through interpretation, but it is not produced by interpretation. (Umberto Eco arrives at much the same conclusion in his *Theory of Semiotics,* in which he discusses the interaction of semiotic freedom and semantic constraints).[41]

For the literary historian this suggests a history derived solely from the intertextuality of documents, requiring no verification other than the cross-reference of interpretants. Yet, as the work of the *Annales* historians has shown, the actual use of language is determined by what people eat, drink, and wear, where and how they buy and sell. The fact that the Prioress fed "wastelbreed" to her dogs doesn't mean very much unless you know the way in which the hierarchy of breads reflects the social structure. Foucault's genealogy is not, like Nietzsche's, an exhumation of buried motives; it is a tracing of superficially similar practices which have shifted from their role in one period of cultural history to serve a totally different function in a new social context. He is not concerned with what people say they are doing, or with what they think they are doing, but with what they are actually doing. He rejects all hermeneutics (including the Freudian, Marxist, and Nietzschean hermeneutics of suspicion) because it centers on the individual rather than the interplay of social rules, the game in which the individual is a chess piece, not a player.

For a general introduction to hermeneutics and its role in literary history, nothing has superseded David Hoy's *The Critical Circle: Literature, History and Philosophical Hermeneutics.* Chapter 5, "Hermes and Clio," deals with the application of hermeneutics to literary history and concludes that Gadamer's *Wirkungsgeschichte* offers the best possibilities.[42] The practice of hermeneutic criticism is best represented by Gerald L. Bruns, *Inventions: Writing, Understanding, and Textuality in Literary History.*[43] Bruns is always both erudite and readable, whether he is working on the traditional texts of religious hermeneutics or modern literary texts. His review of Jonathan Culler's *On Deconstruction,* "Structuralism, Deconstruction, and Hermeneutics," is more analytic than polemic and urges a hermeneutic dialogue with the text rather than the deconstructive dissolution of textual unity.[44] His essay "The Problem of Figuration in Antiquity" examines the function of figuration in Philo, Origen, and Augustine as a mode of pragmatic hermeneutics whose primary purpose is to make the text readable rather than to offer a reading of the text.[45]

Stanley Fish's hermeneutics is also pragmatic rather than normative. His pragmatism led him to the extreme of accepting any interpretation, but he has since retreated from that position. As Umberto Eco has suggested, wherever signs are used, lying is a possibility. For deconstructive readings a text can only belie itself, purporting to do one thing but actually doing another. For historical readings, however, it may be that and something more: a failure to link itself in some way to an actual state of affairs. When a student informs me that Shakespeare and Abraham Lincoln were contemporaries, it is not usually necessary to look for textual evidence to show that he is mistaken. The trouble with any form of pragmatics that is cut loose from an extensional semantic base is that it may be persuasive and apparently well-informed but not necessarily true. Naive students, like naive critics, take Iago's recital of his wrongs at face value, but the semiotic characteristic that marks *his* pragmatics is that he lies—to himself as well as to others.

There is a clear distinction between Frye and Kermode, who are closer to traditional hermeneutics, and Bruns and Fish, whose hermeneutics is more aesthetic than philological. To borrow a phrase from Nietzsche, literary history becomes justifiable as an aesthetic phenomenon, not because it is an accurate description of anything. As Jauss's scheme for a history of reception demonstrates, it is possible—even desirable—to write a kind of literary history that includes the aesthetic. On the other hand, Hayden White's *Metahistory* suggests that an aesthetic history, even if it deals with the aesthetics of historiography, is an Apollinian history, a history of illusion, of repetitive rhetorical forms that mask an unknown and unknowable reality. Is a Dionysian literary history possible, one wonders, a history rooted in that reality?

If anyone can claim to have attempted a Dionysian literary history, it is Harold Bloom, the last of our hermeneuts. There is no need to rehearse the strident debate over the value of his work. Lentricchia's discussion of Bloom in *After the New Criticism* is as balanced as one could wish. Instead, I would like to take up the single question: Is Bloom's theory of literary history a valid and viable source of historiography?

No one has come closer to the answer than Susan Handelman, whose scholarly study, *The Slayers of Moses: The Emergence of Rabbinic Interpretation in Modern Literary Theory*, groups Freud, Derrida, and Bloom in a modern school of "heretic hermeneutic" which seeks to impose radical or revisionist readings on the canonical texts and normative commentaries of the hermeneutic tradition. As Handelman points out, Bloom's knowledge of Kabbalah is based entirely on his reading of Gershom Scholem's *Major Trends in Jewish Mysticism,* which first appeared in 1941.[46] If there is anything missing from Handelman's discussion of Bloom's place in the counter-history which heretic hermeneutic has created, a history much like Hillis Miller's deconstructive literary history, it is the similarity between Bloom's shifts of discourse and the discourse of that historical figure in Scholem's book who, like Bloom, passed through Kabbalism and then abandoned it for a radically antinomian gnosticism. Scholem tells us more about Bloom than Bloom has ever told us about Scholem.

Scholem contrasts Sabbatai Zewi, the "weak" Messiah who founded the Sabbatian heresy in the seventeenth century, with Jacob Frank, the eighteenth-century pseudo-Messiah: "Only towards the end of the Sabbatian movement do you find in Jacob

Frank a strong personality whose very words exercise a considerable though sinister fascination. But this Messiah, who for once is a personality in every fiber of his being, is also the most hideous and uncanny figure in the whole history of Jewish Messianism." Scholem describes Frank's gnosticism as an antinomian revolt which outstrips the worst excesses of historical Gnosticism: "The ideas he adduced in support of his preaching constitute not so much a theory as a veritable *religious myth of nihilism.*" Summing up his impression of Frank, Scholem singles out his will to power as his dominant characteristic: "Jacob Frank (1726–1791) is a Messiah with a thirst for power; indeed, his greedy lust for power dominated him to the exclusion of every other motive. There is a certain demonic grandeur about the man. . . . This almost sensuous love for power, which Frank possessed in the highest degree, is the stigma of nihilism. To Frank the grand gesture of the ruler is everything."[47]

Bloom is not writing literary history, he is creating a historical myth whose goal is the annihilation of historical time. Mythical time, as Ernst Cassirer has pointed out, is not historical time. In the universe of myth, Cassirer writes, "all configurations of being show a peculiar fluidity; they are differentiated without being separated from one another. Each of them is, as it were, ready at any moment to transform itself into another, seemingly antithetical configuration."[48]

The limitations of Bloom's hermeneutic history, and perhaps of all hermeneutic histories, are inherent in the model of perspective, which is so fundamental to Husserl's phenomenology. The horizon of the reading, which is ideally fused with the horizon of the text, is only one element of this model; the fine adjustments of focus in close reading are important, but so is the breadth of the field of vision. The critic who peers into history by using a magnifying glass on texts may see further but see less than the critic on a mountain top using his own unaided vision. Bloom's field of vision is very narrow indeed, a fact obscured by a desperate search for models whose structure can be mapped on literary texts: Freud, Kabbalah, even catastrophe theory. What remains constant in a practical criticism that jumps from one discourse to another in a series of category mistakes is Bloom's boasted will to power. For Bloom, all poets (and critics) are players in a mythical drama of dominance and submission, of parricide and incarnation, a drama on a stage outside history, neither preceded nor followed nor surrounded by history. Bloom's final authority is his authority as reader, not the authority of his reading.

There appear to be only two paths for the literary historian who wishes to move beyond the limits of traditional scholarship (which is far from dead): the dialectical history of Hegel and Marx or Foucault's discontinuous periods penetrated by the filiations of genealogy. Except for these, there appears to be no great interest in the philosophy of history. It is disheartening to open a new book on history and modern poetry, for example, and find that Spengler's name is not even mentioned, when the sense of the end of a civilization that marks the period between the two world wars owes so much to his work. The most useful theory of history may come from the history of science and technology. The work of Thomas Kuhn is well known in literary circles, Foucault wrote as one who had learned from Canguilhem, and Michel Serres is now dazzling his readers with a bold new approach to the interpretation of texts, an approach broad enough to encompass both myth and science.

Perhaps René Wellek, who lamented "The Fall of Literary History" in 1973, sums up best the following decade of American appropriation of Continental literary theory: "The abolition of aesthetics, the blurring of the distinction between poetry and critical prose, the rejection of the very ideal of correct interpretation in favor of misreading, the denial to all literature of any reference to reality are all symptoms of a profound *malaise*. If literature has nothing to say about our minds and the cosmos, about love and death, about humanity in other times and other countries, literature loses its meaning."[49]

NOTES

1. Douglas Bush, "Literary History and Literary Criticism," in *Literary History and Literary Criticism*, ed. Leon Edel (New York: New York University Press, 1965), p. 1.
2. René Wellek, "The Fall of Literary History," in *Geschichte: Ereignis*

und Erzählung, ed. Reinhart Kosseleck and Wolf-Dieter Stempel (Munich: W. Fink Verlag, 1973), pp. 439–40, reprinted in Wellek, *The Attack on Literature and Other Essays* (Chapel Hill: University of North Carolina Press, 1982), pp. 75–77.

3. Geoffrey Hartman, "Toward Literary History," *Daedalus,* 99 (1970), 335–83, *The Fate of Reading and Other Essays* (New Haven: Yale University Press, 1980), p. 299, *Saving the Text: Literature/Derrida/Philosophy* (Baltimore: Johns Hopkins University Press, 1981).
4. Wesley Morris, *Toward a New Historicism* (Princeton: Princeton University Press, 1972), *Friday's Footprint: Structuralism and the Articulated Text* (Columbus: Ohio State University Press, 1981).
5. Morris, *Friday's Footprint,* p. 201.
6. Jacques Derrida, "Cogito and the History of Madness," in *Writing and Difference,* trans. Alan Bass (Chicago: University of Chicago Press, 1978), pp. 31–63.
7. Michel Foucault, "Cogito Incognito: Foucault's 'My Body, This Paper, This Fire,' "trans. Geoff Bennington, *Oxford Literary Review,* 4 (1979), 5–28.
8. Jacques Derrida, *Edmund Husserl's Origin of Geometry: An Introduction,* trans. John P. Leavey, Jr. (New York: Nicholas Hays, 1977), p. 149.
9. Ibid., p. 153.
10. J. Hillis Miller, "Tradition and Difference," *Diacritics,* 2 (1972), 12, 13.
11. J. Hillis Miller, "Deconstructing the Deconstructors," *Diacritics,* 5 (1975), 31.
12. See Michel Serres, "Platonic Dialogue," in *Hermes: Literature, Science, Philosophy,* ed. Josué V. Harari and David F. Bell (Baltimore: Johns Hopkins University Press, 1982), p. 67, and *The Parasite,* trans. L. R. Schehr (Baltimore: Johns Hopkins University Press, 1982).
13. Rodolphe Gasché, "Deconstruction as Criticism," *Glyph* 6 (1979), 202–3.
14. Paul de Man, "Literary History and Literary Modernity," in *Blindness and Insight: Essays in the Rhetoric of Contemporary Criticism,* 2nd ed., rev. (Minneapolis: University of Minnesota Press, 1983), 162–63.
15. Martin Heidegger, *Sein und Zeit* (Tübingen: Max Niemeyer Verlag, 1960), p. 391.
16. Suzanne Gearhart, "Philosophy *Before* Literature: Deconstruction, Historicity, and the Work of Paul de Man," *Diacritics,* 13 (1983), 80.
17. Frank Lentricchia, *Criticism and Social Change* (Chicago: University of Chicago Press, 1983), pp. 48–53.

18. Timothy Reiss, *The Discourse of Modernism* (Ithaca: Cornell University Press, 1982), pp. 31–44.
19. Timothy Reiss, "The Environment of Literature and the Imperatives of Criticism: The End of a Discipline," *Europa*, 4 (1981), 64.
20. Michel Serres, "Turner Translates Carnot," *Hermes*, p. 59.
21. Frank Lentricchia, *After the New Criticism* (Chicago: University of Chicago Press, 1980), p. 200.
22. Ibid., p. 205.
23. Michel Foucault, "Nietzsche, Genealogy, History," in *Language, Counter-Memory, Practice*, ed. Donald F. Bouchard, trans. Donald F. Bouchard and Sherry Simon (Ithaca: Cornell University Press, 1977), p. 140.
24. Edward Said, *The World, the Text, and the Critic* (Cambridge: Harvard University Press, 1983), p. 292.
25. Edward Said, "The Problem of Textuality: Two Exemplary Positions," *Critical Inquiry*, 4 (1978), 673–714.
26. David Carroll, "The Subject of Archaeology or the Sovereignty of the Episteme," *Modern Language Notes*, 93 (1978), 710–11.
27. David Carroll, *The Subject in Question: The Languages of Theory and the Strategies of Fiction* (Chicago: University of Chicago Press, 1982), p. 125.
28. Joseph N. Riddel, "Redoubling the Commentary," *Contemporary Literature*, 20 (1979), 241.
29. Michel Foucault, *The Order of Things* (New York: Pantheon Books, 1971), pp. 46–50 and 303–6.
30. Riddel, "Redoubling the Commentary," p. 250.
31. Michel Serres, "Michelet: The Soup," *Hermes*, p. 38.
32. Jonathan Morse, "History in the Text," *Texas Studies in Language and Literature*, 24 (1982), 340.
33. Michael Sprinker, "Textual Politics: Foucault and Derrida," *Boundary 2*, 8 (1980), 83.
34. Ibid., 88–92.
35. E. M. Henning, "Foucault and Derrida: Archaeology and Deconstruction," *Stanford French Review*, 5 (1981), 263.
36. Gary F. Waller, "Deconstruction and Renaissance Literature," *Assays*, 2 (1982), 69–91.
37. Dominick LaCapra, "Rethinking Intellectual History and Reading Texts," *History and Theory*, 19 (1980), 259, 274.
38. Hans-Robert Jauss, *Toward an Aesthetic of Reception*, trans. Timothy Bahti (Minneapolis: University of Minnesota Press, 1982).
39. See Hans-Georg Gadamer's Introduction to *Seminar: Philosophische*

Hermeneutik, ed. Hans-Georg Gadamer and Gottfried Boehm (Frankfurt: Suhrkamp Taschenbuch Verlag, 1976), pp. 7–40.

40. Jean Granier, "Perspectivism and Interpretation," *The New Nietzsche,* ed. David B. Allison (New York: Dell, 1977), pp. 190–200.

41. Umberto Eco, *A Theory of Semiotics* (Bloomington: Indiana University Press, 1976), pp. 125–29.

42. David Hoy, *The Critical Circle: Literature, History and Philosophical Hermeneutics* (Berkeley: University of California Press, 1978).

43. Gerald Bruns, *Inventions: Writing, Understanding, and Textuality in Literary History* (New Haven: Yale University Press, 1982).

44. Gerald Bruns, "Structuralism, Deconstruction, and Hermeneutics," *Diacritics,* 14 (1984), 12–22.

45. Gerald Bruns, "The Problem of Figuration in Antiquity," in *Hermeneutics: Questions and Answers,* ed. Gary Shapiro and Alan Sica (Amherst: University of Massachusetts Press, 1984), pp. 147–64.

46. Susan Handelman, *The Slayers of Moses: The Emergence of Rabbinic Interpretation in Modern Literary Theory* (Albany: State University of New York Press, 1982), p. 197.

47. Gershom Scholem, *Major Trends in Jewish Mysticism,* rev. ed. (New York: Schocken Books, 1946), pp. 308, 316, 336–37.

48. Ernst Cassirer, *The Phenomenology of Knowledge,* vol. 3, *The Philosophy of Symbolic Forms,* trans. Ralph Manheim (New Haven: Yale University Press, 1957), p. 61.

49. René Wellek, "Destroying Literary Studies," *The New Criterion,* 2 (1983), 7.

EVA CORREDOR

Sociocritical and Marxist Literary Theory

THE MIXING OF LITERATURE AND SOCIETY continues to be viewed as a scandal by some literary purists. For others, such as Fredric Jameson, Marxism, which operates within an all-encompassing cultural framework, is the ultimate horizon of all literary inquiry.[1] In retracing the theoretical intermingling between text and society, it is best to approach it historically. While the plethora of influences on the main sociocritical current are impossible to assess, one can identify some of the theoreticians and works that have had the greatest impact on its development within the past twenty years.

It began with the early sixties: the Kennedy years; Algeria, Cuba, and Vietnam; and the racial and sexual revolutions in America. Departments of literature at U.C.–San Diego and Berkeley in the west and Columbia University in the east became political hothouses that transgressed the former boundaries of literary analysis and entered into passionate and provocative dialogues with the radical theories of Marx, Engels, and Lenin. Many of the same radical voices are still heard today. Most of the then influential, so-called "Marxists" have remained active contributors to the huge critical wave that has swept academic establishments in the last two decades. Historically, sociological and Marxist criticism in the United States developed most forcefully from the mid-sixties to the early seventies, a time which coincides roughly with the critical writings of Fredric Jameson and Edward Said, the publication of journals such as *Telos,* and the activities of a Marxist scholarly group that has conducted seminars in the summer (in Minneapolis and other midwestern towns) and has been responsible for the organization of the Marxist literary sessions of the Modern Language Association.

Almost from the beginning, Fredric Jameson emerged as the center of this sociocritical and so-called "Marxist" movement. His career and writings are paradigmatic of the direction sociological and Marxist theory has taken and the "fortune" it has known in this country. Not so much "godfather" as "semio," signifier, Jameson himself has been drawn into several competing modes of discourse of which Marxism has remained the one stable dialectical pole, the others being psychocriticism, structuralism, deconstruction, and various other modernist and postmodernist voices that have emerged on the critical scene. Jameson's very first publications are revelatory of his sustained interest in the relationship between history, politics, and literature.[2] Among the authors he addresses are Adorno, Walter Benjamin, Marcuse, Bloch, and Georg Lukács. In *Marxism and Form* he makes his initial, somewhat cautious "Case for Georg Lukács."[3] Maybe because of the relative novelty of the topic—by then only two of Lukács's works listed in Jameson's bibliography had appeared in English[4]—Jameson begins his study by quoting the critique of others: Susan Sontag, Adorno, and Georg Steiner. Yet he remarks that they "pay lip service to Lukács as a figure, but the texts themselves were not what they had had in mind at all."[5] On the other hand, and already in this early study, Jameson gives Lukács the benefit of his doubt: "What if, far from being a series of self-betrayals, Lukács' successive positions proved to be a progressive exploration and enlargement of a single complex of problems . . . a continuous lifelong meditation on narrative, on its basic structures, its relationship to the reality it expresses, and its epistemological value?"[6] In these few lines, in which Jameson summarizes his comprehension of Lukács's interest in literature, he also defines what will be his own constant theoretical inquiry into the epistemological value of a text and its relationship to reality. As in this chapter on Lukács, punctuated by the dialectical use of *yet, therefore,* and especially *thus* to introduce his forceful arguments and conclusions, Jameson sets out to demonstrate, before Lukács had the time to publish his *Ontologie,* what he himself finds in Marxism: for him it is not "merely a political or economic theory but above all an ontology and an original mode of recovering our relationship to *being* itself."[7]

In 1971 and 1972 Princeton published two of Jameson's books. At the same time, Jameson and Marxism gained tremendous "respectability" in this country. James H. Kavanagh reports that "largely through the work of one man, Fredric Jameson, the unimaginable has become commonplace." The most prestigious gatherings, such as the meetings of the English Institute, include sessions on "Marxism, History and Textuality," the central theme of which are "the unabashed propagation of Marxist critical discourse."[8] After earning M.A. and Ph.D. degrees from Yale and holding a Harvard professorship for ten years, in 1969 Jameson went west to join the liberal faculty of U.C.–San Diego, only to return to Yale less than ten years later. At the Ivy League bastion, Jameson felt relegated to the margins of the academic mainstream dominated by Hillis Miller, Paul de Man, Geoffrey Hartman, and the rising star, Jacques Derrida. During these years at Yale, Jameson practiced his "disciplined, comprehensive, and immanent appropriation-critique of virtually every critical language issuing from the crevices of the Western ideological apparatus," from Volochinov's theories on language (1974) to Robbe-Grillet as anticolonialist (1976), science fiction (1976 and 1980) and "futuristic visions that tell us about right now" (1982).[9] To the academic world of the 1970s, he offered *The Prison-House of Language: A Critical Account of Structuralism and Russian Formalism.*[10] As his title suggests, Jameson exposes what he considers to be the pitfalls of structuralism and formalism: their linguistically based methodology, which neglects the input of the human experience, time, and history. Jameson tackles works such as Lévi-Strauss's *Tristes tropiques* (1955) and *La Pensée sauvage* (1962), the texts of *Tel Quel* (founded in 1960), Lacan's *Ecrits* (1966), and Derrida's *De la grammatologie, L'Ecriture et la différance,* and *La voix et le phénomène* (all three of 1967). He deliberately excludes from his critique of structuralism the work of Jean Piaget, Lucien Goldmann, and Yuri Lotman, who, according to Jameson, have merely appropriated structuralism and formalism for their own systems. Jameson's approach, typically, is *not* an a priori rejection of structuralism. On the contrary, he considers structuralism to be one of "the seeds of time" which fascinate him. As he says, "To 'refuse' structuralism on ideological grounds amounts to declining the task of integrating present-day linguistic discoveries into our philosophical system; my own feeling is that a genuine critique of structuralism commits us to working our way completely through it so as to emerge, on the other side, into some wholly different and theoretically more satisfying philosophical perspective."[11]

Such conciliatory, open-minded attitudes put forth by the top Marxist critic in the U.S. have prompted criticism from the more orthodox left, while they did not suffice to reconcile Jameson's work with the master-thinkers at Yale, dominated by the vestiges of Wellek, Warren, de Man, and Derrida. Nevertheless, Jameson's *The Political Unconscious*, a confrontation between Marxism and Freudian-Lacanian psychoanalysis, prompted an unprecedented attention to Jameson's work. In this study, Jameson argues "the priority of the political interpretation of literary texts . . . not as a supplemental method . . . but rather as the absolute horizon of all reading and all interpretation." For him history provides the unity of all collective narrative, of all texts and cultural manifestations. Lacan's psychoanalysis, stylistics, semiotics, ethical and structuralist criticism fall into the same all-encompassing cultural category. Jameson views literature, and we could say *any* text, as a "Socially Symbolic Act."[12]

While *The Political Unconscious* extended the realm of Jameson's theoretical inquiry into the field of psychoanalysis much in favor at Yale, it also signaled the critic's departure from the Ivy League and return to California and the airy, open horizons of Santa Cruz. In 1983 he reformulated, with his characteristic ideological vigor and determination, an again more orthodox Marxist position, seemingly inspired by one of Lukács's most important chapters in *History and Class Consciousness,* "What Is Orthodox Marxism?", where Lukács says: "Let us assume for the sake of argument that recent research had disproved once and for all every one of Marx's individual theses. Even if this were to be proved, every serious 'orthodox' Marxist would still be able to accept all such modern findings without reservation and hence dismiss all of Marx's theses *in toto*—without having to renounce his orthodoxy for a single moment. Orthodox Marxism, therefore, does not imply the uncritical acceptance of the results of Marx's investigations. It is not the 'belief' in this or that thesis, nor the exegesis of a 'sacred' book. On the contrary, orthodoxy refers exclusively to *method*."[13] Similarly, Jameson himself stresses not the historically determined end product of a specific investigation but a generally valid approach to analysis: "Marxism is not a set of propositions about reality, but a set of categories in terms of which reality is analyzed and interrogated. To see Marxism as a problematic rather than as a system thus means displacing (but not effacing) older notions of orthodoxy, heterodoxy, or revisionism: to be a Marxist . . . means to agree that the central categories of Marxism continue to designate the most basic interesting problems to be solved. . . . Being a Marxist . . . means remaining and working within the Marxist problematic, whatever position one may take about its fundamental categories." Jameson says further: "The explanatory power of Marxist (class) analysis remains undiminished by political developments which might from a different (but to my mind misconceived) perspective seem to have invalidated it." Finally, Jameson stresses the "urgent need" to reinvent Marxism, quoting verbatim Lukács, who, toward the end of his life, made the following remark: "We are no longer in a revolutionary, not even in a pre-revolutionary, situation: we are not even in the 1840s any longer. In fact, we find ourselves back in the situation of the first Utopian socialists; our task is to work from that situation, in slow, original, unforeseeable ways, towards our own reinvention of the Manifesto of 1848."[14] This remark by Lukács is not as "astonishing" as Jameson sees it, but rather in keeping with Lukács's fundamental, but frequently neglected, theoretical position based on the belief in a continuously dynamic and valid Marxist methodology as opposed to a firmly established system or norm.

Jameson's return to liberal California and Lukácsean orthodoxy was followed by trips to Cuba and China, and a successful ideological survival on the margins of an academia that has become increasingly critical of itself but has remained still more critical of Marxism and Marxists such as Jameson. Jameson's most recent dialectical exchange of residency between east and west boasts a renewed comeback to the Ivy League, a new fashionable mode of existence, and a lucrative appointment at Duke University. No other theoretician in the U.S. can quite compare to Jameson's figure. No other Marxist has the intellectual power, the erudition in contemporary theory, the forceful dialectical thinking combined with the ideological rigor and political commitment that have been the trademarks of Jameson's career. Furthermore, among the self-avowed Marxists, only Gayatri Spivak has managed to even approximate the brilliance of Jameson's academic success.

Parallel to Jameson's activities, there are other signs and figures that support the direction left-wing theory has taken in this country. In 1968 a group of graduate students began to publish a student journal called *Telos,* which in its style and contents reflects the radical positions of left-wing academia in the last two decades. Its young editors and contributors, Paul Piccone, Paul Breines, Andrew Arato, Jean Cohen, and Robert d'Amico, to name only a few of those who are still with the journal, undertook to question and discuss in a provocative, enthusiastic, youthful, and sometimes chaotic style any "mastertheoretician" or intellectual novelty that appeared on the theoretical horizon. What unites them is less a clearly defined ideological position than the mode and realm of inquiry. Their subtitle for *Telos* has changed from "An International Cultural Quarterly" (Fall 1972) to "A Quarterly Journal of Radical Theory" (Winter 1972), from "A Quarterly Journal of Radical Social Theory" (Spring 1974) to "A Quarterly Journal of Radical Thought" (Fall 1982); and their topics, similar to those of Jameson, range from Marxism, existentialism, phenomenology (no. 7), Husserl, Heidegger (no. 13), Marcuse (no. 8), Max Weber (no. 14), the Frankfurt School (no. 20), Baudrillard (no. 20), Habermas (nos. 19, 25), Alvin W. Gouldner (no. 26), Lyotard and Foucault (no. 19), Spain, Algeria, Hungary (no. 53), terrorism (no. 54), Mitterrand (no. 55), and the German peace movement (no. 56) to the Soviet antinuclear movement (no. 57).

In 1971 and 1972 *Telos* devoted two consecutive issues to the work of Georg Lukács (nos. 10 and 11). Having received their first theoretical education from the young Lukács, two of the editors of *Telos,* Andrew Arato and Paul Breines, published *The Young Lukács and the Origins of Western Marxism,* which reflects their own intellectual apprenticeship as much as Lukács's contributions to Western Marxism.[15] A more complex and representative publication of the *Telos* group is *The Essential Frankfurt School Reader,* edited by Arato and E. Gebhardt and introduced by their, then and in 1986 again, general editor, Paul Piccone. The collection presents the disruptive and modernizing force of the Frankfurt School within Marxist critical developments. The young editors seize upon these writings to discredit any form of domination and to "refute the myth of a single, unified critical theory of society."[16] Their attitude obviously signals a rapprochement with the intellectual spirit of the late 1970s, symbolized in the right-wing polls at the 1978 elections in Giscard d'Estaing's France and the unprecedented media success of the charismatic anti-Marxist (and anti-almost-everything-except-themselves) *Nouveaux Philosophes* in the Paris of 1977.[17]

Paul Piccone's "General Introduction" to *The Essential Frankfurt School Reader* expresses the actuality, in 1977, of the theories elaborated by the pessimistic left-wing theoreticians of the Frankfurt Institute of Social Research. Founded in the mid-1920s in Germany, the institute relocated to the U.S. in the late 1930s and published the last volumes of its journal, *Zeitschrift für Sozialforschung,* in English. Even though its members, such as Theodor Adorno, Walter Benjamin, Erich Fromm, Max Horkheimer, and Herbert Marcuse, kept a relatively low-key profile in those early years, their theories became instrumental, as we have remarked, in a rejuvenation of Marxist critical thinking in the 1970s. The revolutionary editors of *Telos,* increasingly impatient with "the unwarranted retention of too much traditional Marxist baggage," welcomed the departure from orthodox Marxism, the "collapse of the Lukácsean project" with its totalizing tendencies and its articulation of a concrete social theory. Instead, they opted in favor of a new epistemological foundation of social critique. Eager to destroy any totalizing or normative political and theoretical model, they felt inspired by "two antimonic yet complementary theories of American society": first, Adorno's *micrological* theory, expressed in such works as *Minima Moralia,* which puts forth that social theory was possible only by escaping into esthetics, where it succeeds in salvaging revolutionary subjectivity but at the price of destroying any possible normative political mediational function; second, Marcuse's *macrological* theory, unfolded in the *One-Dimensional Man,* which constitutes a more orthodox approach similar to the Lukácsean project but without its promise of a happy ending.[18]

The pessimistic evaluation of emancipatory prospects implied in the writings of these authors seemed to bother *Telos* less than what Piccone describes, in the Freudian-Marxist terminology typical of the Frankfurt School, as "the logic of domination," "the colonization of consciousness," and "the ontologization of the socio-historical predicaments of American society." Characteristic of *Telos,* as of the post-1968 young intellectuals in Paris, is, on the one hand, Piccone's pessimistic view of the "collapse of any hope for the Marxist model" and, on the other hand, a surprisingly optimistic hymn to the present, based on what he sees as a "freedom to formulate even emancipatory projects . . . within the *newly* created institutional *free* space." Piccone says, "Critical theory can not only *renew* itself but can also seek the kind of broad popular base previously ruled out in earlier formulations of the theory." He speaks of "theoretical *renewal,*" a "*new* critical sociology and a *new* philosophy of history," which is much in line with the discourse of the French *New* Philosophers.[19] Thus the theories of Adorno on art and society and his statements, "Science needs those who disobey it" and "Empirical science has to prevent the cognitive concept of a 'law' from becoming a mythological concept," and Horkheimer's essay on critical theory in *The Eclipse of Reason*, his *The Authoritarian State,* and *Materialism and Metaphysics* furnished a methodology that has infused the left-wing critical thinking of the, it would seem, eternally youthful *Telos* group.[20] Jürgen Habermas's scientifically grounded social theory, which is based not on a metaphysical interpretation of the meaning of history but rather on a practical, scientifically and quantitatively derived projection of its goals and future dimension, has also held a tremendous appeal for these social philosophers of our technological age.[21] To judge from a phone conversation with Piccone in January 1986, "neo-Adornian and Habermasian" theories are currently, or should one say "still," *Telos*'s theoretical passion.

It was also in the early 1970s, during the same years in which Princeton published two of Jameson's major works, that MIT Press began to publish several translations of Lukács's major works: *The Theory of the Novel* (1971), *History and Class Consciousness* (1971), *Lenin* (1971), *Solzhenitsyn* (1970), *Soul and Form* (1974), and *The Young Hegel* (1976). In Europe Luchterhand undertook the publication of Lukács's *Werke,* a monumental enterprise of, so far, thirteen published volumes, the last of which, *Ontologie,* came out in 1984. In the late sixties and early seventies, Marxist scholars from abroad, such as Lucien Goldmann, were invited as visiting professors to several prestigious institutions in the United States, including the Johns Hopkins and Columbia universities. An ever-increasing number of articles appeared on Lukács's work. At the 1978 congress of the Modern Language Association, for the first time an entire session was devoted to the work of Georg Lukács. Conferences, papers, dissertations, and books on Lukács followed as far away as Australia, where three of Lukács's original disciples, Agnes Heller, Ferenc Fehér, and György Márkus, had emigrated. In 1976 Edward Said published a lengthy review on Lukács in the *Times Literary Supplement.*[22] Said's comments on Lukács, among the first made by a scholar in this country, were quite revelatory of Said's own views and position. Lukács, for Said, "was interesting not only as a Marxist, but also for the kind of Marxism he produced, which was eccentric, and with regard to his own pre-Marxist period, eclectic and inclusive." Said also states, "Nothing can be more moving, surely, than the themes of yearning (*Sehnsucht*) and unfocused irony in his early works before his conversion to Marxism." "Consider," says Said, "the main problematics, even the idioms, to which Lukács gave currency. Most of them have less to do centrally with history than with marginality and eccentricity vis-a-vis history, or with imputations about and potentialities in history." Said projects a Lukács who is surprisingly similar to Said himself: "eccentric," "eclectic," moved by "themes of yearning" and in a position of "marginality." Said's comments are thus significant for several reasons. The fact itself that he undertook to write the review could be seen as a wish to demonstrate his thorough familiarity with a theoretical body that was still a relative novelty to the Western world of that time. Lukács's work was rapidly acquiring the reputation, and with it the distinction, of being difficult and accessible only to an intellectual elite well versed both in several European languages and in Western philosophy. Said not only wished to be counted among that intellectual elite but aspired to become its leader.

While Said unquestionably belonged to the U.S. pioneers of sociocritical theory in the 1970s and partook in prestigious encounters with all the figures of the *Who's Who?* in radical, left-wing letters and politics, his position on the sociocritical scene has differed considerably from that of most other theoreticians. He continued to occupy a prestigious position as Parr Professor of English and Comparative Literature at Columbia University, where he was hailed for dedication and charisma as teacher-scholar, and enjoyed the *quasi* unlimited freedom and adulation of a professorial star. At the same time, as a "Palestinian," born in Jerusalem, Said felt naturally drawn to the promise of revolutionary social theory. His psychological, intellectual, and political need to understand and vindicate his own position as a "U.S. Ivy-League-Pro-Palestinian" at intervals tipped him, if not into a Marxist, definitely into the sociocritical camp. This resulted in impassionate letters to the *New York Times* and an intellectual commitment against all forms of discrimination and social injustice without prompting him to leave the prestigious Ivory Tower of Columbia University. With *Beginnings,* particularly in chapter 5, "Abecedarum Culturae: Absence, Writing, Statement, Discourse, Archeology, Structuralism," and chapter 6, "Vico in His Work and in This," Said entered full-fledged upon the terrain of critical theory, being among the first to tackle the intricacies of the French *nouvelle critique* in the works of Roland Barthes, Lévi-Strauss, Althusser, Genette, and, most of all, Michel Foucault. Antonio Gramsci's *The Prison Notebooks* also provided him with much inspiration.[23] Characteristically, Said again stressed analytic plurality, heterogeneity, and variety as the most interesting aspects of Gramsci's social theory. According to Said, such views distinguished "Gramsci from nearly every other important Marxist thinker of his period."[24] Even though Said's discourse has never been explicitly Marxist, in the 1970s it prompted a strong, somewhat romantic, revolutionary response among his students and followers, based as much on his own charismatic image as on the then mostly mystical ring to the names and titles of theoreticians he discussed: Vico, Williams, Gramsci, Foucault, and Lukács.

The Palestinian crisis precipitated Said into an almost exclusively political direction which saw the publication of *The Question of Palestine* and his magnum opus, *Orientalism.*[25] In Said's own words, the latter "elicited a great deal of comment, much of it positive and instructive, yet a fair amount of it hostile and in some cases (understandably) abusive." Said felt misunderstood in his plea to challenge the "muteness imposed upon the Orient as object . . . the silent Other" of European "Orientalism," which he saw as a "science of incorporation and inclusion" and "an ideology and praxis" on the part of the European colonialists of the Orient. Said still sees himself as a victim of such "Orientalism" today, "an Oriental responding to Orientalism's asservations," as he puts it.[26] Understandably, his theories provoked the sensitivities of many intellectual and ethnic groups. Their hostile responses, however, have not stopped him from assuming what he believes is his role as an intellectual within a hostile context that he is dedicated to change. In his erudite *The World, the Text, and the Critic,* Said takes a closer look at what he calls the "critical hurly-burly" in this country. His skepticism toward all kinds of extreme, yet always academic, forms of criticism expresses a kind of personal fatigue with the eternal contentious discourse of Academia. "There is oppositional debate without real opposition," he complains, and he seems annoyed at that "rhetorical individualism in criticism" that seems cultivated for its own sake. Borrowing from Williams's terminology, he indictes the "cultural materialism prevalent among today's critics and intellectuals. "What is lacking in contemporary oppositional criticism is . . . some sense of involvement in the affiliative processes that go on, whether we acknowledge them or not, all around us."[27] While arguing that the various critical tendencies had a crippling effect on the understanding of works of literature by forcing them to meet certain theoretical requirements, Said—in a winning theoretical stance—distances himself from all dogmas and orthodoxies of what he perceives as dominant culture—academic, social, critical—and advocates freedom of consciousness and responsiveness to the exigencies of the text, to political, social, and human values, to the heterogeneity of the human experience. Said's position, even though influenced by French critics such as Roland Barthes and Michel Foucault, reflects quite clearly his own individualistic and brilliant intellectualism. It also speaks, one feels, of his recent theoretical aloneness, not to say exile and intellectual loneliness on the terrain of Western critical discourse.

Sociocritical and Marxist tendencies have thus been closely tied to general and personal liberationist trends that have gradually spread all over the world. Yet the theoretical impetus for revolutionary thought has unquestionably emanated from Europe, in particular from cities such as Budapest, Oxford, and cosmopolitan Paris, which, in the last two decades, has become the mecca for many of the most influential theoreticians of our era.

At Oxford, after an early success with *Culture and Society,* Raymond Williams published *Marxism and Literature,* a thorough analysis of literature and culture from a traditional Marxist point of view.[28] In this text, Williams managed to make his concepts of "base and superstructure," "reflection theory," "hegemony," and other cultural phenomena accessible to a broad audience that included not only intellectuals but many followers from the working class. Yet to his student, Terry Eagleton, Williams was "neither sufficiently theoretically rigorous nor sufficiently politically engaged." It looked to Eagleton "as though Williams was standing still, or perhaps even regressing."[29] Eagleton therefore left Oxford for Cambridge, where he set out to develop Williams's lessons on Marxism in the light of more recent Continental theories from France. Eagleton's *Marxism and Literary Critique, Criticism and Ideology,* and *Literary Theory* are in their theoretical interest similar to the work of Fredric Jameson.[30] Both attempted to enrich their views by the lessons learned from other theories and disciplines. The two men differ considerably, however, in the *mode* of their discourse. Eagleton's is more linear, less dialectic, and less searching. He is simpler in his views and developments. His work, therefore, is more appropriate to serve as an introduction or as a textbook on left-wing critical theory.

Today, Eagleton is again in the process of redefining himself. He views Williams more positively, not only as a kind of "*eminence grise* on the left in Britain" but as someone who "has never succumbed to the various tides of fashionable post-Marxist pessimism." One cannot say as much of Eagleton himself; he plunged without much hesitation into the waves of more revisionist Marxist theory, including that of the Frankfurt School, in particular Walter Benjamin's "dramatic and violent hermeneutics," and his study of the relationship between past and present. Eagleton was fascinated by Gadamer's hermeneutics and Macherey's structuralist literary production theory. More recently, he has expressed much admiration for Jacques Derrida's deconstructions of the institution as stated in his "Manifesto" for the newly founded "College International de Philosophie."[31] This vacillation in Eagleton's theoretical position appears in the difference between his deconstructive rhetorics in *Walter Benjamin* and his explicit appropriation of rhetoric for the purposes of political criticism in *Literary Theory*.[32] Similarly, Eagleton rejects both extreme positions implied in the notion of "the text itself" on the one hand and a reading based "on a plurality of interpretations" on the other.[33] He clearly belongs to a group of theoreticians, now in their mid-years (Ryan, Spivak, Jameson) and well versed in contemporary critical discourse, who struggle to find valid responses to questions concerning cultural and literary problems which Marxism—despite their fundamental allegiance to it—has been unable to provide for them.

Quite influential and far more controversial in their Marxist revisionism than Eagleton's work in England were the theories of Louis Althusser in France. Althusser was a former Catholic turned Communist in 1948. His structuralist Marxism occupied the center stage of Marxist theory for a good number of years, due to his *For Marx* and *Reading Capital*, published during the fatal years of the 1968 May revolution in Paris and the student upheavals at various U.S. campuses.[34] For Althusser, Marx's foundation of the science of history was a theoretical and political event unprecedented in human history. But Althusser's major attempt was to examine what he saw as "the contradictions inherent in Marxist philosophy which might have led to totalitarian practices."[35] His individualistic reading of Marx outside any established school attracted followers from all over the world, in particular the Third World. Influenced by the Freudian and structuralist discourse prevalent around him, Althusser located epistemological breaks in Marx's work and redefined Marx's relationship to Hegel. Althusser assumed the role of a "super-reader" who liberated Marx from his customary audience. Perceiving parallels between Lacan's scientific psychoanalysis and his own scientific socialism, he decoded Marx according to Marx's historical, personal crises and rejected the early, pre-1948 humanist Marx as an adolescent Hegelian. Althusser's approach led to a new definition not only of Marxism but of philosophy altogether. The novelty of his nonhumanistic, structuralist theory of Marxism has been well captured by the translator (Ben Brewster)—and applauded by Althusser himself—in the Glossary appended to the English edition of *For Marx*. "Consciousness," we are told there, is profoundly *unconscious* in Althusser's views; it is "a structure imposed involuntarily on the majority of men." With respect to "Humanism," we are told, "As a science . . . historical materialism, as expressed in Marx's later works, implies a theoretical anti-humanism." According to Althusser, the Hegelian notion of "totality," conceived as a structure around a center does not apply to the Marxist idea of "totality," where each element is the condition of existence of all the others and therefore "has no center." The Marxist totality is "a decentered structure in dominance," claims Althusser.[36]

Althusser's theoretical views were shared by disciples and contemporaries such as Pierre Macherey, who, in 1966, published *A Theory of Literary Production*.[37] Macherey answers questions concerning the laws of literary production with a purely materialist theory, superseding all earlier mythologies of literature based on notions of creation. The writer, for him, is not the creator, but more prosaically the mere "producer" of a text. He is a workman.

Many of Althusser's ideas have also found a fertile ground in the mind of his disciple Michel Foucault. The master, however, protested this influence slightly in his "Letter to the Translator" of *For Marx,* saying that "even the meanings he [Foucault] gives to formulations he has borrowed from me [Althusser] are transformed into another, quite different meaning than my own."[38] Although Foucault was at one time a member of the Communist party, his philosophical position, his revolutionary epistemology, and his opposition to what he calls the "logocentrism" of our culture clearly separate him from the mainstream of sociocritical and Marxist theory. Neither a Marxist, a structuralist, a deconstructivist, a historicist, nor a postmodernist, Foucault escapes classification and reduction to one approach. Yet despite such eccentricities, the wealth of his research into social problems, human suffering, and institutionalized exploitation provide abundant case histories for even the most traditional sociocritical and Marxist analysis. Any survey of the sociocritical theory of the last two decades would be utterly incomplete without at least the mention of the *phenomenon* Foucault. He was named one of the top ten intellectuals of our era shortly before his premature death in 1984. His critical "archeology" of the modern self, Western culture, and the all-encompassing power of discourse has found its echo in nearly all disciplines of the academic world. He had a profound influence on Edward Said and many young scholars critical of established canons, institutions, systems, and language itself, not only within the field of academia, but also in the realm of medicine, law, prison surveillance, morality, and sex. His works, such as *Madness and Civilization, The Birth of the Clinic, The Order of Things,* and *The Archaeology of Knowledge,* followed shortly before his death by two more volumes on *The History of Sexuality*, had an all-pervasive influence on contemporary thinking that has to be recognized, even though today neither the socialist left nor the traditional right in France seem very interested in keeping his theories alive.[39] Scandalous, marginal, a pariah who enjoyed phenomenal stardom for at least a decade before his death, Foucault is one of the signs that signify the course sociocritical theory has taken in the last twenty years.

Parallel to such eccentric developments in left-wing literary theory in France, a more orthodox Marxist ideology has continued to assert its presence. In the 1960s and 1970s, Lucien Goldmann was among its strongest proponents. His *Hidden God* of 1956 was one of the first detailed Marxist analyses of literature available to the Western world.[40] Inspired by several of Georg Lukács's pre-Marxist texts, such as *Soul and Form* and *The Theory of the Novel,* and by Lukács's first Marxist credo, *History and Class Consciousness*, Goldmann produced a Marxist political critique of seventeenth-century France which consists essentially of a theoretical analysis and practical application of Lukács's concept of the "tragic vision" to the works of Racine and Pascal.[41] In 1964 Goldmann published *Pour une sociologie du roman,* in which he attempted to furnish proof of the timeless validity of the Lukácsean theory of the novel. He compared Lukács's views to those of René Girard in *Mensonge romantique et vérité romanesque,* published twenty years *after* Lukács's *The Theory of the novel* by a critic who, at the time he wrote his work, had not even known of Lukács but nevertheless arrived at astonishingly similar conclusions.[42] The interest of Goldmann's work lies in this attempt to update Lukács's pre-Marxist theories in the light of Lukács's later Marxist ideology. Unlike Lukács, Goldmann accepted the form of modern literature and attempted to demonstrate its "realism" in the works of Robbe-Grillet, the plays of Jean Genet, the poetry of Saint-John Perse, and even the paintings of Chagall. He also analyzed such phenomena as the appearance of the "Livre de Poche," the "flower children," and Marilyn Monroe. It may be significant to note that Lukács never reciprocated or even thanked his most faithful disciple in France. On the contrary, the Hungarian philosopher expressed dissatisfaction and embarrassment at Goldmann's extraordinary interest in his early, pre-Marxist texts, which the later Marxist had not only recanted on several occasions but apparently wished to erase from his memory.

Since Goldmann's death in 1970, followed shortly by Lukács's in 1971, most scholars, both in the East and in the West, have taken a position toward Lukács's theories ranging, almost equally on both sides, from extreme hatred to sincere admiration—never complete indifference. It has become nearly fashionable today to either use or abuse Lukács. However, despite the continuous polemics surrounding his work, his prestige within sociological and Marxist theory has remained unequaled. The vitality and power of his theories appear not only in the innumerable references to his work in the last fifteen to twenty years but even more in the silent appropriations of his thought by recent critics who have written and talked about the novel, the drama, and cultural and social problems discussed by Lukács without going as far as even acknowledging his ideas in a footnote or reference. This may be seen as a sign of academic opportunism—not to say plagiarism—but it may also be taken, and thus possibly excused, as a sign of cultural assimilation of Lukács's ideas. While many critics—not just Lucien Goldmann but others such as Jacques Leenhardt and Michel Lowy—have tried to update Lukács's concepts of realism, the novel, the epic, irony, and the so-called "imputed consciousness" using the results of contemporary research in linguistics and psychoanalysis, others have tried to assimilate Lukács's theories to enrich their own. His views have been applied to the analysis of such cultural and social manifestations as music, painting, feminism, consumer society, and the new working class. In the course of the last two decades, Lukács's work has joined the classics to which the most far-fetched sociocritics, such as the editors of *Telos,* still refer as an immense source of information and inspiration and to which the most traditional critics, such as René Wellek, devote a surprising amount of published attention. What is the specificity of Lukács's theories or of his personality which makes him into such a formidable philosophical interlocutor?

Lukács is for many the meta-Marx of esthetics and literary interpretation. In the eyes of some critics, such as Michel Löwy, Lukács is the paradigm of the revolutionary intellectual of the twentieth century who "lived his thought."[43] This interpretation seems to be supported by the title of his recently discovered autobiographical sketch—"Gelebtes Denken" or "lived thought." Most of Lukács's theories have indeed paralleled his philosophical development and existential experiences. His work deals essentially with the problem of the modern human being who has lost the possibility of an authentic human existence, feels alienated, alone, and finds neither a home nor himself. Such observations appear very early in Lukács's work, even in his pre-Marxist writings, where he speaks of "longing" and the problematic hero's journey toward himself and his search for a home.[44] According to Lukács's sociological theories, such experiences find their expression, their *mimesis,* in the form and content of literature, which Lukács takes as one of the voices of human communication. Lukács's early Kantian analyses in *Modern Drama* (1911), *Soul and Form* (1910), and the Hegelian *The Theory of the Novel* (1920) identified human experiences and problems which later, after his adoption of Marxist ideology and materialist dialectics in *History and Class Consciousness* (1923), he reassessed as mediations of a negative social and economic reality and endowed with political significance. This led to Lukács's critical work written in Stalinist Russia but published much later, such as *The Historical Novel* (1955) and the historical justification of "irrationalism" and naziism in *The Destruction of Reason* (1954). It inspired the many volumes on realism in literature such as *Studies in European Realism* (1950) and his indictment of "modernism" in contemporary literature expressed in *Realism in Our Time* (1957). It led to his post-World-War-II confrontation and polemics with Sartrian existentialism, documented in *Existentialisme ou marxisme* (1961), and his more recent, post-1956 work in esthetics and ontology which continued his early interest in philosophy and esthetics, expressed in the recently discovered *Heidelberger Philosophie der Kunst* (1912–14) and *Heidelberger Aesthetik* (1916–18).[45]

One of the noted strengths of Lukácsean and, in a more general sense, of sociocritical and Marxist critique, is the interest in the totality of the human experience. All aspects of human existence become significant to their investigations. Since orthodox Marxism adheres to the Hegelian idea of a totality within which all human experience takes place, Lukácsean analysis also operates within the constraints of known human history, in which it finds its norms and points of reference. Lukács's questions usually address problematic situations that develop at one specific moment of history between the individual, or a trans-individual group, and a certain form of society. A subject-object dichotomy characterizes Lukács's thought from the very beginning of his writing career. It receives its first thorough theoretical treatment in his 1918 essay entitled "The Subject-Object Relationship in Esthetics" but continues to dictate the nostalgia for subject-object harmony that shapes his use of irony in the analysis of the novel and, later, seems to inspire the utopian goals of his Marxist dialectics.[46] The subject-object predicament appears in Lukács's theories of the historical function of the proletariat, seen as the agent of its own destiny. It serves Lukács's analyses of "reification," the total objectification of the human being who has lost all faculty to direct its life according to its human needs and desires. What has motivated Lukácsean and most sociocritical and Marxist theory is the recuperation of an authentic, free, and normal human existence jeopardized by man himself.

The year 1985 marked the one-hundredth anniversary of Lukács's birth and with it one must recognize that since its inception a sociocritical and Marxist theory has been constantly attacked. As we have seen, what has survived most forcefully are not the detailed results of Marxist or sociocritical interpretation—they have in fact been the most rapidly dated—but rather a method and an awareness of an increasingly complex task to assess all the things and circumstances that contribute to the form and content of human creation and so also to the creation of a text, a piece of art, a society, and, ultimately, the individual and the human self. The plethora of influences on sociocritical and Marxist theory has prompted a plurality of voices that have carried it from its initial "Marxist" to its current "post-Marxist" phase. At the same time, the *post* prefix signifies that a theory originally inspired by Marxism has not died nor stood still but is alive and claims to have updated and corrected itself. By continuously challenging itself and other existing discourses, it has contributed to the modification and "correction" of extreme structuralism, modernism, deconstruction, and reader-response theories. Its dialogue with its own past and the other theoretical present curtailed the arrogance and possible monopoly of any one of them. At the same time, neither its own self-critique nor the critique of others has managed to eliminate it from the critical debate of the eighties. Sociocritical and Marxist theory constitutes an interlocutor who has to be reckoned with today and will, no doubt, have to be confronted tomorrow.

NOTES

1. Cf. Steve Nimis, "Introduction," *Critical Exchange*, 14 (Fall 1983), iii.
2. Fredric Jameson, "T. W. Adorno; or, Historical Tropes," *Salmagundi*, 5 (1967), 3–43, "On Politics and Literature," *Salmagundi*, 2, no. 3 (1968), 17–26.
3. Fredric Jameson, *Marxism and Form: Twentieth-Century Dialectical Theories of Literature* (Princeton: Princeton University Press, 1971), pp. 160–205.
4. Georg Lukács, *The Historical Novel*, trans. H. and S. Mitchell (London: Merlin, 1962), and *Studies in European Realism*, trans. Edith Bone, with a preface by Roy Pascal (London: Hillway, 1950), and its American edition, with an introduction by Alfred Kazin (New York: Grosset and Dunlap, 1964).
5. Jameson, *Marxism and Form*, p. 160.
6. Ibid., p. 163.
7. Ibid., p. 205.
8. James H. Kavanaugh, "Jameson Effect," *Critical Exchange*, 14 (Fall 1983), 29.
9. Ibid., 30.
10. Fredric Jameson, *The Prison-House of Language: A Critical Account of Structuralism and Russian Formalism* (Princeton: Princeton University Press, 1972).
11. Ibid., p. vii.
12. Fredric Jameson, *The Political Unconscious: Narrative as a Socially Symbolic Act* (Ithaca: Cornell University Press, 1981), quote on p. 17.
13. Georg Lukács, *History and Class Consciousness: Studies in Marxist*

Dialectics, trans. Rodney Livingsone (Cambridge, Mass.: MIT Press, 1971), p. 1.

14. Fredric Jameson, "Science versus Ideology," *Humanities in Society: Marxists and the University,* ed. Robert M. Maniquis, 6, nos. 2 and 3 (Spring and Summer 1983), 282, 295, 302.
15. Andrew Arato and Paul Breines, *The Young Lukács and the Origins of Western Marxism* (New York: Seabury, 1979).
16. A. Arato and E. Gebhardt, eds., *The Essential Frankfurt School Reader* (New York: Urizen, 1978), quote on p. ix.
17. Cf. their publications: Bernard-Henri Levy, *La Barbarie a visage humain* (Paris: Grasset, 1977), and André Glucksmann, *Les Maitres penseurs* (Paris: Grasset, 1977).
18. Paul Piccone, "General Introduction," in Arato and Gebhardt, *The Essential Frankfurt School Reader,* pp. xvii, xviii.
19. Ibid., pp. xviii, xxii. Emphasis mine.
20. Arato and Gebhardt, *The Essential Frankfurt School Reader,* p. 369; Max Horkheimer, *The Eclipse of Reason* (New York: Oxford University Press, 1947, rpt. New York: Seabury, 1974), *The Authoritarian State,* trans. and published by *Telos* (1973), *Materialism and Metaphysics* (New York: Seabury, 1972).
21. Cf. Jürgen Habermas, *Theory and Practice,* trans. John Viertel (Boston: Beacon, 1973); *Legitimation Crisis,* trans. Thomas McCarthy (Boston: Beacon, 1975); *Communication and the Evolution of Society,* trans. Thomas McCarthy (Boston: Beacon, 1979).
22. Edward Said, "Between Chance and Determinism," *Times Literary Supplement,* 6 February 1976. All quotations in this paragraph refer to p. 126 of this publication.
23. Edward Said, *Beginnings: Intention and Method* (New York: Basic, 1975), pp. 277–343, 347–81; Antonio Gramsci, *The Prison Notebooks: Selections,* trans. and ed. Quintin Hoare and Geoffrey Nowell Smith (New York: International, 1971).
24. Edward Said, *The World, the Text, and the Critic* (Cambridge, Mass.: Harvard University Press, 1983), pp. 168–72.
25. Edward Said, *The Question of Palestine* (New York: Times Books, 1979), *Orientalism* (New York: Random House, 1978).
26. Edward Said, "Orientalism Reconsidered," *Cultural Critique,* 1 (Fall 1985), 89, 93, 94.
27. Said, *The World, the Text, and the Critic,* pp. 158, 160, 173, 177.
28. Raymond Williams, *Culture and Society* (Oxford: Oxford University Press, 1958), *Marxism and Literature* (Oxford: Oxford University Press, 1977).

29. Andrew Martin and Patrice Petro, "Interview with Terry Eagleton," *Socialtext*, 13/14 (Winter-Spring 1986), 85.
30. Terry Eagleton, *Marxism and Literary Critique* (Berkeley and Los Angeles: University of California Press, 1976), *Criticism and Ideology: A Study in Marxist Literary Theory* (London: Verso, 1978), *Literary Theory: An Introduction* (Minneapolis: Minnesota University Press, 1983).
31. Martin and Petro, "Interview with Terry Eagleton," 86, 87, 90, 99.
32. Terry Eagleton, *Walter Benjamin; or, Towards a Revolutionary Criticism* (New York: Schocken, 1981).
33. Martin and Petro, "Interview with Terry Eagleton," 94.
34. Louis Althusser, *For Marx* (New York: Pantheon, 1972), originally published as *Pour Marx* (Paris: Maspero, 1965); Louis Althusser and Etienne Balibar, *Reading Capital* (London: New Left Books, 1976), originally published as *Lire le capital* (Paris: Maspero, 1968).
35. Cf. Edith Kurzwel, *The Age of Structuralism* (Berkeley and Los Angeles: University of California Press, 1980), p. 35.
36. Louis Althusser, *For Marx* (London: New Left Books, 1977), pp. 250, 251, 255–56.
37. Pierre Macherey, *Pour une Theorie de la production litteraire* (Paris: Maspero, 1966), trans. *A Theory of Literary Production* (London: Routledge and Kegan Paul, 1978).
38. Althusser, *For Marx*, p. 257. Names in parentheses added by author.
39. Michel Foucault, *Madness and Civilization* (New York: Random House, 1965), originally published as *L'Histoire de la folie a l'age classique* (Paris: Gallimard, 1961); *The Birth of the Clinic* (New York: Pantheon, 1973), originally published as *Naissance de la clinique* (Paris: Presses Universitaires de France, 1963); *The Order of Things* (New York: Pantheon, 1971), originally published as *Les Mots et les choses* (Paris: Gallimard, 1966); *The Archaeology of Knowledge* (New York: Pantheon, 1972), originally published as *L'Archeologie du savoir* (Paris: Gallimard, 1969); *The History of Sexuality*, vol. 1 (New York: Pantheon, 1978), originally published as *La Volonte de savoir* (Paris: Gallimard, 1976).
40. Lucien Goldmann, *Le Dieu caché* (Paris: Gallimard, 1956).
41. Georg Lukács, *Die Seele und die Formen: Essays* (Berlin: Egon Fleischel, 1911), trans. by Anna Bostock as *Soul and Form* (Cambridge, Mass.: MIT Press, 1971); *Die Theorie des Romans* (Berlin, Paul Cassirer, 1920), trans. by Anna Bostock as *The Theory of the Novel* (Cambridge, Mass.: MIT Press, 1971); *Geschichte und Klassenbewesstsein: Studien über Marxistische Dialektik* (Berlin:

Malik Verlag, 1923), trans. by Rodney Livingstone as *History and Class Consciousness: Studies in Marxist Dialectics* (Cambridge, Mass.: MIT Press, 1971).

42. René Girard, *Mensonge romantique et vérité romanesque* (Paris: Grasset, 1961).

43. Michel Löwy, *Littérature, philosophie, marxisme 1922–1923* (Paris: Presses Universitaires de France, 1978), pp. 147–53.

44. In German, Lukács uses the word "*Sehnsucht*" for "longing" in *Soul and Form;* he develops this theory of the hero's journey in *The Theory of the Novel.*

45. The most complete edition of Lukács's works has been published in German by Hermann Luchterhand Verlag in Neuwied and Berlin. The most complete bibliographical reference to Lukács's works and critics in English, French, German, and a few other languages has been compiled by François H. Lapointe, *Georg Lukács and His Critics: An International Bibliography with Annotations (1910–1982)* (Westport, Conn. and London, England: Greenwood, 1983).

46. Georg Lukács, *Heidelberger Aesthetik (1916–1918)* (Darmstadt und Neuwied: Hermann Luchterhand Verlag, 1974), pp. 91–132.

IRENE HARVEY

The Wellsprings of Deconstruction

THIS ESSAY WILL SEEK TO OUTLINE a pseudohistory of deconstruction or what might be called a recovery of origins and sources. This is *pseudo*history for the following reasons: (a) deconstruction as practiced by Derrida is unique in the history of philosophy (and a fortiori of criticism) and has no precursors as such; (b) deconstruction does share similar aims with respect to its target of operation and overall goals of the process with Kantian critique, Nietzschean genealogy, and Heideggerian destruction; (c) there is no continuity in this series nor between deconstruction and any of these earlier approaches, yet there are analogies and parallels; and (d) the differences between these four strategies—deconstruction, critique, genealogy, and destruction—are undoubtedly more significant than their similarities.

Nevertheless, it still seems important for us here to situate deconstruction within a pseudohistory in order to illuminate precisely these points of departure from this tradition and thus reveal its bonafide originality. The contribution that Derrida is making with respect to current philosophic and textual problems can only be seen against the background of this tradition in which his work is still necessarily situated.

Our procedure here will be one of oscillation between past and present, between precursor and inheritor, between Derrida and his "fathers" in order to reveal the locus of identification or parallel and to articulate the differences at precisely these points. We will also proceed chronologically—from Kant to Nietzsche to Heidegger—since there may be some reason to believe that their respective "methods" asymptotically approach deconstruction. This problem will thus form the focus of our investigation here. We shall not address the *effects* of deconstruction, in particular those in America, since this will be undertaken by Richard A. Barney in his essay in this collection.

Kant's Critique of Metaphysics (and the deconstruction of logocentrism)

In Kant's brief summary of his project of the First Critique, he articulates his general aims: "The world is tired of metaphysical assertions; it wants to know the *possibility* of this science, the *sources* from which certainty therein can be derived, and certain criteria by which it may distinguish the dialectical illusion of pure reason from truth. To this the critic seems to possess a key, otherwise he would never have spoken out in such a high tone."[1] Thus he is concerned to ground metaphysics legitimately, scientifically, once and for all. He wants to show the *limits* of Reason and to curtail its "unbounded use." He wants to demonstrate the *conditions of the possibility* of metaphysics and establish certain criteria to distinguish truth from "dialectical illusion." We might just as easily situate Derridean deconstruction here, since it also aims to elucidate the "conditions of the possibility" of metaphysics (and the conditions of its impossibility). These conditions and their elucidation are not and cannot simply be metaphysical, according to both Derrida and Kant. The results of their investigations are of course very different, but for now let us continue with the parallels.

Kant also claimed that he wanted to "limit the pretensions of pure reason" and to "guard its bounds with respect to its empirical use." He wanted to know "just how far Reason is to be trusted and why only so far and no further."[2] Thus he showed via critique or transcendental philosophy that Reason left to its own devices—playing only with itself—necessarily led us into the labyrinth of antinomies. The Antinomies of Pure Reason—one of Kant's greatest discoveries—reveal the conflicting results of Reason's unbounded use.[3] More concretely, they show that contradictory propositions can equally well be defended by Pure Reason itself. The way out for Kant was, of course, to distinguish between the noumenal realm and the phenomenal, and subsequently to situate the conflict of arguments as violating this distinction. The point here is that, for Kant, Reason necessarily extends itself into a domain wherein fictions are created and no judgments or decisions based on truth can be made. Reason perverts itself with respect to the "search for truth" in the very process of its unbounded, free, unlimited extension.

Paradoxically, Derrida too, by way of deconstruction, is concerned to limit this unbounded use of pure reason which he will call logocentrism.[4] The Logos, Derrida claims, has always determined the meaning of truth, from Plato at least until Hegel. In the tradition and history of metaphysics, Reason has always been considered its own ground, its own reason for being, and equated with the Good and the True.[5] In his search for the conditions of the possibility of this metaphysical tradition, Derrida finds that nonmetaphysics and the nonrational can be seen to inhabit essentially metaphysics and reason. Rather than seeking to limit this contamination, which Kant had revealed to a certain extent in spite of himself, Derrida shows the essential necessity of such contamination. In the process Derrida too is aiming to curtail the unbounded use of our Reason—logocentrism—but not in order to ground metaphysics and Reason in the service of an absolute certainty, as Kant sought to do. Rather, the deconstruction of the metaphysical tradition shows the limits of rational, metaphysical, and speculative control with respect to discourse, writing, the sign, language, and, in more general terms, textuality itself.

Concerning the relations between critique and deconstruction one might aptly characterize it in the following way: deconstruction can be seen as a critique of critique in the Kantian sense. Derrida, in many respects, focuses on the conditions of the possibility of what Kant took for granted, such as the idea of science (which Kant sought to ground by critique on the one hand and to obey as the ground of critique itself), the ideal of absolute certainty, absolute criteria, fixed boundaries and borders, rigid limits, and transcendent structures which were to be essentially ahistorical, atemporal, and aspatial and thus could serve as the conditions of the possibility of our experience of the opposites of these phenomena.[6] Thus deconstruction, although parallel to critique, reaches more deeply into the ground upon which Kant and his critique stood.

Derrida distinguishes deconstruction from critique on the basis of his own concern with "materiality" (that which is always reduced, overcome, suppressed, or *Augehoben* in philosophy) and with "material" institutions. Deconstruction, he says, "extends to solid structures, to 'material' institutions, and not only to discourses or meaningful representations," and hence it "is always distinguishable from an analysis or a *critique*" (my emphasis).[7]

On the contrary, for Kant criticism operates by "ascending from the data of actual use (of the sciences and of experience), as shown in its consequences, to the grounds of its possibility."[8] It is indeed on the level of semantics (or, as Derrida says, of "meaningful representations") rather than syntactics that Kant operates. To illuminate further the radical differences between Kant's project and Derrida's, let us give the final word here to Kant himself: "By criticism, however, a standard is given to our judgment whereby knowledge may be with certainty distinguished from pseudo-science and firmly founded, being brought into full operation in metaphysics—a mode of thought extending by degrees its *beneficial influence* over every other use of reason, at once infusing into it the true philosophical spirit" (my emphasis).[9] When one realizes that all of the above here—as Kant's aim—must be considered the target for deconstruction, the discontinuity between Derrida and Kant can no longer be ignored.

Nietzschean Genealogy (and the dissemination of polysemy)

Nietzsche was not uninfluenced by Kant, and despite the former's attempts to rid himself of "Kantian dogma," he nonetheless enlists a strategy known as genealogy which has its roots in critique. For instance, if we consider Nietzsche's framing of the problem of morality in his well-known text, *The Genealogy of Morals,* we find the claim that "we need a *critique* of all moral values; the intrinsic worth of these values must, first of all, be called into question." Further, he says, "To this end we need to know the conditions from which those values have sprung and how they have developed and changed: morality as a consequence, symptom, mask, tartuferie, sickness, misunderstanding; but also, morality as cause, remedy, stimulant, inhibition, poison." Thus the project of a genealogy of morals and morality can be seen as a critique in the sense that Nietzsche is seeking the origins and conditions of possibility of what was in his day considered morality and, in particular, of "good" and "evil." But the differences from Kant appear in a number of ways. First, Nietzsche is concerned with historical origins, historical conditions, and historical grounds—not transcendental ones. Second, he is concerned with etymology, philology, and language in general in its role in the constitution of "what is taken for granted as eternal" (truth). Third, he is concerned with the biological, the psychological, and the physiological in "man" and how these aspects relate to the origin of his ideas, philosophies, and ethics and values, in particular.[10] Thus far from the ascent into the eternal, essential, and absolute ground that Kant aimed toward in critique, Nietzsche turns toward all of those "forgotten" spheres that philosophy traditionally has sought to abandon, overcome, transcend, exclude, or at least ignore. The body, the temporal, spatial, the specificities of history and life, and perhaps above all the role of what is today called textuality become crucial already with Nietzsche's perspective and his strategy of recovery known as genealogy.

The movement of genealogical analysis is, however, not simply a return to origins. It is the transformation of the given, actual situation, expression, or experience into a *sign* for something else which is hidden yet represented therein. The past becomes a resource for Nietzsche, and hence he relies on etymology as in turn providing signs or clues to original meanings and original uses and ways of life. Historical, socioeconomic, and religious transformations can be traced in the philological analysis of words themselves. Prior to structural linguistics, Nietzsche's reliance on such a strategy would today be seen as diachronic analysis—focusing on individual terms without regard for their system relation synchronically to other terms.[11] Nevertheless, we can see the philological influence of Nietzsche's strategies still at work in Derridean deconstruction. Let us continue with Nietzsche here for a moment further, however, before turning to Derrida.

Not only does the "present" become a sign or symptom for a hidden, yet presupposed and represented, "past" or "origin" for Nietzsche, but this situation is also reversible. As he says above in our opening quotation, current morality is at once a symptom (or a consequence) and a cause, at once a remedy and a poison. Thus genealogy as a movement back and forth between times in no way reduces the present simply to a derivation from the past. The "present" is also an origin and provides a guiding thread by which we can trace its effects on the "past." In other words, what Nietzsche discovers here without formulating it as such is the doubling of presentation/representation or origin/result or cause/effect such that each relation is reversible, or what de Man would call "undecidable." It is the nonorigin of origin, as Derrida might say, or the supplement itself which is always at the "origin."

With respect to Derrida and these issues in general, there is much coincidence or contamination. It is clear that, like genealogy, deconstruction is not in search of a transcendental ground (signifier or signified) but rather aims to reveal the conditions of the possibility of such a desire (for an absolute ground).[12] Deconstruction also steps outside the "bounds" of philosophy in its unravelling of sources, origins, and hidden, yet effaced, grounds. Temporality and spatiality, desire and the unconscious, textuality and difference, rather than their nineteenth-century translations such as history, the body, etc., step in for Derrida as the results of his deconstructive process.

Deconstruction too relies on language, or textuality, as genealogy relies on etymology. The parallel stops here, however. Where Nietzsche finds that "good" as a term houses within it a history of meanings which represent a "real" history and reveal the origin of the meaning of "good" to be noble, Derrida discounts the value of etymology itself. The isolation of one term already destroys its meaning, which depends necessarily upon the synchronic relations of that term to others in a system of discourse and language. Derrida might argue that Nietzsche relies here on a process of decontextualization and, ultimately dehistoricization and that, in this mapping of the present on the past, he privileges an origin and wishes in the end to *re-establish* that original meaning. The claims to reversibility are only strategic, therefore, and in fact genealogy exhibits a romantic desire to "return to the origin" as a return to authenticity and a restoration. The roots of Heideggerian retrieval clearly appear here; we shall address them in some detail shortly.[13]

Despite an apparent overlap, Derridean deconstruction parts

company with genealogy on a number of issues. Derrida refuses the primacy of a past that is not necessarily mediated by the present, refuses a privileging of an origin, and refuses the possibility of a return and a restoration.[14] Just as for Nietzsche the "truth is that there is no truth," for Derrida, the "origin of origin is a non-origin" and the "trace of the trace is itself a trace." Thus deconstruction does not seek to privilege what it reveals as the "source." The hidden side(s) of the text—its shadows and plays of presence and absence—do not become solidified with the work of deconstruction. On the contrary, the apparent fixity of interpretations, readings, meanings, and strategies exhibited by texts (readers and writers) are shown to be much more fluid and fluctuating than previously imagined. There is no continuous history of terms sought, needed, or presupposed by the work of deconstruction as there is for genealogy. And there is no simple mapping possible of the "linguistic truth" upon an actual reality. Language and world, far from having a one-to-one correspondence as they appear to have within the work of genealogy, are mutually constituting and deconstituting for Derrida. The limits of language are not, as some have suggested, the limits of our world from a deconstructive point of view.[15] Further, for Derrida, language is not identical to textuality. What archi-ecriture, or what we might call the movement of textuality, entails beyond simply language and a fortiori discourse (as its usage in message form) includes force, the idiom, and thinking.[16] It is no accident, therefore, that Derrida does not call his work philology, hermeneutics, or a philosophy of language. The study of writing—grammatology—entails the very elements that language as such excludes.[17]

A final note of caution with respect to the Derrida-Nietzsche connection seems in order here. Although Nietzsche's theory of artistic creation depended upon the notion of two forces interrelating and battling with each other for supremacy, and Derrida speaks of "force" as one of those elements which language and structure cannot and do not control, they speak here of very different issues. Derrida does not identify *differance* (the movement of textuality) with either Apollonian or Dionysian forces as Nietzsche describes them but declares that differance articulates their relation—as it does all metaphysical oppositions—in a double movement of differing and deferring.[18] Apollonian force is Dionysian deferred and vice versa. Thus differance is neither and does not fit within the Nietzschean schema.

Ultimately it is clear that Derrida's relation to Nietzsche in general cannot be explored here and we have not made such an attempt due to spatial constraints.[19] However, with respect to our issue at hand, the parallels between deconstruction and genealogy, there is a profound contamination yet at the same time more profound differences. It is appropriate here to recall that Derridean deconstruction moves toward the dissemination of polysemy, not the sinking of a shaft into a dominant meaning of a term to find its acorn-like origin deep in the recesses of a past that can then be brought back to life. Ultimately it is no accident that Nietzsche was considered a life philosopher whereas Derrida is concerned with a deconstruction of the privileging of humanism.[20]

Heideggerian Destruction of Tradition (and the deconstruction of textuality)

In his early work Heidegger explains the task of destruction with reference to a notion of tradition which itself is never fully fleshed out.[21] It is this concept of tradition as such which we will explore here initially as it is pointed toward and presupposed by Heidegger in his text, in order to then explicate the remedy which destruction is claimed to provide. Since it is clear that the notion of deconstruction in Derrida's work is most closely related to Heideggerian destruction, we will focus exclusively on Heidegger in this section in order that in our final section we can address in precise detail how Derrida goes beyond or transforms Heidegger's project. Of course, this task would require a book-length study in itself, but we wish here only to point toward the areas which we consider most significant for the focus of that more profound analysis. Thus we will attempt here to provide a wedge and a bridge between Heidegger and Derrida specifically on the basis of the analogical affinity between destruction and deconstruction.

Heidegger introduces the *task* of the destruction of the history of ontology via an analogy initially between "tradition" in general and the "history of ontology."[22] He then considers that history itself to be a "tradition" in his sense of the term, which we will describe presently. The final, or perhaps essential, focus for destruction is in turn directed toward that ontology that determines all other ontologies in the history of philosophy—Greek ontology. This must be "destroyed," Heidegger tells us, in order that the most primordial possibilities of tradition, ontology, and of course the question of the meaning of Being itself may be *restored,* recuperated, brought to light, or (as he will later call the process) retrieved. We wish here to trace these *shifts* in the target of destruction as we describe the *task* and the "method" for that task in the process.

Tradition, Heidegger insists, captures and has captured Dasein and has thrown it off the track of authenticity.[23] Dasein's truth has been concealed or hidden from itself by the overpowering sway of tradition. For example, "Dasein is inclined to fall back upon its world (the world in which it is) and to interpret itself in terms of that world by its reflected light, also . . . Dasein simultaneously *falls prey* to the *tradition* of which it is more or less explicitly taken hold. This tradition keeps it from providing its *own* guidance, whether in inquiring or in choosing." "Tradition" thus masks Dasein's own potentiality for being itself—being its *own* (proper) guide and leader. Instead, tradition usurps the role of master (or father) and masks the truth "transmitted" to Dasein: "When tradition thus becomes *master,* it does so in such a way that what it 'transmits' is made so *inaccessible*, proximally and for the most part, that it rather becomes concealed."[24] What we have revealed/concealed here is what in Heidegger's later work will have the structure of Being as it presences/absences itself, reveals/conceals itself, withdrawing as it appears and so on. But let us for the moment stay with the so-called early Heidegger and his "theory" of tradition.

Precisely why or how this "tradition" becomes Dasein's master is not elucidated by Heidegger. Of course he reveals the ontological possibility of Dasein's inauthenticity, but this is not precise enough with respect to "tradition" in particular to account for the usurpation of Dasein. It is a battle of forces that Dasein has lost here? Is it an Oedipal struggle with the father that on the first round Dasein is condemned to lose only to overcome and dominate on the second round (via destruction)? Is Dasein condemned a priori to be lost in tradition as man was corrupted by society for Rousseau? Of course there are many other possibilities, but we must leave these for further speculation elsewhere. Suffice it to say that the meaning of "tradition" for Heidegger at this stage is a process that overtakes Dasein's world, Dasein's judgments, perceptions, and Being, and hides or blocks the access to what is more primordial, authentic, and true *within* that tradition but covered up there. Finally, Heidegger says: "Tradition takes what has come down to us and delivers it over to self-evidence; it blocks our access to those primordial sources from which the categories and concepts handed down to us have in part been quite genuinely drawn. Indeed it makes us forget that they have had such an origin and makes us suppose that the *necessity* of going back to their sources is something that we need not even understand."[25] Tradition thus dehistoricizes the past on the one hand, making the historical into a present self-evidence or nature, and on the other hand, it conceals the past as past. It is as if tradition as master of Dasein, its Father, has itself overtaken and attempted to bury *its* Father—Dasein's grandfather. Thus what is at stake here is the Father of the Father, or the original violence that is then handed down to Dasein as repeated on the one hand and invisible on the other. Dasein presumably is not only unaware of all of this but goes along with "what tradition says is the case"—a dutiful son. But, Heidegger says, Dasein must reject such a patriarchy in order to find for itself its *own* proper roots—the authentic Father, the Father of the Father—the origin.

Destruction enters the scene at this point. It is by the process of the *destruction of tradition* that these "hidden possibilities" latent within it become visible or apparent for Dasein. Destruction is thus an *ought* for Dasein as well as simply one of its possibilities. As Heidegger says above, there is a "*necessity* of going back" to these sources despite traditions' desire to have us believe that "we need not even understand" them.

The shift from *tradition* in general, in its masking role as a relation of "bad faith" to Dasein, is made at this point to *ontological understanding*.[26] The history of philosophy as the history of ontology now serves a parallel function for the Dasein of such thinkers as Descartes and Kant.[27] They have systematically yet unknowingly adopted as self-evident an ontology or way of thinking (and not thinking) about Being which has come down to them from the Greeks. Greek ontology has been turned into a tradition (in the above sense of the term) and has dominated (mastered) the entire history of ontology. In order to release Dasein (philosophic especially) from this hold upon it, the tradition (history of ontology) itself must be destroyed. Ultimately, Greek ontology (from Aristotle in particular) must be destroyed in order to reach the pre-Socratic origins and possibilities of ways of thinking about Being, but first let us consider destruction as a methodological approach to philosophy's history/tradition, as Heidegger explains it.

If one were to ask, "What is destruction?" Heidegger might have answered by focusing on its aim, its task, its purpose, its goal. He might thus have responded as if the questions were "Why destroy?" and "What is to be destroyed?" However, he never systematically addresses the question of "What is destruction?" If he had, he would have had to *thematize* the *way* he was doing what he was doing in much of *Being and Time,* and especially his work on Kant (the principle target, I would argue), but he did not. What is left *unthematized* is thus the very *process* by which Heidegger does *what* he does and discovers *what* he discovers. The syntax of these discoveries is not addressed, however, except, as mentioned above, in terms of its place in a larger system of "Why destruction?" and "What is to be destroyed, for what aims?"

We cannot begin here to explicate or thematize this as yet unthematized (prior to Derrida, to a certain extent) aspect of Heidegger's work, but we shall attempt to outline some of his signposts or guidelines of operation. He is concerned with the so-called blind spots and dogmatic prejudices lurking within the philosophic systems of his predecessors. His analysis focuses on the presuppositions made by the thinker as evidenced by certain turns and conclusions made within the particular philosophic system. For example, with respect to Kant, Heidegger focuses on why Kant *could not* have discovered or addressed certain issues, what prevented him from seeing certain problems, what tradition blocked his access to particular issues: "In pursuing this task of destruction with the problematic of temporality as our clue . . . we shall show *why Kant could never* achieve an insight into the problematic of temporality." Further, "There were two things that *stood in his way:* in the first place, he altogether *neglected* the problem of Being; and in connection with this, he *failed* to provide an ontology with Dasein as its theme or . . . to give a preliminary ontological analytic of the subjectivity of the subject. Instead of this, Kant took over Descartes's position quite *dogmatically*." It is tradition and its effects of blindness on Kant's philosophy that Heidegger is thus seeking to reveal by destruction. The method is one of revealing the limits of Kant's thinking and where those limits become evidence for dogmatism, or where thinking stops and tradition takes over. As Heidegger says, "Because of this double effect of tradition the decisive connection between time and the 'I think' was *shrouded in utter darkness;* it did not even become a problem."[28] It is of course the task of destruction to illuminate, to bring to light what has been hitherto "shrouded in utter darkness." These metaphors are by no means innocent or neutral, as we shall see shortly through Derrida's position.

From the destruction of the history of ontology Heidegger wants to move to the destruction of Greek ontology itself. By first finding the latter throughout philosophy's history, he can show how the question of the meaning of Being itself has been systematically neglected, ignored, or assumed since the inception of Greek way of seeing things. This is not sufficient or adequate, Heidegger insists, and it is time to overturn that conception by destruction. Overturning it means finding other possibilities hiding within it yet never made actual until now. The Greeks too are thus blind with respect to their inheritance from the pre-Socratics and have themselves turned "their past" into a tradition which in turn conceals its own possibilities. Thus we have a third-order tradition here which is, just as much as the first in which Dasein found itself initially, serving to mask the authenticity of the Western inheritance from itself. Yet destruction can reveal such hidden, latent aspects and in turn can, Heidegger hoped, "work out the principles of the question of Being." This is of course the ultimate task of destruction, although it must operate initially at only preparatory stages. We shall not submit Heidegger's procedure or *his* dogmatic assumptions here to an interrogation but rather save that project for another time.

Let us now turn to Derrida and his "deconstructive strategy" in order to reveal how he, more than anyone, has addressed and taken up Heidegger's project yet radically transformed it as well. Derridean deconstruction might well be seen as the thematization of what Heidegger left unthematized, but it is also much more than this, as we shall see.

Derrida and Deconstruction

Derrida elucidates his "practice of deconstruction" more by exemplary instances or cases than by a general theory or systematic treatise on the matter. Indeed, he claims explicitly that "deconstruction is not a theory, nor a method" and certainly not a hermeneutics.[29] Rather, it can be called—tentatively, of course— a "textual strategy" and more precisely a "practice" instead of a theory. For our purposes here, we wish to examine not a case study of deconstruction in action but rather some general claims as to the telos, purpose, or aims of deconstruction which Derrida does indeed make on occasion. Although he does not systematize them, these propositions concerning the general work he is doing—albeit as a strategy of analysis, without essence, without ideality, and hence essentially nonrepeatable—do in fact *cohere,* form a single project, and designate a single, unifiable process. It is this process we shall attempt to elucidate here and in turn focus on the presuppositions concerning the nature of textuality which they entail. This latter aspect, of course, is as yet unthematized by Derrida and perhaps necessarily so. Finally, we wish to insist that this analysis is itself far from a so-called "deconstruction of deconstruction." Such a project seems nothing less than naive if one has not clarified in advance more precisely *what* the "strategy of deconstruction" is and what notions of meaning, language, textuality, and understanding it entails as such.

Derrida himself claims that the following are aims or intentions which orient the work of deconstruction:

(1) to articulate the relation between what a writer *commands* and *does not command* of the patterns of language that he/she uses;
(2) to deconstruct onto-theology, logocentrism, the metaphysics of presence, the proper;
(3) to reveal the economy of a written text;
(4) to show the relations between metaphysics and nonmetaphysics;
(5) to reveal the logic of the supplement or the play of differance.[30]

Let us consider the implications of these claims and, more precisely, *how* they operate within the work of deconstruction. The "relation between what a writer commands and does not command of the patterns of language that he/she uses" can also be described as that between what a writer *declares* (a stated argument or claim) and what a writer *describes* (what is actually done in the text/writing itself).[31] This duplicity—and it is significant here—is characterized in the following ways: (a) something is controlled by the writer and something is not; (b) both of these aspects can be revealed by the work of deconstruction and, indeed, distinguished by textual evidence from each other; and (c) each level requires both a certain univocity which identifies it and a "hinge," or linking term, which plays a role in both systems and is parasitic on/in each, thereby having the function of betrayal by contradiction.[32]

For example, in the deconstruction of Rousseau's texts, Derrida focuses on the hinge term "supplement" as playing this double role—situated on both levels yet on neither absolutely, revealing the connections between the levels. It is, in short, a third term, at least in appearance. In fact, however, the hinge is not a synthesis and does not unite the levels of the text therein described. Rather, it allows for the switch in focus, perspective, or vision which Derrida describes by the term "economy." Indeed, it is the economy of differance which describes this movement as such of the interplay of presence and absence of these levels. Another way of elucidating this economy might be by considering first that a text, for Derrida, is structured in levels, each of which can be identified via a certain systematic nature or completeness. Yet the text as such, as a whole, cannot be understood according to such a schema. The reason for this is that these levels which inhabit it become visible/understandable via a disjunctive relation which, when presenting one aspect, shifts the others "discretely into the background," or into the realm of "absence." Hence the economy of presence and absence prohibits the closure, the absolute visibility, and the finitude of interpretation. Instead, we have a shifting ground of perceptions—indeed, as Merleau-Ponty described, a figure/ground relation which does not allow for total visibility of both at the same time.[33]

The second aim is the "deconstruction of onto-theology," of logocentrism, of phallocentrism, of the metaphysics of presence and of the proper. There are a number of ways that all of these "objects" of deconstruction can be linked together, but in fact they are not to be identified as a single concept (i.e., evil, the enemy, etc.) according to Derrida. Analogous to Heidegger's concerns with the "destruction of metaphysics and onto-theology," Derrida's "deconstruction" substitutes for Heidegger's method or approach. The difference is significant since Heidegger's work also comes under the deconstructive project. The quest for the "meaning of Being" is an onto-theological one, Derrida claims, and the aim to reveal "a hidden meaning of Being" within all philosophic systems since Plato's is itself a metaphysically ordered project, he claims.[34] The difference between Being and beings, or the ontological difference, is not an ultimate ground for Derrida and neither is the meaning of Being the "most primordial" level of analysis. What this leaves hidden in its wake is the constitution of meaning itself—the transformation of non-meaning into meaning, from nonsense to meaning, the excluding process that has already taken effect within Heidegger's own framing of the issue and the problem. Hence, one could argue that Derrida is deconstructing Heidegger's text, if not his thought. Logocentrism and the metaphysics of presence work hand in hand, Derrida claims, to construct the privileged system of immediate relations between the voice, consciousness, reason, essence, goodness, meaning, and truth. The constitution of what is taken as, or given as, true is the realm of Derrida's concern here. In this sense, his analysis of textuality is an analysis of the *embodiment* of Truth—of its materiality, of its signifying structure which of itself has always been systematically reduced and considered radically exterior to that which it produces/exhibits: truth. We shall not examine this in further detail here but suffice it to say that deconstruction for Derrida is not a haphazard, disorganizing, or anarchic play with textuality, as some have claimed. Instead, it entails a process more analogous to Kant's notion of critique but in addition takes into account the textual, inscribed body in which knowledge is not only written, found, but produced and constituted originally for what Husserl called intersubjective availability or accessibility. In short, *the text* is the locus of the constitution of objectivity for Derrida, and thus his *interest* in revealing its internal structures and the play of the economy he calls *différance*.

Before we address the presuppositions within Derrida's own claims here, let us consider further implications on the surface of his strategic intentions. He claims above all that "no practice is ever totally faithful to its principle," particularly with respect to articulated principles within textuality and their manifest betrayal by that same text. Once again, let us begin with an example. In the deconstruction of Aristotle, Derrida analyzes the *concept of metaphor* that the former elucidates.[35] The multiple claims themselves are individually examined with respect to presuppositions required yet not thematized by Aristotle himself. This, however, is not the main issue. The second level of Aristotle's text is the actual *usage of metaphor* that he requires in the format of his argument as such. This level of analysis can be considered the *how* of the text as opposed to its *whatness*—its form as opposed to its context, or in contemporary French terminology, its signifi*er* as distinct from its signifi*ed*. What he finds is that Aristotle's use of metaphor (or metaphor's use of Aristotle, perhaps) is in opposition to his claims concerning metaphor in general. The details of this study should not concern us here except with respect to the *frame of disjunction* that Derrida has located in this text and, indeed, one could argue, in *every* text that he analyzes. It is no accident that "differance," the name for this interrelation of levels, is called "the most general concept of economy itself."

Finally, let us consider the presuppositions for interpretation, meaning, and the structure of textuality that inhabit Derrida's notion of deconstruction here. First, it is clear that univocity, unity, coherence, and systematic totality are not the aims of interpretation for him. Indeed, the nature of textuality radically excludes these possibilities a priori. This nature entails at least two levels: one controlled by the author, one not; one declared by the author, one described; one metaphysical, one not; one entailing form, one content; one entailing a principle, one a practice, and so on. However, these levels are not related in an oppositional manner nor in a hierarchical one. Instead, they are disjunctive with respect to their presentation to the "reader"/interpreter. The appearance of one necessitates the disappearance of the other. Further, there is a linking term, or many, in fact, which could be located, which plays a *double role* (plurivocally, essentially), and which inhabits both levels at the same time. It can be perhaps called something like a two-way mirror, reflecting an image from one point of view and, from another, piercing through to another realm. There is, we repeat, no synthesis possible of levels and no reduction of plurivocity legitimate without simply overruling various other "hidden" (disjunctive, disordering, discontinuous) and evidently threatening terms or aspects within a logic of identity known as the metaphysics of presence or logocentrism. This latter, of course, is assumed uncritically by Ricoeur, as we have shown.

There are clearly some problems with this framework, however. Some of these include the *identity* of the levels articulated; the *distinction* between the controlled and uncontrolled aspects of language; the location of the hinge term or links in the text; the radical exclusivity of the presence of both or many levels at once. Let us consider these one at a time.

First, the identity of the levels of the text presupposes a certain *closure* or system to each level in order to locate it, identify it. Indeed, this also presupposes a reduction of plurivocity of terms in order to constitute a meaning of one level. Second, the claim to distinguish what a writer commands and does not command of the patterns of language that he/she uses rests on certain very questionable presuppositions. Paul de Man has made such an objection. On the basis of the systematic nature of the contradictions in Rousseau's text, he claims that Rousseau was evidently well aware of "what he was doing," contrary to Derrida's claim with respect to the difference between the declared and described levels. This seems a weak argument to us since, as Lacan and Freud have adequately shown, "*repetition automatism*" or compulsively repeating structures can certainly be a sign for the unconscious or nonconscious production in a text "by an author," or, as Derrida says, that which he/she is not in control of.[36] The problem is how can one tell the difference between controlled systematicity and uncontrolled systematicity and, what is more, between controlled contradiction, paradox, and the like and uncontrolled versions of the same. Derrida would no doubt argue that the tradition of Western metaphysics necessitates a submission to the law of noncontradiction should one wish one's claims to be taken as veridical. Hence, the emergence or revelation of *contradiction* within textuality can only be an embarassment to the author aiming toward a contribution of knowledge. Further, he might claim that since such contradictions are not to be avoided and not reducible—that no practice is ever totally faithful to its principle—they are instead to be embraced, not as disorder, chaos, or a principle of Dionysian revelry, but rather as an element that although not present in the consciousness of the writer can be made evident via interpretative strategies, in particular that of deconstruction.

One might also object to the "finding of a hinge term" as analogous to finding a needle in a haystack or to simply pretending to have found one there by making the needle equivalent to any arbitrarily chosen bit of straw. Despite the fact that Derrida would be the first to admit, as we have shown, that he has no method, no key, and no hidden agenda here for his strategy, one can unravel a certain coherence in his project with respect to this issue as well. The term, as mentioned, is not simply "any term at all" but rather is indicated by the author him-/herself as that which is to be *excluded* from consideration. The nature of this exclusion can be multivariant, but the point is that an explicit claim is always made to reduce, dominate, capture, and, in effect, *exclude* something in order to constitute the apparent closure—indeed a finite and closed totality of the work, as Ricoeur argues, or of the text. What deconstruction reveals in tracing the path of the excluding gestures is that whatever it is that is thematized as excluded or irrelevant is always, albeit unthematized as such, lurking within, inhabiting and, indeed, constituting (from the shadows or offstage) the production or presentation that in turn (as a result) becomes visible. Hence, the excluded issue or term leads us into that other side of the palimpsest to the other levels of the text and behind that which only seems to be a mirror.

Our final suggested objection concerns the apparently arbitrary structure of this disjunctive relation of one side of the text to its others. It does not seem to take into account the process of memory itself or, indeed, the element of imagination in the constitution of the object as Husserl explained it. In short, what has happened to protension and retension here with respect to Derrida's most general concept of economy, differance? It would clearly take us too far afield here to examine the complex relation of dependence and differentiation that Derrida's work has to Husserl's and, more specifically, that the notion of differance has to Husserl's of internal time consciousness. However, it must be recalled that Derrida's textual strategy of analysis does not claim that the "two sides" of the text are never simply available to consciousness via the synthetic imagination. He does claim that (a) nothing is ever totally available or presented to consciousness in its full concreteness; (b) the horizon of absence is internal to presence and that which is taken to be present to consciousness at any given instant, as with Husserl; (c) the two sides or two levels of the text are *not legible simultaneously*, that is, they are not visible to the reader at the same instant, but rather require a shift, a return, and a repetition which allows the other side or level to appear for a reader. In this second reading, or repetition, the first does not disappear without a trace but rather its very suspension (albeit in the memory, mind, or retention of the reader) is what allows for the appearance of the *disjunctive relation* itself; (d) the abyss, and in turn the hinge between levels, is only visible when the two levels are realized as such. It is this *undecidability,* oscillation and the impossibility of both choices (of priority, privilege, hierarchy, etc.), and synthesis into one unified whole that is perceptible *only if* both levels are *juxtaposed* at least by the reader, if not the writer. It is this *impossibility* of choice that Derrida claims is almost inconceivable to Reason; it is, in short, a violation of its most fundamental law, noncontradiction. The dictates of Reason and hence of all hermeneutics to date involve choice of alternatives, evaluation of readings/interpretations according to the criterion of adequacy, wholeness, completeness. In short, a one-dimensionality is presupposed concerning the text itself. It is this that Derrida's deconstruction will unilaterally revoke as a legitimate or justifiable possibility for textuality as such, in its very structure. The meaning of this impossibility has subsequently been taken up in America in various ways, as we shall see in Barney's analysis in this collection.

NOTES

1. Immanuel Kant, *Prolegomena to Any Future Metaphysics,* trans. Lewis White Beck (Indianapolis: Bobbs-Merill, 1958), p. 126, my italics.
2. Ibid., pp. 76, 96, 98, 102.
3. Immanuel Kant, *Critique of Pure Reason,* trans. Norman Kemp Smith (New York: St. Martin's Press, 1965), pp. 384–484.
4. Jacques Derrida, *Of Grammatology,* trans. Gayatri Spivak (Baltimore: Johns Hopkins University Press, 1976), pp. 12–13. In this

section Derrida explains this term as logos determining the meaning of truth.

5. Irene E. Harvey, "Derrida and the Concept of Metaphysics," *Research in Phenomenology*, 13 (1983), 113–49. This article focuses exclusively on Derrida's sense of the term "metaphysics."
6. Derrida, *Of Grammatology*, pp. 74–93. In this section Derrida's notion of science and its preconditions is discussed in detail.
7. Jacques Derrida, *La Vérité en Peinture* (Paris: Flammarion, 1978), pp. 23–24.
8. Kant, *Prolegomena to Any Future Metaphysics*, p. 132.
9. Ibid.
10. Friedrich Nietzsche, *The Genealogy of Morals*, trans. Francis Golffing (New York: Doubleday, 1956), pp. 155, 163, 178, 210–11.
11. Ferdinand de Saussure, *Course in General Linguistics*, trans. Wade Baskin (London: Collins, 1974), pp. 140–89.
12. Derrida, *Of Grammatology*, pp. 10–18. He discusses here the desire in philosophy for a transcendental signified.
13. Martin Heidegger, *Being and Time*, trans. John Macquarrie and Edward Robinson (New York: Harper and Row, 1962), pp. 41–55. In this section Heidegger gives a clear thematic explanation of retrieval as destruction.
14. Jacques Derrida, *Speech and Phenomena and Other Essays on Husserl's Theory of Signs*, trans. David B. Allison (Evanston: Northwestern University Press, 1973). See also Derrida's text entitled *Writing and Difference*, trans. Alan Bass (Chicago: University of Chicago Press, 1978), pp. 64–79, 79–154, 278–341.
15. Derrida, "Force and Signification," in *Writing and Difference*, pp. 3–30.
16. Irene E. Harvey, *Derrida and the Economy of "Différance"* (Bloomington: Indiana University Press, 1986), pp. 128–38 passim.
17. Derrida, *Of Grammatology*, pp. 74–93. In this section Derrida discusses the possibility and preconditions for a science of writing, or grammatology.
18. Jacques Derrida, "Differance," in *Margins of Philosophy*, trans. Alan Bass (Chicago: University of Chicago Press, 1982), pp. 1–27.
19. Jacques Derrida, *Spurs: The Styles of Nietzsche*, trans. Barbara Harlow (Chicago: University of Chicago Press, 1978). See also, concerning the issue of forces, Derrida's text *Of Grammatology*, pp. 18–26.
20. Derrida, "The Ends of Man," in *Margins of Philosophy*. This essay relates directly to Heidegger's text, *Letter on Humanism*, in *Philoso-*

phy in the Twentieth Century, vol. 2, trans. E. Lohner (New York: Random House, 1962).

21. Heidegger, *Being and Time,* pp. 41–45.
22. Ibid.
23. Ibid., pp. 312–80. In this section Heidegger explicates his notion of authenticity as distinct from inauthenticity.
24. Ibid., pp. 42, 43.
25. Ibid.
26. Jean-Paul Sartre, *Being and Nothingness,* trans. Hazel Barnes (New York: Philosophical Library Press, 1956), pp. 47–73. In this section Sartre introduces his concept of "bad faith" and gives the following brief definition in addition: "We shall willingly grant that bad faith is a lie to oneself, on condition that we distinguish the lie to oneself from lying in general" (p. 48). Further, "in bad faith it is from oneself that I am hiding the truth" (p. 49).
27. Heidegger, *Being and Time,* pp. 128–45. In this section he performs a destruction of Descartes. For his destruction of Kant, see also his text *Kant and the Problem of Metaphysics,* trans. James S. Churchill (Bloomington: Indiana University Press, 1962).
28. Ibid., pp. 44, 45.
29. Derrida, *Of Grammatology,* p. lxxxix.
30. Ibid.: on the issue of "presence," p. 67; on "onto-theology," p. 68; on "economy," p. 142; on the economy of the written text, p. 142; on the supplement, pp. 144–45, 148–49; on the limits of the author's control of language, p. 158; on the relation between metaphysics and non-metaphysics, pp. 162–63.
31. Ibid., p. 313.
32. Ibid., pp. 65–74.
33. Maurice Merleau-Ponty, *Phenomenology of Perception,* trans. Colin Smith (London: Routledge and Kegan Paul, 1962), pp. 13, 101.
34. Derrida, "Ousia and Gramme," in *Margins of Philosophy,* and *Of Grammatology,* pp. 18–26, are two particularly good sources for Derrida's deconstruction of Heidegger.
35. Derrida, "White Mythology: Metaphor in the Text of Philosophy," in *Margins of Philosophy,* pp. 207–73.
36. Jacques Lacan, "Seminar on the Purloined Letter," trans. Jeffrey Mehlman, *Yale French Studies,* 48 (1972), 38–72.

HERMAN RAPAPORT

Phenomenology and Contemporary Theory

CRITICAL INFLUENCE is often spread by short position papers composed by major thinkers, and in the field of phenomenology one can locate papers which, if not manifestos, are, nevertheless, extremely important condensed outlines of significant shifts in thought. Certainly contemporary critical thinking has been indebted to major philosophical paradigm shifts initiated from within phenomenology, and this essay will outline four important position papers written by major phenomenologists in order to demonstrate how phenomenology has been crucial for much contemporary theory. It is presupposed that the reader will look at the primary works discussed and will understand that no paraphrase can do justice to condensed papers that are very suggestive and complex. Yet paraphrases have their place, too, in that they help orient readers unfamiliar with recondite concepts and frames of reference. In this essay I will discuss Edmund Husserl's *Paris Lectures,* Jean-Paul Sartre's *Transcendence of the Ego,* Martin Heidegger's "Letter on Humanism," and Maurice Merleau-Ponty's "Indirect Language and the Voices of Silence" from a relatively postmodern perspective. The point is not simply to contextualize phenomenological ideas within the fields of postmodernism, for one can do such contextualizing with any philosophy, but to show that phenomenology itself is the basis out of which the newer languages of criticism and theory arise. To that extent, this survey is largely historical in outlook.

Edmund Husserl's *Paris Lectures,* delivered for the first time at the Sorbonne in Paris on February 25 and 29, 1929, can be read as an overall sketch of Husserlian phenomenology.[1] Anyone who reads *The Paris Lectures* today will be struck, of course, by its strong contemporary resonances, and, indeed, these lectures stand as a basic critique of a reflective tradition which today is perceived as distinctly "metaphysical."

Husserl's starting point is Descartes and the emphasis upon the self-givenness of the ego from which the philosopher begins his inquiry, *cogito ergo sum. The Paris Lectures* argues that Descartes erred by regarding "the apparently insignificant yet fateful transformation of the ego to a *substantia cogitans,* to an independent human *animus,* which then becomes the point of departure for conclusions by means of the principle of causality."[2] Descartes is credited with having made assumptions about that which could not be observed. Therefore, Husserl posited the *phenomenological epoche,* the "methodology through which I come to understand myself as that ego and life of consciousness in which and through which the entire objective world exists for me, and is for me precisely as it is."[3] At issue is the suspension of the "natural attitude," the ordinary commonsense manner in which worldly phenomena are observed. Unlike Descartes, Husserl de-objectifies the notion of the ego. For this reason Husserl says that Descartes stood before the gates of phenomenology but was blinded, because he saw the "I" as an object and not as a reflection. Perhaps a contemporary structuralist would say that Descartes conceptualized the "I" semantically rather than syntactically. The phenomenological epoche, however, "eliminates as worldly facts from my field of judgement both the reality of the objective world in general and the sciences of the world. *Consequently, for me there exists no 'I' and there are no psychic actions, that is, psychic phenomena in the psychological sense.* To myself I do not exist as a human being, nor do my *cogitationes* exist as components of a psycho-physical world. But through all this I have discovered my true self."[4] The Cartesian notion of the cogito is only a falsification or false appearance of the "I" which, in fact, must be conceived in transcendental terms. In other words, there is an ego structure behind the notion of a cogito, what Husserl calls the "transcendental ego." (In Husserl, the word "transcendental" refers to a structure anterior in the mind to other structures, while the term "transcendent" refers to things out in the world.)

Definition of the "transcendental ego" is somewhat problematized by the fact that Husserl develops the concept differently in various studies: "We call 'transcendental' the progressing object-index which is part of a very definite yet universal structure belonging to the ego. It is a progression which advances towards the ego's real *cogitata* as well as towards potentialities and capacities."[5] In this passage from *The Paris Lectures* Husserl emphasizes how structures of thought are revealed as the interpretation of objects. Husserl insists that consciousness is always consciousness of something, and it is in this context that structures of consciousness lead to the discovery of a "transcendental ego." In *Cartesian Meditations* the "transcendental ego" is defined as part of an experience in which "an infinite realm of being of a new kind" is intuited.

> The bare identity of the "I am" is not the only thing given as indubitable in transcendental self-experience. Rather there extends through all the particular data of actual and possible self-experience . . . a *universal apodictically experienceable structure* of the Ego (for example, the immanent temporal form belonging to the stream of subjective processes). Perhaps it can also be shown, as something dependent on that structure, and indeed as part of it, that the Ego is *apodictically predelineated*, for himself, as a concrete Ego existing with an individual content made up of subjective processes, abilities, and dispositions—horizontally predelineated as an experienceable object, accessible to a possible self-experience that can be perfected, and perhaps enriched, without limit.[6]

The "transcendental ego" is, then, a prearticulation of the ego, and in *The Crisis of European Sciences* Husserl describes it as "the motif of inquiring back into the ultimate source of all the formations of knowledge, the motif of the knower's reflecting upon himself and his knowing life in which all the scientific structures that are valid for him occur purposefully, are stored up as acquisitions."[7] This source is the "I-myself," though it is not a character or persona but a structure archaeologically viewed. The "I-myself" is a formation of knowledge, a "motif" of the knower's mode of reflection upon the self.

The "transcendental ego" as "formation of knowledge" has

been developed by Michel Foucault, who has talked about society as a network of discourses which map "knowledge formations" through which an individual is articulated as a relationship to the formation itself.[8] For Foucault, social structures are not fully explained in terms of people who dominate because of force or will, or merely because of a social power resulting from their own actions, but rather social structures must be considered as formations of knowledge creating relationships which make possible those social agencies perceived as acting of their own accord. Social relations are revealed through knowledge formations which, like language itself, cannot be controlled by a person or group. And yet knowledge formations represent the interests of some people and not those of others. To the extent that such formations come about through the arduous labor of some and the passive consent of others, there is a sense that the system has been determined or set up by a free agent. And this appearance is close to what Husserl terms the ego, though the formations of knowledge anticipating it are "transcendental."

Husserl's notion of the transcendental ego has influenced Julia Kristeva, who views it less as a formation of knowledge than as a pre-Oedipal fore-structure which is revealed once a paternalistic and Oedipal formation of consciousness is stripped away. The Oedipal formation guarantees fixed symbols, whereas the pre-Oedipal formation discloses much more fluid forms of signification. The Oedipal is thus demystified by Kristeva much as the cogito was demystified by Husserl. In *Polylogue* Kristeva shows how a transcendental ego structure concerns pulsion, passion, music, dissemination, the rhapsodic.[9] Such consciousness formations have transcendental horizons which are feminine, and it is in this sense that Kristeva introduces feminist concerns into phenomenological speculations. One of these aims is to show that the feminine is a mode of "de-centered" consciousness, meaning that Cartesian thought was from its inception a masculine philosophical system which was centered on a male consciousness purporting masculine values of difference, logic, unity, truth, clarity, ground, and certainty. To decenter ideological foundations of philosophy, Kristeva has consciously turned to Husserlian thought in order to define consciousness formations which are not expressions of what she views as phallocentric desire.

Decentering, however, can be viewed from another perspective that concerns a group of phenomenological thinkers called the Geneva School, which includes Charles du Bos, Marcel Raymond, Jean Starobinski, Jean Rousset, Gaston Bachelard, Albert Béguin, and Jean-Pierre Richard. They developed a decentered notion of literary consciousness as various formations of literary patterns, attitudes, rhythms, fixations, mise en scènes, and themes which were not so much the expression of an author's selfhood but of modes of consciousness-apprehension, modes which stretch back into an infinite realm termed the "transcendental ego" by Husserl. Gaston Bachelard's investigations of spatial experience in *The Poetics of Space* and his studies on a poetic consciousness saturated with perceptions and emotions about the natural elements are not exercises in impressionism, but rather serious attempts to disclose fore-structures of consciousness where knowledge is still bound with emotions, fleeting fantasies, memories, vague desires, and so forth.[10] For Bachelard, the image of a house or shell is not merely what Roland Barthes would call a "seme" (a word with largely cultural connotations) but an envelope for consciousness, a thought formation in which consciousness can become aware of itself as a word index revealing very subjective and intimate thought patterns. These mark a literary expression as not so much a cultural artifice as a modality of conscious expression, one that operates on a transcendental level in the Husserlian sense.

Many of the Geneva critics focus on particular aspects of consciousness: Poulet stresses temporality, Richard the emotions, Starobinski the cognitive formations, Rousset the gaze, Béguin the religious. While some people might wonder how these critics differ from pattern critics like Northrop Frye—it could be argued that Frye's *Anatomy of Criticism* describes the literary consciousness of the seasons as expressed through archetypes and genres of literature—it is evident that in large part the Geneva critics focus on intuitive approaches to reading through structural formations of consciousness rather than upon preestablished cultural codes and idealist conceptions of an authorial ego.[11] For the Geneva School, intentionalism means not uncovering patterns which could be viewed as transcendent ideas but rather revealing phenomenological structures which are extremely subjective, intimate, personal. Reading is not so much an uncovering of forms as a participation between consciousness so that forms become a guide to an interaction between reader and author.

This brings us back to *The Paris Lectures*. Husserl argues that consciousness is not a recognition of a split betwen mind and world but an "intentional" structure: the articulation of two formations which interpenetrate, the formations of consciousness (noesis) and the formations of worldly phenomena (neoma). These formations cannot be detected except in terms of how they are interpreted or intended by consciousness. It is not that mind struggles against world in order to gain perspective on itself but that mind and world cannot be bifurcated by beings who have consciousness enough to recognize that a split is conceivable. The paradox, of course, is that although we are capable of recognizing that mind and world are, however much related, different this *rational* understanding is itself a great philosophical stumbling block. For we ought to recognize that noesis and noema are interpretive horizons of one another and that in reflecting upon them clues will be revealed to the philosopher who would attempt to make a description of mental formations that are not obscured by a naive notion of the self as opposed to world.

Husserl noticed that "*the same* hexahedron may thus appear to mean a variety of recollections, expectations, or distinct or vacuous conceptions as intentionally the same."[12] That is, the object is always part of a formation of conscious interpretation and its form acts as a privileged structure for the flux of thought at a particular time. This object is not a thing but a formation of knowledge and perception, an interpretive structure allowing for synthesis of noesis and noema. Such synthesis allows one to posit a synthetic notion of consciousness in which an object can appear as a unified "field" or "concretization." Husserl thought that consciousness posited horizons or fields of expectation, a pointing towards: "Each series, in turn, carries potentialities with it, such as the fact that I can look in one direction rather than another, and can redirect the run of my perceptions. Each recollection leads me to a long chain of possible recollections ending in the now."[13]

Roman Ingarden in *The Literary Work of Art* developed this idea with respect to what he called "schematized aspects," those apprehensions of literary meaning which pose as a formation with a perspective disclosing the possibilities for new apprehensions or interpretations.[14] But Husserl himself writes: "What is the nature of that particular infinity which pertains to the actual and possible perception of objects? The same question applies to every class of objects. What is the intentional structure of the horizon without which an object cannot be an object? This intentionality points to the cohesion of the world, without which . . . no object can be thought." Husserl notes that, given such perception, one must also consider the formation of a structure like the Cartesian *cogito:* "It is above all important to notice that the many modes of the *cogito* possess a point of identity, a center, in the fact that I—always the same I—am the one who carries out now the act of thinking."[15] In addition to object polarization, there is ego polarization. Yet the unity of these formations is not static as in the Cartesian "natural attitude," and the ego at the so-called center is not the origin of perception but itself a perceptual construction arising out of a manifold of intentional experiences. The central ego is only an index of synthesized perception, a locus where identity triumphs over differences. Phenomenology acknowledges the centrality of the ego while allowing for a decentered understanding of consciousness, a transcendental ego that discloses a multiplicity of ego formations not reducible to a center of control, an origin of thought. In this sense, Husserl can maintain that "consequently for me there exists no 'I.' "

The phenomenological critique of the Cartesian *cogito* has had deep influences on recent European philosophy, and in large part the structuralist and poststructuralist movements carry out phenomenological critiques in ways that encourage new interpretive approaches in many fields of research. The work of Roman Jakobson in linguistics, Claude Lévi-Strauss in anthropology, Jacques Lacan in psychology, and J. F. Lyotard in social science is very much indebted to Husserlian thinking. Of course, already in the 1930s some thinkers, though recognizing the radicality of Husserl's project, wanted to go beyond Husserlian limitations. Heidegger's *Being and Time* (1929) was a major revision of Husserlian epistemology contextualizing phenomenology within an ontological framework. Jean-Paul Sartre was also deeply influenced by Husserl and, like Heidegger, set out to radicalize phenomenology, though within a more dialectical and ethical perspective. Also, Jacques Lacan's critique of ego psychology reflects an indebtedness to Husserlian thinking. In Germany and in France the phenomenology of Husserl was perceived simultaneously both as a significant new direction for philosophy and as an insufficiently radical approach. Contemporary critical theory is the legacy, then, of a desire to use Husserl in order to go beyond Husserlianism, a legacy which we see reflected in contemporary concepts such as deconstruction, decentering, polylogue, the death of the subject. In this sense contemporary theory, however new it may appear within academic frameworks of thinking, must be viewed from the standpoint of intellectual history as very much indebted to ideas and issues beginning to be established in the 1930s, a period that in the last few years has begun to receive renewed attention and interest.

Jean-Paul Sartre's *Transcendence of the Ego* was published in the late 1930s and is in many respects a critique of Husserlian phenomenology, though one which was intended to bring out the more radical aspects of Husserlian thought: "We may reply without hesitation: the phenomenological conception of consciousness renders the unifying and individualizing role of the *I* totally useless. It is consciousness, on the contrary, which makes possible the unity and the personality of my *I*. The transcendental *I*, therefore, has no *raison d'être*."[16] By the end of the thirties, intellectuals reflect impatience with Husserl's notion of the transcendental ego, the idea that anterior to the Cartesian *cogito* there must be a fore-structure. Sartre notices in *Transcendence of the Ego* that Husserl's project vacillates between overturning Cartesian reflection and reestablishing it yet once more on different premises. In contemporary terms, the decentering of the subject has been subjected to recentering by Husserl. Sartre's project is to argue consciousness has no self-given structures of thought: "The *I* with its personality would be a sort of center of opacity." For this reason psychoanalysis is anathema and phenomenology must be subjected to close scrutiny and revision. Sartre is extremely close to the criticisms made of subject-oriented theories and metaphysical naivete by Jacques Derrida, and, in fact, Derrida's philosophical orientation is far more indebted to Sartre than we may suspect. For Sartre writes, "But if the *I* were a necessary structure of consciousness, this opaque *I* would at once be raised to the rank of an absolute. We would then be in the presence of a monad."[17]

Sartre argues that the phenomenological I of Husserl is curiously superfluous. "This superfluous *I* would be a hindrance," Sartre says. "If it existed it would tear consciousness from itself; it would divide consciousness; it would slide into every consciousness like an opaque blade." For this reason, Husserl's "transcendental *I* is the death of consciousness."[18] These comments indicate Sartre believed Husserlian phenomenology was essentially Cartesian and that the transcendental I only arrested reflection since it was reified consciousness. Moreover, the transcendental I functioned to bifurcate subject from object. By interpreting Husserl's philosophy as a continuation of Cartesianism, Sartre justifies his theoretical stand: consciousness is simply consciousness of being conscious. In short, consciousness is a *mise en abyme* of being *conscious of*.[19] Sartre specifies consciousness is not positional. Therefore, consciousness cannot be reduced to a structure, model, or object. "Consciousness is not for itself its own object. Its object is by nature outside of it, and that is why consciousness *posits* or *grasps* the object in the same act."[20] In addition, Sartre maintains that consciousness as that which posits, grasps, and acts must be viewed as volitional and considered as motivated. Indeed, Sartre differs from Husserl in that Sartre does not believe reflection is a passive activity, something that happens whether we intend it or not. Rather, for Sartre consciousness is implicitly an ethical engagement with the whole that posits an interpretation of self derived from understanding that the self is an object valorized in world. This awareness does not occur as a private apprehension of self but as a relating with the "self" through a network of worldly values in which we become apparent to ourselves. This view is developed in *Being and Nothingness*, but already in *Transcendence of the Ego* we notice Sartre views *consciousness of* as a "relative existent," a mode of reflection that takes itself for the object in the world it has constituted relative to a system of worldly values.

Sartre is, of course, not willing to be trapped in solipsism, in reflection as *mise en abyme*. Sartre takes care to outline that consciousness is necessarily positioned by the production of a "me" as found in the world. This finding is a positing, though the me is also "found" insofar as consciousness must reflect within a world of values. However, Sartre insists that this positing of a me is by no means a prerequisite for consciousness. In fact, there are many experiences that do not engage a me, the nonpositional consciousness of consciousness. And this raises the objection that reflection is, indeed, a *mise en abyme,* though Sartre insists it is inherently stabilized, for "I am then plunged into the world of objects; it is they which constitute the unity of my consciousnesses; it is they which present themselves with values, with attractive and repellant qualities—but *me,* I have disappeared: I have annihilated myself. There is no place for *me* on this level."[21] Even though this is an unreflective and passive action which occurs in the annihilation of self, it remains an action involving a world of objects. Moreover, Sartre suggests that this involvement signifies a choice not to constitute a me, that such passivity implies a responsibility on the part of the subject. In this sense, then, action is always already an ethical or social matter and reflection, no matter how passive, anything but solipsistic, since it always implies a relation to others or otherness.

Sartre is well known for positing the difference between an I and a me in *Transcendence of the Ego,* and he defines the ego as the unity of I/ME. "I" signifies the ego "as a unity of actions," but "me" signifies "the ego as the unity of states and of qualities." This means the I is posed at the level of thought and the me is considered at the level of objects. The I and the me are correlates of each other, and they belong to the same manifold of relations. In addition, the ego is composed of states (a manifold of attitudes in which consciousness comes to know itself in a particular way), actions (the concrete results of consciousness), and qualities (objective passivities, i.e., prejudices, taste, habits, etc.). An action for Sartre is not merely a reflected thought but the result of concrete reflection, or "concrete realization." Actions result from processes of passive and active reflection as well as from the energizing of attitudes, states, and qualities which make up automatic and objectified modes of behavior. The ego in its relays between the poles of the I and the me realizes reflection as actions that are both interpretations of world and how the me is situated in it.

Though Sartre has been considered part of an old guard which structuralism and poststructuralism sweep aside, his philosophy has been influential on thinkers like Jacques Lacan and those who have considered his ideas: Julia Kristeva, Roland Barthes, Shoshana Felman, and others. Without doubt, Lacan was already influenced in the 1940s by Sartre's reading of Husserl, and the well-known Lacanian mirror stage may well be derived from Sartre's discussion of the I and the me in *Transcendence of the Ego*. The mirror stage refers to that moment when an infant recognizes itself in a mirror and realizes in the reversal and alienation of its own image that it is an object in the world and not simply a part of the mother's body. This is the break with primary narcissism and the onset of secondary narcissism: the adequation between image and self. In looking at the mirror, the child can perceive "that is me." In Sartrean terms this constitutes the emergence of the ego in the sense that the two poles of reflection—I and me—*know* about one another as both different and identical. As the child develops, he or she will realize a cardinal Lacanian point which is, in fact, Sartre's: "Thus, 'really to know oneself' is inevitably to take toward oneself the point of view of others, that is to say, a point of view which is necessarily false."[22] By false, Sartre means there is inadequation in the representations of the self through others, and Lacan calls this "méconnaissance" or misrecognition.

Sartre ought to be considered along with figures like Jacques Lacan, Jacques Derrida, Louis Althusser, Michel Foucault, and Maurice Blanchot, since like them Sartre wanted to transcend the limits of a classical thought grounded in the texts of Plato, Aristotle, Descartes, Locke, and Kant. Like Husserl and Heidegger, Sartre wanted to challenge the basis of Western thinking by questioning its metaphysical assumptions. In *Being and Nothingness,* Sartre expands thoughts from *Transcendence of the Ego*.[23] He attempts to prove on a much larger scale that the ego is not the "owner" of consciousness but is an object of consciousness. Hence, Cartesianism is inverted. However, already in *Transcendence of the Ego* we can read that

> we may therefore formulate our thesis: transcendental consciousness is an impersonal spontaneity. It determines its existence at each instant, without our being able to conceive anything *before* it. Thus each instant of our conscious life reveals to us a creation *ex nihilo*. Not a new *arrangement,* but a new existence. There is something distressing for each of us, to catch in the act this tireless creation of existence of which *we* are not the creators. At this level man has the

> impression of ceaselessly escaping from himself, of overflowing himself, of being surprised by riches which are always unexpected. And once more it is an unconscious from which he demands an account of this surpassing of the *me* by consciousness. Indeed, the *me* can do nothing to this spontaneity, for *will is an object which constitutes itself for and by this spontaneity*. The will directs itself upon states, upon emotions, or upon things, but it never turns back upon consciousness. . . . Consciousness is frightened by its own spontaneity because it senses this spontaneity as *beyond* freedom.[24]

In such passages, the philosophical tradition is redefined through a reversal of traditional relations concerning the centrality of "man" as maker, actor, creator, doer. Claude Lévi-Strauss also argued that "man" does not come into the world with a set of pregiven qualities to which the world is made to adapt but that the notion of who and what we are has to be interpreted or created after reflection has had an opportunity to unfold, or to put it another way, an existential hermeneutics has had time to establish itself late in the history of mankind. Culture is not the result of an ego at work in the world, but rather the ego is itself a cultural production or fiction which once established appears as if it had been there from the start. In this sense, Sartre says, "consciousness is frightened by its own spontaneity."

It is well known, of course, that in the 1960s Lévi-Strauss attacked Sartre on the grounds that existential-Marxism, as developed by Sartre in *The Critique of Dialectical Reason,* still demanded a fiction of selfhood to which history itself was subordinated.[25] Lévi-Strauss argued that for thinkers like Sartre history was a sub-set of events which justified a universal framework into which "man" could be positioned. The radical ideas advanced in texts like *Transcendence of the Ego* were compromised by a historical approach allowing for the interpretation of humanist man through the careful selection of event sub-sets. Every universal history, Lévi-Strauss says in *Savage Mind,* is only the bringing together of very local histories, and thus any universal history leaves more out of any given context than it includes.[26] History is never neutral but exists for some group or subject, and Sartre's view of history is precisely that of a consciousness frightened by its own spontaneity.

Indeed, Sartre would agree with Lévi-Strauss that we are constituted by the institutions which select event structures for their histories, but Sartre would not accept that such a constitutive principle can be thought to elide existential positioning of the subject as an essential feature of its capacity to articulate subjectivity. For Lévi-Strauss and other structuralists, the emphasis upon existential reflection suggests a history of consciousness which is continuous and encyclopedically fashioned in an egocentric manner. And it is this egocentrism which the structuralists want to avoid, though in so doing their theories elide conceptualization of consciousness and the existential perspectives stressing the responsibilities that individuals bear for the institutions and practices whose effect on others is ethically determined.

Without doubt, one of the most influential phenomenologists with respect to literary criticism has been Martin Heidegger. In the work of Paul de Man, Geoffrey Hartman, J. Hillis Miller, and others, the influence of Heideggerian thought is more than slight. In part, contemporary literary theory considers an interpretation of textuality viewed from the perspective of the "later" Heidegger, meaning not the Heidegger of *Being and Time,* who was mainly concerned with an ontological phenomenology of being in the world, but rather the Heidegger who had made a "linguistic turn" in order to phenomenologically transcend the limitations of a philosophy starting and ending with a notion of Dasein. Dasein itself is an existential notion of the subject that, like Sartre's, takes account of the ego as that which is always already transcendent, an ego whose structure is that of a consciousness of Being in relation to being. A student of Husserl, Heidegger studies the "transcendental ego" from an ontological, rather than an epistemological, perspective, and this, of course, raises the question of metaphysics generally, just as Husserl's investigation of mind raised the question of the cogito. Just as Husserl demystifies the cogito, Heidegger demystifies metaphysics, unearthing transcendental clues within the field of metaphysics in order to show that structures can be intuited which precede the notion of a metaphysics, structures which themselves play havoc with metaphysical concepts of presencing, revelation, truth, logos, and being.

In the essays on art written during the 1930s, Heidegger discusses the poetic work of art as an object that discloses our relation to being through our relation to the work itself. In "The Origin of the Work of Art" (1935–36), Heidegger says of the construction of a Greek temple that its being-in-the-world, "in its standing there, first gives to things their look and to men their outlook on themselves. This view remains open as long as the work is a work, as long as the god has not fled from it. It is the same with the sculpture of the god, votive offering of the victor in the athletic games. It is not a portrait whose purpose is to make it easier to realize how the god looks; rather, it is a work that lets the god himself be present and thus *is* the god himself."[27] The presence of the work both discloses and conceals relations to Being. That a work may present itself to us as a temple means that as work it discloses our relation to being as god. But this is only the potential the temple holds open, and in our interpretive recognition of that potential, the temple reveals relations to being which will necessarily be articulated as a "unity of paths and relationships." The work of art, then, gathers together an interpretive manifold of relations, a hermeneutics, in which our own being is foregrounded and backgrounded, and this manifold is disclosed to us in terms of a strengthening and destruction that occurs through time or history. The "meaning" of the temple is disclosed as a temporal manifold of relations in which man's relationship to Being is established and concealed. The work of art, then, is a clue to the destiny not only of man's being but of Being itself, and this destiny is the horizon for self-understanding, that hermeneutical perspective which views Dasein as a proximity relative to the destiny of Being. In Heidegger's later writings, it is in the context of language that such a view will be developed more from the standpoint of Being and less from the standpoint of Dasein.

In Heidegger's very important "Letter on Humanism" (1946) language, not art, is under discussion, for Heidegger notices that language is itself the key to understanding how our perception of being is mediated by a system of relations essentially temporal and historical. Unfolding in time, relations of language reveal and conceal ontological premonitions. The "Letter" is the most specific announcement of such a "linguistic turn," and it is important in that we are introduced to a phenomenological antihumanism which has become basic to poststructuralist attitudes. Interestingly enough, it is this antihumanism which is developed in terms of a somewhat acrimonious confrontation with Jean-Paul Sartre.

Clearly, given the new critical interest in language as an autotelic entity, critics in both England and America have been attracted to that part of Heidegger's work which privileges language as an ontological medium. This pull is already anticipated in "Wanted: An Ontological Critic" by John Crowe Ransom: "Poetry intends to recover the denser and more refractory original world which we know loosely through our perceptions and memories. By this supposition it is a kind of knowledge which is radically or ontologically distinct."[28] Ransom is concerned with demystifying the Enlightenment notion of language as a purely denotative or referential medium, and he argues that the notion of "man" is severely reduced by such scientific or referential contexts. Poetry, Ransom argues, makes possible a recovery of an ontological relation that has been concealed by Enlightenment thought. In the "Letter," Heidegger takes up a similar line of argument, though he has developed it by means of a much more complex and refined philosophical approach. Heidegger writes: "Thought brings to fulfillment the relation of Being to the essence of man, it does not make or produce this relation. Thought merely offers it to Being as that which has been delivered to itself by being. This offering consists in this: that in thought Being is taken up as language. Language is the house of Being. In its home man dwells. Whoever thinks or creates in words is a guardian of this dwelling. As guardian, he brings to fulfillment the unhiddenness of Being insofar as he, by his speaking, takes up this unhiddenness in language and preserves it in language."[29] Like the temple, thought and language offer the potential for an ontological relation as part of mankind's metaphysical destiny. To create or think in words is to preserve the structure whereby our relation to being is revealed but also concealed. It is a structure already given by language as language, though the structure is also shaped by the one who would bring it to various fulfillments. Crucial is the idea that language is not merely an expression of our will—this is the romantic view upheld by National Socialism—but that our ontological or metaphysical destiny is prefigured and disclosed by language. Whatever we are must be understood hermeneutically as posited by language rather than as some essence preceding it, i.e., the ego. The linguistic turn in Heidegger recognizes that Dasein (being-there) is an effect or interpretive relation made possible by the potentials which language as a temporalizing agency articulates. For this reason, our being is revealed in the unfolding of thought as a reflection through language, a historical relation that illuminates itself as the history of metaphysics: the clarification and withdrawal of ontological relations. It ought to be noted that whereas the Anglo-American New Critics were interested in ontology and textuality as a means whereby to establish the construction of the work of art as something independent of the ego, Heidegger stresses the work of art much more in terms of its nihilistic or destructive capacities, particularly in his essays on Nietzsche.

Heidegger's thoughts on language have had much influence on the French novelist and essayist Maurice Blanchot, whose writings develop the production and dissolution of conceptions of subjectivity which are brought forward through linguistic reflection. In an essay entitled "Absence of the Book," Blanchot writes:

> The book is a labor through which writing, changing the givens of a culture, of "experience," of knowledge, that is to say of discourse, obtains another product that will constitute a new modality of discourse as a whole and will integrate itself with it even as it claims to disintegrate it. And everywhere that there is a system of relations that arranges, a memory that transmits, everywhere that writing gathers in the substance of a mark that reading regards in the light of a meaning (tracing it back to an origin whose sign it is), when emptiness itself belongs to a structure and allows itself to be adjusted, then there is the book: the *law* of the book.[30]

For Blanchot, writing at once establishes and unworks all those ontological relations upon which culture, experience, and knowledge are based, and it is in this interplay between emergence and oblivion of the relatedness to Being that the "work" of the artist comes to be. The law of the book, Blanchot says, is the impossibility of establishing ontological certainty, absolute truth of being. Indeed, Blanchot extends and develops consequences of Heideggerian philosophy, particularly the recognition that by way of the linguistic turn one can go beyond the possible recovery of writing as a particular expression of being, consciousness, selfhood. Whereas the existentialists noticed the threat of nothingness from within the project of writing, they thematized it in the context of the absurd hero. Samuel Beckett's *Malone Dies,* for example, typifies an existential novel in that the failure to compose a text always reveals itself as endemic to the ego, that person the novel names Malone. From Malone's human perspective the inevitability of narrative collapse is sure; however, it is Malone's human emotions or moods which recover that failure as something pathetic and hilarious, ironic and anomalous. In Blanchot the failure is not ridiculed and recovered by way of consciousness of the absurd. Rather, Blanchot sees the failure as the law of writing, what he calls de-scription. For the failure or un-working of the text reveals absence or oblivion with regard to Being such that we must accept the impossibility of the text's metaphysical closure and the author's presence. In Blanchot, language and text defy closure, presencing, authority, certainty, truth, or what amounts to the construction of a meaning which asserts itself in a determinant manner independent of consciousness. The problem Blanchot's readers must recognize is that the failure of writing forecloses an independence of the work from the author while at the same time it forecloses a reductionism of text to consciousness. Textuality is reducible to neither noema nor noesis; rather, it marks those instances in which "intentionality" is itself disclosed as a site of impasses or aporeas through which the dialectics of phenomenological epistemology is deconstituted.

Heidegger's orientation toward language is significant not only for Blanchot but for Paul de Man as well. In "Autobiography As De-Facement" de Man ends on some very familiar Heideggarian terrain: "As soon as we understand the rhetorical function of prosopopoeia as positing voice or face by means of language, we also understand that what we are deprived of is not life but the shape and the sense of a world accessible only in the privative way of understanding. Death is a displaced name for a linguistic predicament, and the restoration of mortality by autobiography (the prosopopoeia of the voice and the name) deprives and disfigures to the precise extent that it restores. Autobiography veils a defacement of the mind of which it is itself the cause."[31] De Man, like Heidegger and Blanchot, understands the representation of the subject in language as a relation to being marked by both revelation and concealment. In fact, for de Man, the illumination of the self can only occur through its occlusion and defacement, through the medium of the trope which in deflecting the possibility of unmediated vision manages through the disclosure of death or oblivion to bring us closer to a restoration of mortality. Autobiography veils defacement. This is precisely Blanchot's law of the book, which contends that the space of literature manifests the failures of consciousness, its defacements and unworkings. For de Man, autobiography is the impossibility of the subject's self-constitution and self-representation; it is the interpretation of the self by way of an excursion into death. And this, of course, parallels Heidegger's thought that art refers us ontologically to a destiny in which being is illuminated and obscured, in which insight is interpenetrated with blindness.

In the "Letter" Heidegger not only talks about language as the house of being but also attacks Sartre's cliché that "existence precedes essence." This existential slogan suggests that one is not born into the world with an a priori essence or identity. We recall that Sartre maintains the ego is constituted "from without," not from essentialist or Cartesian premises. Yet Sartre does make ethical delimitations which localize notions like "I" and "me" in what are easily recovered as Cartesian or rationalist moments of selfhood. Heidegger is aware of this, though he begins the attack on Sartre from much more fundamental positions: "Sartre formulates . . . the basic principle of existentialism as this: existence precedes essence, whereby he understands *existentia* and *essentia* in the sense of metaphysics, which since Plato has said *essentia* precedes *existentia*. Sartre reverses this phrasing. But the reversal of a metaphysical phrase remains a metaphysical phrase. As such it remains with metaphysics in the oblivion of the truth of Being." This passage demonstrates that Heidegger was committed to the overcoming of metaphysical formulas, especially those based on the presupposition that strict differences or differentials can be conceptually established as a logical precondition for the rhetoric of philosophical analysis. In the 1940s Heidegger wrote seminars on the pre-Socratics, arguing that before Plato the history of philosophy was not structured by means of absolute distinctions or categories (i.e., of difference) but that philosophical thoughts are viewed as bundles of relations whose terms are not reducible to a logic of difference/identity. The attack on Sartre presupposes that, in talking about existence and essence, Sartre maintains a reductionism to absolute difference. Sartre fails to understand that it is not the order of the terms which matters but the logical preconditions of their difference which ought to be at issue. This is a fundamental error, according to Heidegger, and from it the consequence will always be a form of egocentrism. Heidegger remarks: "One must first of all ask, through what destiny of Being this difference in Being as *esse essentiae* and *esse existentiae* precedes thought. It remains to be considered why this question about the destiny of Being has never been asked and why it could never be thought."[32]

"The destiny of Being" is a phrase which appears in much of Heidegger's later writings; it refers to the "sending of Being," its dispatch, through a temporality that is not linear or chronological but multidimensional as both an appropriation and an expropriation. In this manifold of Being and time we see that Dasein constitutes itself within differences which are not strictly different in the metaphysical or absolute sense. Rather, these differences are indeterminate or undecidable. For this reason the relationship between difference/identity, or the stable ground of existence upon which modern man would like to depend, is deconstituted from within a philosophical perspective that sees metaphysical certainty as a wrong turn, obscuring Being as well as the question "What is man?" In this sense Heidegger is antihumanistic, yet he says quite emphatically that this does not mean he supports inhumanity: "The opposition to 'humanism' by no means implies the defense of the inhuman."[33]

Heidegger's antihumanism is crucial to Derrida's notion of a "decentering" of the "subject."[34] And it is important to recall that such decentering is suggested from within a phenomenological tradition which Heidegger gleans from Husserl. But although Heidegger's ontological approach is more radical in the development of new philosophical perspectives than Husserl's epistemological project or Sartre's dialectical formulations, there is the impression that a thinker like Sartre is better able to address ethical and social issues, whereas Heidegger's philosophizing remains abstract and verges on what Theodor Adorno called magical thinking. In his "Memorial Address" of 1955, Heidegger says that what threatens mankind is our being uprooted from the "homeland," for man's work ought to thrive in fertile ground. When man is uprooted, calculative thinking results, and the atomic age, in Heidegger's opinion, is evidence of this fact. Without doubt, the 1955 address contains strong nationalistic presuppositions nostalgically looking back to a more "landed," if not pastoral, society in which the relation between blood and soil results in a meditative thinking that focuses specifically on the question of one's relatedness to being-in-the-world from an authentic point of view. At the same time Heidegger maintains that man can adapt to the new forms of technology through preserving an "openness to the mystery." That is, we must be prepared to release ourselves for the sake of a technology whose mystery contains the key to our being: "For the time being . . . man finds himself in a perilous situation. Why? Just because a third world war might break out unexpectedly and bring about the complete annihilation of humanity and the destruction of the earth? No. In this dawning atomic age a far greater danger threatens—precisely when the danger of a third world war has been removed."[35] Perhaps some readers will find this is more like inhumanism than antihumanism. Heidegger's suggestion is that catastrophe is preferable to a safe world in which meditation is superseded by calculative or automatic thinking because a world in which technology thinks for us is already a place where man is extinct. Only the horizon of man's annihilation gives him the opportunity, now that he is homeless, to think the question of Being in a meditative manner. Here, as in Heidegger's well-known essays on Nietzsche, the question of Being is posed from within the question of oblivion and nihilism. And characteristic of Nietzschean thinking, the nature of our humanness is dependent upon our courage to release our being in the face of a danger which we may not survive. This echoes Heidegger's closing quote to his rectorate speech of 1933, "Alles Grosse steht im Sturm . . . "

Post-Heideggerian and poststructuralist thinking must make an uneasy alliance with such attitudes while justifying an antihumanist order that supersedes Cartesianism. But at what cost does culture transcend Cartesianism and the rationalist notions of thought which have such an effect on us ethically and politically? Is it that of an "inhumanism"? Needless to say, the Frankfurt School thinkers—i.e., Theodor Adorno, Herbert Marcuse, Jürgen Habermas, etc.—find that Heideggerian modes of philosophical analysis become extremely suspect when applied to political frames of reference, but Jacques Derrida, in a forthcoming book on the term *Geschlecht* in Heidegger, also attempts to come to terms with Heideggerian inhumanism, particularly with respect to a meditation on the image of the hand in philosophy and how this hand participates in the historically monstrous. Derrida's own post-Heideggerianism is by no means insensitive to the political resonances in Heidegger, and it is clear within a Derridean perspective not only that there is a certain political contamination of philosophy within the oeuvre of Heidegger but that such contamination cannot be localized to Heideggerianism per se. That is, Derrida is sensitive to the suspicion that the "difference" between humanism and inhumanism is itself anything but absolute and determinate and that it is this "difference" which mystifies an ethics purporting to detect the "difference" between good and evil, humane and inhumane. What is the basis of such difference, Derrida asks, if not a metaphysical ground which is itself a phantasmal politics? It is, quite evidently, through such questioning that the ethics of an existentialist like Sartre is severely challenged, if not undermined.

Maurice Merleau-Ponty's "Indirect Language and the Voices of Silence" was published in *Signs* in 1960.[36] The date of publication is significant because it shows that Merleau-Ponty had provided much of the groundwork for what was later to become known as "deconstruction"; *Signs* develops within a phenomenological perspective and vocabulary many of the key terms which belong to the more exotic vocabulary of Jacques Derrida's *Of Grammatology* (1967). A major achievement of "Indirect Language and the Voices of Silence" is the demonstration of the relevance of structuralist linguistics to a phenomenological understanding of language, and Merleau-Ponty's appropriation of Saussurean linguistics, in particular, marks a "linguistic turn" in French phenomenology while preserving close ties with Husserlian thought.

Most striking about Merleau-Ponty's consideration of Ferdinand de Saussure's *Course in General Linguistics* (1915) is that from a phenomenological view such a treatise might at first appear quite unworthy of consideration for two major reasons.[37] First, Saussure is only interested in "signs" on the level of conventional symbols in a restricted denotative sense. In his *Logical Investigations* Husserl terms such signs "indicative" and opposes them to "expressive" signs, which refer to those signs relevant at levels of more complex conceptualization, intuition, apprehension, and interpretation.[38] Second, since Saussure ignores "expressive" signs, he can at best merely assume that somehow we attach concepts to words through the agent of a sound shape. That is to say, Saussure depends entirely upon a very simplistic notion of naming which takes no account of the cognitive processes involved. Husserl, quite to the contrary, spent much effort in *The Logical Investigations* attempting to demonstrate precisely how logical processes of thought—naming, signification, syntax, etc.—occur within complex levels of symbolic formations that concern the modalities in which consciousness apprehends and synthesizes perceptions at the levels of both noema and noesis. Husserl finds that signification comprises a complex network of overlapping structures which are not reducible to the kinds of simplistic naming assumptions common in a field like Saussurian linguistics.

Therefore, given the obvious limitations of Saussure, it is quite surprising that Merleau-Ponty, himself deeply committed to a Husserlian phenomenology, would turn to structuralism in general and Saussure in particular. However, Merleau-Ponty saw in Saussurean linguistics the perception that apprehension through language is inherently indirect and that meaning is not a given conceptualized by mind but a horizon which the subject constitutes "intentionally" in the phenomenological sense. Since Saussurean linguistics assumes meaning is not a latent reserve transcending discourse, structuralism becomes another means through which the phenomenologist can talk about language acquisition as a constitutive network of relations within which the subject is articulated as an effect of language rather than as its cause. What especially attracted Merleau-Ponty to Saussure was the notion that the subject is, in fact, the effect of a signifying chain constituted out of distinctive features or differences which are naturally given through man's voicings of sound, that is, given as a somatic effect. In other words, the capacity to speak is biologically determined as difference, as the capacity to produce phonemic features which are "distinctive." Hence, it is not so much that man invented language as a tool in order to achieve practical aims, such as hunting food, but that the very fact man has a voice, a tongue, a certain oral cavity, and so on, destines him to speak. Speech, then, is achieved indirectly as a somatic effect rather than directly by force of intellectual will, and in this sense, man can be said to be constituted by language rather than being its inventor or author.

The Saussurean orientation led Merleau-Ponty to criticize classical notions of rhetoric or writing as established by eighteenth-century figures like Jean de la Bruyère. Indeed, Roland Barthes had already conducted a similar critique in the late 1940s within his long essay "Writing Degree Zero." And the new novelists—Alain Robbe-Grillet et al.—had similarly begun to think about "writing" in relation to ideology and materialist conditions. Yet Merleau-Ponty initiates a critique of classical writing which will be developed more or less point by point in *Of Grammatology* by Derrida and which contains a passage of particular relevance on La Bruyère: "As La Bruyère would have it, speech has no other role than finding the exact expression assigned in advance to each thought by a language of things themselves; and this double recourse to an art before art, to a speech before speech, prescribes to the work a certain point of perfection, completeness, or fullness which makes all men assent to it as they assent to the things which fall under their senses."[39] Merleau-Ponty outlines three philosophical assumptions which are merely metaphysical or idealist presuppositions, attitudes toward language which have no phenomenological veracity. First, La Bruyère holds a denotative and mimetic theory which presupposes words are tools that must be able to adequately refer to all those things we already know without recourse to language. Second, La Bruyère presupposes a speech before speech. This is an intentionalism which again assumes that ideas exist independently of words and that all signs are merely conventional translations of ideas. Third, La Bruyère distinguishes between the presence of a true thought in a private and inspired form and a corrupted translation of thought in a public or conventional system of marks. For La Bruyère, then, the artist is one who produces a medium of signification whose conventions most adequately approximate or reflect an incommunicable truth. Thus the work of art communicates plenitude of meaning and achieves perfection through wholeness.

"Indirect Language and the Voices of Silence" invalidates these assumptions and clarifies that they are merely mystifications derived from both a Platonic and a Cartesian point of view. Like Merleau-Ponty, Derrida questions the classicist view of language and takes issue primarily with the notion of a speech before speech. This idea presupposes a ground or origin for language; moreover, it justifies a curious hierarchy in which voice reigns over writing.

Derrida questions the classical attitude, strongly set out in Plato, that writing is inferior to speech and finds that the privilege of speech is necessary to maintain and resolve a philosophical contradiction without which a theory of mimesis could not stand. This contradiction insists that meaning or truth is at once present and absent, determinate and indeterminate. That "writing" gives us access to the fullness of speech even while it is offered as a debasement of speech's plenitude allows for an ideology of art which agrees with La Bruyère's statements about expression. Derrida, like Merleau-Ponty, is suspicious about the notion that writing or expression ought to reflect a totality of relations, since this notion of totality is itself but a ruse to support the contradiction that a text is at once everything and nothing, that it is a golden world, to use Sir Philip Sidney's term, but yet a fraud.

Merleau-Ponty is, of course, not particularly interested in demystifying the notion of "voice"; in fact, one could argue that he also privileges it. Nevertheless, *Of Grammatology* is very much an expansion of the kinds of critiques initiated by Merleau-Ponty on La Bruyère, an expansion which raises the level of critique to that which questions Western writing as a whole. Taking a position which Derrida will later elaborate, Merleau-Ponty writes, "Now if we rid our minds of the idea that our language is the translation or cipher of an original text, we shall see that the idea of *complete* expression is nonsensical, and that all language is indirect or allusive—that it is, if you wish, silence."[40] The silence reflects Saussure's thought that meaning is constituted within semiotic differences, these distinctive features which reveal gaps, spaces, silences. Meaning is the total movement of speech, Merleau-Ponty says, and meaning is constituted in linguistic space. This idea is transferred to artistic creation when Merleau-Ponty concludes that when Matisse painted the hesitations of the brush produced the painting's meaning. Signs do "not so much express a meaning as mark a divergence of meaning between [themselves] and other signs."[41] Perception is saturated with differences or spaces, and this allows consciousness to intend indirectly through hesitation, pause, interruption. Language, in its broadest sense, is the medium through which phenomenological intentionality transpires, and, in fact, one could say that consciousness cannot be separated from language as difference or spacing, though consciousness, like language, is subjected to the punctuations of silence, spaces.

In *Of Grammatology* Derrida similarly argues that being does not escape the movement of the sign and must be considered in terms of "espacement." It is in this context that writing is determined from within the notion of the trace, the idea that expression or marking occurs from within a trajectory of trace effects through which our apprehension of ourselves as grounded beings necessarily takes place. Indeed, Derrida's thought on the structure of the trace is also greatly indebted to Heidegger's essay "The Anaximander Fragment" from *Holzwege,* though it must be taken into account that, insofar as this Heideggerian context of the trace is contextualized within a critique of a speech before speech and a determination of language within "espacement," Merleau-Ponty's influence is strongly felt at such moments and functions to radically alter the way in which Heidegger had been perceived prior to Derrida's reformulations.[42]

Merleau-Ponty's situating of language at the center of his philosophy has allowed him to argue that "meaning arises at the edge of signs" and that the synthesis consciousness seeks is only indirectly apprehended through the linguistic medium, which is itself characterized by silence. Language is not a means but "much more like a sort of being. . . . Because meaning is the total movement of speech, our thought crawls along in language. Yet for the same reason, our thought moves through language as a gesture goes beyond the individual points of its passage." Moreover,

> As algebra brings unknown magnitudes under consideration, speech differentiates significations no one of which is known separately; and it is by treating them as known (and giving us an abstract picture of them and their interrelations) that language ends up imposing the most precise identification upon us in a flash. Language signifies when instead of copying thought it lets itself be taken apart and put together again by thought. Language bears the meaning of thought as a footprint signifies the movement and effort of a body. . . . It goes without saying that language is oblique and autonomous, and that its ability to signify a thought or a thing directly is only a secondary power derived from the inner life of language. Like the weaver, the writer works on the wrong side of his material. He

> has to do only with language, and it is thus that he suddenly finds himself surrounded by meaning.[43]

Not unlike the early Sartre, Merleau-Ponty engages interpretation within an exterior realm in which the ego is itself constructed. But in *Signs* that realm is language. Not an alien medium through which thought is itself a copy of a speech before speech, language is a medium to be taken apart and put together by thought, part of a process which is itself thinking and which is not preceded by any originary language or speech. In a sentence adumbrating Derrida's thoughts on the trace, Merleau-Ponty says language bears the meaning of thought "as a footprint signifies the movement and effort of a body." That is to say, language is itself residual, supplementary, but a print. And yet nothing comes before this print which is more authentic or originary. Meaning is nothing but the exertion of an impulse to think on language. If we consider the voice as a somatic effect, we will immediately notice that vocalization itself is but the imprint of a bodily impulse, a pressure or gesture. This vocalization is not the presencing of thought, only that which is impacted upon. And yet, prior to this impacting on voice, there is nothing that could be called speech, meaning, intention, truth. In the use of the bodily apparatus for speech, in this very inhabiting of voice, its very experimentations in language acquisition, we have what Merleau-Ponty is calling language, thought: a taking apart and putting together. And such taking apart and reconstitution cannot occur except by way of silence, space, absence. Like the weaver, the *speaker* works from the wrong side of the materials, from the inside of his voice. We are all inside our voices, our minds, our apparatuses for signification. And yet, given that there are others similarly oriented, we also find ourselves suddenly surrounded by meaning, find ourselves also on the outside. But this difference of inside/outside, is it not, Merleau-Ponty suggests, always one that is "invaginated," a difference where the opposites saturate one another? It is in this sense that when Merleau-Ponty considers the constitution of the ego as transcendent he too goes beyond the dialectics of Sartrean existentialism.

For Merleau-Ponty, the writer is not a user of a ready-made

language but an agency both constituting and constituted by language as that which is never fully present, that which is itself saturated by difference, space, disarticulations. The subject does not apprehend language as totality but as a medium that is incomplete, fragmentary. And it is in terms of the "not said," or unspoken, that the artist must find a way, that the subject comes to be as an articulation indirectly arrived at through language as the voices of silence, as dis-articulation. This idea is well anticipated by Maurice Blanchot, who in *The Space of Literature* writes that "in the language of the world, language as the being of language and as the language of being keeps still. Thanks to this silence, beings speak, and in it they also find oblivion and rest."[44] Blanchot summarizes by saying, "Poetry expresses the fact that beings are quiet." Merleau-Ponty's essay "Indirect Language and the Voices of Silence" investigated such an attitude, as we have seen, from a very detailed phenomenological perspective, and many of the notions so peculiar to what is today called deconstruction are, quite obviously, closely allied to Merleau-Ponty's stress on silence, absence, trace, indirection. Unfortunately, Merleau-Ponty died in the early 1960s, and there is good cause to believe that, had he lived, the Derridean analyses which followed *Signs* would have influenced Merleau-Ponty to develop his phenomenological investigations in ways that would have allowed us to follow a deconstructive path less hostile to the notion of consciousness and more open to epistemological researches. Certainly, Merleau-Ponty remains an immensely important modern thinker whose work is extremely suggestive for those interested in pursuing new approaches to deconstructive philosophy.

Few theorists would dispute that phenomenology is a most significant precursor to contemporary critical movements. In our brief resumé of four major phenomenological thinkers, it should be quite evident that phenomenology has, indeed, played a major role in the development of contemporary critical thought. Clearly, many other thinkers could have been included—for example, Gabriel Marcel, Emmanuel Levinas, Paul Ricoeur, and Aron Gurwitsch. However, our discussion should alert the reader to some of the general pathways by means of which these other phenomenologists have also traveled, though, of course, along very original and innovative lines of their own.

NOTES

1. Edmund Husserl, *The Paris Lectures,* trans. Peter Koestenbaum (The Hague: Martinus Nijhoff, 1975).
2. Ibid., p. 9.
3. Ibid., p. 8.
4. Ibid., p. 10.
5. Ibid., p. 25.
6. Edmund Husserl, *Cartesian Meditations,* trans. Dorion Cairns (The Hague: Martinus Nijhoff, 1973), pp. 28–29.
7. Edmund Husserl, *The Crisis of European Sciences,* trans. David Carr (Evanston: Northwestern University Press, 1970), pp. 97–98.
8. Michel Foucault, *The Archaeology of Knowledge* (New York: Pantheon, 1972).
9. Julia Kristeva, *Polylogue* (Paris: Seuil, 1977).
10. Gaston Bachelard, *The Poetics of Space* (Boston: Beacon, 1969).
11. Northrop Frye, *Anatomy of Criticism* (New York: Atheneum, 1957).
12. Husserl, *The Paris Lectures,* p. 18.
13. Ibid.
14. Roman Ingarden, *The Literary Work of Art* (Evanston: Northwestern University Press, 1970).
15. Husserl, *The Paris Lectures,* pp. 21, 25–26.
16. Jean-Paul Sartre, *The Transcendence of the Ego,* trans. Forrest Williams and Robert Kirkpatrick (New York: Farrar, Straus and Giroux, 1957), p. 70. The original French version was published in *Recherches Philosophiques,* 6 (1936–37).
17. Ibid., pp. 41, 42.
18. Ibid., p. 40.
19. "*Mise en abyme*" is a term used by André Gide to describe an infinity of mirrored reflections. For Gide, consciousness could be described as that which has no ground or privileged basis for the representation of ideas (André Gide, *Journal d'André Gide* [Paris: Gallimard, 1939], p. 41).
20. Sartre, *The Transcendence of the Ego,* p. 41.
21. Ibid., p. 49.
22. Ibid., p. 97.
23. Jean-Paul Sartre, *Being and Nothingness,* trans. Hazel Barnes (New York: Philosophical Library, 1956).

24. Sartre, *The Transcendence of the Ego,* pp. 98–100.
25. Jean-Paul Sartre, *The Critique of Dialectical Reason,* trans. Alan Sheridan-Smith (Atlantic Highlands, N.J.: Humanities Press, 1976).
26. Claude Lévi-Strauss, *Savage Mind* (Chicago: University of Chicago Press, 1966).
27. Martin Heidegger, *Poetry, Language, Thought,* trans. A. Hofstadter (New York: Harper and Row, 1971), p. 43.
28. John Crowe Ransom, *Beating the Bushes* (New York: New Directions, 1941).
29. Martin Heidegger, "Letter on Humanism," in *Philosophy in the Twentieth Century,* vol. 4, trans. E. Lohner (New York: Random House, 1962), p. 271.
30. Maurice Blanchot, "The Absence of the Book," in *The Gaze of Orpheus and Other Literary Essays,* ed. P. Adams Sitney, trans. Lydia Davis (New York: Station Hill, 1981), pp. 149–50.
31. Paul de Man, "Autobiography As De-Facement," in *The Rhetoric of Romanticism* (New York: Columbia University Press, 1984), pp. 80–81.
32. Heidegger, "Letter on Humanism," p. 280.
33. Ibid., p. 292.
34. Jacques Derrida, "Structure, Sign, and Play," in *Writing and Difference,* trans. Alan Bass (Chicago: University of Chicago Press, 1978).
35. Martin Heidegger, *Discourse on Thinking* (New York: Harper and Row, 1966), pp. 55–56.
36. Maurice Merleau-Ponty, *Signs,* trans. Richard McCleary (Evanston: Northwestern University Press, 1964).
37. Ferdinand de Saussure, *Course in General Linguistics* (New York: McGraw-Hill, 1959).
38. Edmund Husserl, *Logische Untersuchungen* (Halle: Niemeyer, 1913), translated as *Logical Investigations* by J. N. Findlay (New York: Humanities Press, 1970).
39. Merleau-Ponty, *Signs,* p. 47.
40. Ibid., p. 43.
41. Ibid., p. 39.
42. Martin Heidegger, *Early Greek Thinking* (New York: Harper and Row, 1975).
43. Merleau-Ponty, *Signs,* pp. 43, 44–45.
44. Maurice Blanchot, *The Space of Literature,* trans. Ann Smock (Lincoln: University of Nebraska Press, 1982), p. 41.

RICHARD A. BARNEY

Uncanny Criticism in the United States

WRITING AN ACCOUNT of deconstruction in the United States is difficult if only because two main methods for approaching it—either as a coherent body of work or as a historical development—have been severely criticized by deconstructors themselves. In fact, all the "uncanny critics" this essay will discuss—Paul de Man, J. Hillis Miller, Geoffrey Hartman, Barbara Johnson, Gayatri Spivak, and Michael Ryan—have in some way or another attacked the use of these methods. They have argued that the first approach, by making deconstruction into a synchronic phenomenon, would ignore the differences created by historical change and be inclined to create a system relying on spatial unities. A historical approach, while registering the differences produced by temporal change, would be no less problematic, for it consistently tends to create a misleading continuity by establishing an origin whose character effectively determines the nature of the succeeding events or by positing an end, or telos, toward which the events in its narrative all lead.

These writers also point out, however, that such totalization cannot be entirely avoided and that it is even necessary for the act of writing. The trick is to diminish its effects. My strategy for doing so will be to use both a synchronic and a diachronic approach, playing their respective similarities and differences off each other. The result, I hope, will be a provisional, historical description in which the work of Jacques Derrida will not function as the origin of deconstructive practice in the United States nor the Marxism of Spivak or Ryan supply its fulfillment.

Deconstruction: An Overview

Since the rumblings of its first appearance in the United States during the late 1960s and early 1970s, deconstruction has garnered a number of American practitioners and advocates.[1] These include not only the members of the so-called Yale School but also critics such as Cynthia Chase, Jonathan Culler, Eugenio Donato, Carol Jacobs, Richard Rand, and Joseph Riddell, to name only a few. All these critics merit consideration in a more comprehensive study, but for our present purposes we shall focus on six major figures: de Man, Miller, Hartman, and Johnson, who comprise the Yale School, and Ryan and Spivak, who represent an important extension of deconstruction to social and political concerns.[2] Although Harold Bloom shares some important ideas with his Yale colleagues—such as the claim that criticism can exhibit the same dynamic as literature—he has been omitted because, as Hartman himself says, he is not in fact a "boa-deconstructor."[3] Bloom has consistently been more interested in authors' psychological strategies for writing than have his deconstructive counterparts, and he has deliberately avoided their terminology, recently even disavowing any status as a deconstructor.[4] His denial suggests that the "Yale School" has been more the creation of the rhetoric of its opponents than the result of programmatic intellectual agreement; even when the Yale critics have responded by presenting a unified front, it has often been in the demeanor or tone of institutional solidarity.[5] In any case, the Yale School (or Yale Critics) has had a profound effect on the practice of literary criticism in the United States. It may be argued, however, that the Yale School, which had its heyday in the 1970s and early 1980s, has ceased to exist. Paul de Man's unfortunate death in 1983 and Barbara Johnson's recent move to Harvard University suggest that Yale's central role in American deconstruction is approaching an end. In the future, the influence of Miller and Hartman will probably be due more to their work as persuasive individuals than their putative membership in a particular "school" of thought.

If there is anything that unifies deconstructionists, it is, as

Miller himself has noted, "a focus on language as the central problematic of literary study" (SRII, 332). Miller's use of the term "problematic" suggests an important distinction between deconstructors' approach and that of their structuralist predecessors, who were among the first to turn to language as the focal point of literary study: instead of treating language as a complex but stable system whose constituents can be securely established, deconstruction considers it an unreliable structure that violates its own rules and thereby makes its features difficult to grasp. This view brings a number of changes to the traditional relation of consciousness to language, world to language, and language to itself. First, rather than the human subject confidently directing language to express intentions, thoughts, or emotions, language in fact constitutes the subject by being the *form* of consciousness; therefore, consciousness cannot "possess" language. For deconstructors, as for their predecessors, language is not intrinsically mimetic. Its status is primarily determined not by the arrangement of the outside world but by its own internal rules of grammar, syntax, and so on. This establishes a major premise, derived from Saussure: sign and meaning (or referent) are divided. But deconstruction goes further than structuralist theories by claiming that language is also divided against itself. The rules that govern its structure are inconsistent, thus creating a text that at the simplest level is contradictory and that at the most complex level states the impossibility of its own unity.

Certainly this is to state the case in a most schematic fashion, but it clearly indicates where deconstructionists part company with more traditional critics, especially M. H. Abrams, Wayne Booth, E. D. Hirsch, Gerald Graff, Denis Donoghue, and Walter Jackson Bate, who have vigorously challenged these claims about language because of what they fear to be adverse consequences for literary criticism and history. These critics, the humanist guard, have argued that deconstruction eliminates both the role of the human author and historical context, thereby dismantling the very model of communication which is necessary for the interpretation of texts' meaning.[6] These kinds of charges have, unfortunately, produced a highly combative atmosphere of polemic, often resulting, on the one hand, in exaggerated attacks on deconstruction and, on the other, in staunch reentrenchment on the part of deconstructors.[7]

We shall also observe ways, however, in which the deconstructionists (especially Hartman) attempt to answer humanist concerns.

The work of Jacques Derrida differs significantly from that of the American deconstructionists, even while having influenced it profoundly. These differences mainly take the form of narrowing the scope of deconstruction as Derrida conceives it. (This is particularly true of the Yale Critics; later we will see how Ryan and Spivak attempt to extend deconstruction's analytical scope.) As it should be clear from Irene Harvey's discussion in this volume ("The Wellsprings of Deconstruction"), Derrida has been concerned with the entire history of philosophical metaphysics. For those critics in the United States, however, the focus has generally been localized to the nature of Romanticism and its legacy in the nineteenth and twentieth centuries. This is often true even of de Man, who has written penetrating analyses of various philosophers. Derrida has also gone beyond the normal boundaries of philosophy by bringing to his analysis a formalist, even literary, approach (see Harvey, p. 141), thereby beginning to erase the distinction between philosophical and literary texts. If Derrida has brought literature to philosophy, the critics at Yale have brought philosophy to literature, creating what Hartman calls "philosophical criticism" and bringing larger philosophical questions within the domain of literary structure. This is most evident in their contrasting treatments of language. Though Derrida introduces the problem of language to philosophical discourse, he does not reduce his procedure to linguistic analysis. When he defines the term "*écriture*," for example, he explains that it entails more than the literal "substance" of language (its properties of syntax, etc.), which exemplifies only one instance of the differential structure that is in the general nature of things.[8] In contrast, the Yale Critics have tended to stress the mechanics of grammar, rhetoric, and tropes. This is most clear in de Man's conclusion about the "random" structure of Rousseau's *Confessions:* "The resulting predicament is linguistic rather than ontological or hermeneutic."[9]

We need to consider one more point before discussing the American critics individually. Despite its contrasts, Derrida's work has developed along a trajectory similar to that of his American counterparts. In the essay "La Différance" (1968), Derrida defines the term "*différance*" as the starting point of his analysis, in opposition to the term "presence." Presence, generally defined, has been the underlying concept or quality in traditional metaphysics' attempt to posit a fundamental moment or region that is an essence or a replete fullness; it constitutes the assumption that at some level there is a primordial element or principle that is thoroughly coherent. Since any opposition is also hierarchical, presence has been the more valued or "privileged" term in its relation to absence, division, or incompleteness. Derrida reverses this relation by making *différance* "*provisionally* privileged" and making its attributes—a spatial differentiation and a temporal deferral of closure—the basis for his procedure.[10]

Later, in "Signature Event Context" (1972), Derrida reflects on this strategy and describes a further step: "Deconstruction cannot limit itself or proceed immediately to a neutralization: it must, by means of a double gesture, a double science, a double writing, practice an *overturning* of the classical opposition *and* a general *displacement* of the system. It is only on this condition that deconstruction will provide itself the means with which to *intervene* in the field of oppositions that it criticizes."[11] Since the mere reversal of oppositions cannot escape a metaphysical system but only reestablish its contours in negative form, displacement includes both shifting the system away from its traditional operation and placing the newly formulated opposition back *into* that system—what Rodolphe Gasché calls "reinscription."[12] For Derrida, this procedure takes many forms because he does not want it to harden into a fixed method. In general terms, it allows the overall structure of the metaphysical system to remain but also undermines its stability by indicating that the privileged terms in its classical oppositions are in fact supplementary or derivative. Such a displacement erodes the purity of each binary term and demonstrates their interdependence and ultimate interchangeability—their "indeterminacy" or "undecidability."

This sequence from reversal to displacement by no means characterizes the entirety of Derrida's career, but it does suggest a useful analogue for discussing the development of deconstruction in the United States. The American critics, it should be pointed out, move from reversal to displacement over a longer period of time than does Derrida, and they explore the possibilities of reinscription in different ways; in this sense their development is "displaced" from Derrida's. To summarize this pattern: Miller presents the starkest instance of this shift in his endorsement of difference in the early 1970s and later study of repetition in *Fiction and Repetition* (1982). De Man's work is a less pronounced version of this change, though his focus on "negative insight" in *Blindness and Insight* (1971) moves to undecidability eight years later in *Allegories of Reading*. Hartman and Johnson enter the scene during the mid-1970s, when the term "undecidability" is broached; and Spivak and Ryan attempt to broaden the description of undecidability in order to introduce a political agenda.

Paul de Man and J. Hillis Miller: Toward Undecidability

Paul de Man has undoubtedly been the most influential practitioner of deconstruction in the United States. He brought an intense rigor and a broad background in Continental philosophy and literature to many subjects, which ranged from Romanticism to Nietzsche to phenomenology. Like Derrida, he proceeded more by exemplary instances than by a comprehensive theoretical framework and as early as 1966 was developing ideas analogous to Derrida's, though it was not until 1979 that he acknowledged that the term "deconstruction" best described the nature of his approach (*AR*, x).

In *Blindness and Insight*, a collection of essays written between 1966 and 1970, de Man analyzes the work of critics such as Lévi-Strauss, Poulet, Lukács, and Derrida in order to understand the relation between criticism and literature.[13] The main thesis of these essays is that the intended or explicit statement of a critic's work is consistently belied by its implicit, more accurate findings. De Man uses the terms "blindness" and "insight" metaphorically, giving them at least two senses. Blindness, on the one hand, entails the conceptual limitations that result from a writer's particular critical assumptions; on the other, it marks the moment when the implicit statement of a critic's text violates the premises of those assumptions. Insight follows suit: it describes a critic's explicit claim, but it also refers to his text's implicit "truth." In analyzing the relation between these two terms, de Man focuses particularly on their latter senses. He finds that the American New Critics, for example, came to describe literary diction as a language of irony and ambiguity, despite their avowed commitment to a Coleridgean notion of organic form.

This pattern is more than a simple case of logical contradiction. De Man argues that the inevitable structure of criticism is one in which insight *depends* on blindness: "This insight could only be gained *because* the critics were in the grip of this peculiar blindness" (*BI*, 106, my italics). De Man's thesis about "negative insight" effectively reverses the traditional assumptions about knowledge and its articulation, and he stresses this kind of reversal especially in the essays composed from 1966 to 1967. Rather than conscious intent preceding and directing the form of a text, "the concept of intentionality is neither physical nor psychological in its nature, but structural. . . . The relationship of the particular state of mind of the person engaged in the act of structurization to the structured object is *altogether contingent*."[14] We can roughly represent the shift from the valuing of conscious insight "over" blindness to the opposite arrangement in diagrammatic fashion:

$$\frac{\text{Insight}}{\text{Blindness}} \text{ ——(reversal)——→ } \frac{\text{Blindness}}{\text{Insight}}$$

This pattern could even lead to overturning *any* traditional authority so that "there are no longer any standpoints that can a priori be considered privileged, no structure that functions validly as a model for other structures."[15]

But if this is the initial inclination in de Man's analysis, it is countered by the arguments in the latter part of the book (written after 1967), creating a tension within the work as a whole. Even in the early essay "Criticism and Crisis," de Man points out that the attempt to overturn the assumption that there is any legitimate authority, a gesture characteristic of what he calls "demystification," must itself depend on such an unacknowledged assumption: "All structures are, in a sense, equally fallacious and are therefore called myths. But no myth ever has sufficient coherence not to flow back into neighboring myths or even has an identity strong enough to stand out by itself without an arbitrary act of interpretation that defines it. The relative unity of traditional myths always depends on the existence of a privileged point of view to which the method itself denies any status of authenticity."[16] The act of demystification itself can therefore be mystified or blind. The pattern of "flowing back" into the larger cultural network of myths (or what Derrida might call "metaphysics") suggests a Derridean reinscription, but with a crucial difference: instead of being a *deliberate* move in a critical approach, it seems to be an inherent structural feature of myth or interpretation. In order that this return not be blind, de Man proposes a kind of knowledge that admits its fictionality and is modeled on literary language: "Consciousness does not result from the absence of something, but consists of the presence of a nothingness. Poetic language names this void with ever-renewed understanding and . . . it never tires of naming it again. This persistent naming is what we call literature" (*BI*, 18). De Man elaborates on this description of literature and the potential knowledge of criticism in subsequent chapters.

In "The Rhetoric of Blindness," de Man explains that although blindness may now be the valued term in his analysis, it is not a stopping point. This is partly because blindness is itself divided: on the one hand, it marks a limitation in a critic's explicit statement, but on the other, it is positive because it enables a critic to read or interpret a text. Reading, therefore, "can never be taken for granted" (*BI*, 107), and de Man connects this unreliability with the nature of language, particularly literary language. He derives his description of language from Rousseau, who bases language on passion, "because passion . . . is precisely the manifestation of a will that exists independently of any specific meaning or intent and therefore can never be traced back to a cause or origin" (*BI*, 132). De Man therefore highlights language's nonmimetic, rhetorical dimension. Still, this description does not eliminate language's literal and referential dimension, though it clearly resituates its significance. Literary language, as the most exemplary instance of language's new character, now has a "necessarily ambivalent nature," which always allows the possibility that its figural level will be mistaken for a literal one (*BI*, 136). Since a literary text "implicitly or explicitly signifies its own rhetorical mode and prefigures its own misunderstanding as the correlative of its rhetorical nature" (*BI*, 136), this pattern can be described, but it forecloses the possibility of clearly true or untrue readings. Hence "truth and error exist simultaneously, thus preventing the favoring of the one over the other" (*BI*, 165). Translated into diagram form, this is a move from a hierarchical relation between blindness and insight (on a vertical plane) to a relation that circumvents hierarchy altogether (on a horizontal plane):

$$\frac{\text{Insight}}{\text{Blindness}} \xrightarrow{\text{(rev.)}} \frac{\text{Blindness}}{\text{Insight}} \xrightarrow{\text{(displ.)}} \text{Blindness/Insight}$$

In a sense, this displacement tilts the reversed opposition "on its side"; the result is turning the literary text into "a fictionally diachronic narrative" that tells the story of the problem of reading it (*BI*, 135).

In *Allegories of Reading* (1979), de Man extends his approach to the domains of literature, history, and philosophy, submitting them to the rigors of what he calls "rhetorical deconstruction," which is both more involuted and technically exacting than his strategy in *Blindness and Insight*. He sets out to break down the kind of rigid opposition that has characterized literary criticism as either referential or formalist, "realistic" or focused on self-referentiality. For de Man, rhetoric entails both aspects, but in an ambivalent fashion: rhetoric "is precisely the gap that becomes apparent in the pedagogical and philosophical history of the term"—that is, the gap between rhetoric as a system of tropes within a text and rhetoric as persuasion, which acts outside its boundaries (*AR*, 131). Rhetoric constitutes, then, "a disruptive intertwining of trope and persuasion" (*AR*, ix). Furthermore, the grammatical structure of a text cannot provide the qualities usually assigned to it—including coherence, logicality, and truth—because it depends on and is undone by the tropological or figural level of the text. This does not, however, allow the figural dimension to achieve a totalization of its effect, what de Man calls "rhetorical mystification." Instead, he demonstrates that each feature both constitutes and disrupts the other, producing indeterminacy: "The grammatical model . . . becomes rhetorical not when we have, on the one hand, a literal meaning and on the other a figural meaning, but when it is impossible to decide by grammatical or other linguistic devices which of the two meanings (that can be entirely incompatible) prevails" (*AR*, 10).

Within this theoretical framework, de Man examines the way a set of oppositions in a text is transformed by a series of substitutions until there results a sequence of reversals of the opposing terms. This transformation is gradually produced by the process of metaphor, which he defines as "an exchange or substitution of properties on the basis of resemblance" (*AR*, 146). Since this exchange, however, in fact conceals "the difference[s] necessarily introduced by the substitution" (*AR*, 62), the totalizing potential of the process is finally undone by the accumulation of these differences. In Rilke's poetry, for instance, these substitutions of the traits associated with the opposition self/world finally "allow a reversal of their categorical properties, and this reversal enables the reader to conceive of properties that would normally be incompatible . . . as complementary" (*AR*, 40). In the end, polar terms and their associated qualities substitute for each other and reverse positions in vertiginous fashion:

$$\frac{\text{Term \#1}}{\text{Term \#2}} \longrightarrow \frac{\text{Term \#2a}}{\text{Term \#1a}} \longrightarrow \frac{\text{Term \#1b}}{\text{Term \#2b}} \longrightarrow \text{and so on.}$$

If this characterization seems overly schematic, we should remember two things. First, de Man claims that "deconstruction is not something we have added to the text but it constituted the text in the first place" (*AR*, 17). Second, the metaphor for a text that de Man uses when discussing Rousseau—a machine—suggests the regularity that he finds in all the works he discusses: the text as machine, he says, presents "the implacable repetition of a preordained pattern" (*AR*, 294). De Man insists on this polar structure even when a third term enters the picture and does not seem immediately assimilable to the working opposition. Such a third element, he emphasizes, "becomes productive . . . only when it is conceived as a polarity rather than a mere positional relationship, that is, from the moment that a principle of articulation connects an inside with this outside in a way that allows for the exchange of properties" (*AR*, 235).

In the end, however, de Man will submit this regularity to undecidability: "The wisdom of the text is self-destructive . . . but this self-destruction is infinitely displaced in a series of successive rhetorical reversals which, by the endless repetition of the same figure, keep it suspended between truth and the death of this truth"

(*AR*, 115). Furthermore, since the description that rehearses this self-de(con)struction is itself a totalizing gesture that cannot escape rhetoric, it can be brought to a "deconstruction to the second degree." This process de Man calls "allegory," which, rather than provide a narrative based on metaphoric similarity and closure, relates an open-ended, metonymic sequence: "Allegories are always allegories of metaphor"—that is, of metaphor's inability to secure certain meaning—"and, as such, they are always allegories of the impossibility of reading" (*AR*, 205). If reading is the ability to create a consistent description of a text, then the nature of allegory postpones this possibility indefinitely in a potentially endless series of deconstructions.[17]

J. Hillis Miller's shift to deconstruction in about 1970 occurs in a much more dramatic fashion than de Man's for at least two reasons. First, Miller had already established a distinguished career in a more traditional vein by his work on Victorian and early modern writers, which included *Charles Dickens: The World of His Novels* (1958), *The Disappearance of God* (1963), *Poets of Reality* (1965), and *The Form of Victorian Fiction* (1968). Next, during the 1960s he had worked under the theoretical tutelage of Georges Poulet, the patriarch of the Geneva school of phenomenological critics. Miller's switch, then, becomes a thorough revaluation of his past critical assumptions and ultimately a rejection of the father figure who had helped establish them. In his essay "Geneva or Paris? The Recent Work of Georges Poulet" (1970), Miller attempts a kind of rapprochement between Poulet's criticism and the newer ideas of Derrida and Deleuze. Miller finds, however, that Poulet's failure to maintain a "metaphysics of presence" cannot be fully reconciled with the strategy *deliberately* undertaken by Derrida. Only a complete break, as is suggested in the title—"Geneva *or* Paris"—will satisfy: "A critic must choose either the tradition of presence or the tradition of 'difference,' for their assumptions about language, about literature, about history, and about the mind cannot be made compatible."[18]

Miller chooses the tradition of difference, and perhaps the clearest example of his commitment to a radical reversal is in the essay "Tradition and Difference" (1972), in which he reviews M. H. Abrams's *Natural Supernaturalism* as an exemplary instance in the humanist tradition. For Miller, Abrams's work both identifies and embodies "a basic paradigm of Occidental metaphysics—the picture of an original unity, lost in our present sad dispersal, to be regained at some point in the millenial future."[19] Against this, Miller claims that "the dream of primal and final unity, always deferred, never present here and now, is generated by the original and originating differentiation" (TD, 12); significantly, he cites Derrida's essay "La Différance" in support of this claim. This kind of reversal also applies to Miller's definition of language, for rather than accept that it can be a transparent representation of meaning or the outside world, he says that "the notion of a literal or referential use of language is only an illusion born of the forgetting of the metaphorical 'roots' of language. Language is from the start fictive" (TD, 11).[20]

Though at first extremely resistant to Miller's position, Abrams eventually begins to consider its possible merits, providing perhaps the most painstaking and sympathetic account of deconstruction offered by those opposed to its premises.[21] By the mid-1970s, Miller's trenchant tone similarly diminishes, and he begins to examine issues of undecidability. By then de Man had already introduced this term in important essays on Nietzsche and Rousseau,[22] but Miller attributes a very different structure to the suspension of a text's determinate meaning. This difference can be partially explained by Miller's combination of concepts from both de Man and Derrida.[23] Miller frequently uses a de Manian tropological analysis, identifying the uncertainty of rhetorical meaning, but he characteristically extends this beyond a polar opposition to a kind of Derridean *dissémination*—a refraction of linguistic meanings. When analyzing Stevens's "The Rock," he finds not only "an undecidable play between literal and figurative" meaning but a "bewildering multiplication of different chains of figurative terminology superimposed, juxtaposed, interwoven, [in] a final form of *mise en abyme*."[24] This is a stark contrast to de Man, for whom the pattern of reversibility is indeterminate but nevertheless mechanically predictable. Miller's metaphors for the structure of a text are decidedly nonmechanical: a web, woven cloth, labyrinth, *mise en abyme*, and so on. For this reason, Miller's deconstructive critic follows a more tenuous and sinuous process than does de Man's: "The critic feels his way from figure to figure, from concept to concept, from mythical motif to mythical motif. . . . [He] seeks to find, by this process of retracing, the element in the system studied which is alogical, the thread in the text in question which will unravel it all" (SRII, 341).

In *Fiction and Repetition* (1982), a collection of essays on nineteenth- and twentieth-century English novels, Miller makes the structure of undecidability more dualistic, but not in de Manian form. He defines two kinds of repetition: the first, which he had discounted in "Tradition and Difference," is based on the fundamental similarity between the repeated elements; the second is based on the elements' inherent dissimilarity. The relation of these two types of repetition, however, is not that of opposite terminals, between which a text's meaning must shuttle. Instead, both types asymptotically converge to form a third aspect of the text: what Miller calls "the image." In this imagistic structure, "each form of repetition calls up the other, by an inevitable compulsion. The second is not the negation or opposite of the first, but its 'counterpart,' in a strange relation whereby the second is the subversive ghost of the first."[25] This relation, he explains, "defies the elementary principle of logic . . . which says: 'Either A or not-A'" (*F&R*, 17).

The difference between Miller's earliest deconstructive approach and the one here can best be seen in the differences between the 1970 essay on Conrad's *Lord Jim* and its revised version in chapter 2 of *Fiction and Repetition*. In the first version of the essay, entitled "The Interpretation of *Lord Jim*," Miller claims that this novel "has nothing outside itself by which it might be measured . . . , no thematic or structuring principle which will allow the reader to find out its secret, . . . untie all its knots and straighten all its threads."[26] The revision of this claim, though slight, is indicative of the larger shift in Miller's perspective: now *Lord Jim* "has nothing *certainly* identifiable outside itself by which it might be measured . . . " (*F&R*, 25, my italics). Rather than assert with assurance that Conrad's work is "an example of [the] absence of origin, center, or end" (ILJ, 213), Miller says that it is one of "the intertwining of the two modes of repetition" (*F&R*, 22), a relation that reintroduces the "tradition of presence" while also suspending its usual coherence. In the first version, Miller finds that "the temporal structure of the novel is open" and that "it has the openness of that authentic temporality which Martin Heidegger describes . . . as being fundamentally constituted by repetition" (ILJ, 223). In the second version he omits this endorsement of fundamental openness, which could lead to an unlimited set of explanations of the novel, and adds a section explaining that the linear order of the novel's events "is shared by any reader and that it establishes a large background of agreement about what happens and even about the meaning of what happens" (*F&R*, 34–35). The result is nevertheless undecidable, since "the text does not permit the reader to decide among alternative possibilities, even though those possibilities themselves are identified with precise determinate certainty" (*F&R*, 35).[27]

We should make it clear that this historical pattern of Miller's shift from "pure" difference to undecidability is also one of *emphasis*. To give only two examples: even in the 1970 essay on *Lord Jim,* Miller mentions that "the novel creates its meaning out of the . . . interplay of sameness and difference" (ILJ, 224); and in a revised essay on Poulet, he acknowledges that the relation between Poulet and Derrida is more than "an irreconcilable either/or."[28] The differences *between* his work in 1970 and 1982 could in fact be seen as a development generated by the differences *within* even his earliest pieces. Miller's criticism has frequently had a double focus that is perplexing and may seem the symptom of theoretical inconsistency.[29] Miller has said in "Tradition and Difference," for instance, that "the reading of a work involves an active intervention on the part of the reader" (TD, 12); but in "Deconstructing the Deconstructors," he claims that the critic does "no more than to identify an act of deconstruction which has always already . . . been performed by the text on itself."[30] This later statement, however, does not indicate a mere change of mind.[31] Miller has been justifiably uncomfortable with the characterization of critical reading as a kind of Nietzschean will-to-interpret, for it suggests that criticism can proceed without attending to the unsettling linguistic features he has already encountered in texts. However, he has also mistrusted the claim that deconstruction merely identifies what a literary text has already accomplished, because that position implies that deconstruction is purely referential, able to represent the text in a decisive, transparent fashion.

This double, even self-divided, nature of his work signifies more than inconsistency; it is endemic to deconstructive criticism as Miller conceives it. First, from the start, he has seen his main commitment to be to interpreting specific texts rather than formulating a systematic theory,[32] and therefore he is ready to try various theoretical concepts according to the demands of particular instances. Second, this often leads him to consider one aspect of a problem such as interpretation to the exclusion of other aspects usually expected in a more complete picture. Third, and most important, Miller's double perspective indicates that indeterminacy affects more than the linguistic structure within a text; it also applies to the relationship between the critic and the text itself. Miller's work, probably more than that of the other Yale Critics, illustrates that the relative importance of the critic's point of view to the text's form is a problem whose final solution is continually deferred by virtue of its undecidability. Deconstructive indeterminacy—as a thematic and structural principle of his essays—has formed Miller's career as a necessary movement between the poles of origin and abyss, reader and text, certainty and uncertainty.

Geoffrey Hartman and Barbara Johnson: On the Margins

For most of the 1970s, though thoroughly familiar with the work of his Yale colleagues and Derrida, Geoffrey Hartman remained wary of deconstruction. His book *Beyond Formalism* (1970), a collection of essays written since 1958, focuses mainly on the issues of structuralism, literary history, and hermeneutics. In *The Fate of Reading* (1975), Hartman includes remarks on Derrida and de Man but for the most part attempts to distinguish his position from theirs. We can nevertheless see in these two books some interests that will later move Hartman to engage deconstruction more readily.

One essay in *Beyond Formalism*, "The Voice of the Shuttle: Language from the Point of View of Literature" (1969), demonstrates that Hartman was interested in the vagaries of language a good deal before the time he would call such an interest deconstructive. In this essay he sketches out a "rhetorical analysis" or "playful poetics" that can explain the need for the interpretation of texts.[33] He claims that the figures of speech that constitute a text's meaning are "characterized by overspecified ends and indeterminate middles, . . . and that . . . the very elision or subsuming of middle terms allows, if it does not actually compel, interpretation" (*BF*, 339). This indeterminacy of figures "makes room in meaning itself" (*BF*, 352); it is a kind of generative fecundity in literary texts that produces imaginative signification.

Later, in *The Fate of Reading,* Hartman explores some issues concerning deconstruction, but only in the most cautious, even resistant, manner. He aligns his position with Derrida's in their mutual attack on the tendency in the writing of history to mythologize, but Hartman says he does so "in a tentative and critical, rather than transcendently reductive, way." He adds with characteristic wryness: "Some will accuse me, no doubt, of deconstructing without a license."[34] With or without a license, Hartman distrusts a liaison between rhetorical analysis and literature, calling it "dangerous" (*FR*, ix) and retracting his thesis in "The Voice of the Shuttle." "The danger," he explains, "is that interpretation may interpose itself too much and relativize all terms as middle terms. The experienced reader soon fights a growing sense that . . . everything tends . . . to become echo or quotation, until we fall into . . . [a]n insipidity which seems to have been caused . . . by overdoses of reading" (*FR*, 263). He remains leery of the licentiousness of language as it is described by licensed deconstructors.

By the time he writes *Criticism in the Wilderness* (1980), Hartman more readily accepts deconstruction, or "revisionist criticism," as he calls it, a shift already in progress in his earlier essays on Derrida in 1975 and 1976. His strategy for coming to terms with indeterminacy is to redefine it—or perhaps we should say, to reestablish it in a new *position.* For Hartman, the term "indeterminacy" suggests "that where there is a conflict of interpretations or codes, that conflict can be rehearsed or reordered but not always resolved" and that "even where there is no such conflict we have no certainty of controlling implications that may not be apparent or articulable at any one point in time."[35] Now, however, Hartman does not locate uncertainty primarily within a text but in the position of the literary critic: "I favor moving 'indeterminacy' from the area of grammatical, semiotic, or phenomenological reduction to that of hermeneutic criticism itself" (*CW*, 270).

Hartman describes criticism as caught between the two camps of Continental "philosophical criticism" and Anglo-American "practical criticism," each having its own general set of orientations. Philosophical criticism opens literary texts to larger philosophical contexts, exercises theoretical rigor, and tends toward deconstructive "revision"; practical criticism, descended from the New Criticism, confines itself to formalistic analysis of specific texts while also allowing for interpretive subjectivity. While persuaded by the rhetorical analyses offered in deconstruction, Hartman points out its limitations: deconstruction "accepts . . . figurative language too readily," it fails to account for "how books or habits of reading *penetrate* our lives," and it reduces the complexities of a human product "to the concept of *writing*" (*CW*, 31, 203, 112, author's italics). In these objections we see Hartman's tenacious commitment to the values of humanism which deconstruction would undermine. His goal is to articulate a delicate connection between the two by claiming that "the *character* or *role* of being a critic is implicated in this conflict between mastery and mystery, or rhetoric and hermeneutic hesitation" (*CW*, 36, Hartman's italics). In this way, he transforms the institution of criticism into an exemplary case of his own uncertain relationship to both traditional and revisionist arguments.

By placing himself in the "wilderness" between these two perspectives, and given his interest in biblical hermeneutics, Hartman establishes himself as a kind of Pauline apologist for deconstruction. Rather than play the role of a John the Baptist who staunchly preaches the truth of a new dispensation, Hartman carefully attempts to explain a relation between the old and new views. Unlike the Apostle Paul, of course, he is not completely converted to the new way, but this uncertainty in fact strengthens his persuasiveness. By remaining sympathetic to humanism, he can more effectively convince readers of the values of deconstruction, even to the extent of locating its creative, spiritual import. One of his main ways for doing this is to make the revisionist devaluation of the distinction between literature and criticism or philosophy into more than a matter of linguistic form. He establishes the commonality of these discourses on the fact that both kinds of writing "are institutions of the human mind, and one cannot foretell where the creative spirit may show itself" (*CW*, 256). Concerning revisionism itself, he sees "mainly the *creative* force of the *critical* spirit, as it questions such honorific terms as *creative* or *primary* or *visionary*" (*CW*, 248, author's italics). Hence criticism in general becomes "a relatively free, all-purpose genre" that can reside in this indeterminate but productive region (*CW*, 233).

In *Saving the Text* (1981), Hartman applies this concept of criticism to an extended meditation on Derrida's *Glas* (1974) in the attempt to evaluate Derrida's contribution to literary studies. In Derrida's text, which is a playful and simultaneous discussion of Hegel and Genet, Hartman finds the fundamental reorientation of critical writing he had hoped for in *Criticism in the Wilderness*. Derrida's writing proves to be as richly imaginative as literature proper, in a style—characterized by cunning allusions, puns, and ambiguity—that can revitalize the creativity of criticism. Significantly, if there is any critic on this side of the Atlantic who can match Derrida's intriguing elusiveness, it is Hartman, whose own style during at least the last decade has tended toward an indirection and teasing suggestiveness that reach their apotheosis here.

Despite his enthusiasm, Hartman is concerned that such literary critical virtuosity be limited or controlled in order to avoid the "real danger of literature getting lost."[36] Although "*literary* language [is] the name we give to a diction whose frame of reference is such that words stand out as words . . . rather than being, at once, assimilable meanings," he wants to preserve its communicative function: "To call a text literary is to *trust* that it will make sense eventually, even though its quality of reference may be complex, disturbed, unclear. It is a way of 'saving the phenomena' of words" (*ST*, xxi, author's italics). He is intent on "taking away" from precarious textuality "a perception similar to that offered by myths and positive interpretation" (*ST*, 107). Hartman's project ultimately becomes "a counterstatement to Derrida" in order to establish "a restored theory of representation" (*ST*, 121). He thereby hopes that the deconstructive trek in the wilderness is a process that will finally lead to the Promised Land of a new critical stability. In this respect, even while resisting the inclination, Hartman wants to substantiate the thesis of romantic philosophies of history, which claims, he says, that "we would emerge from the dark passage of an age of doubt and criticism into a new, more organic or total belief" (*CW*, 43). To the extent that Hartman's engagement with deconstruction forms a narrative, it is a wishful pilgrimage; this contrasts sharply with the pattern in de Man's and even Miller's project, which is an open-ended allegory.

If Hartman remains on the margins of deconstruction by deliberate choice, Barbara Johnson has been there not because she is cautious about its radical nature but because of the odd way in which critical movements or groups are constituted in the academy. Despite the fact that since 1974 she has published two books and a number of essays that follow deconstructive lines, and also translated Derrida's *Dissemination* (1981), Johnson has received disproportionately little attention. With one notable exception, the books that survey deconstruction have given her contribution little more than passing remarks, including the recent collection entitled *The Yale Critics: Deconstruction in America.*[37] Without attempting to investigate all the reasons for this fact—which would include her status as a young woman starting out in the profession and her role as a "second generation" deconstructor—it may be productive to examine Johnson's marginal status as indicative of important differences in her approach.

Readers of Johnson's *The Critical Difference* can readily find strong similarities between her strategy and that of de Man or Miller. She concentrates on the instability of hierarchical oppositions, the relation between referentiality and figurality, and so on. But there are also critical differences in her appropriation of the terms "difference" and "undecidability." In adopting from Derrida the term "difference," she immediately introduces indeterminacy to its definition: "Difference can . . . be seen both as an uncertainty over separability and as a drifting apart within identity."[38] Hence she avoids the initial inclination in Miller's work by claiming that "difference as such cannot ever be affirmed as an ultimate value because it is that which subverts the very foundations of any affirmation of value" (*CD,* 12). Johnson sets out to emphasize both the spatial and temporal aspects of difference, but instead of considering this process to be an allegory, which would be the second stage of analysis, she characterizes it mainly by the metaphor of a *drama* that emerges simultaneously with the act of reading. Rather than submit to a de Manian deconstruction "to the second degree," texts "dramatize" the "twisted relations between knowing and doing, . . . reading and judging," and so on (*CD,* 108). In addition, since " 'undecidability' can no more be used as the last word than 'destination' " (*CD,* 146), she is wary of making even undecidability into the ultimate goal of her interpretations.

A more important difference arises in Johnson's description of the reading or interpretive process. For her, reading "proceeds by identifying and dismantling differences by means of other differences that cannot be fully identified or dismantled. The starting point is often a binary difference that is subsequently shown to be an illusion created by the workings of differences much harder to pin down. The differences *between* entities (prose and poetry, man and woman, literature and theory, guilt and innocence) are shown to be based on a repression of differences *within* entities, ways in which an entity differs from itself" (*CD,* x-xi, author's italics). This contrasts with Miller's description, in which, we may recall, the critic looks for the "thread in the text in question which will unravel it all." Johnson does not start with the putative continuity of the text in order to reveal its fragmentation, but with its more apparent distinctions. Therefore she neither avoids the categories offered by the text itself nor immediately moves to using metalinguistic terms from philosophy. Her procedure in dismantling differences is to work from one set of oppositions to the next underlying set, thereby peeling away layers of a text's conceptual and figurative framework until no further distinctions can be clearly made. This last stage is the moment of undecidability, though it is by no means a necessary or complete impasse, since viewed from another angle it could yield a further set of terms. By characterizing this strategy as the "careful teasing out of warring forces of signification within the text" (*CD,* 5), Johnson does not attempt to claim, as has de Man (agreeing with Miller), that deconstruction "takes place independently of any desire" and records only what the text has already accomplished (*AR,* 298). There is instead a necessary, seductive bias in critical reading.

These differences in Johnson's approach indicate at least two reasons why she is sometimes overlooked, and these reasons are related as much to the content of her claims as they are to her general tone or style in presenting them. Unlike de Man or Miller, who have often tended toward authoritative declarations of theoretical principles—a tactic which has undoubtedly garnered the attention, if not the agreement, of their readers—Johnson employs a candid style that is much less doctrinaire. Perhaps equally important is that she has refrained from emphasizing that deconstruction is already performed by literary texts themselves, a move that can be extremely effective in attempting to persuade more traditional colleagues who have inherited the critical assumption that a text's "truth" must be *in* that text and be objectively demonstrable. But we can understand Johnson's marginal status further if we take a cue from deconstruction that any marginalized or excluded minority element is frequently the crux on which the majority is founded. In fact, Johnson investigates issues that the other Yale Critics have left largely unexplored, often providing implicit critiques of their unexamined assumptions. These issues include the alleged totalization in Marx's writing and psychoanalysis, the reduction of politics and history to physical texts, and the relation of sexuality or gender to writing.

When Hartman briefly considers the possibility of taking a Marxist approach to literature in *Criticism in the Wilderness,* he concludes, as have de Man and Miller, that "dialectic points to an intent or current . . . which may become forceful or inquisitional and which leads necessarily to a higher, all-embracing truth" (*CW,* 164). As a program that conceives of history as teleological and of culture as reducible to economics, Marxism counts as another version of Western metaphysics. But without evaluating the entirety of Marxism, Johnson finds in Marx's *Capital* a structure of textuality and theme that is similar to that in Baudelaire's poetry. The poetry is "organized around a signifying surplus that transcends the mere exchange [of meaning] between signifiers and signifieds, between tenors and vehicles," a pattern which corresponds to Marx's description of the relation between a system of direct exchange and the emergence of capitalism (*CD,* 36). We cannot go into the details of her argument here, but Johnson finds that both have in common the indeterminate structure of "transcending a system of equivalences *in the very process of perpetuating it*" (*CD,* 38, author's italics). Johnson also points out such indeterminacy in Lacan's psychoanalysis, despite Derrida's claim that Lacanian theory is "logocentric." In an elaborate reading of Derrida reading Lacan reading Poe's "Purloined Letter," she points out that, like deconstruction, psychoanalysis "has no identity apart from its status as a repetition of the structure it seeks to analyze" (*CD,* 142). Here too there is no necessary, systematic autonomy.

Finally, Johnson resists the tendency to reduce social or political life to linguistic texts or a tradition composed of books, a move that is especially strong in de Man—such as in his claim that "the bases for historical knowledge are not empirical facts but written texts, even if these texts masquerade in the guise of wars or revolutions" (*BI*, 165). In contrast, Johnson makes a subtle but important distinction: "Our very relation to 'reality' already functions *like* a text."[39] This distinction is comparable to Derrida's explanation that a text is "no longer a finished corpus of writing, some content enclosed in a book or its margins, but a differential network, a fabric of traces."[40] Seeing the structures in a text as *analogous* to those in life enables Johnson to investigate the relation between sexual difference and writing, an issue usually overlooked by the other Yale Critics (is there presumption, for instance, in Hartman's remark that "much reading is indeed, like girl-watching, a simple expense of spirit"? [*FR*, 248]). By such an approach Johnson can outline useful parallels between the contradictory structure of a text and the cultural milieu in which it appears, an approach that has characterized her most recent work. She connects, for example, the recurring portrayal of the self as both monstrous and humane by female autobiographers to the problem of needing "on the one hand, to resist the pressure of masculine autobiography as the only literary genre available . . . , and, on the other, to describe a difficulty in conforming to a female ideal which is largely the fantasy of the masculine, not the feminine, imagination."[41] By describing such contexts or "scenes" of writing, Johnson begins to expand the possibilities of a purely formal analysis, thereby offering a most important contribution to deconstructive practice.

Gayatri Spivak and Michael Ryan: On the Politics of Discourse

Barbara Johnson's move to enlarge the focus of deconstruction is indicative of the more far-reaching goals of a number of critics who, since the mid-1970s, have sought to extend deconstruction to historical, social, and political contexts. These critics include Edward Said, Frank Lentricchia, John Brenkman, Gayatri Chakravorty Spivak, and Michael Ryan. To be sure, their commitment to a particular political program or to a thorough-going deconstructive project varies significantly. Lentricchia and Brenkman, for instance, have conducted their analyses along Marxist lines, while Said has avoided what he perceives as the limitations in a strictly Marxist approach. On the other hand, Brenkman has absorbed deconstruction to a greater extent than have either Said or Lentricchia, who have appropriated only those strategies most amenable to their interests and have frequently preferred the hypotheses offered by Michel Foucault over those of Derrida.[42]

The Marxist critics Spivak and Ryan are by no means entirely representative of the new interest in extending deconstruction, but a brief look at their work is appropriate for at least two reasons. First, their critical positions have emerged from a close association with the "first generation" deconstructors: Spivak did her doctoral work under de Man's tutelage while he was still at Cornell, and she translated the first of Derrida's books to appear in English (*Of Grammatology*); Ryan did postdoctoral work with both de Man at Yale and Derrida at the École Normale Supérieure. In addition, unlike many of their historically oriented counterparts, Ryan and Spivak have maintained a firm commitment to a full-scale deconstructive approach.

Critics such as Ryan and Spivak, while being initially sympathetic with the Yale Critics' purposes, have found their practice of deconstruction to be severely limited. Their criticisms have included the following: (1) While attacking the premises of New Criticism, Yale School deconstruction has in fact reinstated a new kind of analytical formalism. (2) Though challenging the clear-cut distinctions between literature and criticism or philosophy, it has in the end reinforced the traditional concept of the literary canon by defining the structure of the nonliterary genres in terms of "literariness." (3) The Yale Critics' formulation of undecidability has led to an impasse in criticism by producing "infinite regression" in texts. (4) Despite its purportedly radical nature, the Yale approach has proven to be conservative in leaving unquestioned the academic, institutional, or political bases of its own operation or of the texts it analyzes.[43] These certainly are serious charges, which we cannot fully examine here. We shall focus instead on the last two points to see how Ryan and Spivak treat them.

Perhaps the most suggestive example of how the Yale Critics' definition of literariness leads to political conservatism is in de Man's analysis of Rousseau's *Second Discourse*. In Rousseau's description of the social contract, de Man finds that the formation of human community is based on the unreliable use of metaphorical language. Therefore the "political destiny of man is structured like and derived from a linguistic model" (*AR,* 156). Since politics, like literature, is constituted by the undecidable relation between literal and figural language, "literature is condemned to being the truly political mode of discourse" (*AR,* 157). As a result, the "social contract . . . is a complex and *purely defensive* verbal strategy by means of which the literal world is given some of the consistency of fiction, an intricate set of feints and ruses by means of which the moment is temporarily delayed when fictional seductions will no longer be able to *resist* transformation into literal acts" (*AR,* 159, my italics). Since the social structure is based on this strategic defensiveness—however undecidable that relation may be—it is resistant to change or action, even if they may be inevitable. Though we should be careful in attributing this attitude entirely to de Man, it is significant that he consistently finds this pattern in his other studies of Nietzsche and Rousseau (*AR,* 111–13, 266–76). Spivak or Ryan would consider this consistency of his findings, I think, not only as evidence of what is *in* Rousseau's texts but also as evidence of the kinds of assumptions de Man or the other Yale Critics make, consciously or not, about bourgeois political stability and the arrangements of social class.[44]

Ryan and Spivak reject this conservativism, their goal being the examination and eventual change of all forms of social domination—including capitalism, patriarchy, and racism. Since, as Ryan notes, "how we read or analyze and how we organize political and social institutions are related forms of practice," both he and Spivak turn from the example of deconstruction proffered by the Yale Critics to that described by Derrida.[45] While having criticized Marx's metaphysical tendencies, Derrida has also said that he "would reaffirm that there is some possible articulation between an open marxism and what I am interested in."[46] But before being able to associate, each in distinct ways, the project of Marxism with deconstruction, Ryan and Spivak face a potential stumbling block to the very possibility of political action—undecidability itself.

Ryan probably summarizes the problem best in an article called "Anarchism Revisited": "At worst, it [Derrida's strategy] would engender a paralysis of all radical action. . . . By problematizing the very structure of oppositions, deconstruction neutralizes the specific oppositions which sustain radical political practice—conservative/radical, fascist/socialist, reactionary/revolutionary—and it thus theoretically, and for all practical purposes, suspends the possibility of radically opposing any system from a position outside that system."[47] The structure of undecidability thus makes it impossible to be "purely" radical or revolutionary without being implicated in the very system one opposes. Ryan's initial solution is also one Spivak accepts, though they will later develop it in different directions: "That the radical stance of opposition is undercut by Derrida's argument seems undeniable, but this should not become an excuse for existential, romantic lamentation. It should justify opting to undermine rather than overwhelm or reject if one wishes to undo a system."[48] Spivak will work out from indeterminacy in a number of ways that we can briefly sketch. Citing Foucault, she points out the necessity of making a "cut" in a particular direction in order to make any analysis possible.[49] She also adopts Derrida's claim that any reading is a "forced reading," that is, to some extent coercive in accounting for the facts of a case.[50] Most important, with the Yale Critics in mind, she indicates the impossibility of maintaining a position that "is politics free, oscillating freely in 'the difficult double bind' of an aporia."[51] Instead, she sets out to describe a "*productive* undecidability of the borderlines of politics, art, law, and philosophy."[52]

For his part, Ryan attacks the problem of undecidability by way of partially reformulating its definition. He indicates that Derrida borrowed the term from Gödel's work on metamathematics, in which undecidability describes the necessary condition that any system "generates elements that can be proved both to belong to the system and not to belong to it at the same time" (*M&D*, 16–17). The result is at least two-fold. "Deconstruction," he says, "both opens the possibility of an infinite regress in the determination of final, absolute truths and implicitly promotes an infinite progress in socially reconstructive action" (*M&D*, 8). Although in theory both orientations are possible, Ryan shuns the first as characteristic of the Yale Critics and chooses the second on the basis of the particular historical conditions in which he is inextricably enmeshed. He cannot eliminate the first aspect, but he can make a difference in the role it will play by "celebrat[ing] undecidability as the constant possibility of modifying . . . any given system" (*M&D*, 21).

Having confronted undecidability, both writers set out to ally Marxism and deconstruction. Spivak's project is actually tripartite, for she adds the third perspective of feminism. She associates these three fields on a basis of analogy and what she calls "translation," without attempting to fuse them into a coherent enterprise; these approaches function in a relation of interanimation and correction. Marxism provides deconstruction a needed socio-political context for its operation, and it gives feminism a much more effective means for analyzing the social and economic position of women. Deconstruction brings to both its collaborating perspectives a set of powerful strategies for locating the philosophical and metaphysical assumptions that undergird the phenomena of social organization. It also alters, for instance, Marx's idealization of labor and the rigid opposition between politics and technology that appears in varieties of Marxism. Spivak suggests instead a politics-technology-economics triad, in which technology (as *techne*) is "the disruptive middle term" (E&C, 219 n. 10). Feminism is by no means the least contributor, for it can correct Marx's masculine bias, particularly the inability of his description to account for female production such as childbearing.[53] In addition, although Derrida effects "a 'feminization' of the practice of philosophy," Spivak finds that "the woman who is the 'model' for deconstructive discourse remains a woman generalized and defined in terms of . . . varieties of denial."[54] She proposes instead to make deconstruction focus on the more material situation of women.

Spivak is deliberately micrological in her approach: she does not attempt to construct a synthesis or propose a coherent theory of culture, economics, or literature. In this sense, Marxism, deconstruction, and feminism are kinds of heuristic trajectories for exploring various areas. The feminist, for example, while reversing the traditional values in a masculine culture, must prevent that reversal "from freezing into a dogma" (E&C, 201). The most telling description of her approach, therefore, may be the title of an essay she has written on Derrida (which also cites him): "Revolutions That as Yet Have No Model."[55]

Although in *Marxism and Deconstruction* (1982) Ryan also

provides no synthetic model of the two projects, he does present an "articulation"—a textual connection, if you will, that locates intersections, overlappings, analogies, as well as differences. His articulation resembles Spivak's description but also differs in substantial ways. Though giving a significant role to a feminist perspective in his discussion, Ryan focuses more attention on the nature of humanistic liberalism and its institutional manifestations in the relations between businesses and universities. Although he analyzes in detail the relation between Marx and Derrida, as does Spivak, Ryan also makes a distinction between two kinds of Marxism: scientific Marxism, which proceeds on a reductive system of "dialectical materialism," and critical Marxism, which is more compatible with deconstruction because it favors "models of socialism which are dehierarchized, egalitarian, and democratic" (*M&D,* xiii). He finds that critical Marxism and deconstruction "supplement" one another in Derrida's sense of the word: each supplies a lack in the other in an asymmetrical fashion. Out of this relation emerges a new version of the pattern we have been considering in this entire essay: "The political-economic equivalent of the deconstructive operation is to reverse the hierarchy that places capital over labor (the moment of revolution) and to displace it so that such an opposition no longer exists (the moment of socialization)" (*M&D,* 68). Here Ryan goes a step further than Spivak, for he claims that "deconstruction can supply conceptual models for economic and political institutions required in egalitarian and nonhierarchic socialist construction" (*M&D,* 44). He sketches out this prospect, however, in extremely brief fashion.

The questions that both these writers leave unanswered—such as to what extent deconstruction can offer specific *con*structive guidelines for social change—may be pressing ones, but they are also inherent in the provisional nature of deconstructive practice. Put another way, the book isn't in yet—particularly since that "book" has now been described as a complex weave of textuality that exceeds its traditional boundaries. Certainly neither the Yale Critics nor the Marxists have had the last word on deconstruction; they have instead contributed versions of its operation which concurrently offer various choices or possibilities. De Man provides the most technical means for analyzing grammar and trope, critical insight and its requisite blindness. While drawing on these techniques, Miller's more exploratory project is willing to concede theoretical consistency in favor of the specificity of particular texts. For his part, Hartman heeds more traditional imperatives and attempts to maintain a productive, though tense, relation between humanist vision and deconstructive *re*vision. Johnson has extended deconstruction to include problems of sexuality and gender in writing and general social contexts. Going still further, Spivak's Marxist commitment is particularly telling in its analysis of the political position of women. And Ryan emphasizes the additional possibility that deconstruction can provide concepts for reconstructing social order. These writers' examples indicate the disseminating nature of deconstruction, which functions not as a strict methodology or dogma but as a loosely related set of strategies that are altered and transformed in the process of shifting their particular applications.

NOTES

1. These "rumblings" include Jacques Derrida's lectures at American universities, the translation of Roland Barthes's critical experiments, and Paul de Man's seminal essays. Derrida, for example, presented his lecture "La Structure, le signe et le jeu dans le discours des sciences humaines" at the International Colloquium on Critical Languages and the Sciences of Man, Johns Hopkins University, on 21 Oct. 1966. It now appears as "Structure, Sign and Play in the Discourse of the Human Sciences," in *The Languages of Criticism and the Sciences of Man: The Structuralist Controversy,* ed. Richard Macksey and Eugenio Donato (Baltimore: Johns Hopkins University Press, 1970), pp. 247–65; another translation appears in Derrida, *Writing and Difference*, trans. Alan Bass (Chicago: University of Chicago Press, 1978), pp. 278–93. Roland Barthes's critical writings, which began to appear in English in 1970, were particularly influential during the next decade. His texts that began to study deconstructive issues include *S/Z,* trans. Richard Miller (New York: Hill and Wang, 1974) and *The Pleasure of the Text,* trans. Richard Miller (New York: Hill and Wang, 1975). De Man's essays include "Georg Lukács's *Theory of the Novel,*" *MLN,* 81 (1966), 527–34; "Literary History and Literary Modernity," *Daedulus,* 99, no. 2 (1970), 384–404; and "Lyric and Modernity," in *Forms of Lyric: Selected Papers from the English Institute,* ed. Reuben A. Brower (New York: Columbia University

Press, 1970), pp. 151–76. These later appeared in *Blindness and Insight* (1971); see also nn. 14–15.

2. For bibliographies on the critics who are discussed in this essay and also those who are not, see Richard A. Barney, "Deconstructive Criticism: A Selected Bibliography," supplement to *Society for Critical Exchange Reports,* 8 (1980), 1–54; Jonathan Culler, *On Deconstruction: Theory and Criticism after Structuralism* (Ithaca: Cornell University Press, 1982), pp. 281–302; Tom Keenan, "Bibliography of Texts by Paul de Man," *Yale French Studies,* 69 (1985), 315–22; Christopher Norris, *Deconstruction: Theory and Practice* (London: Methuen, 1982), pp. 143–52; *Rhetoric and Form: Deconstruction at Yale*, ed. Robert Con Davis and Ronald Schleifer (Norman: University of Oklahoma Press, 1985), pp. 239–51; *Textual Strategies: Perspectives in Post-Structuralist Criticism,* ed. Josué V. Harari (Ithaca: Cornell University Press, 1979), pp. 423–63; and *The Yale Critics: Deconstruction in America*, ed. Jonathan Arac, Wlad Godzich, and Wallace Martin (Minneapolis: University of Minnesota Press, 1983), pp. 203–12.

3. Geoffrey Hartman, "Preface," in Harold Bloom et al., *Deconstruction and Criticism* (New York: Continuum, 1979), p. ix.

4. In an interview with Robert Moynihan (*Diacritics,* 13, no. 3 [1983], 68), Bloom says: "I now find myself in the ridiculous position that the younger, the second or third generation deconstructionists, attack me as a moldy fig, while the moldy figs continue to attack me as a deconstructionist. I'm neither." Norris, in *Deconstruction: Theory and Practice,* pp. 116–25, provides an insightful description of the similarities and differences between Bloom and the Yale Critics.

5. Critics who have contributed to this impression include William H. Pritchard, "The Hermeneutical Mafia; or, After Strange Gods at Yale," *Hudson Review,* 28 (1975–76), 601–10; and Walter Jackson Bate, "The Crisis in English Studies," *Harvard Magazine,* Sept.-Oct. 1982, pp. 46–53. The critics cited in n. 6 are also occasionally guilty of this tendency. See in addition Colin Campbell, "The Tyranny of the Yale Critics," *The New York Times Magazine,* 9 Feb. 1986, pp. 20–28, 43, 47–48. Miller, for example, wants to keep Bloom in the company of these "uncanny critics" in "Stevens' Rock and Criticism as Cure, II," *Georgia Review,* 30 (1976), 336; hereafter cited in the text as SRII.

6. Abrams, Booth, and Hirsch have focused mainly on the issue of authorial intention. See, e.g., M. H. Abrams, "The Deconstructive Angel," *Critical Inquiry,* 3 (1977), 425–38, and Wayne Booth, "'Preserving the Exemplar'; or, How Not to Dig Our Own Graves," *Crit-*

ical Inquiry, 3 (1977), 407–23. Hirsch explicitly addresses himself to deconstruction in "Derrida's Axioms," *London Review of Books*, 12 July–3 Aug. 1983, pp. 17–18; he briefly refers to it in *The Aims of Interpretation* (Chicago: University of Chicago Press, 1976), pp. 13, 147. His most thorough argument for authorial intention is in *Validity in Interpretation* (New Haven: Yale University Press, 1967).

Gerald Graff has specifically attacked deconstruction's disengagement of language from a mimetic relation to the world. See *Literature Against Itself: Literary Ideas in Modern Society* (Chicago: University of Chicago Press, 1979), "Fear and Trembling at Yale," *American Scholar*, 46 (1977), 467–78, and "Deconstruction as Dogma; or, 'Come Back to the Raft Ag'in, Strether Honey!' " *Georgia Review*, 34 (1980), 404–21.

7. Denis Donoghue and Jackson Bate have invoked a rhetoric of crisis, claiming that deconstruction threatens virtually all the values invested in academic humanism since the Renaissance. See Donoghue, "Deconstructing Deconstruction," *New York Review of Books*, 12 June 1980, pp. 37–41, and Bate, "The Crisis in English Studies."
8. Jacques Derrida, *Of Grammatology*, trans. Gayatri Chakravorty Spivak (Baltimore: Johns Hopkins University Press, 1976), p. 68: "Arche-writing as spacing cannot occur *as such* within the phenomenological experience of a *presence*." See Harvey's discussion of the "force" beyond language on p. 133 in this volume.
9. Paul de Man, *Allegories of Reading: Figural Language in Rousseau, Nietzsche, Rilke, and Proust* (New Haven: Yale University Press, 1979), p. 300; hereafter cited as *AR*.
10. Jacques Derrida, "Differance," in *Speech and Phenomena and Other Essays on Husserl's Theory of Signs*, trans. David B. Allison (Evanston: Northwestern University Press, 1973), pp. 131, 132–38. The essay first appeared as "La Différance," *Bulletin de la Société française de philosophie*, 62, no. 3 (1968), 73–101, and in *Théorie d'ensemble* (Paris: Seuil, 1968), pp. 41–66.
11. Jacques Derrida, "Signature Event Context," in *Margins of Philosophy*, trans. Alan Bass (Chicago: University of Chicago Press, 1982), p. 329, author's italics. He first presented this essay to the Congrès international des Sociétés de philosophie de langue française, Montreal, in August 1971. It was later published in *Marges de la philosophie* (Paris: Minuit, 1972), pp. 365–93.
12. Rodolphe Gasché, "Deconstruction as Criticism," in *Glyph 6: Textual Studies* (Baltimore: Johns Hopkins University Press, 1979), p. 192.
13. Paul de Man, *Blindness and Insight: Essays in the Rhetoric of Contem-*

porary Criticism, 2nd rev. ed. (Minneapolis: University of Minnesota Press, 1983), hereafter cited as *BI*.

14. Paul de Man, "Form and Intent in the American New Criticism," in *Blindness*, p. 25, my italics. First delivered in 1966 as a paper for the History of Ideas Club at the Johns Hopkins University.
15. Paul de Man, "The Crisis of Contemporary Criticism," *Arion*, 6 (1967), 47; he uses the same wording in the revised version of this essay, "Criticism and Crisis," in *Blindness*, p. 10.
16. De Man, "The Crisis of Contemporary Criticism," p. 47; and *Blindness*, pp. 10–11.
17. For more extensive discussions of de Man's work, to which my views are partially indebted, see Gasché, "Deconstruction as Criticism," pp. 206–9, and " 'Setzung' and 'Ubersetzung': Notes on Paul de Man," *Diacritics*, 11, no. 4 (1981), 36–57. See also Suzanne Gearhart's response to Gasché in "Philosophy *Before* Literature: Deconstruction, Historicity, and the Work of Paul de Man," *Diacritics*, 13, no. 4 (1983), 63–81; Barbara Johnson, "Rigorous Unreliability," *Critical Inquiry*, 11 (1984), 278–85; Allan Stoekl, "De Man and the Dialectic of Being," *Diacritics*, 15, no. 3 (1985), 36–45; and the special issue of *Yale French Studies*, 69 (1985), entitled *The Lesson of Paul de Man*.
18. J. Hillis Miller, "Geneva or Paris? The Recent Work of Georges Poulet," *University of Toronto Quarterly*, 39 (1970), 223; revised as "Georges Poulet's 'Criticism of Identification,' " in *The Quest for Imagination*, ed. O. B. Hardison, Jr. (Cleveland: Press of Case Western Reserve University, 1971), pp. 191–224.
19. J. Hillis Miller, "Tradition and Difference," *Diacritics*, 2, no. 4 (1972), 12; hereafter cited as TD. For another example of Miller's overturning his previous critical views, see "The Fiction of Realism: *Sketches by Boz, Oliver Twist*, and Cruikshank's Illustrations," in *Charles Dickens and George Cruikshank* (Berkeley: W. A. Clark Memorial Library, 1971), pp. 1–69, rpt. in *Dickens Centennial Essays*, ed. Ada Nisbet and Blake Nevius (Berkeley: University of California Press, 1971), pp. 85–113. Rather than assume, as he had in previous work, that Dickens's novels represent a coherent "world," Miller corrosively penetrates beneath the surface of formal realism.
20. This critique sparked a series of exchanges in *Critical Inquiry*, between not only Miller and Abrams but also Morse Peckham and Wayne Booth. See n. 6, above, and Booth, "M. H. Abrams: Historian as Critic, Critic as Pluralist," *Critical Inquiry*, 2 (1976), 411–45; Abrams, "Rationality and Imagination in Cultural History: A Reply to Wayne Booth," *Critical Inquiry*, 2 (1976), 447–64; Morse Peckham, "The Infinitude of Pluralism," *Critical Inquiry*, 3 (1977), 803–

16; Abrams, "Behaviorism and Deconstruction: A Comment on Morse Peckham's 'The Infinitude of Pluralism,'" *Critical Inquiry,* 4 (1977), 181–93; and Miller, "The Critic as Host," in *Deconstruction and Criticism.*

21. See, e.g., M. H. Abrams, "How to Do Things with Texts," *Partisan Review,* 46 (1979), 566–88; I am also referring to his lecture "Construing and Deconstructing," given during a lecture tour on 11 Apr. 1983 at the University of Virginia.

    At a conference in his honor at Cornell University in 1978, Abrams goes one step further when confronted with Jonathan Culler's analysis of his *Mirror and the Lamp* (1953), in which Culler claims that by examining the unstable metaphorical constitution of philosophies of mind Abrams *anticipates* the work of Derrida. Abrams responds that "I am compelled to agree that I can indeed be plausibly represented as a precursor of the disseminating strategies of Jacques Derrida," while retaining his commitment to authorial intention and the referentiality of language. "Despite immersion in the deconstructive element of our time," he says, "I remain an unreconstructed humanist." See Abrams, "A Reply," in *High Romantic Argument: Essays for M. H. Abrams,* ed. Lawrence Lipking (Ithaca: Cornell University Press, 1981), pp. 167, 174. Culler's essay is "The Mirror Stage," pp. 149–63.

22. See, e.g., Paul de Man, "Action and Identity in Nietzsche," *Yale French Studies,* 52 (1975), 28, and "The Timid God: A Reading of Rousseau's *Profession de foi du vicaire savoyard,*" *Georgia Review,* 29 (1975), 548. These become chapters 6 and 10 in *Allegories of Reading.*

23. I owe this initial insight to Vincent Leitch in *Deconstructive Criticism: An Advanced Introduction* (New York: Columbia University Press, 1983), p. 244, though I develop it here in different ways. See also his cogent essay, "The Lateral Dance: The Deconstructive Criticism of J. Hillis Miller," *Critical Inquiry,* 6 (1980), 593–607.

24. Miller, "Stevens' Rock and Criticism as Cure," 16–17. He reiterates this point in "The Critic as Host," in *Deconstruction and Criticism,* p. 224.

25. J. Hillis Miller, *Fiction and Repetition: Seven English Novels* (Cambridge: Harvard University Press, 1982), p. 9; hereafter cited as *F&R.* In strict terms, the image is produced by the differences in the *second* form of repetition. But since the differences between the two distinct forms of repetition are analogous to those in the second, we can consider the text itself to be constituted by such an image.

26. J. Hillis Miller, "The Interpretation of *Lord Jim,*" in *The Interpreta-*

tion of Narrative: Theory and Practice, ed. Morton W. Bloomfield (Cambridge: Harvard University Press, 1970), p. 215; hereafter cited as ILJ.

27. Miller's revision of the essay on Virginia Woolf, ("*Mrs. Dalloway:* Repetition as the Raising of the Dead," in *Fiction and Repetition,* pp. 176–202) produces a similar, though less pronounced, shift in perspective. The essay first appeared as "Virginia Woolf's All Souls' Day: The Omniscient Narrator in *Mrs. Dalloway,*" in *The Shaken Realist,* ed. Melvin J. Friedman and John B. Vickerey (Baton Rouge: Louisiana State University Press, 1970), pp. 100–127.
28. Miller, "Georges Poulet's 'Criticism of Identification,'" p. 216.
29. See William E. Cain's useful overview of Miller's work in "Deconstruction in America: The Recent Literary Criticism of J. Hillis Miller," *College English,* 41 (1979), 367–82, which comes to this conclusion.
30. J. Hillis Miller, "Deconstructing the Deconstructors," *Diacritics,* 5, no. 2 (1975), 31.
31. In later work such as *Fiction and Repetition* (p. 23), for example, Miller reasserts the active role of the reader/critic.
32. Miller reaffirms his commitment to this project in *Fiction and Repetition,* p. 21.
33. Geoffrey Hartman, "The Voice of the Shuttle: Language from the Point of View of Literature," in *Beyond Formalism: Literary Essays 1958–1970* (New Haven: Yale University Press, 1970), pp. 338–39; hereafter cited as *BF.*
34. Geoffrey Hartman, *The Fate of Reading and Other Essays* (Chicago: University of Chicago Press, 1975), p. x; hereafter cited as *FR.*
35. Geoffrey Hartman, *Criticism in the Wilderness: The Study of Literature Today* (New Haven: Yale University Press, 1980), p. 265; hereafter cited as *CW.*
36. Geoffrey Hartman, *Saving the Text: Literature/Derrida/Philosophy* (Baltimore: Johns Hopkins University Press, 1981), p. 79; hereafter cited as *ST.* The first chapters were previously published as "Monsieur Texte: On Jacques Derrida, His *Glas,*" *Georgia Review,* 29 (1975), 759–97, and "Monsieur Texte II: Epiphony in Echoland," *Georgia Review,* 30 (1976), 169–204.
37. See *The Yale Critics,* already cited in n. 2. Only Jonathan Culler, in *On Deconstruction,* pp. 235–42, considers Johnson's work at any length. In *Deconstruction: Theory and Practice,* Norris cites her work only in a bibliographical list called "Notes for Further Reading," pp. 147, 150; in his later book, *The Deconstructive Turn: Essays in the Rhetoric of Philosophy* (London: Methuen, 1983), pp. 138, 143, 170–71,

Norris mentions Johnson as a critic whose work confirms the theoretical premises of Derrida and de Man. In what provides the most thorough overview of deconstruction's philosophical background, *Deconstructive Criticism,* Leitch cites her work in three places: pp. 102, 272 n. 9, 281 n. 15. The recent collection of essays *Rhetoric and Form: Deconstruction at Yale*, ed. Davis and Schleifer, has taken a first step in correcting this imbalance.

38. Barbara Johnson, *The Critical Difference: Essays in the Contemporary Rhetoric of Reading* (Baltimore: Johns Hopkins University Press, 1980), p. x; hereafter cited as *CD.*

39. Barbara Johnson, "Translator's Introduction" to Derrida's *Dissemination* (Chicago: University of Chicago Press, 1981), p. xiv, my italics.

40. Jacques Derrida, "Living On/Border Lines," in *Deconstruction and Criticism,* p. 84.

41. Barbara Johnson, "My Monster/My Self," *Diacritics,* 12, no. 2 (1982), 10. For a similar tactic, see "Teaching Ignorance: *L'Ecole des Femmes,*" *Yale French Studies,* 63 (1982), 165–82.

42. See, e.g., John Brenkman, "Narcissus in the Text," *Georgia Review,* 30 (1976), 293–327, and *Culture and Domination,* forthcoming from Cornell University Press; Frank Lentricchia, "History or the Abyss: Poststructuralism," in *After the New Criticism* (Chicago: University of Chicago Press, 1980), pp. 156–210; and Edward Said, *Beginnings: Intention and Method* (New York: Basic, 1975) and "The Problem of Textuality: Two Exemplary Positions," *Critical Inquiry,* 4 (1978), 673–714. Said's and Lentricchia's approaches have nonetheless taken on a distinctly deconstructive coloration, particularly in Said's analysis of the concept of orientalism in Western culture and in Lentricchia's theorizing about the structure of history. See Said, *Orientalism* (New York: Pantheon, 1978) and *Covering Islam* (New York: Pantheon, 1981); and Lentricchia, *Criticism and Social Change* (Chicago: University of Chicago Press, 1983).

For examples of those on the British front who have explored the ways deconstruction can assist the analysis of the social production of texts, see Terry Eagleton, *Criticism and Ideology: A Study in Marxist Literary Theory* (London: Verso, 1978) and "Marxism and Deconstruction," in *Walter Benjamin; or, Towards a Revolutionary Criticism* (New York: Schocken, 1981), pp. 131–42; and Catherine Belsey, *Critical Practice* (London: Methuen, 1980).

43. For a sampling of these criticisms, see Cain, "Deconstruction in America," pp. 381–82; Joseph Riddell, "A Miller's Tale," *Diacritics,* 5, no. 3 (1975), 56–65 (Leitch discusses these remarks in *Deconstructive*

Criticism, pp. 93–100); Edward Said, "Reflections on Recent American 'Left' Literary Criticism," *Boundary 2*, 8 (1979), 11–30; and Gayatri Spivak, " 'Draupadi' by Mahasveta Devi," *Critical Inquiry*, 8 (1981), 382.

44. It seems that de Man's political conscience was pricked, so to speak, by this kind of criticism, as is evidenced in the title of the seminar he later taught in the summer of 1982 at the School of Criticism and Theory (Northwestern University): "Rhetoric, Aesthetics, Ideology." He unfortunately could not finish the last half of that seminar because of illness. To what extent he shifted his approach is yet to be seen in his writings that will be published posthumously, including *The Rhetoric of Romanticism* (New York: Columbia University Press, 1984), which appeared after this essay was written.
45. Michael Ryan, *Marxism and Deconstruction: A Critical Articulation* (Baltimore: Johns Hopkins University Press, 1982), p. xv; hereafter cited as *M&D*. Most recently, however, Ryan has revaluated de Man's work to conclude that his analyses are in fact relevant to a critique of bourgeois liberalism. See "The Marxism Deconstruction Debate," *Critical Exchange*, 14 (Fall 1983), 59–68.
46. James Kearns and Ken Newton, "An Interview with Jacques Derrida," *The Literary Review*, 14 (18 April–1 May 1980), 22.
47. Michael Ryan and Gayatri Spivak, "Anarchism Revisited: A New Philosophy," *Diacritics*, 8, no. 2 (1978), 75–76. This article is a dialogue between Ryan and Spivak. For other critics who also point out this difficulty, while rejecting the prospect of linking deconstruction with Marxism, see Norris, *Deconstruction: Theory and Practice*, p. 80 (Ryan specifically answers Norris's objections in "The Marxism Deconstruction Debate"); Culler, *On Deconstruction*, p. 159; and Miller, "Theory and Practice: A Response to Vincent Leitch," *Critical Inquiry*, 6 (1980), 612–13.
48. Ryan and Spivak, "Anarchism Revisited," p. 76.
49. Gayatri Spivak, "Explanation and Culture: Marginalia," *Humanities in Society*, 2 (1979), 216 and 221 n. 26; hereafter cited as E&C. She refers to Foucault's "Nietzsche, Genealogy, History," in *Language, Counter-Memory, Practice*, trans. Donald F. Bouchard and Sherry Simon (Ithaca: Cornell University Press, 1977), pp. 156, 154.
50. Gayatri Spivak, "Marx After Derrida," in *Philosophical Approaches to Literature*, ed. William E. Cain (London: Associated University Presses, 1984), p. 232.
51. Gayatri Spivak, "Sex and History in *The Prelude* (1805): Books Nine to Thirteen," *Texas Studies in Literature and Language*, 23 (1981), 357.

52. Gayatri Spivak, "The Politics of Interpretations," *Critical Inquiry,* 9 (1982), 262, my italics.
53. Gayatri Spivak, "Feminism and Critical Theory," *Women's Studies International Quarterly,* 1 (1978), 243–44.
54. Gayatri Spivak, "Displacement and the Discourse of Woman," in *Displacement: Derrida and After*, ed. Mark Krupnick (Bloomington: Indiana University Press, 1983), pp. 173, 170.
55. Gayatri Spivak, "Revolutions That as Yet Have No Model: Derrida's *Limited Inc,*" *Diacritics,* 10, no. 4 (1980), 29–49. She is working on a forthcoming book whose manuscript is presently entitled "Literary Criticism and a Critique of Imperialism."

BARRIE RUTH STRAUS

Influencing Theory: Speech Acts

The Foundations of Speech-Act Theory: Austin and Searle

Why have literary critics been attracted to speech-act theory (SAT)? Its originator, J. L. Austin, stipulated his theory of language did not apply to literature, which he excluded as a nonserious and parasitic use of language.[1] How do we account for this paradoxical, if not perverse, desire to defy Austin's exclusion? Since the attractions are as multiple and complex as the literary critics who responded, we will never know for sure. Our speculations, however, can reveal what concerns SAT and literary studies share, what issues the theory raises, and what answers it has been seen to provide. What follows traces the development of the response to SAT in literary studies to show three different paths: the initial response to Austin and Searle, the response to Grice, and the deconstructive response.

SAT began at Oxford University in part as Austin's reaction against the methodology of logical positivism predominant before and after World War II. Austin came to philosophical studies with extensive training in classics and philology. Interested in scientific research but disliking and distrusting its "rhetoric, pretentions, and obscurity" and its addiction to pseudo-scientific jargon, Austin focused his attentions instead on a minute analysis of language.[2] A similar attraction to science with some repulsion for its excesses is seen in the trend in literary studies to move beyond philological foundations and acquire scientific validity from the relatively new discipline of linguistics. The emergence of stylistic criticism, an attempt to replace impressionistic description with more precise, rigorous, and therefore objective linguistic description reveals this trend.

Desiring to avoid philosophy's "occupational disease" of oversimplification, Austin held all theory up to scrutiny. The result was the sometimes maddeningly step-by-step procedure of *How to Do Things with Words*.[3] These lectures, delivered at Harvard in 1955 and published posthumously, with refinements by Strawson, Grice, and Searle, lay out the tenets of SAT. The basis of SAT—to speak is also to act—reveals the oversimplification of traditional distinctions between speech and action. Austin felt meaning was not *merely* propositional, as philosophy's practice of studying sentences alone implied. Moreover, he felt holding sentences up to criticism based on the logical categories of truth and falsity oversimplified what was complex in life. His corrective for the "true-false fetish" was a distinction between "constative" and "performative" utterances.

The distinction between constatives and performatives is Austin's distinction between "just saying" and "doing by saying." "Constative utterances" are traditional statements, where saying is a matter of reporting or describing that can be categorized as true, false, or nonsensical. But Austin focused on performatives. To utter a performative is not merely to describe or report but actually to be doing or performing an action by saying.[4] For example, in saying during a marriage ceremony "I do take you to be my lawfully wedded husband," a speaker is neither describing what she is doing, nor stating that she is doing it, but is actually performing an action that constitutes, as part of a marriage ceremony, becoming a wife. Performatives are not judged as true or false, but happy or unhappy. The degree to which certain conditions under which they are uttered, called felicity conditions, are met determines whether they can be considered felicitous or happily executed, or infelicitous, misfires, misinvocations, etc. For example, if the speakers above were already married or engaged to others, the implications of her utterances, that they were free, are violated, and their utterances are infelicitous. Similarly, promises made without the intent to keep them that uttering a promise implies are infelicitous, as is the declaration "I hereby open this meeting" made by a speaker who has no authority to open the meeting.

As Austin developed his theory, he abandoned the constative-performative distinction. Coming to believe *all* utterances are ultimately performatives, he described utterances as the simultaneous performance of three speech acts: the locutionary act, an act *of* saying something; the illocutionary act, an act performed *in* saying something; and the perlocutionary act, the act performed *by* saying something. The locutionary act, to which he gave little attention, is simply the traditional act of saying: uttering sounds or words. Similarly undeveloped is the perlocutionary act: effects the speaker's utterance may achieve on the listener, from informing, convincing, reassuring, to alarming, embarrassing, or annoying. Austin was most interested in his category of illocutionary force, which indicates how to take an utterance. For example, "I shall be there" could be a simple illocutionary statement of information. However, depending on context, it could also have the illocutionary force of a promise, threat, or warning.

Austin was the first to admit he had left "numerous loose ends" (*HTD*, 148). John Searle, an American Rhodes Scholar studying philosophy at Oxford in 1952, attempted to tie up Austin's looseness, making SAT more accessible outside philosophy. Searle saw the primary distinction between the propositional act or content of an utterance and the way to take it—illocutionary force.[5] Rejecting the term "locutionary" altogether, in his influential *Speech Acts* Searle redefined speech acts as the performance of four interconnected acts: utterance acts (uttering strings of words, that is, morphemes and sentences), propositional acts (referring and predicating), illocutionary acts (stating, questioning, promising, commanding, etc.), and perlocutionary acts (affecting hearers' actions, thoughts, beliefs).[6]

Searle's refinements of Austin's theory led to an emphasis on speech acts as rule-governed behavior. Searle distinguished between regulative and constitutive rules. Regulative rules, such as rules of etiquette, control behavior which exists independently of those rules. However, constitutive rules, such as rules for games like football, don't just regulate those games but create the very possibility of playing them (*SA*, 33). Language for Searle is the conventional realization of the underlying constitutive rules, and speech acts are utterances expressed in accordance with those rules. Searle also distinguishes between "brute" and "institutional" facts. Brute facts, based on the scientific model for knowledge, are essentially made up of physical or mental data. Institutional facts, however, take into account the social agreements inherent in the systems of constitutive rules which make up human institutions. The performance of speech acts based on constitutive rules involves institutional, rather than brute, facts. The difference this makes is that a description of a football game based on brute facts alone reduces that game to "physical" laws of clustering. To describe those movements as the game of football as we know it requires such institutional facts as the constitutive rules of kickoffs, downs, touchdowns, etc.

Searle's expansion of the notion of illocutionary acts intensified the sense of the social, rule-governed, interactional nature of speech acts. His stated goal was to capture both the intentional and conventional aspects of illocutionary acts and the relationship between them. Searle substituted for Austin's "happy" or "felicity conditions" the more scientific notion of "successful and nondefective" performances. He gave new prominence to the listener's role in SAT by insisting that the fully successful performance of a speech act depends not only on the speaker's intention to act but also on the listener's recognition of that intention. Searle also developed a more precise schema of conditions for successfully performing speech acts. Using the promise as a model, he established three general categories of conditions. The essential condition, dependent on the speaker's intention, is undertaking an obligation to perform a certain act. Its preparatory condition, dependent on both speaker and listener, is promising both what wouldn't ordinarily be done and what the speaker knows the listener wants done. Its sincerity condition is intending and believing the speaker is able to do the promised act.

Austin presented a broad program for a theory, which he constantly and prosaically held up to scrutiny. He left to his readers "the real fun of applying it in philosophy" (*HTD*, 164). Searle systematized that program into a general theory, incorporating the work of Strawson, Grice, and others, especially in conversational implicature. The writings of Austin and Searle reveal great differences in thinking and style. Whereas Searle, a no-nonsense man, focuses on the center, "ignoring marginal, fringe, and partially defective promises" (*SA*, 55), Austin focuses on the marginal "types of nonsense" engendered in performing "possible slips between cup and lip" (*HTD,* 147). This distinction is fully exploited in the famous exchange between Searle and Jacques Derrida, discussed later.

First Uses of Speech Acts: The Uses of Literature

Whatever their differences, both Austin and Searle were concerned with the performance of serious speech acts in everyday, ordinary life. Both took care to exclude literary utterances as nonserious and parasitic on normal use. The assumption behind the distinction is that ordinary language, also called "propositional," "literal," "denotative," or "serious," is more objective and closer to reality or the objective world than literary language. How then did SAT become appropriated by literary studies? One reason surely lies in the spirit of the sixties, when Austin's and Searle's major books appeared. Renewed interest in the scientific contributions of linguistics to knowledge about literature was intensified by the assault on all humanistic learning that the sixties saw. The spirit of revolt against much that traditional academics had taken for granted forced a still-continuing reappraisal of all aspects of literary studies.

The banner cry of "relevance" raised two main questions about literary studies: what is literature and what is its "real" or practical use? Richard Ohmann's pioneer incorporation of SAT in applying linguistics to literary studies shows the usefulness of SAT to work out some answers.[7] Austin and Searle's distinction between "serious" and "nonserious" utterances continued the separation of literature from ordinary life associated with formalist and new critical literary theories. Ohmann accepted Austin and Searle's definition of literary utterances as nonserious or parasitic by "waiving the unfortunate tone of the term[s]" (SLS, 52). But he established continuity between literature and ordinary life by expanding Austin's statements that literary utterances are "in a peculiar way hollow or void" (*HTD,* 22). Ohmann used their nonserious nature to define literary utterances as simply a special kind of speech act. Literary utterances are parasitic on speech because written discourse alters conditions of utterance in special ways: the audience is dispersed and uncertain; we have only internal evidence to judge the appropriateness of a writer's beliefs and feelings, and no evidence at all about the appropriateness of the writer's behavior after the utterance. Ohmann then defined literature as discourse "detached from the circumstances and conditions which make illocutionary acts possible; hence . . . a discourse without illocutionary force" (SAD, 13).

Ultimately, Ohmann used SAT to show what use literature could have. He focused on literature as a social contract between writer and reader, and gave increased attention to the competence of the reader, forced to make inferences, largely "by putting to work his tacit knowledge of the conditions for performance of illocutionary acts" (SLS, 55). Ohmann's expansion of the nature of the rules and conventions of speech acts paid new attention to the political and moral implications of the relationships that govern speech acts. Using speech acts to oppose an elitist emphasis on literary works as "structures, objects, artifacts" (LA, 1), Ohmann ultimately articulated a theory of literature that gave political relevance to reading. Speech acts show how literature is not just symbolic action, a surrogate act, but "really doing something" (LA, 96). Written literary texts preserve purported speech acts which readers "bring alive" and "re-enact": "The stage of a literary work is the reader's mind, the action on the stage is illocutionary. Like illocutionary action outside literature, it is inescapably ethical" (LA, 101). In fact, a "strong case can be made, from the nature of speech and action, that in literature everything is indeed politics, so long as we resist the unwarranted inference that literature comprises nothing *but* politics" (LA, 104).

In the seventies, the tentative efforts of such disparate theoreticians as Wolfgang Iser, Monroe Beardsley, and Barbara Herrnstein Smith to use speech-act terminology to define literature (by distinguishing between fiction and nonfiction) mark a growing awareness of the need to take SAT into account.[8] These attempts also show the attractiveness of SAT for critics concerned to replace the notion of literary texts as static objects with an emphasis on reading as a process of constructing, rather than discovering, meaning. SAT became allied not only with the recovery of authorial intention but with a new emphasis on the role of the reader and ultimately with the communal nature of reading conventions. These two different ways SAT allowed critics to go beyond the text can be seen in two different attempts to use SAT to define literature appearing the same year. Searle focuses on the role of the author while Iser emphasizes the role of the reader.[9]

In "The Logical Status of Fictional Discourse" Searle uses SAT to bring more precision and rigor to the vague, unhelpful terminology he finds in literary theory. Carefully cleaning up terms, Searle distinguishes "fiction" from "literature," categories he feels are created by attitudes rather than textual properties. His concern for authors is seen in his decision to focus on fiction, created by the attitudes of authors, rather than on literature, determined by readers. Searle accepts the definition of fictional utterances as nonserious and parasitic. "Nonserious," he explains, is a nonpejorative term and implies not that writing fiction is not a serious activity but that the writer is not committed to the truth of direct reference: "For example, if the author of a novel tells us that it is raining outside he isn't seriously committed to the view that it is at the time of the writing actually raining outside." (LSFD, 321).

Fictional utterances are parasitic because there is suspension of ordinary illocutionary rules, a suspension that leads Searle to consider how words in fictional stories can have their ordinary meanings, while "the rules that attach to those words . . . and determine their meanings are not complied with" (LSFD, 319). He rejects the notion that writers perform a separate class of illocutionary acts, the acts of telling a story or writing a novel, rather than performing the ordinary illocutionary acts of asserting, commanding, and so on.[10] If this were the case, Searle argues, words would not have their normal meanings in fiction, and we would not be able to understand what was going on. Searle agrees with others that writers imitate ordinary illocutionary acts. He rejects the term "mimesis" as unhelpful, however. Shifting attention to authorial intention instead, he proposes that writers *pretend* to perform a series of illocutionary acts: "By way of uttering (writing) sentences . . . the *illocutionary act* is pretended, but the *utterance act* is real" (LSFD, 327). Since this pretense is nondeceptive, *pace* Plato, fiction is clearly distinguished from lies. Searle explains *how* language in fiction is parasitic on ordinary language: "The pretended illocutions which constitute a work of fiction are made possible by the existence of a set of conventions which suspend the normal operation of the rules relating illocutionary acts and the world." For Searle, telling stories is "a separate language game" to be played by a separate set of conventions, which are not meaning rules and "parasitic" on the ordinary language game (LSFD, 326).

In "The Reality of Fiction," Iser uses speech-act terminology to focus on the role of the reader. Unlike both Ohmann and Searle, Iser questions literature as imitating speech acts and rejects the negative corollary, that such speech acts are "parasitic," "void," or "hollow." He observes that, for example, no one in the audience perceives Hamlet's abuse of Ophelia as a void speech act. Unlike Ohmann as well, Iser feels fictional language not only has illocutionary force; its potential effectiveness arouses attention, guides the reader's approach to the text, and elicits responses to it as well. Conceding that fictional language doesn't lead to real actions in a real context, Iser argues that fictional language is not without real effect. The reader may well end up transcending the fictional context of speech and "find himself contemplating the real world, or experiencing real emotions and real insights" (RF, 12).

Speech Acts and Literary Criticism: Fish's Critique

The first attempts to use speech acts for literary criticism and theory were understandably imperfect. The work of Ohmann and Iser, subject to criticism of misunderstood terminology and overstated claims for the usefulness of SAT for literature as they were, paved the way for further refinements and applications. Both the prominence of SAT and resistance to its applications to literary studies are clear in the Midwest Modern Language Association panel devoted to "Speech Act Theory and Literary Criticism" in 1975.

The centerpiece of the MMLA panel was Stanley Fish's presentation, "Speech-Act-Theory, Literary Criticism and Coriolanus." If Ohmann put SAT on the map for literary studies, Fish's clear articulation of its strengths and weaknesses made SAT more broadly available to literary critics. In a series of crucial articles, Fish developed a major statement of the use and abuse of SAT and its relationship to literary studies.[11] Austin had mocked himself and scientific pretensions, noting he said "third power of ten" rather than 1,000 to look "impressive and scientific" (*HTD,* 150). In "What Is Stylistics . . . ," delivered at the same English Institute session as Ohmann's "Literature as Act," Fish uses SAT to show that while stylisticians intended to replace subjective interpretation with objective linguistic descriptions, they in fact practised a more subjective methodology than the one they replaced. Their "pseudo-scientific paraphernalia," "anchorless statistics," and self-referring categories are covert impressionism producing circular or arbitrary interpretations (*ITT*, 86). Not surprisingly, for the founder of reader-response criticism, pursuers of scientific truth fail to recognize that meaning is acquired in the context of an activity that is reading. Like Ohmann and Iser, Fish uses SAT to shift attention from texts to readers. Fish attacks stylisticians' assumption that texts and the world are already ordered and filled with significance that readers are required to get out. Looking for data is not a neutral process but an interpretation itself: readers' purposes and concerns mark out what facts get observed. Stylisticians' view of humans as passive, disinterested comprehenders of objective, external knowledge is an unworthy denial of the remarkable human ability to give, rather than extract, meaning.

Fish's work presents an important moment in the history of the use of SAT for literary studies. In a dazzling analysis of the speech acts of *Coriolanus,* Fish shows how the entire play can be seen as the unfolding of the necessary consequences of the hero's illocutionary behavior. Coriolanus constantly declares his independence from the system of conventional speech acts: he "is always doing things (with words) to set himself apart" (*ITT,* 213). Critical of overextensions of SAT, however, Fish warned against generalizing from the success of his speech-act reading of the play. Initially, he attributed his success to the special condition of *Coriolanus* being a "speech-act play," that is, "about" conditions for the successful performance of certain conventional acts and commitments—a position he later corrected (*ITT*, 200). Criticizing its abuses, Fish articulates the limits of SAT. It deals with conventions rather than perlocutionary or social effects. It is not a rhetoric or a psychology or a theory of narrative.

Fish's work is also important for drawing attention to the problematic nature of the traditional distinction between ordinary, or "serious," and literary, or "nonserious," language. His challenge to that distinction in "How Ordinary Is Ordinary Language" not only marked a departure from the acceptance of Ohmann and

Searle, it challenged the basis of Austin's and Searle's exclusion of literature from SAT. Fish argued that the traditional distinction separating literature from everyday life approves a diminished quality of everyday life that impoverishes both ordinary and literary language.

Fish uses linguistics and SAT to show how "*there is no such thing as ordinary language*" (*ITT,* 106). The "new semanticists" Charles Fillmore, James MacCauley, and George Lakeoff demonstrated that philosophical, psychological, and moral concepts are *built into* language. And SAT emphasizes utterances as purposeful behavior referring not to affairs in the real world but to the commitments and attitudes of those who produce them in the context of specific situations. Both show how ordinary language is in fact extraordinary because it contains the very values, intentions, and purposes often assumed to belong exclusively to literature. By restoring human content to language, then, these theories unite literature with a norm that is no longer trivialized and so restore legitimate status to literature. The resulting reversal of the separation between literature and the rest of life also widens the scope of what can be considered literary.

The question of ordinary versus literary language raises questions about the nature of reality, the self, the text, the autonomy and relationships among all of these—all crucial questions for literary studies. What is implicit argument in "How Ordinary Is Ordinary Language" becomes explicit in "How to Do Things with Austin and Searle." There Fish draws attention to problems in SAT itself as he admittedly takes Searle and SAT farther than they would want to go: "The very words 'pretense,' 'serious,' and 'fiction' have built into them the absolute opposition I have been at pains to deny, between language that is true to some extra-institutional reality and language that is not" (*ITT,* 243). Fish doesn't deny a standard of truth exists that can distinguish between different kinds of discourse, but he asserts that standard is not brute or natural but institutional and made. For Fish, "what we know is not the world but stories about the world." SAT is one of these stories of interpretations and so cannot serve as an all-purpose interpretive key.

After Fish (though not dependent on him), responses to SAT take two different paths, linguistic and philosophical, as exemplified by the critiques of Mary Louise Pratt and Jacques Derrida, both appearing in 1977 but speaking very differently. Derrida's philosophical response points out the problems inherent in the theory presented by Austin and used by his heirs. Pratt's first book-length study of SAT shows clear affinities with Fish. Both share a linguistically-based and pragmatic concern for SAT, a concern also seen in the work of Charles Altieri. Altieri and Pratt both base their utilization of SAT on the modifications of that theory by the philosopher H. P. Grice.

Rewriting Speech Acts: Uses of Grice

Grice, in his 1967 Henry James Lectures, "Logic and Conversation," set out, like Austin, to restore status to "conversation," his term for ordinary language, against the claims that the imperfections of ordinary language (which is loose and metaphysically loaded) mandated the more pure scientific language of formal logic. Grice maintained that differences between ordinary and scientific language were a matter of use, not meaning. He sought to clarify and correct traditional thinking about appropriateness conditions by showing that many cases of inappropriateness, usually seen as violations of conditions governing the applicability of a particular word or expression, were best viewed as violations of other more general rules governing all discourse. In short, Grice converted Austin's appropriateness conditions to general rules governing all verbal discourse and, in fact, all goal-directed human behavior, rather than focusing on specific conditions and contexts for specific speech acts.[12]

The development from Austin to Searle to Grice can be seen in the shift from Austin's focus on words, to Searle's focus on rules, to Grice's articulation of maxims. Grice formulated a Cooperative Principle, which spelled out the most generalized version of the shared mutual assumptions he felt normally prevail in most speech situations: "Make your conversational contribution such as is required, at the stage at which it occurs, by the accepted purpose or direction of the talk exchange in which you are engaged."[13] He saw this principle maintained by the following maxims:

I. Maxims of Quantity
   1. "Make your contribution as informative as is required (for the current purposes of the exchange)."
   2. "Do not make your contribution more informative than is required."

II. Maxims of Quality
   Supermaxim: "Make your contribution one that is true."
   Maxims 1. "Do not say what you believe to be false."
   2. "Do not say that for which you lack adequate evidence."

III. Maxim of Relation
   1. "Be relevant."

IV. Maxims of Manner
   Supermaxim: "Be perspicuous."
   Maxims 1. "Avoid obscurity of expression."
   2. "Avoid ambiguity."
   3. "Be brief (avoid unnecessary prolixity)."
   4. "Be orderly."

Grice's concern with interpretation, not shared by Austin and Searle, is an obvious attractiveness for literary critics. Meaning, for Grice, is both what is said and what is implied, or in his terms, "implicated." Consequently, his Cooperative Principle also involves a theory of conversational "implicature," Grice's term for the different "calculations" by which we make sense of what we hear. For Grice, felicity depends on accurate strategic use of the Cooperative Principle and the function of each maxim is to clarify meaning, to guide interpretive strategies.

In *Toward a Speech Act Theory of Literary Discourse,* Pratt, like Fish, further challenges the distinction between ordinary and literary language.[14] Unlike Fish, Pratt, following Grice, seeks to confer status on ordinary, rather than literary, language. Like Fish, Pratt finds the distinction morally and politically reprehensible, fostering exclusivist attitudes about the superiority of literature to other verbal activities. Both Fish and Pratt find claims of a "scientific" theory of literature the culprit. Scientific objectivity, which separates literature from other human activities, frees critics from seeking out poets', critics', or society's values. In this way it masks the ideological assumptions and values built into the concept of literature. To overturn the distinction, Pratt points to literature as a social institution and shows how literary and nonliterary uses of language are similar in ways the distinction denies.

Pratt's work is based on the analyses of the American sociolinguist William Labov and on SAT. Labov showed both that natural, everyday, inner-city oral narratives of personal experience shared a structurally similar core with novels and that daily discourse is full of other kinds of fictive speech acts. Pratt notes the clear fictivity requiring suspension of illocutionary force in such daily activities as speculation, imagining, planning, dreaming, wishing, fantasizing, or postulating hypotheses. This work showed Pratt what had been identified as "literariness" was not literary at all but rather that natural narratives and novels both belonged to a larger category of speech acts.

Pratt, like Fish, is interested in SAT's emphasis on context, shifting attention away from self-sufficient texts onto authors and readers. Using Labov's emphasis on context and the clear fictivity of daily discourse, Pratt argues that ultimately SAT will have to enlarge its notion of what constitutes normal illocutionary force. She feels "the real lesson" SAT can provide is "that *literature is a context,* too, not the absence of one," as Ohmann and others imply (*TSAT,* 99). Criticizing Ohmann, Pratt argues that reading presupposes not aesthetic detachment but commitment, tied to exceedingly elaborate conventional responsibilities. Moreover, that commitment and those responsibilities define the literary speech situation.

Pratt is especially concerned to articulate and define the unspoken, culturally shared rules and conventions guiding literary speech acts as systems of appropriateness conditions. She provides a description of the context of the literary speech situation which relates the roles of readers and authors to the similar roles of speakers and audiences in other everyday speech situations. She replaces an exclusivist rhetoric of fiction with a rhetoric of audiences related to a rhetoric of conversation. In this view the relationship between any audience and any speaker or writer is based on a mutual exchange. In listening or reading the audience gives up their turn to speak, obligating the writer/speaker to make worthwhile the time during which they remain silent and listen to another, and giving the audience the right to judge the writing/speaking. Definitiveness, pre-paration, and pre-selection, the "conventional procedures" for making a literary speech act, reveal the normative nature of the very notion of literature which the denial of value in intrinsic definitions of literature conceals.

As a critique of such theories of reading as Ohmann's, which erroneously restrict reconstruction by implicature to literature, Pratt works out a theory of literary cooperation and implicature based on Grice's notion of the way speakers may knowingly fail to fulfill his maxims, conditions she terms general appropriateness in a speech exchange:

1. Speakers may unobtrusively *violate* a maxim, perhaps to mislead.
2. Speakers may *opt out* or *openly refuse to cooperate,* saying, for example, "I can say no more."
3. Speakers may be faced by a clash, making them unable to fulfill one maxim without violating another.
4. Speakers may *flout* a maxim, that is, blatantly fail to fulfill it, a condition Grice considers *exploiting* a maxim.

In the first three cases the Cooperative Principle is jeopardized and may even break down. Only flouting does not put the principle in danger. While one of Pratt's main points is that flouting is not restricted to literature, Grice's subcategories of flouting make its interest for literature especially clear: irony, metaphor, meiosis, and hyperbole flout the maxims of quality, while ambiguity and obscurity flout the maxims of manner. According to Pratt, in literature any violation of a maxim will most likely be an exploitation of that maxim in the service of some implicature.

For Pratt, Grice's theory shows the problem of defining literature in terms of intentional deviance because intentional deviance is not restricted to literature. She uses Grice's relation maxim to define literature instead as a subclass of both literary and nonliterary assertions, such as exclamations, which she calls "display texts." Unlike informing texts, such display texts are characterized by their detachability from the immediate context and their susceptibility to elaboration. The only hearer-based appropriateness condition is that the hearer be able to recognize and appreciate the tellability of what is being asserted. Pratt distinguishes between the author's display text utterance, where all violations of the Cooperative Principle will be interpreted as flouting, and the fictional speakers' utterances, where all kinds of nonfulfillment are possible.

Pratt uses Grice's observation that the Cooperative Principle is as much a social as a grammatical construct to explain why readers are ready to "enter into an aesthetic relationship with deviant grammaticality" (*TSAT,* 221) through literature. In the literary speech situation, the Cooperative Principle is so singularly secure and well protected that it is hyperprotected. In literature, then, the Cooperative Principle can be jeopardized or even cancelled without exposure to chaotic consequences. As a result, literature enables us to display and explore "one of the most problematic and threatening experiences of all, the collapse of communication itself" (*TSAT,* 221).

Grice's maxims differ from Austin's and Searle's rules by being regulative and nonconventional rather than constitutive. Pratt's extension of Grice's maxims to define genres and subgenres as systems of appropriateness conditions has been criticized as stretching the term "speech act" beyond usefulness. Pratt's "appropriateness conditions" simply seem to indicate some sort of constraining conditions.[15] The result is to assimilate every linguistic or literary distinction to the speech-act model, without showing either how this is to be managed or in what sense relevant constraining maxims governing the implicit "conversational context" of literary discourse may be detailed. Her very broad extension of appropriateness conditions, moreover, would seem to limit literary criticism to being relatively informal, relativized to admitted genres and practices, and fundamentally retrospective. No conversational maxims may be produced that actually bind discourse.

Pratt, however, also uses the distinction between rules governing the author's and the fictional speakers' utterances to develop an intricate scheme of generic deviance. For example, in Sterne's *Tristram Shandy* deviance of one kind results from Shandy's opting out of the rules governing manner, relevance, and quantity in autobiographies and deviance of another kind comes from Sterne's flouting the rules for both novels and autobiographies.

Ultimately, although Pratt's first book-length extension of SAT to the literary speech act is extremely interesting, the greater contribution of her work would seem to lie in her attempt to bring literary and linguistic theory together in order to correct not only literary critics but linguists as well. She asserts that as utterances literary works by definition form part of the data for which linguistic theory must account, and she faults the desire of both critics and linguists to see linguistic analysis of literature as some kind of special case of applied linguistics.

Working independently, Charles Altieri came to see the usefulness of Grice's SAT for literary criticism at about the same time as Pratt. Altieri's attraction to Grice is a development from his early attempts to use Austin's and Searle's SAT to define literature and the activity of reading, and to refine the concept of mimesis. Initially, Altieri, like Ohmann and Iser, saw SAT as a way to transcend the limits of formalist, contextualist, and structuralist criticism.[16] He sought to replace a static model of the text as an end with a temporal textual model and an emphasis on the activity of reading. Critical of Ohmann's need to see poetry as social criticism, however, Altieri espouses a Burkean view of language as symbolic action instead. Above all, Altieri shares with Fish and Pratt a humanistic view of the value of literature in a world that grants scientific models great prestige. He seeks to use speech acts to "justify the humane value of poetry" by "showing how certain forms of cognition disclose qualities which are not adequately explained by scientific models of human experience" (PA, 107).

Altieri first used SAT against the old orthodoxies; later he used it against newer ones. In "The Hermeneutics of Literary Indeterminacy: A Dissent from the New Orthodoxy," Altieri uses SAT to counter the growing tendency to view literary meaning as not fixed but indeterminate.[17] Altieri is attracted to SAT as a model for focusing on criteria of meaning based on use rather than truth or falsity and on reading as an activity based on rule-governed procedures or conventions. Altieri locates the problem in current theories of indeterminacy using theories of language based on an inadequate dichotomy between emotive and referential language. This dichotomy leads to a theory of meaning needing to be updated by SAT's focus on use and procedure. Psychological theories of indeterminacy practise a "naive empiricism" which "reduces objectivity to discussions of physical properties and banishes all other forms of meaning to essentially individual acts" (HLI, 77). According to SAT, reading is not a matter of physical properties, which are brute facts, but of the institutional facts of procedures for reading that members of a culture share through their education.

In *Act & Quality,* Altieri counters Derrida's philosophical scepticism by presenting a modified SAT based on Wittgenstein's later views on language and an expansion of the theories of Grice.[18] For Altieri, within a system without grounds for absolute truth, Wittgenstein's focus on making sense of experiences by relating them to language games provides a modicum of certainty and an analysis of public agreement preferable to Derrida's scepticism.

Altieri criticizes Austin's reliance on rule-governed procedures and conventions, finding Austin's conventions neither clear nor complex enough to explain institutional features of illocutionary acts. He faults Searle for reducing what one does in saying something to merely functional, typical attitude types. Interested in just that aspect of Austin's work Searle ignores, Altieri would replace Austin's reliance on conventions with more flexible forms of determinacy based on Wittgenstein's theory of grammatical competence.

Like Pratt, then, Altieri is interested in the way Grice's theories provide attention to interpretation that Austin's and Searle's theories lack. Whereas Pratt seems to adopt Grice's regulative sense of convention without distinguishing it from Austin's constitutive sense of the term, Altieri is specifically attracted to Grice's nonconventional model of implicature as an improvement over Austin's reliance on rules. Altieri criticizes those who wrongly hold Grice accountable to the charges of vagueness more rightly attributable to Austin's rules. In fact, Altieri feels Austin probably confined himself to conventions in order to avoid problems of interpretation and intention precisely by staying within a constitutive, rather than a regulative, framework. Altieri prefers Grice's maxims, or moral reasonings, because they specify pragmatic principles speakers understand as conditions of communication and so establish the probable hermeneutic strategies speakers assume an audience will apply.

Altieri attempts to correct Austin's and Grice's lack of attention to the specific *way* utterances are said by his own theory of expressive implicature, which like Pratt's is interested in the deliberate flouting of maxims. Altieri adds to the semantic and syntactic bases of Austin's and Searle's linguistic choices a behavioral framework based on Grice's work. Altieri's model makes a difference in its accommodation of attention to tone, style, or the *way* an utterance is said.

"I warn you that I shall come," an explicit performative according to Austin and Searle, becomes problematic if intended as a somewhat ironic, self-deprecating promise. Neither they nor Grice can account for the way "the utterance seems to vacillate between what it says and what it conventionally accomplishes" (*AQ*, 89). For Altieri, the tone represents not only a projection of the speaker's self-knowledge and self-conscious control but also an invitation to the listener to assess the speaker's dramatic stance, the intersection of literary and existential meaning.

Like Fish and Pratt, Altieri is concerned with an over-reliance in literary studies on scientific models which explain human behavior in terms of causal laws. Altieri's interest in correcting a denial of human agency in textualism parallels Fish's earlier criticism of stylistics. Altieri, however, is interested in specifying principles for understanding as publicly determinate, the terms in which agents might understand and describe the purposive qualities of their acts, in order to prevent "the inherent reductionism in forcing significant particulars into premature generalizations" (*AQ*, 101). He is concerned to use SAT to show the way bundles of possible meanings take on a single coherent communicative or expressive role in specific situations.

Rewriting Speech Acts: Deconstructive Responses

If Ohmann put SAT on the map for literary studies and Fish established the critique of the relationship between speech-act and literary theory, Jacques Derrida took the possibilities and limitations of SAT itself to new heights. His critique burst on the scene through a battle of words with Searle, which exploded such oppositions as "serious" and "nonserious" and the question of the subject on which SAT is based.

In 1977 *Glyph* published "Signature Event Context," Derrida's critique of the concepts of context and intention at the heart of Austin's SAT.[19] This essay displays Derrida's affinity for Austin's "critique of linguisticism," in which the emphasis on force rather than the truth value of utterances seems Nietzschean. Derrida's main interest, however, lies in Austin's expressed doubts and objections to his own changing train of thought. In fact, Derrida finds Austin's analysis "often more fruitful in the acknowledgment of its impasses than in its positions" (SEC, 187). Clearly attracted to the problematic aspects of Austin's work, Derrida presents implications of that work Austin did not seem to see.

Derrida seems attracted by the revolutionary possibilities of many of Austin's insights. He points out that while Austin emphasizes speech acts as communication, his notion of performatives changes the traditional notion of communication as transferring a semantic content "already constituted and dominated by an orientation toward truth" (SEC, 187). The performative seems to eliminate the idea of a referent existing "outside of itself." Rather than describing "something that exists outside of language and prior to it," it "produces or transforms a situation" (SEC, 186).

For Derrida, however, Austin does not go far enough. His concept of performatives ultimately relies on the ability to determine absolutely what Austin calls the total context. This total context is inextricably intertwined with the idea of intention, because an exhaustively definable context necessarily involves the sense of "a free consciousness present to the totality of the operation, and of absolutely meaningful speech" (SEC, 188). Derrida, however, proceeds to "show why a context is never absolutely determinable, or rather why its determination can never be entirely certain or saturated" (SEC, 174). As he does so, he reveals how Austin's observations do not go far enough.

Derrida argues that communication is structured by the necessity of repeatability in the necessary absence of the communication from its author, as most readily seen in the example of writing. For Derrida, what constitutes a writing is its ability to continue to "act" and be readable even when its "author" "no longer answers for what he has written" due to his temporary absence or death or because he hasn't used "his absolutely actual and present intention or attention, the plenitude of his desire to say what he means" (SEC, 181). Furthermore, Derrida argues, that communication (like *all* language) "must be repeatable—iterable—in the absolute absence of the receiver" or "any empirically determinable collectivity of receivers" as well (SEC, 179).

The idea that all linguistic utterances are structured on the possibility of being repeated requires a rethinking of the traditional concept of context. Since iterability is a structure of language in the broadest sense, he states that because "every sign, linguistic or nonlinguistic, spoke or written" always has the possibility of being cited, or "put in quotation marks," it always has the possibility of breaking with every given context, "engendering an infinity of new contexts in a manner which is absolutely illimitable" (SEC, 185). For Derrida, this means not "that the mark is valid outside of a context" but rather "that there are only contexts without any center or absolute anchoring." This citationality, a form of iterability, then, is similarly not an accident but rather that aspect which structures the possibility of the mark (SEC, 186).

Ultimately, Derrida sees Austin as teetering on the brink of revolutionary insights whose consequences he fails to develop. Thus, Austin did give some notice to the phenomenon Derrida describes. In fact, Derrida supplies that "very general high-level doctrine" Austin noted would be required. Because his own interests were local and specific, however, Austin was unconcerned to sketch the general theory himself. Describing felicitous and infelicitous performative conditions, Austin carefully noted that "infelicity is an ill to which *all* acts are heir which have the general character of ritual or ceremonial, all *conventional acts,*" but Austin characteristically also noted that this observation "failed to excite" him (*HTD,* 18–19). Consequently, he relegated the phenomenon to a possible exception from his rules, one he excluded from further consideration.

Not surprisingly, Derrida locates problems in SAT in Austin's failure to understand that his exception in fact constitutes the structure of all locutions. Derrida criticizes Austin's consideration of conventionality *solely* in terms of the "contextual surroundings of the utterance," rather than paying attention to "a certain conventionality intrinsic to what constitutes the speech act itself" (SEC, 189). Derrida also faults Austin's failure to "ponder the consequences issuing from the fact that a possibility—a possible risk—is *always* possible, and is in some sense a necessary possibility" (SEC, 189). Ultimately, Derrida sees this failure to take the structure of locutions into account as blinding Austin to the way his entire opposition between successful and unsuccessful performative utterances is "quite insufficient and secondary" compared to the constituting structure (SEC, 189). Of most interest to literary studies, however, is Derrida's similar objection to Austin's famous exclusion of literature in favor of focusing on ordinary language:

> A performative utterance, will, for example, be *in a peculiar way* hollow or void if said by an actor on the stage, or if introduced in a poem, or spoken in soliloquy. This applies in a similar manner to any and every utterance—a-sea-change in special circumstances. Language is in special ways—intelligibly—used not seriously, but in ways *parasitic* upon its normal use—ways which fall under the doctrine of the *etiolations* of language. All this we are *excluding* from consideration. Our performative utterances, felicitous or not, are to be understood as issued in ordinary circumstances. (*HTD*, 22)

Derrida argues that here again what Austin excludes as "anomaly, exception, 'non-serious,' *citation* (on stage, in a poem, or a soliloquy)" is instead *one* manifestation of "a general citationality—or rather, a general iterability—without which there would not even be a 'successful' performative" (SEC, 191). In short, according to Derrida, citationality in plays, philosophical references, or recitations of poems differs from other utterances not in *kind* but in degree.

What we have then is a chain of marks, rather than Austin's opposition between "citational utterances, on the one hand, and singular and original event-utterances, on the other" (SEC, 192). In this way, Derrida demonstrates that Austin's larger opposition between serious and nonserious uses of language, or ordinary and nonordinary language, does not hold. The collapse of this distinction involves a critique of Austin's concepts of intention and context. Derrida carefully points out that intention does not disappear: "It will have its place." But that place will be different: "It will no longer be able to govern the entire scene and system of utterance" (SEC, 192). Most significantly, because of the structure of iteration, "the intention animating the utterance will never be through and through present to itself and to its content" (SEC, 192). Austin's concept of an exhaustively determinable context, implying a "conscious intention that would at the very least have to be totally present and immediately transparent to itself and to others" (SEC, 192), can no longer be maintained.

Derrida does not argue that there is no performative effect. Rather, he says that "those effects do not exclude what is generally opposed to them" but "presuppose it, in an asymmetrical way, as the general space of their possibility" (SEC, 193). For Derrida, that general space is "first of all spacing as a disruption of presence in a mark" which he calls writing (SEC, 193). Thus Derrida finally presents a critique of Austin's concept of the source of an utterance. Derrida notes Austin's assurance that the source of an oral utterance, which Austin locates in grammatical terms as the first person present indicative active voice, "is *present* to the utterance and its statement" (SEC, 193). Austin similarly assumes that the presence of the origin of a written utterance "is simply evident in and assured by a *signature*" added to it (SEC, 193).

Derrida uses the phenomenon of the signature as an example of the problem of attributing any utterance to a simply identifiable and identical source. Presenting the signature as another manifestation of the structure of iteration, Derrida argues that it functions or is readable only by having a repeatable, iterable, imitable form capable of being "detached from the present and singular intention of its production." Each production of a signature is necessarily a unique event, necessarily *removed* from its originating impulse: its sameness, "by corrupting its identity and its singularity, divides its seal" (SEC, 194).

Searle's "Reiterating the Differences: A Reply to Derrida," appearing in the same issue of *Glyph*, makes clear the differences between Searle's philosophy and Derrida's.[20] Their different approaches are characterized by their different styles of writing. Derrida presents a dialogue, with carefully chosen quotations from Austin woven into a long, complicated (some claim tortuous), step-by-step development of his arguments. Searle's writing, on the other hand, characterized by its tendency toward summation, brevity, clarity, and assertion, adopts the authority of the scientific model.

Searle attacks Derrida's notion that the three features traditionally attributed to writing alone—the fact that something remains after its inscription, that it constitutes a break with its context of production, and that the written sign constitutes a space—are in fact characteristics of all language. Asserting that the most important difference between written and spoken language is "the (relative) permanence of the written text over the spoken word" (RD, 200), Searle argues that Derrida assimilates features of written and spoken texts only by confusing iterability with the permanence of the text. Searle sees two different principles involved in the way written texts are weaned from their origins and the way "any expression can be severed from its meaning through the form of 'iterability' . . . exemplified by quotation" (RD, 200). Only the principle of permanence allowing written texts to be weaned from their origins is "genuinely graphematic."

More importantly, however, Searle disputes Derrida's argument that texts are not vehicles of intentionality. For Searle, in both writing and speaking intentionality plays the same role. "There is no getting away from intentionality, because *a meaningful sentence is just a standing possibility of the corresponding (intentional) speech act*." Accusing Derrida of being under the illusion that in order to exist or matter, intentions have to "*lay behind* the utterances," Searle asserts that intentions are neither separate processes from expressions nor necessarily conscious (RD, 202).

Ultimately, Searle accuses Derrida of presenting an "unrecognizable" Austin bearing "no relation to the original" (RD, 204), a misrepresentation based on a complete misunderstanding of Austin's intentions and attitudes. Derrida's questioning the status of parasitism entirely misunderstands Austin's attitude towards parasitism and reasons for excluding it from SAT. Claiming to "hold no brief for the details of Austin's theory of speech acts," Searle also claims his own article on the status of fictional discourse already answers Derrida. For Searle, Derrida fails to understand that Austin's exclusion of parasitic forms of discourse was a temporary matter of research methodology, completely without metaphysical import. Derrida also fails to see that for Austin parasitism is a "relation of logical dependence," completely devoid of the pejorative moral connotations Derrida finds. Derrida is "similarly mistaken" in claiming Austin thought parasitic discourse was not part of ordinary language. According to Searle, Austin simply uses "ordinary language" as opposed to "technical or symbolic or formalized language" (RD, 206). And Austin's point was not that plays and novels were not written in ordinary language but that quotations in them were not produced in ordinary *circumstances.*

Finally, Searle asserts that Derrida confuses "no less than three separate and distinct phenomena: iterability, citationality, and parasitism" (RD, 206). Derrida confuses parasitical with citational discourse, overlooking their great differences. For Searle, writing a poem or novel is not a matter of quoting anyone, while lines said on stage are repetitions of the author's words but not quotations. The difference is that in parasitic discourse "expressions are *used* and not mentioned" (RD, 206). Even more important for Searle, however, is his sense that parasitic discourse is a "determined modification of the rules for performing speech acts" but *not* a modification of iterability or citationality (RD, 206).

Derrida's confusion of "use" and "mention" here is similar to one Searle noted as an example of Derrida's "penchant for saying things that are obviously false" (RD, 206). Searle similarly finds Derrida's supposition that parasitism necessarily involves an exclusion of iterability, and thus the possibility of all performatives, invalid. And he finds Derrida's supposition "more than simply a misreading of Austin" (RD, 206). According to Searle, Derrida uses iterability in "the trivial sense" and fails to distinguish between the relation of logical dependency between fiction and nonfiction and the "contingent fact about the history of human languages" of the dependency of writing on speech (RD, 207).

Ultimately, Searle denies Derrida's contention that an understanding of iterability involves an understanding of the "essential absence of intention to the actuality of the utterance" (RD, 207). Searle asserts that iterability should be understood as both the repeated use of the same word type and the recursive and repeated application of the rules which allow speakers to recognize intentions. Thus, despite being "datable singular events in particular historical contexts," it is the recognition of speakers' intentions that enables speech acts to communicate an infinite number of different contents. For Searle, then, rather than being in conflict with intention, iterability is "a necessary condition of the particular forms of intentionality that are characteristic of speech acts" (RD, 208).

"Limited Inc a b c," Derrida's response to Searle's "Reply," is a tour de force which exposes and exploits the differences between Searle and Derrida.[21] In effect, "Limited Inc a b c" enacts a confrontation which "never quite takes place" between the suppositions to which Searle firmly adheres and the questioning of those suppositions Derrida seeks (LI, 198). In a dazzling display of wit and erudition, "Limited Inc" demonstrates the way differences between Searle's insistence on seriousness, science, and logic and Derrida's contrasting spirit of expansiveness, parody, and play are more than simply a matter of style. Of most interest to literary studies is the way "Limited Inc" explodes the opposition between serious and nonserious discourse on which the exclusion of literature from SAT is based. "Limited Inc" accomplishes this end by employing such "nonserious" techniques as parody to question the certainty with which SAT maintains its clear separation between what is serious and what is not.

Through its spirit of parodic play "Limited Inc" presents an example of how there is always the possibility of "a certain element of play" inscribed in the structure of iterability. "Limited Inc" plays with the seriousness and dogmatic assertion of an authoritive hold on truth that are part of the scientific stance of Searle's "Reply." Its complexity and ingenuity are part of its point about oversimplifications in Searle's assumptions. But "Limited Inc" also plays with its own stance. Questioning its own sincerity and intentions as well as those of Searle's reply, it raises the problem of establishing the certainty about sincerity and intentions that SAT requires. Thus, beyond the problems of Searle's reply and Derrida's response, it enacts the problems of the speech acts of all philosophical discourse.

The title "Limited Inc a b c" plays on the simplified notions of ownership of truth, texts, and meaning displayed in Searle's "Reply." It plays at once with Searle's need to "own" or copyright the truth or words of his reply and with his need to establish himself as the "owner" of the meaning of Austin's words, authorized to take Derrida to task for his misreadings. "Limited Inc" also plays with Searle's simple attribution of the authorship of his text. In a spirit reminiscent of Austin's mockery of scientific precision, Derrida notes that philosophical tradition and Searle's footnotes call for a more accurate attribution of authorship to at least "three + n authors." In order to avoid the ponderousness of the scientific expression "three + n authors," however, Derrida calls the collective authorship of Searle's "Reply" the "Société à résponsabilité limitée—literally, 'Society with Limited Responsibility' . . . normally abbreviated to *Sarl*" (LI, 170). This change of Searle's name to Sarl—like the changes Derrida rings on his own name ("Is my name still 'proper,' . . . when, in proximity to 'There. J. D." [pronounced, in French, approximately Der. J. D.], in proximity to 'Wo? Da.' in German, to 'Her. J. D.' . . . they begin to function as integral or fragmented entities?" [LI, 167]) and the way he plays with titles (abbreviating "Signature Event Context" to SEC, which he calls a "dry text")—questions the certitude with which Searle can posit a singly identifiable source for any utterance. For Derrida, at the origin of any utterance there can only be societies with limited responsibility. This challenge to simple ownership is continued in Derrida's feat of managing to quote the entire text of Searle's reply in separate quotations scattered throughout his response.

The "a b c" of Derrida's title suggests (in addition to his self-imposed restriction to the letters of the alphabet) a primer of basic principles of reading. "Limited Inc," however, is a primer that scrutinizes the conventions of reasonableness and good faith on which reading relies. At stake is Searle's stance as objective scientist. Derrida claims an analysis of the speech acts of the "Reply," its denials, seductions, and initiation of a confrontation that does not quite take place, reveals not a disinterested but a self-interested reading of Derrida. Derrida does not claim that Sarl's reading is wrong, for the ambiguity of Austin's words leaves room for both Sarl's and his points of view. What he shows, however, is the way the reading of Derrida in the "Reply," which Derrida is careful not to attribute to Searle himself, is partial—both incomplete and interested in maintaining the proprietary hold of the sole legitimate heir of Austin's ideas: "Something identifying itself so much with Austin that it can only read *Sec* feverishly" does not allow the possibility that someone else can question the "limits or the presuppositions of Austin's theory" (LI, 177). Ultimately, "Limited Inc" presents Sarl's reading as a domestication, an avoidance of the difficulty and uncertainty of questioning traditional concepts in order to provide the rest and certitude of maintaining them. According to Derrida, these interests do not let Sarl see the possibility that SEC might be doing something else: presenting a staged provocation of debate or providing a performance which defines the limits of the structure of oppositions on which SAT is based.

"Limited Inc" does not present a simple opposition between Sarl's interested reading and its own; it also probes the partiality of its own stance. Its refrain constantly questioning whether it is serious, when its seriousness might begin, and how we might know presents the problem of speech act's clear opposition between what is serious and what is not. This questioning refrain also shows the problem of ascertaining the sincerity on which the felicity of speech acts relies. By questioning Sarl's motives and its own, "Limited Inc" reveals the problems in SAT's reliances on the simple criteria of known intentions, desires, and needs to distinguish one speech act from another.

According to SAT, a promise is distinguished from a threat by the speaker's intention to do something for the hearer that the speaker is aware the hearer wishes done. To promise something the hearer does not want done is to issue a warning or a threat. "Limited Inc" explodes the neatness of this distinction by introducing the problem of unconscious desires. "Suppose that I seriously promise to criticize implacably each of Sarl's theses," states Derrida (LI, 216). Whether this constitutes a promise or a threat depends on knowing what Sarl wants. If Sarl doesn't want this critique, according to SAT, Derrida's statement constitutes a threat. But what if unconsciously Sarl wants to be threatened? Similarly, with Derrida. What if his unconscious wants to please Sarl by gratifying his wish to be criticized or to cause Sarl unhappiness by refusing to be critical or, conversely, wants to please Sarl by being uncritical or to cause pain by being critical? SAT is based on the exclusion of the unconscious to allow a clear and simple identification of speakers' and listeners' identities and intentions with the conscious ego. By introducing the question of the unconscious, "Limited Inc" makes the locations of the identities of speakers, hearers, and intentions unclear. In this way it questions the certitude with which we can know clearly both what the identities of speakers and listeners are and what their intentions and desires might be.

"Limited Inc" re-presents the main critique of SAT set forth in "SEC": the structure of iteration does not allow the structure of oppositions on which SAT is based—serious/nonserious, literal/metaphoric, ordinary/parasitic—to remain intact: "Iterability blurs *a priori* the dividing line that passes between these opposed terms, 'corrupting' it if you like, contaminating it parasitically, *qua* limit. What is remarkable about the mark includes the margin within the mark. The line delineating the margin can therefore never be determined, rigorously, it is never pure and simple" (LI, 210). Since such terms as "nonserious," "parasitic," and "metaphoric" are therefore purely external, they cannot simply be excluded in the way SAT attempts. "Parasitism," for example, "does not need the theatre or literature to appear. Tied to iterability, this possibility obtains constantly," as Austin was aware (LI, 232). Thus, according to "Limited Inc" SAT "neither can nor should begin" by excluding the possibility of theatrical or literary fiction because "this 'possibility' is part of the structure called 'standard'" (LI, 231). A promise that could not be reiterated (repeated, reproduced, cited, or mimed) would not be a promise, and therein lies the possibility of parasitism, even in what Sarl calls "real life": "as though literature, theatre, deceit, infidelity, hypocrisy, infelicity, parasitism, and the simulation of real life were not part of real life" (LI, 232). At work here, for Derrida, is a different kind of mimesis: "The 'pretended' forms of promise, on the stage or in a novel, cannot be 'pretended' except to the extent that the so-called 'standard' cases are reproduced, mimed, simulated, parasited, etc., as being in themselves reproducible, already 'parasiticable,' as already impure" (LI, 232).

Similarly, SAT tries to maintain a clear separation which does not hold between the serious, literal language of science and nonserious, metaphoric language. It justifies its idealizing methodology by analogy with the model for other sciences. Since this idealization means that SAT is based on nonliteral metaphoric language, however, the distinction SAT seeks cannot be maintained. In addition, the analogy does not take into account the crucial way SAT differs from other sciences by having as its object the speech acts of ordinary language.

Ultimately, "Limited Inc" presents a critique of SAT's stance as impartial science. SAT presents itself as uninvolved in the value system of the structure of oppositions which it inherits. Derrida agrees that its theoreticians do not morally advocate preference of the serious over the nonserious or the normal over the parasitic in ordinary language. But Derrida claims that since the opposition serious/nonserious cannot become the object of a strict, rigorous, and serious analysis without one of the two terms determining the value of the theoretical discourse itself, the discourse becomes an integral part of the object it claims to be analyzing. Determined by the hierarchy, the discourse can no longer be impartial or neutral but must produce speech acts that are in principle serious, literal, strict. "Because the model of speech act theory claims to be serious, it is normed by a part of its object and is therefore not impartial. It is not scientific and cannot be taken seriously" (LI, 211).

Derrida's crucial critique restores a complexity to SAT that Austin saw and Searle lost. The critiques of Paul de Man and Shoshana Felman emphasize differently the complex ways SAT must be rewritten.[22] De Man's contribution emphasizes the relationship between speech acts and rhetoric and the question of the self-reflexivity of literature.[23] Like Kenneth Burke, de Man regrets Austin's basing SAT on grammar at the expense of neglecting rhetoric.[24] In "Semiology and Rhetoric" de Man points out that SAT assumes an illocutionary realm governed by grammatical rules (usually considered generative and universal) and a perlocutionary realm governed by rhetoric seen exclusively as persuasion (as actual action on others rather than as an intralinguistic figure or trope).[25] The theory also assumes the movement from grammar to rhetoric is direct and uncomplicated, a continuity de Man finds naive.

In "Resistance to Theory," de Man praises "the most astute practitioners of a speech act theory of reading," especially Fish, for "rightly" insisting on the necessary separation of actual performance (illocutionary force) of speech acts from their causes and effects (perlocutionary function). The problem of this "exile" of persuasion to a "purely affective and intentional realm," however, is that it "makes no allowance" for rhetorical modes of persuasion in literary texts which operate "by *proof* rather than seduction." Characterizing the performative power of language as more properly called "positional" (that is, speaking from a subject) rather than "conventional," de Man states that "speech act oriented theories of reading read only to the extent that they prepare the way for the rhetorical reading they avoid."[26]

In contrast to de Man, however, Shoshana Felman is precisely interested in persuasion by seduction. Her analysis of SAT, *The Literary Speech Act: Don Juan with J. L. Austin; or, Seduction in Two Languages*, extends de Man's Nietzschean critique in a Derridean spirit of play.[27] *The Literary Speech Act* invites the reader to contemplate the seductive aspects of Austin's SAT as well as the implications for SAT, language, and theory in general in both Lacanian psychoanalysis and the literary drama of seduction and revenge of Molière's *Don Juan.* Like Derrida, Felman dispels the notion of the "impartial observer" and enacts the positional nature of language by declaring partiality for Austin. She is "seduced," she says, by the openness of Austin's theory as well as its potential for scandal. Like Derrida, too, Felman embraces the problematic Austin rather than seeking in him the security of scientific authority. Ultimately, she presents a critique of the limits of theory and of the scientific stance.

Felman likes not only what Austin says but what he does. Her critique emphasizes doing things with Austin's notion of the performative. In substituting the criterion of pleasure for that of truth, Felman sees Austin issuing a Don Juanian invitation to share both the pleasure and desire of language. Austin's teaching tries not to say but to *do,* not to incite to knowledge so much as to incite to desire and enjoyment. It enacts a theory of desire that seeks above all to communicate the desire of theory. Austinian "force" is constantly in excess over the meaning of the theoretical statement. And this excess of energy is continually discharged through humor, which is not a "saying" but a "doing." Austin invites his readers not just to pleasure but to the pleasure of scandal: "We shall most interestingly," as Austin put it, " 'have committed the act of bigamy' " (*LSA,* 113). This scandal is articulated indirectly, through the disparity between Austin's theoretical statements and his incongruous examples, which Felman likens to the case histories of psychoanalytic practise. These decentering examples subvert the cognitive evidence inherent in the constative. Through humor, Felman feels Austin presents an assault not only on constative knowledge but on power, political and analytical repression as well.

Felman finds that, like Lacan, Austin conveys the importance of the unconscious not through theses but through style. Criticizing Austin's followers for focusing on what Austin *says* while neglecting the importance of what Austin *does* with words, Felman analyzes Austin's style. She shows how through constant word play, ironic self-deprecations and qualifications, and parodic titles Austin doesn't merely add the criterion of pleasure but puts pleasure into play as something specific to speech acts. For example, Austin's title, "How to Do Things with Words," both parodies the facile instruction of fashionable how-to-do-it manuals and comments ironically on the authorial promise of teaching, suggesting that we are dealing with the "unteachable" noncognitive. The titles, subverting their own promises of new subjects, authorial authority, knowledge, or learning, show how Austin's knowledge "is no longer what is to be *seen* in *representation,* a spectacle" to be contemplated, but "what is to be *tasted* in a *feast* of language" and enjoyed (*LSA,* 102).

Fish showed readers how to do things with Austin and Searle; Felman shows the great difference between what Austin and Searle do. She emphasizes that this subversion of cognitive knowledge—achieved through Austin's ironic style—is precisely what Austin's followers have not been able to accept. Desiring cognitive knowledge made Austin's heirs focus on his statements—rather than acts—and miss what Austin actually does with words. Theoreticians have needed to know with certainty whether Austin was serious or unserious. But Felman feels these critics, by excluding Austin's jokes, fail to take Austin seriously. For her, Austin "displays seriousness" "not in order to 'play an unserious role' but—in his own words—'to play the devil'" (*LSA,* 131). Theory is "by definition foreign to humor" and "in the habit . . . of playing God: of 'underwriting,' by its authority of 'supposed knowledge' the values or theses it proposes." But Austin underwrites neither seriousness nor nonseriousness. With him, "the devil's chief characteristic is precisely that [like de Man and Derrida] 'he does not know' whether he is playing seriously or not" (*LSA,* 131). His performance doesn't turn seriousness against unseriousness but blurs the boundaries between them.

Because Austin's heirs have been unable to accept the play of undecidability that Austin presents, some have reproached him for a too-serious adherence to what is supposedly normal. Grice's theory of conversational implicature, on the other hand, attempts to correct Austin's adherence to the abnormal by eliminating the infelicities and normalizing the acts of language. The same is true for rule-makers like Searle. According to Felman, Austin's SAT is only accepted into the institution at the expense of its cutting edge, "the subversive aspect of seduction." Felman sees this process as emblematic of the historical *doing* of theory and the way "history *integrates* this doing in the very gesture of repressing its force and denying it (*LSA*, 144).

Felman's analysis brings us back to Austin where SAT began but with a difference. She emphasizes performatives and play over constatives and cognition. Returning to the beginnings of SAT, we can see a common thread pulling SAT and literary studies together. For Austin's original exclusion of literary language was an attempt to rid the language of philosophy of the jargon of the logical positivists, an attempt which would democratize philosophical language by connecting it to the language of the rest of society. The same thread runs through the application of SAT to literary studies. Ohmann and Fish, who tend to follow Searle, and such followers of Grice as Pratt and Altieri all attempt to relate literary language to the language of the rest of society. A main attraction between SAT and literary studies is their joint need to deal with the question of referentiality: the relationship between language, literature, and the rest of society. The deconstructive rewritings of SAT and the linguistically oriented applications see the question of referentiality in different ways. Linguistically oriented followers of Searle and Grice, seeking the certitude of science, focus on laws, conventions, and regulations relating literary and ordinary language. Deconstructive rewritings, on the other hand, question the laws of language that accord a privilege to ordinary language and relegate literature to parasitical status.

What began as an attempt to appropriate the validity of scientific method became a critique, not merely of the scientific method, but of the categories which would separate literature from science or constative from performative on which the original exclusion of literary language from SAT is based. Ultimately, linguistic and deconstructive rewritings reveal that literary language was in speech-act language from the beginning. In this way SAT poses questions which challenge the boundaries separating discipline from discipline, challenge the very intellectual territoriality which would create an opposition between literature and the rest of language. It demonstrates not only that language and its conventions constitute a reality but that that reality is inextricably political.

Fish pointed out that above all SAT is an ideology. It posits a speaking subject based on a human voice for all textuality. Deconstructive rewritings also pointed out the main problem with

SAT: its model of textuality as a human voice. One problem lies in the anthropomorphism of this model which seems to be a retreat from imagining laws of language beyond the conscious and intentional control of human subjects. Another problem lies in the androcentric nature of this model. While SAT centers attention on the question of voice and the nature of the speaking subject, it proceeds without any notion of sexual difference. SAT needs to take into account what difference the presence or absence of women's voices or women as speaking subjects makes in literary and other discourse.[28] Attention to this, which would bring feminist critical theory and SAT together in a new way, might undo another basic category of public discourse, the distinction based on women as plus or minus men.

NOTES

1. For this question with different purposes and results see Rodolphe Gasché, " 'Setzung' and 'Ubersetzung': Notes on Paul de Man," *Diacritics,* 11, no. 4 (1981), 36–57.
2. G. J. Warnock, "John Langshaw Austin, a Biographical Sketch," in *Symposium on J. L. Austin,* ed. K. T. Fann (London: Routledge and Kegan Paul, 1969), p. 6.
3. J. L. Austin, *How to Do Things with Words,* ed. J. O. Urmson and Marina Sbisá, 2nd ed. (Cambridge: Harvard University Press, 1962), p. 38, hereafter cited as *HDT.*
4. In addition to *HDT* see Austin's "Performative Utterances" in *Philosophical Papers,* ed. J. O. Urmson and G. J. Warnock, 3rd ed. (New York: Oxford University Press, 1979), pp. 233–52 (transcript of B.B.C. talk, 1956), and "Performative-Constative" in *The Philosophy of Language,* ed. John Searle (Oxford: Oxford University Press, 1971).
5. John Searle, "Austin on Locutionary and Illocutionary Acts," *The Philosophical Review,* 75 (1968), 405–24.
6. John Searle, *Speech Acts: An Essay in the Philosophy of Language* (Cambridge: Cambridge University Press, 1969), p. 24, hereafter cited as *SA.*
7. Richard Ohmann's articles include "Speech, Action, and Style," in *Literary Style: A Symposium,* ed. Seymour Chatman (New York: Oxford University Press, 1971), pp. 241–59; "Speech Acts and the Definition of Literature," *Philosophy and Rhetoric,* 4 (1971), 1–19;

"Speech, Literature and the Space Between," *New Literary History,* 4 (1972), 47–63; and "Literature as Act," in *Approaches to Poetics,* ed. Seymour Chatman (New York: Columbia University Press, 1973), pp. 81–108; hereafter cited as SAS, SAD, SLS, and LA.

8. See Wolfgang Iser, "The Reality of Fiction," *New Literary History,* 7 (1975), 7–38, hereafter cited as RF; Monroe Beardsley, *The Possibility of Criticism* (Detroit: Wayne State University Press, 1970); "Aesthetic Intentions and Fictive Illocutions," in *What Is Literature?* ed. Paul Hernadi (Bloomington: Indiana University Press, 1978); "The Concept of Literature," in *Literary Theory and Structure,* ed. Frank Brady, John Palmer, and Martin Price (New Haven: Yale University Press, 1973); Barbara Herrnstein Smith, "Poetry as Fiction," *NLH* (1971), 259–81.

9. John Searle, "The Logical Status of Fictional Discourse," *New Literary History,* 6 (1975), 319–32, hereafter cited as LSFD; Iser, "The Reality of Fiction."

10. For writing as a separate speech act of hypothesizing, imagining, etc., see *Pragmatics of Language and Literature,* ed. Teun A. Van Dijk (North Holland: Elsevier, 1976), especially Samuel R. Levin, "Concerning what kind of speech act a poem is," pp. 141–60.

11. Stanley Fish's articles are collected in *Is There a Text in This Class?: The Authority of Interpretive Communities* (Cambridge: Harvard University Press, 1980), hereafter cited as *ITT.*

12. For H. D. Grice's work see "Meaning," *Philosophical Review,* 66 (1957), 377–88, "Utterer's Meaning, Sentence-Meaning and Word-Meaning," *Foundations of Language,* 4 (1968), 225–42, "Logic and Conversation," in *Syntax and Semantics,* vol. 3: *Speech Acts,* ed. Peter Cole and Jerry L. Morgan (New York: Academic Press, 1975), pp. 41–58.

13. All maxims are quoted from "Logic and Conversation," pp. 45–46.

14. Mary Louise Pratt, *Toward a Speech Act Theory of Literary Discourse* (Bloomington: Indiana University Press, 1977), hereafter cited as *TSAT.*

15. For criticism of Pratt see Michael Hancher, "Beyond a Speech-Act Theory of Literary Discourse," *MLN,* 92 (1977), 1081–98, and Joseph Margolis, "Literature and Speech Acts," *Philosophy and Literature,* 3 (1979), 39–52.

16. Charles Altieri, "The Poem as Act: A Way to Reconcile Presentational and Mimetic Theories," *Iowa Review,* 6 (1975), 103–24, hereafter cited as PA, "A Procedural Definition of Literature," in Hernadi, *What Is Literature,* pp. 62–78, "Presence and Reference in a Literary Text: The Example of Williams' 'This Is Just to Say,'" *Critical Inquiry,* 5

(Spring 1979), 489–510, and "The Qualities of Action Part I and II," *Boundary 2,* 5 (1977), 323–50, 899–917.

17. Charles Altieri, "The Hermeneutics of Literary Indeterminacy: A Dissent from the New Orthodoxy," *NLH,* 10 (Autumn 1978), 71–99, hereafter cited as HLI.
18. Charles Altieri, *Act and Quality* (Amherst: University of Massachusetts Press, 1981), hereafter cited as *AQ*.
19. Jacques Derrida, "Signature Event Context," *Glyph 1* (Baltimore: Johns Hopkins University Press, 1977), pp. 162–254, hereafter cited as SEC, reprinted in *Margins of Philosophy,* trans. Alan Bass (Chicago: University of Chicago Press, 1982).
20. John Searle, "Reiterating the Differences: A Reply to Derrida," *Glyph 1,* pp. 198–208, hereafter cited as RD.
21. Jacques Derrida, "Limited Inc a b c," *Glyph* 2 (Baltimore: Johns Hopkins University Press, 1977), p. 198, hereafter cited as LI. See also Gayatri Spivak's "Revolutions That As Yet Have No Model: Derrida's 'Limited Inc,'" *Diacritics,* 10 (1980), 29–49.
22. For an excellent discussion of the difference between Paul de Man's deconstruction and that of Derrida, see Barbara Fletcher, "*Speculations*—on '(Derri)Da,'" diss., University of Florida, 1984.
23. For opposing views on de Man and self-reflexivity see Gasché, "'Setzung,'" and Suzanne Gearhart, "Philosophy *Before* Literature: Deconstruction, Historicity, and the Work of Paul de Man," *Diacritics,* 13 (Winter 1983), 63–81.
24. See Kenneth Burke's review of Austin, *How to Do Things with Words,* "Words as Deeds," *Centrum,* 3, no 2 (Fall 1975), 147–68.
25. Paul de Man, "Semiology and Rhetoric," first appeared in *Diacritics,* 3 (Fall 1973), 27–33. Hereafter cited in the text from de Man's *Allegories of Reading* (New Haven: Yale University Press, 1979), pp. 3–19.
26. Paul de Man, "Resistance to Theory," *Yale French Studies,* 63 (1982), 19.
27. Shoshana Felman, *The Literary Speech Act: Don Juan with J. L. Austin; or, The Seduction in Two Languages,* trans. Catherine Porter (Ithaca: Cornell University Press, 1983), hereafter cited as *LSA*.
28. There has been curiously little attempt to integrate speech-act and feminist criticism. See Susan Snaider Lanser's *The Narrative Act: Point of View in Prose Fiction* (Princeton: Princeton University Press, 1981), my "Women's Words as Weapons: Speech as Action in 'The Wife's Lament,'" *Texas Studies in Literature and Language,* 23 (Summer 1981), 268–85, and my "Feminism and Speech Act Theory," in progress.

TEMMA F. BERG

Psychologies of Reading

POSTMODERN LITERARY THEORY HAS BECOME, almost more than anything else, the problematics of reading, for to examine the process of reading is to raise a host of difficult, though fascinating, questions. Above all, we want to know, How *do* we read? Can we construct a model of reading which will indicate how reading *may* occur without, as is usually the case, insisting on how we believe reading *should* occur? How *do* text and reader affect one another? (Indeed, is there a text?) What purpose does reading serve? How do we assimilate, appropriate, and use what we have read? How does our reading change us? Ultimately, questions about reading lead us to questions about self and its relationship to the world it encounters.

Indeed, the problematics of reading includes within it nearly every other category named in this book. Critics of reading have incorporated much from structuralism, hermeneutics, phenomenology, semiotics, historiography, communication theory, and speech-act theory and have in turn influenced all these fields. Feminist theory is, in some ways, a special case of reader-response theory. How do women read? How should women read? Do women read differently than men? A chapter on reading is, necessarily, concerned with difference. And certainly, as my calculated use of that overdetermined term "difference" might indicate, my essay, as a whole, is meant to suggest that deconstruction has affected and continues to affect the course of reader-response theory. Though a complete historical survey of the reader-response movement and its interrelationships with other twentieth-century literary movements would be beyond the scope of this chapter, I have selected out for extended discussion those critics, those works, and those relationships which have exerted the greatest pressure on the movement as it has taken shape in America during the latter half of this century. I trace the roots of the reader-response movement in I. A. Richards's work with students and locate its branches in the work of Louise Rosenblatt, Stanley Fish, Wolfgang Iser, Hans Robert Jauss, Norman Holland, David Bleich, and Harold Bloom.

Ironically, while I. A. Richards is ordinarily appreciated as the man who first diagnosed reading as a problem and fathered a movement which purported to suppress the reader in support of a positivist text, reexamination of his work reveals some interesting affinities with that of later reader-response critics. Richards's early work was written in reaction to what he viewed as the sterile aestheticism of his precursors and contemporaries. He wanted to take critics like Clive Bell and A. C. Bradley to task for what he saw as their mistaken emphasis on an "aesthetic experience" and their belief that art and the aesthetic should be divorced from life. In *The Principles of Literary Criticism*, Richards suggests that when we talk about our experience of a poem we talk about our state of mind, not about an external autonomous object like the text or quality like beauty.[1] Poems, for Richards, are concrete experiences.

In his work, Richards sought a foundation for the experience of reading poetry in the actual psychological processes of the mind. He sought a biology of the mind which would explain what happened during a "mental event" (*PLC*, 88). As Richards concluded long ago, "A theory of feeling, of emotion, of attitudes and desires, of the effective-volitional aspect of mental activity, is required at all points of our analysis" (*PLC*, 91). Though Richards broke the experience of reading into six parts—seeing the words, seeing closely associated visual images, seeing freer images, "thinking of" various contingent things, feeling emotion, and displaying an attitude (*PLC*, 117–18)—he clearly recognized his explanation was not completely satisfactory. Once he reached stage 4 of his breakdown—thinking of various contingent thoughts—he came to a labyrinth of infinitely branching possibilities: "It is difficult to represent diagrammatically what takes place in thought in any satisfactory fashion. The impulse coming in from the visual stimulus of the printed word must be imagined as reaching some system in the brain in which effects take place not due merely to this present stimulus, but also to past occasions on which it has been combined with other stimulations. These effects are thoughts; and they in their groupings act as signs for yet other thoughts" (*PLC,* 131). His meticulously drawn network of neurological connections could not contain what he wanted it to contain.

Richards sought to contain the reading experience not only by describing the path of the poem across the individual brain but by valuing correct apprehension. He never gave up his early belief that a correct reading could be obtained and that it was the reader's job to get it. The reader must discriminate between and evaluate various experiences of a poem and find the one most adequate to it. Key principles for Richards are communication, value, and discrimination. Ringing with Arnoldian phrases, all of Richards's work attests to his belief that reading rightly enables us to live rightly. "The arts, if rightly approached, supply the best data available for deciding what experiences are more valuable than others" (*PLC,* 33).

In *Practical Criticism,* Richards explains his program for improving the reading experience.[2] First, he asks his students to write down their "free" responses to poems he gives them. Richards does not identify the authors of the poems, so students (ideally) do not know if they are commenting on a poem by Shakespeare or Ella Wheeler Wilcox. The students are given a week to develop their readings and are under no pressure to turn a reading in at the end of that time, so, presumably, the protocols Richards collects are the result of willing and concentrated effort. Nevertheless, the protocols display a bewildering variety of contradictory responses. They are fascinating, and when we realize that some of them may have been written by Joan Bennett, M. C. Bradbrook, and William Empson (to name just a few of Richards's students), they become even more so. They bear witness to how even privileged students (privileged by birth and education) from very similar backgrounds and with very similar goals (to become educators in turn) can yet produce widely divergent readings. After discussing the various protocols, Richards then demonstrates to his students how close reading will help them avoid future mistakes. Richards saw divergence as a problem, and he believed the solution was better education. He did not seem to see how what he saw as one primary reason for error becomes, even in his own book, one primary path toward correction. That is, Richards complains that his readers come to the poems with too many contexts and presuppositions and interests; however, he also complains that they lack enough contexts, the contexts (presuppositions and predispositions) that would enable them to appreciate and value certain poems appropriately. Richards sees and does not see that readings are not found but made—made by the contexts the reader brings to bear on the text. For example, after discussing a series of very negative protocols on the same poem, all dismissing it as sentimental and naive, he writes, "Another reading is possible, one by which the poem becomes a very unusual kind of thing that it would be a pity to miss. That so few read it in this way is not surprising for if there is any character in poetry that modern readers—who derive their ideas of it rather from the best known poems of Wordsworth, Shelley and Keats or from our contemporaries, than from Dryden, Pope, or Cowper—are unprepared to encounter, it is this social, urbane, highly cultivated, self-confident, temperate and easy kind of humor" (*PC*, 170). Clearly Richards here recognizes how large a part context plays in the reading process. We read according to strategies derived from our reading. We approach the unknown in terms of the known. Why then does Richards not go on to suggest that education give us those strategies? Perhaps because there is a part of Richards at war with his increasing insight into the complexity and irreducibility of the reading experience: a desire for unity and agreement, a desire which led him, toward the end of his career, to spend a great amount of energy urging educators to accept Basic English, his proposal for facilitating world communication and bringing world peace.

In general, Richards became more desperate in his attempts to reduce what he called "unnecessary misunderstanding" (*PC*, 318) as he grew to realize how inevitable misunderstanding was, how reading was, in the end, at least from one perspective (the perspective of belief in that elusive "correct" reading), always a matter of misinterpretation. Even in his early works Richards posed the problem of reading as an epistemological one: "As a rule a process of extraordinary complexity takes place between perceiving the situation and finding a mode of meeting it" (*PC*, 102). While here he sees a break between perceiving and interpretation (a mode of meeting), in *Practical Criticism,* this distinction breaks down: "The reception (or interpretation) of a meaning is an activity" (*PC*, 174n). Reception and interpretation are no longer distinct moments, they are one. However, as the above citation goes on to suggest, Richards still hankers after correctness: "an activity which may go astray; in fact, there is always some degree of loss and distortion in transmission." But as eager as he is for correctness, he is aware of its impossibility. In *How to Read a Page,* Richards makes perhaps his most startling admission about the reading experience: "But in all reading whatsoever much must be left out. Otherwise we could arrive at no meaning. The omission is essential in the twofold sense: without omission no meaning would form *for us;* and through the omission what we are trying to grasp becomes *what it is* (gets its essential being)."[3] He goes on to make an even more startling confession: "The Proper Meaning of a passage (what it really means) is a kind of scholastic ghost with very much less in it than a good reader will quite rightly find there" (*HRP,* 94). Richards could scarcely go much farther in anticipating that student of his who used the title of his book as a title for a chapter, making one small but significant change—"To Reap a Page." Of course, even in this Richards anticipated Geoffrey Hartman, for he considered the alternate title: "We assume we know how to read: spell it *reap,* and we begin to wonder how we do it" (*HRP,* 9). Spell it *reap,* and we wonder how far reader-response has been able to take us from the Derridean impasse Richards found himself in.

Louise Rosenblatt, whose *Literature as Exploration* first appeared in 1938, sees herself as deeply influenced by I. A. Richards, noting that while the New Critics drew on him in one way (selecting out his emphasis on close reading as technique), she drew on him in a very different way. Because of her training in phenomenological philosophy (and her abiding belief in the subjectivity of all experience), she drew on that part of Richards which "reinforced [her] interest in the reader's response."[4] However, while Rosenblatt urges educators to pay attention to the individuality of reader-response, she also urges a sense of "responsibility" toward the text. Ultimately, because her emphasis is on the educator's need to enable the student to explore literature as a vital resource for living in the world and because she follows her predecessor in his allegiance to Arnold, Rosenblatt presents literature as a vehicle for shared cultural values, as a means to the good life.

We read, according to Rosenblatt, in order to learn: "The reader seeks to participate in another's vision—to reap knowledge of the world, to fathom the resources of the human spirit, to gain insights that will make his own life more comprehensible" (*LE*, 7). Accordingly, Rosenblatt designed *Literature as Exploration* as a guide for teachers of literature. Just as the reader must be responsible to the text, the teacher must be responsible to the student. Rosenblatt's pedagogy is deeply ethical. For Rosenblatt, the aesthetic and the social are not divorced from one another; they are, in fact, the same. The aesthetic experience is a social experience. Furthermore, it is an educational experience.

Rosenblatt sees the reading process as an interaction between text and reader. Though the reader will bring his psychological, social, and cultural environment to bear during any reading of a particular text, the text will exert its own force on the reader. "Because the text is organized and self-contained, it concentrates the reader's attention and regulates what will enter into his consciousness" (*LE*, 33). However, her descriptions of *how* the text regulates the reader's consciousness remain exceedingly abstract. Since Rosenblatt was taking a position antithetical to the prevailing notion of her day, which reified the text into an unassailable object, to explain how the text worked was superfluous. What *her* reader needed to consider was the neglected reader. And it is here, in the area of expanding and defending the reader's unique experience of the text, that Rosenblatt excels. She cannot repeat often enough her belief in the student's need for a vital "personal sense of literature" (*LE*, 60).

Rosenblatt wants to help the teacher create an atmosphere within which the student can "have an unself-conscious, spontaneous, and honest reaction" (*LE*, 67). In Rosenblatt's first book, literature is presented as a potentially liberating experience. It fosters empathy, facilitates acculturation, and offers us release from narrow provincialism. Though Rosenblatt occasionally wonders about the possibly negative results of reading—"To what extent, for example, can the influence of literature be held responsible for the fact that many women today find within themselves emotional obstacles to their sincere ambition to be independent emotionally and intellectually?" (*LE*, 221n)—and thus can suggest in one compassionate sentence a vital concern of feminist critical theory, in the end she suggests reading is usually beneficent, tutelary, and satisfying (*LE,* 222–23).

In *The Reader, the Text, the Poem* (1978), Rosenblatt retains the widely anthropological view of her first book and continues to look at literature as one of the many interdependent aspects of culture.[5] However, in her second book she elaborates her model of reading in two ways. First, she explains how a reader makes a text a poem. And, second, she formulates a distinction between two different kinds of reading.

The poem is an event, according to Rosenblatt. The reader and the text share a transactional experience. "First the text is a stimulus activating elements of the reader's past experience with literature and with life. Second, the text serves as a blueprint, a guide for the selecting, rejecting, and ordering of what is being called forth; the text regulates what shall be held in the forefront of the reader's attention" (*RTP,* 11). The "poem" is the aesthetic transaction between the reader and text; the "poem" is what reader and text create together. Reader and text interact, condition each other. Rosenblatt presents reading, or the aesthetic transaction, as a vital, organic, synthesizing activity.

To make clearer what she means by aesthetic transaction, Rosenblatt goes on to discriminate aesthetic from efferent reading. When we read efferently, we are reading to obtain information. When we read a textbook, when we read the label on a medicine bottle, we are not interested in the words themselves; we are only interested in what they have to tell us. However, when we read aesthetically, we are paying attention to the whole language experience—sound, rhythm, economy, ambiguity, etc. When we read efferently, we read to take some necessary fact away with us. When we read aesthetically, we read to live through the text (*RTP,* 27–28). This distinction enables Rosenblatt to perceive the reader as directing her reading experience, as choosing to take a cognitive or emotional stance (or one that combines elements of both stances). However, like most critics of reading, Rosenblatt disparages one particular aspect of the reading process—the tendency to be so emotionally carried away that we jeopardize our aesthetic distance. She describes an incident of going to the theater and realizing that the woman next to her was reacting so strongly to the performance that it looked as if she might jump on stage to warn Othello. Rosenblatt suggests the woman was reacting efferently rather than aesthetically to the performance and ends by implying that in this case her response was inappropriate, since the woman lost the necessary aesthetic distance (*RTP*, 80–81).

In sum, though Rosenblatt seeks to open the text to different possible interpretations, to see the text as a tapestry whose threads the reader can pull to create different experiences, still she presents a notion of the appropriate and the inappropriate, the correct and the incorrect. The text is not a Rorschach blot, reading is not a game of free association; reading is the intense aesthetic exploration of as much of a text's potential as possible.

While Rosenblatt's conception of reading remains consistent from her early to her later work, the work of Stanley Fish shifts radically. In 1980, he conveniently telescoped the dialectic in his changing critical position by publishing in a single volume essays which had appeared in various academic journals over a ten-year period. This book, entitled *Is There a Text in This Class?: The Authority of Interpretive Communities*, makes exceedingly clear Fish's movement toward a poststructuralist position, asserting, at the same time, as the title paradoxically implies, that there is no text in the classroom and that there is. While in his early work Fish concentrates on the way in which the reader experiences the text, in his later work he explores the contexts that influence the way the reader reads.

Fish first defined his reader in *Surprised by Sin: The Reader in "Paradise Lost."* Fish suggests in this book that the experience of reading *Paradise Lost* is analogous to the losing of paradise. The reader is continually led into entangling Satanic rhetoric, complex similes, and tortuous syntax in order to be instructed in the limitations of his human and necessarily fallible perspective. The reader will necessarily stumble if she chooses to depend on her own unaided reason to thread the labyrinthine verse of the poem. The poem advocates faith in Jesus Christ, and readers, if they are to demonstrate this faith, must escape the many pitfalls to which the reading of *Paradise Lost* will lead them if they do not hold fast. All those romantic readers who sided with Satan were surprised by sin and led into error. The reader who reads correctly will not side with Satan. Fish's definition of the "informed reader" is ultimately derived from Milton.[6] The reader is fit and, necessarily, part of a very small group. In fact, by the end of *Surprised by Sin,* it becomes clear that Fish is the only fit reader of *Paradise Lost.* Every other reader—Frye, Empson, C. S. Lewis, Watkins, Ricks, etc.—errs in one way or another.

Though Fish at first urged the reader to respond to cues "in the text," as his work progressed his focus changed. In *Self-Consuming Artifacts: The Experience of Seventeenth-Century Literature,* he suggests that the reader formulates the text according to the interpretive assumptions he brings to his reading.[7] For example, when he created the category "self-consuming artifacts," he was not actually accounting for certain anomalies he encountered in his reading but naming a pre-given perceptual category that dictated the shape of his reading. Fish's reading is thus shaped by a version of the hermeneutic circle. Certain aspects of reading catch Fish's eye. He creates a category to account for them. Then this category takes on an active role and shapes his reading. Fish then "discovers" that the category has (already) determined his reading of the texts which led to his discovery of that category.

Fish prefers to see the reader in the grip of an interpretive strategy or perceptual category. Although this concept has now grown to include the notion of interpretive communities, the reader is still tightly controlled. The reader will "write" the text he reads according to the interpretive strategy of the interpretive community to which he belongs. A reader may belong to several different interpretive communities during his lifetime, but it is his membership within a particular interpretive community and his deployment of a particular interpretive strategy that constitutes the text for him. Thus the text changes for any particular reader as he moves from one interpretive community to another or as the communities themselves follow a process of growth and decline.

The text changes, according to Fish, because the operations that bring it into being change. However, the range of change is severely circumscribed because the reader cannot bring just any operations to bear on a particular text. The reader is always already in a situation, a member of an interpretive community, or of a series of interpretive communities, which reads the text for him. The community, or communities, provides the reader with the tools he needs. In an article which appeared in *Critical Inquiry* in summer

1982, "With the Compliments of the Author: Reflections on Austin and Derrida," Fish uses speech-act theory to explain how interpretive communities work.[8] Interpretive communities make "facts." "Facts" are products of conventions, and conventions enable us to understand the activities we engage in, whether we are playing baseball or reading a novel. "The 'facts' of a baseball game, of a classroom situation, of a family reunion, of a trip to the grocery store, of a philosophical colloquium on the French language are only facts for those who are proceeding within a prior knowledge of the purposes, goals, and practices that underlie those activities. Again, this does not mean that there is no difference between them, only that they are all conventional as are the facts they entail" (WCA, 709). Because a "fact" can never be observed in isolation, because a sentence is always part of a context, because a reader is always part of an interpretive community, meaning can be shared. However, an interpreter will only be able to share his meaning if his reading is assimilable to the meanings held by other members of the community.

In the essay, Fish goes on to show how in *How to Do Things with Words,* J. L. Austin anticipated Derrida.[9] Each time Austin took a step to separate constative speech acts (statements of fact) from performatives (speech acts which produce action, for example, "I do" in a wedding ceremony), he found his distinction slipping away from him. In fact, Fish concludes, if one reads Austin as Derrida's precursor, it becomes clear that the "perfectly explicit" constative speech act does not exist (WCA, 719). There are no statements of pure perception (constative speech acts); there are only statements which constitute what they refer to (performatives). Thus, Fish at once radicalizes Austin and suggests speech-act theory can serve as a basis for explaining how interpretive communities act. Fish, Austin, and Derrida come together.

However, Derrida can be a slippery ally. When in the same issue of *Critical Inquiry,* Derrida employs Fish's maneuver of finding unlikely precursors, he uses the maneuver to reach a very different end. In "The Linguistic Circle of Geneva," Derrida suggests that Rousseau might very well serve as Saussure's precursor: both privilege voice, both "make linguistics a part of general semiology," both emphasize the arbitrariness of the sign, both reject any physiological explanation for language, and both believe "articulation" makes language possible.[10] Derrida concludes, "Once more, I am not concerned with comparing the content of doctrines, the wealth of positive knowledge; I am concerned, rather, with discerning the repetition or permanence, at a profound level of discourse, of certain fundamental schemes and of certain directive concepts. And then, on this basis, of formulating questions. Questions, doubtless, about the possibility of given 'anticipations,' that some might ingenuously judge 'astonishing.' But questions too about a certain closure of concepts; about the metaphysics in linguistics or, if you will, about the linguistics in metaphysics" (LCG, 691). Derrida here claims to be looking for moments of permanence "at a profound level of discourse," "fundamental schemes," "directive concepts." This is a rather extraordinary announcement on his part, one which has not yet been heard, and one which makes problematic any easy alliance with him. While Derrida would agree with Fish that philosophers of speech-act theory need to reread Austin (Derrida himself did this in "Limited Inc," and, like Fish, Derrida found elements of the deconstructive project in Austin), he offers a different reason why: "It is up to them [philosophers of speech act] whether they will take advantage of this opportunity to transform infelicity into delight [*jouissance*]."[11] *Jouissance*/ fundamental concepts—Derrida does not oppose them, he suspends them both in the uneasy solution of deconstruction.

In another essay which appeared later that year, "Working on the Chain Gang: Interpretation in the Law and in Literary Criticism," Fish explained once again how interpretive communities work and offered a suggestion as to how change can occur. "Interpreters are constrained," according to Fish, "by their tacit awareness of what is possible and not possible to do, what is and is not a reasonable thing to say, and what will and will not be heard as evidence in a given enterprise; and it is within those same constraints that they see and bring others to see the shape of the documents to whose interpretation they are committed." The interpreter works, in other words, within the guidelines of his community; he cannot convince the members of his community to see anything that their frame of reference will not allow them to see. The interpretive community is, thus, at once the mechanism of stability and the mechanism of change. To explain, according to Fish, is to change: "The distinction between explaining a text and changing it can no more be maintained than the others of which it is a version (finding versus inventing, continuing versus striking out in a new direction, interpreting versus creating). To explain a work is to point out something about it that had not been attributed to it before and therefore to change it by challenging the other explanations that were once changes in their turn. Explaining and changing cannot be opposed activities . . . because they are the same activities."[12] While this argument begins to open up Fish's otherwise somewhat narrow conception of interpretive community as a police force for defending us against outrageous interpretations—"the business of criticism was not (as I had previously thought) to determine a correct way of reading but to determine from which of a number of possible perspectives reading will proceed"[13]—it still sidesteps the issue of the uncanniness of the conversion process. Not every change is incremental. Sometimes changes are abrupt and discontinuous. Sometimes a new "way of seeing" is initiated, as even Fish once asserted in *The Living Temple*.[14]

One of Fish's principal antagonists over the years has been Wolfgang Iser. In contradiction to Fish, Iser insists on the subjectivity of the reading process. However, as we will discover when we look more closely at his model of reading, the subjectivity of Iser's reader is more mythical than real. In his work, Iser seeks to present reading as a dialectical process. Reader and text interact. But time and again, the text seems to emerge as the stronger partner. Perhaps because Iser, like Rosenblatt, seeks to redress an imbalance perceived in others, he, too, merely substitutes one imbalance for another. Just as Rosenblatt was unable to indicate how the text affected the reader, Iser seems unable to indicate how the reader affects the text. Although Iser wants to present reading as a process which balances text and reader, he always presents the reader in the firm grip of the text.

First of all, the reader Iser refers to in his title, *The Implied Reader* and throughout his work is not the actual reader holding a book in her hand; rather, the reader indicated by the title is one brought into being by a text. "The implied reader as a concept has his roots firmly planted in the structure of the text; he is a construct and in no way to be identified with any real reader."[15] Furthermore, though the actual reader uses her emotional and cognitive faculties to fill in the text's gaps and indeterminacies—for example, to flesh out a visualization of the hero or heroine—yet the reader must obey the text. We do not draw visual images of our own; we use the description provided by the author to "try and conceive what is actually to be communicated through it" (*AR*, 138).

At one point, Iser discriminates between implied and actual readers by placing the distinction within a historical context. The actual reader uses the text differently depending upon whether he is its contemporary or of a later generation: "And so the literary recodification of social and historical norms has a double function: it enables the participants—or contemporary readers—to see what they cannot normally see in the process of day-to-day living; and it enables the observers—the subsequent generations of readers—to grasp a reality that was never their own" (*AR*, 74). In other words, the seventeenth-century Puritan read *Pilgrim's Progress* to learn what he could not ordinarily find out (whether or not he was saved), while later readers read it to enter into the Puritan reality, to learn what it would be like to be a Puritan, to become, in other words, the implied reader. It would seem only later generations can *become* implied readers; the contemporary reader already is. Moreover, to become the implied reader is the object of all readings, contemporary or subsequent. However, this is not why all readers have read *Pilgrim's Progress*. Some readers have read it in order to gain an understanding of allegory. Others have read it as a good adventure story. Stanley Fish read it as a "self-consuming artifact." In short, though readers would seem to read for many different reasons, Iser believes readers always read to gain mastery.

The text enables the reader to gain mastery through its use of three principal devices: narrative strategies, blanks, and negations. The author uses narrative strategies to enable the reader to obtain the meaning of the text. For example, in *Humphry Clinker* the narrative strategy of the letter allows the author to present his reader with different perspectives of the same object. The reader then puts the different perspectives together to obtain a picture of the object (Bath, Humphry Clinker, etc.) unavailable to any of the letter-writers in the novel. Narrative strategies help the reader make connections by leaving "blanks" in the text and by guiding the reader's reactions to the "negations" in the text. "Blanks" and "negations" are, according to Iser, "the two basic structures of indeterminacy in the text" (*AR*, 182). Blanks are created in the text by the juxtaposition of various limited perspectives on the characters and situations in a novel. For example, Bath and Humphry Clinker are blanks in the text filled out by the reader according to lines prescribed by the many letters about the city and the person. "Negations" are created when a text points out defects in a prevailing thought system. The contemporary reader is then forced to reevaluate the norms he has always taken for granted. The text exists as a way of communicating failures in perception (which the reader overcomes when he recognizes and responds correctly to the "blanks" in the text) and failures in prevailing social and moral systems (which the reader notices when he recognizes and responds to the way the text negates what he has always accepted). Thus, though the text may raise questions in the reader through the use of various narrative strategies, it is always careful to provide the reader with the answers.

Despite Iser's desire to make reading an interaction, it would seem that, for Iser, the text has more to do with the outcome of a reading experience than the reader. Since the reading process is ultimately controlled by the blanks and negations in the text, reading is not an interaction but a reaction of the reader to the text (*AR*, 169–70).

Iser's model of reading draws from phenomenology. A student of Hans-Georg Gadamer and Roman Ingarden, he seeks to use their theories to understand the process of reading. In *The Implied Reader,* he uses Gadamer to explain how reading proceeds like conversation in that we do not know in advance how a reading will turn out. However, Iser leans much more heavily on Ingarden. He draws on Ingarden's vocabulary and quotes him more often. Moreover, it is Ingarden's over-reliance on "the classical idea of art"[16] that Iser seeks to correct. Ingarden, according to Iser, does not appreciate the *active* experience of reading. Ingarden deplores the gaps in reading; Iser relishes them, for they release the reader's imagination. Iser, unlike his predecessors, wants to emphasize the importance of the reader.

Though Iser's model of reading claims reading proceeds as a dynamic interaction between reader and text, Iser's own performance as a reader demonstrates how reading proceeds by interpretive conventions determined before the reading ever begins. In *The Implied Reader,* Iser reads according to the assumptions of his theory, not according to intentions imbedded in the text. When Iser reads, there is no interaction between him and the text. There is Iser showing us again and again how every text conforms to his pregiven notion of reading as an act of transcendent communication.

My use of the term "interpretive conventions" in the preceding paragraph owes much to Steven Mailloux. In his book, *Interpretive Conventions: The Reader in the Study of American Fiction*, Mailloux criticizes Iser for his inability to move beyond "traditional American literary theory." Mailloux's own work develops along the lines of a Fishean model. Even his titular phrase "interpretive conventions" would seem to owe something to Fish's "interpretive communities." Like Fish, Mailloux's "emphasis is not on the political or cultural constraints on reading and criticism nor on the effects of literature on society, but rather on the literary conventions that influence evaluation and interpretation."[17] Like most reader-response critics, Mailloux skirts history. However, the next critic to be discussed, Hans Robert Jauss, most assuredly does not. Jauss brings history into reader-response.

Jauss's work can be found in two difficult but seminal books, *Toward an Aesthetic of Reception* and *Aesthetic Experience and Literary Hermeneutics,* both of which were published in English in 1982. Jauss's work looks at how "horizons of expectation" change over time so that the same work is understood very differently during different historical periods. Ultimately, Jauss would like to see the process of reading as a way both to stabilize political and social contexts (what he would call the conservative tendency of art) and to renew and revise exhausted cultures (what Jauss might label the liberal reformist tendency of art). In general, Jauss's work breaks down into three areas—aesthetic experience, literary hermeneutics, and reception aesthetics—as the titles of his two books might suggest. Moreover, though his emphasis on the reader changes as he moves his attention from one area to another, in all three areas we can see Jauss caught between his desire for universals and his recognition that art is time-bound.

When Jauss talks about the aesthetic experience, he writes about an experience with four transcendent, supratemporal, and fundamental characteristics. First, the aesthetic experience enables us to discover anew; it lifts, to paraphrase an earlier aesthetician, the veil of familiarity from the world. Second, as psychoanalysis has taught us, it is a way to rediscover buried experience. Third, and this it seems to me is Jauss's major contribution to a theory of aesthetic experience, it serves as a source for identity; it allows us to narrate ourselves. Fourth, and this is Jauss's only concession to what he will occasionally refer to as "the Tel Quel Group," it satisfies a need for play.[18]

Jauss's discussion of literary hermeneutics moves away from the fundamentalism of his view of the aesthetic experience to explain how the reader's activity opens up the text to interpretation. Literary interpretation is the result of a dialectical interchange between text and reader, between the questions the reader asks and the answers the text gives, between the answers the text does not give and the new author (that is, the reader) who asks different questions of it in order to write another text. By introducing the concept of historical process into literary hermeneutics, Jauss shows how the reader is responsible *for* as well as *to* the text. However, too often, as in Iser, the text seems the stronger partner in this dialogue: "The fictive role of the traditional reader is built into Diderot's novel so that the real reader may be refused identification with his representative."[19]

But if we turn to Jauss's analyses of reception aesthetics, we will see Jauss paying more attention to the time-bound reader. In *Toward an Aesthetic of Reception,* Jauss criticizes philological critics like Erich Auerbach and Ernst Robert Curtius, Marxist critics like George Lukacs, and phenomenologists like Hans-Georg Gadamer for accepting the canon of literature as it has been given to them and for supporting a Platonic view of aesthetic experience. According to the chapter "Literary History as a Challenge to Literary Theory," which might serve as Jauss's manifesto, the work of art is not an autonomous, supratemporal aesthetic experience. In this essay Jauss presents seven theses for grounding literary history and, in the process, affirms the importance of the reader. First, Jauss holds that literary history must look at readers and their receptivity to works of art. Most importantly, a literary history must recognize that reader receptivity depends on a "horizon of expectations." Second, the changing horizon of expectations must be related to genre-theory. Third, by looking at "horizons of expectation," we can begin to understand audience reactions whether of approval, or shock, or incomprehension. For example, reception aesthetics can explain contemporary response to *Madame Bovary* and demonstrate why *Madame Bovary* became world famous while Feydeau's *Fanny* (a contemporaneous novel about adultery) faded into obscurity, although initially it was very successful. While Flaubert created a "new canon of expectation," Feydeau's style was outworn.[45] Fourth, by reconstructing the horizon of expectation, we can learn how the contemporary reader viewed and understood the work. Fifth, reception theory explains why certain works meet resistance when they first appear. Posing too great a challenge to their readers' "horizon of expectations," some works may need to wait a long time for an audience capable of appreciating them. For example, Góngora did not find an audience until Mallarmé created it. Sixth, reception aesthetics accepts the plurality of temporal perspectives that must be taken into account when considering the work of art. Seventh, reception aesthetics recognizes the social function of literature. It allows that one's reading has an effect on one's social behavior. Ultimately, according to Jauss, reception aesthetics joins with literature and the other arts to emancipate "mankind from its natural, religious, and social bonds" (*TAR*, 45).

While Jauss is generally optimistic about our ability to transcend our own horizons of expectation in order to understand the horizons of earlier societies and thereby their works of art, there are moments when he seems to see this transcendence as problematic. In his chapter on "Theory of Genres and Medieval Literature," he admits the difficulty of defining medieval genres and establishing their lines of conception, development, and decay. However, Jauss's insights into the myriad difficulties that beset any attempt to define genres for any period are offset by his desire to provide smooth, coherent structures. In fact, Jauss is able to give us an intricate structural analysis of the three dominant Medieval genres—epic, Arthurian romance, and novella (e.g., *Decameron*). It is important to Jauss to see genre development as coherent and "transubjective," for genres provide him with a mechanism to explain historical change.

Jauss denies that genres have essential, timeless qualities. Rather, genres are "*groups* or *historical* families" which can only be described (*TAR*, 80). The history of a genre is the history of its growth, "of the shaping of a structure, its variation, extension, and correction, which can lead to its ossification or can also end with its suppression through a new genre" (*TAR*, 89). Jauss's description of how genres alter over time through accretion ("variation, extension, and correction") begins to look very much like Fish's description of how interpretive communities work. Genres, like interpretive communities, create horizons of expectation (Jauss's name for Fish's interpretive strategies?). In turn, these expectations, or strategies, organize the reading process. Just as, according to Fish, a reader can alter or add to the interpretation of a particular interpretive community, just so, according to Jauss, a reader can alter or add to the conception of a genre. But there seems no way a reader can inaugurate a new way of seeing a text. How are new genres or new interpretive communities created? Isn't there any way to account for discontinuities productive of new ways of seeing? While Fish cannot account for the formation of particular interpretive communities, Jauss can trace certain genres to particular writers. For example, "The invention of the fantasie as a fixed form of poetry is probably to be attributed to Philippe de Remi" (*TAR*, 89). However, the reader cannot create a genre, inaugurate a new way of seeing. The reader merely "sees" what the writer has given him, that is, he describes the genre and the changes it goes through. However, isn't it possible that a reader could create a genre by juxtaposing texts and seeing new connections between them, connections not seen either by their authors or by other readers? Can only writers create new genres? Jauss goes on to give examples of how social conditions can form or change a genre—for example, the passion play—but he never gives any examples of how a reader may create a genre. In the end, since Jauss believes that the most important contribution of reception aesthetics is its emphasis on historical contexts, he emphasizes again and again that social phenomena, not individuals, are responsible for developments in genres.

Though Jauss believes reading depends on the reader's reception of the text, he deplores the possible excesses of intuitive criticism and turns to literary hermeneutics to control them. Horizons may change and alter but they always limit. Literary hermeneutics imposes limits in two ways. One, it suggests the way a literary work's historical progress follows a certain "logic" to form and transform the canon. Two, it enables one to "distinguish absolutely between arbitrary interpretations and those available to a consensus, between those that are merely original and those that are formative of a norm" (*TAR*, 147–48). Again, Jauss's reception aesthetics begins to look like Fish's interpretive communities and seems to serve, as do Fish's communities, as a source of constraint on interpretation. Finally, Jauss's desire to maintain the integrity of the text leads him, when he reads individual texts (for example, Baudelaire's "Spleen"), to sound very like a New Critic exploring the text for its patterns of paradox and ambiguity. Ultimately, Jauss looks for unity—of the text, of the genre, of literary development as a whole.

It would seem that acknowledging the subjectivist element in reading has ever been a bone of contention in reader-response criticism. When, in 1981, Fish reviewed the work of Wolfgang Iser, he took Iser to task for believing there was a subjectivist element in reading: "What I have been saying is that there is no subjectivist element of reading, because the observer is never individual in the sense of unique or private, but is always the product of the categories of understanding that are his by virtue of his membership in a community of interpretation."[21] However, though Iser claims in his response to Fish that there is a subjectivist element in reading ("It is quite true that membership of the community helps to prevent arbitrary ideation, but if there is no subjectivist element in reading, how on earth does Professor Fish account for different interpretations of one and the same text?"[22]), he is as little able as his antagonist to describe it. The only members of the reader-response movement able to talk about the reader as an individual with a "subjectivist element" are Norman Holland and David Bleich.

Holland, who sees himself as continuing the work of his predecessors in psychoanalytic theory—Ernst Kris (*Psychoanalytic Explorations in Art*) and Simon O. Lesser (*Fiction and the Unconscious*)—has written about the way self (reader) interacts with world (text) in four books: *The Dynamics of Literary Response* (1968), *Poems in Persons* (1973), *5 Readers Reading* (1979), and *Laughing: A Psychology of Humor* (1982). All four have been concerned with the reader in one way or another, but it is in the later three books that Holland has elaborated the reader's role in reading. In *Dynamics,* Holland was mainly interested in explaining how texts embody fantasies.[23] Later, as his thinking about texts reversed itself under the relentless prodding of David Bleich (who insisted that texts do not have fantasies, people do), he came to see the reader as embodying fantasies and projecting them onto texts, rather than the other way around. Not that Holland ever really believed that texts have fantasies. He always asserted that people, not texts, have fantasies, but in *Dynamics,* the text provided the fantasy that the reader introjected. In *Dynamics,* Holland was more concerned with the "central meaning" of the text rather than with the identity theme of the reader, though the concept was present as a reservation and clarification of the process of introjection. That is, people internalize differently, and exploration of the different ways introjection proceeds led to a revision of emphasis in the dynamics of reading in the later books. People internalize texts differently because they internalize them according to a core identity theme.

Poems in Persons serves as a transitional work between *Dynamics* and *5 Readers Reading.* In it, Holland not only explains how the reader creates the text but also radically questions the objectivity of the text; for example, he suggests that a poem "is nothing but specks of carbon black on dried wood pulp."[24] He goes on to argue that it is a fiction to suggest that these specks do things to people when actually it is people who do things to these specks. In *5 Readers Reading,* Holland gives more evidence for his belief that the text is the subjective re-creation of the reader.[25] Five readers (six including Holland) read "A Rose for Emily" and in the process create very different stories, stories which inevitably reflect the identity themes of their creators. While it might seem that Holland must move toward the idea of a completely subjective text (which is what David Bleich does), yet he does not. Holland does not want to take one side or the other of the subjective/objective split. Holland is looking for a space where the subjective and objective can meet or at least for a position from which the horizons of the subjective and objective can be seen to recede each toward its own vanishing point: "In technical terms, we introject the literary work. We create in ourselves a psychological transformation, which feels as though it were "in" the work or, more exactly, neither "out there" nor "in here" but in some undifferentiated 'either.' "[26]

It is to situate this "undifferentiated either" that Holland has formulated his concept of the "transactive." With this concept, Holland is able to suggest that perception is not a matter of subtracting out the subjective to reach an impartial objectivity, as has been traditionally assumed, nor is it a matter of accenting subjectivity over objectivity, as Bleich asserts. The new paradigm Holland proposes suggests that "final reality is neither 'objective' nor 'subjective' but the *transaction between them, between the me and what I relate to as not-me*" (Holland's italics).[27]

In a later work, *Laughing*, Holland expands his concept of identity theme to allow for the variations any person's sense of self includes: "To the extent that I can trace in someone's choices in living (as in the choices of a composer) patterns of repetition and contrast, sameness and change, style and content, I can arrive at an identity theme for someone. I can then (perhaps) understand that person's reactions to some new experience, such as Kliban's cartoons, as variations on that theme. I can think of the whole person in his or her history—the person's identity—as the theme plus all the variations, the whole composition."[28] Holland goes on to distinguish between primary identity (which is "in" a person) and identify theme (what one person can infer about another). Thus, while an identity theme is the result of interpretation, identity does exist and when we read a cartoon, "*we laugh when we have recreated our identities through a stimulus suddenly and playfully*" (Holland's italics).[29]

Like Norman Holland, David Bleich focuses on the unconscious responses of the reader to the text, the emotional responses, our infantile, adolescent, or simply "gut" responses. However, while Holland seeks the identity theme of the individual, demonstrating how our infantile responses form our mature ways of relating to the other, Bleich denies that we can ever find another's identity theme: "Even if we explore many responses and in depth, they have to be conceived as local phenomena and related not to permanent character structure, but to immediate motives, preoccupations, and character*istics*. A response always helps us find out something about ourselves" (Bleich's italics).[30] Bleich wants us to know ourselves but insists we do not come to know ourselves by trying to determine identity themes. Rather, we should try to understand our feelings and motivations.

In his first book, *Readings and Feelings: An Introduction to Subjective Criticism,* Bleich focuses on adolescents and how their responses to texts are a result of their developing sexuality, a development which is continuous with life itself but which becomes increasingly anxiety-ridden during the college years. Bleich seeks to show how personal conflicts the reader is undergoing as he reads motivate his feelings about texts. For example, adolescent sexual anxieties aroused by fear of body inadequacy, concern with sexual identification/differentiation, and the American society's insistence on a prolonged adolescence have a lot to do with adolescent reading responses.

In *Readings and Feelings,* Bleich presents us with a detailed account of his teaching techniques during a typical semester. He tells us that before he discusses any literature at all, he introduces himself to the class and discusses the way he wants his students to look at literature. He wants them to feel free to give their own unique responses to literature. The first few classroom sessions are designed to help students become aware of and communicate their subjective feelings. Their idiosyncratic personal responses are not attacked but discussed sympathetically. After a sense of trust has been established, the class turns to poetry. Bleich wants his students to be as personal as possible when they discuss poetry. He wants their affective responses, their free associations, any anecdotal material that occurs to them. The protocols of Bleich's students on Robert Frost's poetry do turn out to be exceedingly personal.

After they have finished working with poetry, Bleich's class turns to short stories. When he is using short stories, Bleich focuses mainly on such questions as the most important word, the most important passage, or the most important aspect of a story. His students' protocols on short stories by D. H. Lawrence, Katherine Mansfield, and Henry James focus on these questions. Thus Bleich believes he moves his class from the personal to the interpersonal. The movement from the interpersonal to the social is then accomplished by reading a novel instead of a short story and by analyzing student responses to the novel to see if a communally held value can be found in them. Though Bleich's movement from poetry to short story to novel would seem to say something about the way in which he views these three categories of literature, it is clear that what guides the movement from personal to interpersonal to social is not the change in genre. What guides the movement is the tenor of the questions Bleich asks. Therefore, the movement from personal to interpersonal to social is something that Bleich has determined beforehand will happen, and he creates a situation which he believes enables it to happen. The question is, Does it happen?

Although Bleich's students come up with a consensus reading of *Vanity Fair,* their reading is the result not of a community-held value or drive, as Bleich holds, but of the way Bleich has collected and assembled their responses. That is, Bleich believes his class agrees unanimously that *Vanity Fair* is sexually repressed because his class is composed of twentieth-century adolescents. However, as Bleich himself notes, his students' consensus of Victorian novels—"a strong intrusive author telling about unsexual women"[31]—matches his own preconception. Unwittingly, Bleich becomes the intrusive author in his own fiction about sexless Victorian novels.

In *Subjective Criticism,* Bleich draws on his philosophical and psychological background to examine his model of reading in greater detail. Any act of interpretation, or meaning-conferring activity, is motivated, according to Bleich, and he believes it is important for us to understand the motives behind our interpretations. And the only way to determine the motivations behind our interpretations of texts is to look at our subjective responses to texts in the supportive environment of a democratic classroom, where each reader's response receives the same respect. In general, however, we are all, according to Bleich, motivated by a desire to increase our self-understanding: "*The logic of interpretation is that its resymbolizing activity is motivated and organized by the conscious desires created by disharmonious feelings and/or self-images; the goal of these desires is increasing the individual's sense of psychological and social adaptability*" (Bleich's italics).[32] We interpret in order to gain some kind of knowledge which will resolve some difficulty we may have had or explain something that was puzzling us.

Though many of his critics have accused Bleich of being left with an infinite number of idiosyncratic readers reading idiosyncratically, that is not where Bleich wants to be left. He seeks ways to negotiate new knowledge by collective consensus. Bleich's movement is always away from the individual toward the group. In *Subjective Criticism,* Bleich introduces the idea of negotiation. New knowledge is the result of free negotiation by members of the group. In other words, in the classroom—or in whatever community of which one is a member—all bring forth their individual responses. Then the group reaches a consensus. I am, of course, oversimplifying Bleich's method, but however complicated one sees his method as being, it is impossible not to see it as other than a conscious weighing and discussing of one's own and others' responses in order to come to a group decision. However, as Thomas Kuhn has suggested, a group may accept a "new" response not because they have negotiated it but because it appeals to them for some reason that cannot be predicted or precisely determined.[33] For an example of this, we can turn to Holland's explanation of how he was convinced by Bleich that people, not texts, have fantasies: "It was not until March 1972 that suddenly one day looking for the I-don't-know-how-manyeth time at Dave's commentary, I realized with the proverbial shock of recognition that he was, quite simply and astonishingly, right."[34] Holland and Bleich did not negotiate a consensus; rather, by some irrational leap, Holland became convinced of what Bleich had to tell him.

Like Bleich and Holland, Harold Bloom leans heavily on psychoanalytic theory. However, unlike Bleich and Holland he is not usually included in the reader-response movement. But a theory of misreading is a theory of reading, and, in practice, Bloom presents a striking image of the courageous reader seeking to understand the process that produces him at the same time that he produces it.

The critic of "belatedness," Harold Bloom appropriately comes last in this chapter. Feeling himself to be at the end of a very long and exhausted tradition, Bloom has, throughout his career, developed and extended his complex and wide-ranging theory of reading and writing poetry in an effort to renew himself. Though he began his career by writing more or less conventional criticism, pitting romantic consciousness or imagination against nature, he quickly moved toward the much less conventional notion of pitting one imagination against its prior imaginations. In his need to keep finding new ways to write about poems that have been written about over and over, Bloom follows a trajectory as erratic as any of the poets he writes about. Bloom ranges from revisionary ratios to tropes to psychoanalytic theory to topoi to Kabbalah to Gnosis in his unending quest for the ultimate antithetical criticism.

In his early work, Bloom, concerned less with the reader/critic, focused more directly on the poet. He wrote about romantic poetry, especially Blake and Shelley and Keats, but even in his early work, he was developing a strong interest in poetic relationships and rivalries. Bloom was always eager to draw the circle of "the visionary company." However, little in Bloom's early work prepared his reader for the radical theory of literary history he presented in *The Anxiety of Influence*. There, literary history was presented as a series of misreadings: "Poetic history . . . is held to be indistinguishable from poetic influence, since strong poets make that history by misreading one another, so as to clear imaginative space for themselves."[35] In order to overcome their sense of belatedness, poets revise their predecessors. Dismissing any similarity to source hunters or literary influence seekers, Bloom insists on the poet's intense pain as he seeks to escape, like Milton's Satan, the authority of tradition.

To flesh out his theory, Bloom names six revisionary movements: *clinamen*, *tessera*, *kenosis*, *daemonization*, *askesis*, and *aphrodades. Clinamen* is misreading proper. The term, indeed, becomes so general that Bloom asks at one point, "[I]s not every reading necessarily a *clinamen*?" (*AI*, 43). The second term, *tessera*, or "completion," comes from Lacan; moreover, Lacan's revisionary work of Freud, according to Bloom, could serve as an example of *tessera*. *Kenosis* traces a movement toward discontinuity with one's precursors. Repetition becomes re-creation and the poet finds himself more than a copy. *Daemonization* is the effort to create a personalized Counter-Sublime, in reaction to the precursor's Sublime. An example of this, according to Bloom, is Shelley's re-writing of Wordsworth's Intimations ode as his "Hymn to Intellectual Beauty." *Askesis* is a movement towards solitude; a contest proper, it is "the match-to-the-death with the dead" (*AI*, 122). *Aphrodades* is the strange possibility that the inheritor has influenced the precursor, for example, when Milton shows the influence of Wordsworth. The six revisionary ratios serve a chronological purpose, outlining the various stages in a maturing poet's career.

While in *The Anxiety of Influence* Bloom traces the poet's progress through the six revisionary ratios, in *A Map of Misreading* and *Figures of Capable Imagination*, he traces the progress of individual poems through these six ratios.[36] Using Kabbalah, as explained by Gershom Scholem, to revitalize his theory, Bloom portrays reading as an interpretive strategy to open the text. The struggle to write a poem or to formulate a reading is a struggle against time. The poet, the reader, defends himself against death by using six tropes: irony, synecdoche, metonymy, hyperbole, metaphor, and metalepsis. Using psychoanalytic theory to bolster this tropical discourse, Bloom aligns tropes and defenses alongside recurring images for the six revisionary ratios to form a map. The reader may then use this map to plot the course of any poem.

Though Bloom claims he practices an "antithetical criticism" in order to escape from reductiveness, one begins to wonder if he has indeed succeeded in doing so. According to Bloom, antithetical criticism is the only criticism that is not reductive: "Rhetorical, Aristotelian, phenomenological, and structuralist criticisms all reduce, whether to images, ideas, given things, or phonemes. Moral and other blatant philosophical or psychological criticisms all reduce to rival conceptualizations. We reduce—if at all—to another poem. The meaning of a poem can only be another poem" (*AI,* 94). One must ask, however, if this "antithetical criticism" does not reduce the poem and its reading to solipsistic tautology. Bloom seems to accept this possibility, indeed, to exalt it as the way of American poets, whom he names, at one point, "gorgeous solipsists."[37] Furthermore, though antithetical criticism follows a carefully outlined program (first analyzing the misreading of the precursor using the revisionary ratios and then examining the tropes, images, and psychological defenses), what ultimately guides the reader through the maze of ratios, defenses, and tropes is the reader's individual "preferences."

In *Agon,* Bloom adds Gnosis to his growing stockpile of literary maneuvers. Like psychoanalysis, tropical analysis, and Kabbalah, Gnosis offers Bloom a way to restore energy to his theory of reading. Gnosis, the only authentic nihilism and the only way to understand one's performance of the poetic text, becomes a revision of Freudian "*unheimlich.*" It becomes a darker version of all that has gone before: "We read to usurp, just as the poet writes to usurp . . . [a] place, a stance, a fullness, an illusion of identification or possession: something we can call our own or even ourselves."[38] In *Agon,* the elements of struggle, dark anxiety, and fear of emptiness reach apocalytic proportions.

In sum, Bloom's theory of misreading follows the Emersonian code of self-reliance. And, in the process, Bloom, the critic most famous for his theory of the anxiety of influence, becomes his own best example. Though Bloom never names him as a precursor—indeed, he names nearly everyone else but him, from Freud and Nietzsche to Kierkegaard and Empson, from Vico and Scholem to Angus Fletcher and Geoffrey Hartman, from Lacan to Luria, Derrida to Burke—the spirit of I. A. Richards seems to float above all of Bloom's criticism. At crucial moments the phrase "practical criticism" will appear, but always Bloom uses it to indicate his difference from his predecessor: "I propose, not another new poetics, but a wholly different practical criticism. Let us give up the failed enterprise of seeking to 'understand' any single poem as an entity in itself. Let us pursue instead the quest of learning to read any poem as its poet's deliberate misinterpretation, *as a poet,* of a precursor poem or of poetry in general" (*AI,* 43). Bloom can generously admit that he has read, appropriated, and exploited many, but he too must find his voice by ignoring what he may once have heard.

I would like to close this essay with an apology in the form of a quote from Bloom. "I have never known a person whose writing was quoted by anyone else who did not believe that he or she had been distorted or misrepresented by being quoted out of context. Yet all quotation is necessarily out of context, and not to a greater or lesser degree. The truth may be that there is no difference between the act of quoting with a favorable or with an unfavorable intention. All quotation may be an un-favoring process, in regard to the text that is being 'read,' 'reviewed,' 'studied.' But this is *not* because 'unity' or 'context' is being violated, but only that 'unity' and even 'context' are revealed as being illusions. We all of us are condemned to do what Emerson did cheerfully, and Benjamin with an elegiac grace: to read any text only for the lustres or *auras.*"[39] I have tried to read I. A. Richards, Louise Rosenblatt, Stanley Fish, Wolfgang Iser, Hans Robert Jauss, Norman Holland, David Bleich, and Harold Bloom for their auras, and if I have now and then quoted them against their own best interest, it was probably because I was quoting them in my best interest. I have, however, tried to make my best interest to give the reader some idea of the multitude of differences that abound in the movement sometimes called reader-response. If I have been unfair, I offer the process of reading as my defense. As I. A. Richards said so long ago, "in all reading whatsoever much must be left out" (*HRP,* 93).

NOTES

1. I. A. Richards, *The Principles of Literary Criticism* (London: Routledge and Kegan Paul, 1924), p. 22, hereafter cited in the text as *PLC.*
2. I. A. Richards, *Practical Criticism: A Study of Literary Judgment* (New York: Harcourt, Brace, 1952), hereafter cited in the text as *PC.*
3. I. A. Richards, *How to Read a Page: a course in effective reading, with an introduction to a hundred great works* (New York: Norton, 1942), p. 93, hereafter cited in the text as *HRP.*
4. Louise Rosenblatt, *Literature as Exploration* (1938; New York: Noble and Noble, 1976), p. viii, hereafter cited in the text as *LE.*
5. Louise Rosenblatt, *The Reader, the Text, the Poem* (Carbondale: Southern Illinois University Press, 1978), hereafter cited in the text as *RTP.*
6. Stanley E. Fish, *Surprised by Sin: The Reader in "Paradise Lost"* (London: St. Martin's, 1967), p. 207.
7. Stanley E. Fish, *Self-Consuming Artifacts: The Experience of Seventeenth-Century Literature* (Berkeley: University of California Press, 1972).
8. Stanley E. Fish, "With the Compliments of the Author: Reflections on Austin and Derrida," *Critical Inquiry,* 8 (Summer 1982), 709, hereafter cited in the text as WCA.
9. J. L. Austin, *How to Do Things with Words,* ed. J. O. Urmson and Marina Sbisá, 2nd ed. (Cambridge: Harvard University Press, 1962).
10. Jacques Derrida, "The Linguistic Circle of Geneva," *Critical Inquiry,* 8 (Summer 1982), 687, hereafter cited in the text as LCG.
11. Jacques Derrida, "Limited Inc a b c," in *Glyph* 2 (Baltimore: Johns Hopkins University Press, 1977), p. 212.
12. Stanley E. Fish, "Working on the Chain Gang: Interpretation in the Law and in Literary Criticism," *Critical Inquiry,* 9 (1982), 211.
13. Stanley E. Fish, *Is There a Text in This Class?: The Authority of Interpretive Communities* (Cambridge: Harvard University Press, 1980), p. 16.
14. Stanley E. Fish, *The Living Temple: George Herbert and Catechizing* (Berkeley: University of California Press, 1978), p. 173.
15. Wolfgang Iser, *The Act of Reading: A Theory of Aesthetic Response* (Baltimore: Johns Hopkins University Press, 1978), p. 34, hereafter cited in the text as *AR.*
16. Wolfgang Iser, *The Implied Reader: Patterns of Communication in Prose Fiction from Bunyan to Beckett* (Baltimore: Johns Hopkins University Press, 1974), pp. 256, 279.

17. Steven Mailloux, *Interpretive Conventions: The Reader in the Study of American Fiction* (Ithaca: Cornell University Press, 1982), pp. 53, 169.
18. Hans Robert Jauss, *Aesthetic Experience and Literary Hermeneutics* (Minneapolis: University of Minnesota Press, 1982), pp. 3–13.
19. Ibid., p. 186.
20. Hans Robert Jauss, *Toward an Aesthetic of Reception,* trans. Timothy Bahti (Minneapolis: University of Minnesota Press, 1982), pp. 27–28, hereafter cited in the text as *TAR.*
21. Stanley E. Fish, "Why No One's Afraid of Wolfgang Iser," *Diacritics,* 11 (Spring 1981), 11.
22. Wolfgang Iser, "Talking Like Whales: A Reply to Stanley Fish," *Diacritics,* 11 (Spring 1981), 86.
23. Norman Holland, *The Dynamics of Literary Response* (New York: Oxford University Press, 1968).
24. Norman Holland, *Poems in Persons: An Introduction to the Psychoanalysis of Literature* (New York: Norton, 1973), pp. 2–3.
25. Norman Holland, *5 Readers Reading* (New Haven: Yale University Press, 1975).
26. Holland, *Poems in Persons,* p. 84.
27. Norman Holland, "The New Paradigm: Subjective or Transitive?" *New Literary History,* 7 (Winter 1976), 337.
28. Norman Holland, *Laughing: A Psychology of Humor* (Ithaca: Cornell University Press, 1982), p. 130.
29. Ibid., p. 174.
30. David Bleich, "Pedagogical Directions in Subjective Criticism," *College English,* 37 (January 1976), 463.
31. David Bleich, *Readings and Feelings: An Introduction to Subjective Criticism* (Urbana, Ill.: National Council of Teachers of English, 1975), p. 88.
32. David Bleich, *Subjective Criticism* (Baltimore: Johns Hopkins University Press, 1978), pp. 83–84.
33. Thomas Kuhn, *The Structure of Scientific Revolutions* (1962; Chicago: University of Chicago Press, 1970), p. 4.
34. Norman Holland, "A Letter to Leonard," *Hartford Studies in Literature,* 5 (1973), 22.
35. Harold Bloom, *The Anxiety of Influence* (New York: Oxford University Press, 1973), p. 5, hereafter cited in the text as *AI.*
36. Harold Bloom, *A Map of Misreading* (New York: Oxford University Press, 1975).

37. Harold Bloom, *Figures of Capable Imagination* (New York: Seabury, 1976), p. 99.
38. Harold Bloom, *Agon: Towards a Theory of Revisionism* (New York: Oxford University Press, 1982), p. 17.
39. Ibid., pp. 241–42.

CAROLYN J. ALLEN

Feminist Criticism and Postmodernism

FEMINIST CRITICISM WAS BORN in the streets during the second wave of feminist activism in the late sixties and early seventies. It was born in those heady days of communal identity, of discovering the pride in being black or gay or female or leftist or some combination thereof. It was born in a consciousness of oppression(s), a sense of a common enemy who turned out to be more complicated and pervasive than we realized in our first days of marching. It was born there, but it didn't grow up there. Instead, at least in the United States, feminist criticism grew up in the academy, where its initial outrage sometimes gave way to intellectual habits of gentility.[1] As a child in the ivory tower, it quickly became subject to disciplines, its wildness tamed and its body divided. While feminist literary criticism produced in English departments looked different from that in French or German studies, neither looked much to written work outside the standard definitions of high art. Film studies, when they occurred in the universities at all, were tiny pockets in various academic disciplines. Feminist criticism of the visual arts happened in art history departments. And all these cultural studies were isolated from feminist social and political history and theory.

Only recently have these divisions begun to come together as feminists from separate vantage points see the necessity for insisting not only on the oppressive nature of patriarchal power but on its systematic construction as well.[2] What used to be feminist literary criticism, with its emphasis on canon reformation and women's literary tradition, is for some feminists becoming cultural criticism, which integrates a revisionist postmodern discourse with feminist social and political theory. In so doing, feminist criticism is returning to its birthplace, keeping its commitment to change. If it has outgrown its overt anger, it maintains in its place a steady sense of the need to demonstrate how different some parts of the worlds of women and men are and how vital it is to imagine a future free of that inequality and those of race, class, and religion.[3]

Seen from one angle, feminism, with its commitment to material change, has nothing in common with postmodernism and its preoccupation with language and the free play of signifiers. Indeed, many feminist critics view such a connection on a scale ranging somewhere from distracting to pernicious. But feminist cultural criticism intersects with postmodernism in considering the construction of "the subject." Postmodernism asserts the ascendance of the subject over what has seemed the safety of "the self," and feminist critics often revise this assertion to understand how "woman" is constructed by cultural practices. In its loosest usage the term "subject" dislodges the individual as a locus of meaning, denies the existence of an ahistorical transcendent self, and marks as ideologically created the myth of the Cartesian cogito, an essential being, a free individual freely choosing life's directions. Feminist semiotician Kaja Silverman suggests that the subject is constituted by "the relationship between ethnology, psychoanalysis, and semiotics" always with "very precise historical and economic determinants." If we understand the subject as a construction, a product of signifying practices which are both culturally specific and generally unconscious, then feminist cultural theory seeks points of intervention in the patriarchal system of meaning and representation by foregrounding sexual and, recently, racial difference.[4]

Feminist criticism both analyzes critical practices grounded in semiotics and psychoanalysis and stresses the construction of sexual difference as crucial to the matrix. At the same time, it critiques both semiotics and psychoanalysis for their neglect of material concerns. It is a social and political as well as a cultural criticism that makes clear the oppressive/repressive practices of patriarchial phallocentrism. From its interrogation it forges its own interpretive strategies. It operates as a dialectic using texts to understand the sex/gender system and constructions of sexual difference, and using theories and constructs of sexual difference to give new interpretations of texts. The following discussion draws on studies of written and filmed texts, but a longer essay would have included other visual arts and the whole range of practices known collectively as "popular culture." If feminist criticism is to continue as a vehicle for social change as well as a variety of cultural analysis, it must not limit itself either in audience or in the kind of signifying practices it investigates.

Feminist critical thinking uses a variety of methods but has at its base at least four assumptions: (1) that the sex/gender system is a primary category of textual analysis, (2) that every act of cultural production and reception occurs in a social, historical, and economic context, (3) that within these contexts people in dominant groups marked by sex, class, and race have greater control over their lives than those in dominated groups do, and (4) that because critical acts occur in the contexts of these power differences, they are never disinterested. Guided by these assumptions I want in what follows to indicate the intersections between feminism and postmodernism by focusing on sexual difference in revisionist semiotic and psychoanalytic perspectives, on critiques of those revisions, and on alternatives to them.

Sexual Difference and Postmodern Discourse: Feminist Film Theory

Even though the many guises of postmodernism threaten the possibility of definition, even as they insist on the instability of meaning, discussions require some explanation of terms, however conventional or problematic. My essay makes conventional use of "female" and "male," using them for categories based on sex, biologically determined. "Feminine" and "masculine" are descriptors based on gender, collections of behaviors and characteristics determined not by biology but by social and cultural prescriptions. One accomplishment of feminist thinking has been to denaturalize these sexual categories, to illustrate how what appears to be "naturally" female, like caring for the needs of others, is a function of gender, of culturally learned expectation rather than of inborn tendencies. I use Gayle Rubin's phrase "the sex/gender system" to stress the way in which biological sex differences take the bulk of their meaning from cultural, social, and economic institutionalization, that is, from ideology.[5]

"Woman" and "man" might seem clear enough at first, but it is at this definitional juncture that feminism meets postmodernism. In looking at postmodernist interest in the subject and feminist insistence on sexual difference, it is apparent that while we might have some idea about "man," we are still looking for "woman." We are in the dark about "the dark continent," as Freud called her. Contemporary French psychoanalyst and semiotician Julia Kristeva maintains that "a woman cannot 'be.' . . . In 'woman' I see something that cannot be represented, something that is not said, something above and beyond nomenclatures and ideologies."[6] Venturing further still, feminist critic Mary Jacobus calls woman "the ruin of representation."[7]

In fact, problems of representation have shifted feminist criticism over the years as critics have developed semiotic readings of cultural practices. Early studies on images of women focused on ways in which male writers used female stereotypes in portraying their woman characters. Articles and books deplored versions of women as whores or virgins, earth mothers or bitches. Such portrayals we thought betrayed the complexities of women in "real life." But that objection assumes that literature and film directly "reflect" or present women as social beings. It does not take into account the mediation of language, of discourse, of the literary or cinematic apparatus. It does not account for *re*-presentation, for the role of the writer, convention, form, for the constructed nature of the portrayal of both woman and man. Recent work, informed by feminist semiotics, interrogates the concept "woman" itself. By examining a literary or filmic text as a system constructed of signifiers, critics focus now on how what appears to take woman as a natural, universally accepted signifier is really an ideological construct. Any textual practice is always unconsciously imbued with cultural versions of what constitutes woman (or man). Feminists recognize that historically in culture, men have controlled the signifying practices that construct woman and that "woman" as created by men must be deconstructed. Feminist semioticians suggest that woman has so often been the object of someone else's articulation, so constructed by her culture as an object, especially an object of desire, that she has yet to speak clearly as subject.[8] Her discourse, when it exists, is muted, buried by the welter of patriarchal textual practice. It is ironic that just when postmodernism argues for a decentered subject woman is struggling socially and economically to become a subject at all.

To date the most impressive work in feminist semiotics has been done in film theory. Teresa de Lauretis, in *Alice Doesn't: Feminism, Semiotics, Cinema,* brings together the concerns of her subtitle to investigate woman as signifier.[9] In a series of brilliant and, as she says, "eccentric" readings of various critical discourses (e.g., by Freud, Lacan, Foucault, Eco, Lotman) and textual practices (by contemporary filmmakers Michael Snow and Nicolas Roeg), she joins the numerous other feminist cultural critics trying to understand "woman." One part of her project in *Alice Doesn't* is to understand how male discourses create woman and what value hierarchies they employ in doing so. Another is to relate the construct "woman" to women, those "real historical beings who cannot as yet be defined outside of . . . discursive formations, but whose material existence is nonetheless certain" (5).

De Lauretis also poses these male discourses against feminist theory, primarily film theory, and its alternative constructions. In this part of her project she is particularly valuable in her linking of semiotics to women's experience, by which she means a process by which subjectivity is constructed (159). In theorizing experience as a process, she frees women from the passive entrapment suggested by some versions of semiotics and social theory in which woman is constructed and thus both passive and fixed. By positing women as participants in an unending struggle against dominant ideology, she suggests possibilities for engagement and change. She focuses on sexuality as the locus of women's experience and in so doing joins a number of feminist theorists exploring sexuality as the locus of identity which most engenders one as woman.[10]

Sexuality, of course, and by extension sexual difference, is basic to theories of psychoanalysis from Freud to Lacan; de Lauretis, Silverman, and other feminist theorists argue the close connection of psychoanalytic and semiotic models in their discussions of sexual difference in film. Feminist critiques of these models have shown them not only to be gendered but also to be male. Freud and Lacan both provide a "path" for females, but in so doing their models lose their explanatory power. At best they provide women with an explanation of why dominant culture provides them the place it does. Both base the acquisition of human subjectivity and sexual difference on the functioning of the castration complex and thus on the primacy of the penis in Freud's model, the phallus in Lacan's.

Freud's lack of interest in female sexuality kept him from writing much about it until well into his career.[11] What he did write, he and others acknowledge as inadequate. That his emphasis on the castration complex was seen as derogatory to women is evident in the concentration on female sexuality in post-Freudian analysts, many of them women (e.g., Karen Horney, Melanie Klein, Helene Deutsch). But as Juliet Mitchell points out, their desire to account for what seemed at best an omission in Freud's theory led some to positions of biological essentialism, that is, to an emphasis on an incontrovertible "female essence" to explain sexual difference, thereby passing over Freud's insistence on cultural intervention in his formation of the castration complex.[12] But theories of psychoanalysis do not suggest why that patrocentricity and other sex/gender structurings of human history exist; feminist social theorists continue their interrogation of the hierarchical models of Western society and its microcosm, the traditional nuclear family, upon which Freud's model of sexual difference is predicated.

Lacan rereads Freud in the light of structural linguistics to understand (among other things) the construction of a subject positioned as user of language. Like Freud, he makes castration the center of his ideas of sexual difference. He maintains that under the perceived threat of castration the subject is split into an unconscious and a conscious by repression of incestuous desires and other early losses. Those losses, or "lack," motivate the subject's entry into the Symbolic, the world of language and the laws of society, called by Lacan "the Name of the Father" and by feminist critics "social identity as involved in patriarchal order."[13] In this order the preoedipal unity of the subject is replaced by knowledge of language, a system of signs based on difference, replacement, and condensation, marking the subject as forever split and forever subject to desire for the lost. The sign of all signs in this system is the phallus, the transcendent signifier. Lacan tries to separate his notion of phallus from the anatomical penis, but as feminist commentators point out, he is not entirely successful and the model carries more than a trace of the male.[14] However, Lacan's model of language, like Saussure's, needs difference and needs woman to mark that difference. Thus woman in Lacanian theory is fantasy, a place where man's lack is projected, the Other, the not-man.[15] Lacan's theory is thus problematic for women both in its phallocentrism and in its relegation of woman to a place of negation.

In France, Hélène Cixous and Luce Irigaray, among others, have questioned psychoanalytic theory in both its Freudian and especially its Lacanian versions. Using sexual difference as a starting point, they write in the gap left from Lacan's negation of woman. They pursue the relation of language to woman's body in general and to female sexuality in particular. Irigaray, a psychoanalyst who was one of Lacan's closest associates until she indirectly critiqued his theory in *Speculum de l'autre femme* and he dismissed her from his institute, works from the premise that " 'language and the systems of representation cannot 'translate' woman's desire."[16] Irigaray asserts that the subject in male psychoanalytic discourse has only the appearance of neutrality, that it is instead always male. She begins *Speculum* by examining Freud's essay "Femininity" (1933) to understand why female sexuality has been omitted not only from Freud but from male Western discourse from Plato forward. She critiques the pre-Freudian idealist tradition with its emphasis on Logos and identity and the Lacanian Freud who treats woman only as man's opposite without a presence of her own. Her next book, *Ce Sexe qui n'en est pas un,* inscribes in its language the disruption of logocentric discourse she calls for in *Speculum.* She counters what she sees as the "unitary representation of [male] identity in analogy with the male sexual organ" by describing the plurality of female sexual desire.[17] In keeping with this plurality, represented by woman's "two lips" and by her multiple orgasmic capacity, she writes part of her text in the fluid, "plural" polysemous style that characterizes "l'ecriture feminine."

Irigaray's poetic style identifies her with a second French writer also interested in the connection of a woman's body to her writing, Hélène Cixous. One of Cixous's essays best known by American feminists, "The Laugh of the Medusa," reads like a manifesto, calling women to write a language of the body in the white ink of a mother's milk, and though Cixous is not specific about how "ecriture feminine" would look, she stresses the need for a kind of writing that would be specifically female.[18] She believes that "it is beyond doubt that femininity derives from the body, from the anatomical, the biological difference, from a whole system of drives which are radically different for women than for men."[19]

Though other essays of Cixous's radically critique Cartesian logic and linear historical, teleological thought and though her more recent work no longer espouses "l'ecriture feminine," this early connection with the biological still makes her the subject of feminist attacks, in France and elsewhere. Many feminist critics find "The Laugh of the Medusa" marred both by the essentialist idea that female sexual difference rests in some biological or spiritual feminine essence that denies the constructing role of the sociocultural matrix and by the universal celebration of female sexual difference without regard to individual women's experiences, especially as they are marked by differences of race, class, and nationality.[20] This emphasis in some of Cixous's work is one version of what Catherine Stimpson has called the maximalist position in feminist theory, an insistence not only on differences between women and men but on the superiority of women and of what in patriarchal contexts might be called stereotypes of the feminine, woman as peaceful plenitude, close to nature and transhistoric in her moral superiority.[21] Cixous attempts to turn those stereotypes in upon themselves and to celebrate the natural bonds between women everywhere.

These feminist revisions of Freud and Lacan, as well as the original models, are central to much feminist film theory. Freudian emphasis on the role of sight in the oedipal process and Lacanian positing of the mirror as the marker of the preoedipal nonlinguistic stage of subject-formation provide obvious connections for a body of work which had already imagined the film screen as first a window, then a frame.[22] In the pages of *Screen* and *Camera Obscura,* the latter a journal devoted entirely to feminist film theory, the screen becomes a mirror. Feminist filmmaker Laura Mulvey, in her 1975 essay "Visual Pleasure and Narrative Cinema," is especially interested in the "looks" in cinema. She maintains that two of them, the look of the camera as it films and the critical reading made by the audience as it "identifies" with the protagonist, are subsumed and made invisible by the ideology of representation in the third, the look between the characters on screen. Illusionist cinema makes the passive woman-as-icon, active male-as-initiator narrative appear "natural" rather than constructed. This "natural" narrative is jeopardized by the woman in cinema who is not only the object of pleasurable looking but also the source of threat because of her role in the castration complex.[23] She must be fetishized by the viewer in order to ward off the threat and produce pleasure. Hence the prominence of glamorous Hollywood stars like Monroe and the filmic focus on their physical beauty, especially on parts of the body. By actively transforming threat into objects, the viewer can continue to enjoy the flow of the narrative.

Obviously, the viewer addressed by the Hollywood cinema Mulvey describes is male. The camera perspective constructs a masculinized position for the spectator just as that viewer with his "male gaze" constructs the woman on the screen. Mulvey does not discuss in this essay the specific nature of the female spectator, but the question has been taken up by others, such as Mary Ann Doane, who argues that the female viewer is constructed in a position of sexual mobility, partially feminine, partially masculine.[24] Doane draws on the work of Irigaray and Cixous to posit the woman's closeness to her body. Unlike the male, she cannot fetishize what is already lacking for her; thus she is constructed differently from the male viewer as she watches the film. She over-identifies passively and narcissistically with the female image because of her involvement in her own body; at the same time she is constructed in a masculinized position in her identification with the male image. As a spectator, she then oscillates between the two in a kind of sexual mobility.

This attention to the woman as spectator as well as to the ideological construction of the woman on the screen characterizes the work of many other feminist film theorists. They extend the idea of the "male gaze" to the entire cinematic apparatus, a construct that feminist critic Annette Kuhn defines as "the product of the interactions of the economic and ideological conditions of existence of cinema at any moment in history."[25] "Ideological" here refers especially to the methods by which cinema prevents the presentation of woman as speaking subject either on the screen or in the audience. In their postmodern concern with the subject, recent feminist film theorists depart substantially from early film studies of women, which, like those in literature, focused on images of women.[26] Current work such as Ann Kaplan's *Women and Film: Both Sides of the Camera* presents readings of classical and contemporary Hollywood cinema and independent feminist films in light of psychoanalytic and semiotic theory.[27] Kaplan begins her book with the question "Is the gaze male?" and goes on to demonstrate the presence of that gaze in dominant cinema. She then examines feminist film in both its avant-garde and realist modes with reference to ongoing feminist debates about form and political efficacy and includes a chapter in feminist film in the third world. Annette Kuhn's *Women's Pictures: Feminism and Cinema* also brings semiotic and psychoanalytic discourse to bear on her discussion of women and film.[28] Its difference from Kaplan's is signaled by the presence of "feminism" in the title. Though both discuss dominant cinema and feminist independent films, Kuhn, as her ideological definition of cinematic apparatus above indicates, is consistently more interested in cultural politics and in possibilities for feminist intervention in cinema as an instrument of social change. Rather than structuring her chapters around readings of individual films as Kaplan does, she focuses on the interrelations between theory and practice. Film theory for Kuhn provides one way to reread dominant cinema; film practice offers a way to replace it.

Sexual Difference and a Woman's Tradition: Feminist Literary Criticism

At present, feminist literary critics interested in Anglo-American texts have not integrated the postmodern discourses of sexual difference into their readings as extensively as feminist film critics have.[29] But sexual difference was not invented in the seminars of Lacan. The history of feminism in England and America includes other, more straightforward, kinds of divisions by sex. The nineteenth-century ideas of separate spheres, of the "feminine ideal," "the proper lady," and the "cult of true womanhood" currently of interest to feminist social and intellectual historians are in their own way also versions of sexual difference. The split between what woman do and what men do has shaped the shifting direction of feminist literary criticism over the years as critics debate whether to address literature by men or literature by women.[30]

Feminist literary criticism of the late sixties and early seventies focuses on images of women in literature by men. It critiques inadequate and stereotypic portrayals of women and evidences of "phallic criticism."[31] Perhaps the most widely known of these critiques is Kate Millett's *Sexual Politics*, notable not only for its scathing analysis of the sexism of male writers such as Lawrence and Mailer but also for its insistence on political analysis as well as literary categorizing.[32] Later studies of male writers argue the damage done by a masculine ethos. Annette Kolodny's *The Lay of the Land* parallels the treatment of women in nineteenth-century American literature to the colonizing of the American landscape; Judith Fetterley, in *The Resisting Reader* also working with nineteenth- and twentieth-century American male writers, delineates the problem of the woman reader who, to read the work, must "identify against herself" (xii).[33]

These relatively early studies were vital in demonstrating how invisible women's perspectives had been in traditional literary criticism. But writing about woman as victim in the works of men seemed limited after the case had been made repeatedly, and attention turned to women writers and the literary canon.[34] Critics began rereading canonized authors (e.g., Austen, Dickinson, G. Eliot, Woolf) from a feminist perspective and putting forth new interpretations of their work. At the same time we began to uncover previously neglected or "lost" women writers and to argue for their merits and their place in the pantheon of important writers (e.g., Kate Chopin, Zora Hurston, Elizabeth Robins, Edith Summers Kelley). Soon we came to question the whole notion of the canon, who stayed in print, who was taught, who made such decisions. Finally feminist literary critics began to argue for a women's tradition in literature, for connections, influences, for, as Woolf put it, "thinking back through our mothers." Much of American's best-known feminist criticism is in this vein: Moer's *Literary Women*, Showalter's *A Literature of Their Own*, Christian's *Black Women Novelists*, and Gilbert and Gubar's *The Madwoman in the Attic*.[35]

The sheer volume of feminist literary criticism in the last twenty years has led critics to attempt to define its goals, its parameters, its taxonomy. These efforts provide the nonspecialist a way into the field and the feminist theorist a chance to see how resistant most American feminist literary criticism has been to theory.[36] Ten years ago articles were resolute in their desire to refrain from definition at all. But as the discipline has grown, models or tentative notes toward them have begun to be put forth. The differences among these models center on the same male-vs.-female-writers debate evidenced by the changing nature of the discipine. Showalter argues strenuously for the study of women writers, "gynocritics," rather than for the study of male texts, "feminist critique." Arguments for the study of women writers have also been made by Catherine Stimpson and Nancy Miller, and it is this focus that dominates American feminist literary criticism. Myra Jehlen suggests instead a continued forging of the path begun by Kate Millett, focusing on "the meshing of a definition of woman, and a definition of the world" (586). Instead of tracing a women's literary tradition, she argues for a method of "radical comparativism" that would examine the cultural myths influential for both male and female writers.[37]

The debate about what should center feminist literary criticism shifts radically among feminist critics working in literatures other than English. Alice Jardine, an American critic of French texts, is typical in her criticism of what might be thought of as standard American approaches. She outlines them as "the sex of the author, narrative destinies, images of women, and gender stereotypes" and continues: "When one turns to France . . . one learns that this bedrock of feminist inquiry has been dislodged; there, in step with what are seen as the most important fictional texts of modernity, the 'author' (and his or her intentionalities) has disappeared; the 'narrative' has no teleology; 'characters' are little more than proper name functions; the 'image' as icon must be rendered unrecognizable; and the framework of sexual identity, recognized as intrinsic to all of those structures, is to be dismantled" (56).

Similarly, Biddy Martin, whose focus as a critic of German literature is on feminism and postmodernism, criticizes the best-known modes of Anglo-American feminist literary study:

> As feminists we have based our critical practice on authorial intentionality and classical notions of language for too long. We have been engaged on the one hand in exposing sexism in male texts on the level of manifest content, condemning what we document to be a history of sexist images and preserving those images of women which seem to conform in isolation to a pregiven conception of a positive portrayal; and on the other hand, we have worked on creating a canon of

> women writers and developing an analysis of their writing that might unify woman as artist. Certainly, both projects have been crucial to the development of a feminist cultural criticism and alternative cultural sphere; however they are limited by an approach to language and culture which interprets images as the more or less authentic reflection of a pre-conceived reality or truth, and assumes that women, by virtue of our powerlessness, can create new meanings without simultaneously engaging in a careful analysis of the processes through which meanings are negotiated across various discursive practices at any given historical moment.[38]

Feminist critical theorists such as Jardine and Martin incorporate the work of European postmodernists even as they critique that work. Gayatri Spivak, for example, has written extensively on the postmodern thought of Jacques Derrida; she finds deconstruction of interest to feminists but acknowledges Derrida's limits. She has articulated her views on the possibilities and problems of Derridean deconstruction for feminists in three related articles. Two of these articles, "Displacement and the Discourse of Women" and "Love Me, Love My Ombre, Elle," may be read together as both presentations and deconstructions of Derrida's figures of woman.[39] The third, "French Feminism in an International Frame," insists on the material conditions of women and women's sexuality as it discusses recent French feminists and their relation to intellectual currents in general and Derrida in particular.[40]

Spivak finds deconstruction useful for feminists in its refusal to accept an opposition between abstract principles and concrete struggle, and in its critique of phallocentricism. But she makes more radical claims for Derrida by arguing that his texts have increasingly come to use "the name of woman" as a counternarrative to traditional philosophical argument: "In texts such as 'La double seance' (the figure of the hymen as both inside and outside), *Glas* (the project of philosophy as desire for the mother), *Eperons* (woman as affirmative deconstruction), 'The Law of Genre' (the female element as double affirmation) and 'Living On: Border Lines' (double invagination as textual effect) a certain textuality of woman is established."[41] Moreover, it is this naming that has engendered such hostility to deconstruction among anti-Derrideans. This "feminizing of philosophy" does not, however, make Derrida anything like a feminist critic since to use woman as a figure of nondeterminancy is again to assign her "a undecidable (non) place."[42] Even as Spivak learns from Derrida, she knows she must go elsewhere with her knowledge. In this series of articles she goes into an exploration of a social text of motherhood that defines woman as object of exchange cut off from her sexual pleasure by symbolic (or literal) clitoridectomy. Her brief discussion is promising for feminist theory and allows her to begin to bring together the textual/sexual "woman" with the material condition of women, a move called for with increasing frequency by many feminist theorists.

Though Spivak is probably the feminist critic best known in this country for her deconstruction of postmodernist texts, other critics are also conducting such interrogations.[43] Both here and in France critics have responded to René Girard's theory of mimetic desire. Most feminist readers probably see intuitively that such a theory, in which desire for an object (usually, despite assurances to the contrary, female) disappears under the increasing rivalry of two (male) subjects, cannot describe female desire and makes the discounting of woman inevitable once again. But Sarah Kofman, Toril Moi, and Mary Jacobus respond in the context of readings of Freud, which in turn provide theoretical discussions from a feminist perspective against which literature can be read. Kofman argues that Girard's reading of Freud on narcissism misses the threat of the enigmatic woman, complete in herself, desirable in her inaccessibility.[44] Moi reads Girard's obsessive denial of Freud in general and the Oedipus complex in particular as a failure to acknowledge the role of the mother in the formation of desire. She maintains further that Girard's refusal to account for female desire or, for the most part, for female characters in literature leads him to skewed literary readings, such as his implicit assumption that Levin, rather than Anna, is the principal character in *Anna Karenina*.[45] Like Moi, Jacobus reads Girard's antagonism to Freud as a need for a rival or, as Jacobus puts it, for "an unmediated dialogue with the psychoanalytic text."[46] In an article that is both a reading of *Frankenstein* and a commentary on Freud, Girard, and the relation of women and theory, she calls on both feminist and postmodernist theory. She suggests, like Kofman, that Girard's "onslaught" on the narcissistic woman reveals something of his own fear, but she does so in the larger context of trying to think through what she calls "textual harassment, the specular appropriation of woman, or even her elimination altogether" (119).

Critiques of Sexual Difference: Women in Social Contexts

Sexual difference, whether invoked by an interest in woman as subject or highlighted in a shared tradition of woman as writer, has not been accepted by all feminist critics as the cornerstone of their work. Some critics object to a preoccupation with the subject, even with woman as subject, or to other versions of postmodernism because they carry the mark of male discourse, of models imagined from male experience.[47] These models, especially in their psychoanalytic form, are at best highly problematic for some feminists and the decision to ignore them is a conscious one. As feminist critics continue to read each other and as the disciplinary barriers break down further, the arguments over the place of male theory in feminist discourse will undoubtedly grow hotter. There is already an established tradition of attacking and eschewing these models, postmodern or otherwise, among feminist cultural critics in both literature and film; this tradition will no doubt continue especially as feminist theorists move away from dominant models to theorize from woman's experience.[48]

Some of those who prefer another direction for feminist criticism are suspicious of sexual difference arguments, not necessarily (or only) because they revise originally male models, but because psychoanalysis disregards women's material place in social and economic contexts and makes invisible differences among women. Not only can dominant models of psychoanalysis not account in general for woman's desire, they have nothing to offer lesbians because of their heterosexual bias and nothing to offer dominated groups (poor and working-class women and women of color) because of their individualist bias and their failure to consider material conditions.

Judith Kegan Gardiner has criticized theories of sexual difference because of their dualism.[49] Dominant psychoanalytic models often focus on a present/absent dichotomy so that woman is always the negative absence in a polarity. If all women are absence, then it is difficult conceptually to see the ways in which some women stand in a privileged position to others. Gardiner calls instead for a move away from such dualism and hopes for a model in which "self and other are both female" so we can "account for women's full and diverse experience as mothers, daughters, sexual beings, speakers, thinkers, and workers." (737).

French writer Monique Wittig goes further still, arguing not only against sexual difference but against "woman" as a category.[50] In opposing both male models and the arguments of Cixous and Irigaray, Wittig argues for a genderless society. She shifts the terms of the discussion from a psychoanalytic to a materialist framework and argues that "woman" and "man" are political and economic categories and that "woman" is marked by economic, political, and ideological dependence on men. She suggests "lesbian" as the subject category marking nonmale dependence.

Other lesbian writers, making arguments different from Wittig's, share her understanding that lesbians confound various heterosexual binary castings of the sex/gender system. There is, however, disagreement about the definition of "lesbian." In a now-famous essay, "Compulsory Heterosexuality and Lesbian Existence," Adrienne Rich critiques a number of feminist theorists because although they see how "woman" is socially constructed they fail to challenge the assumed "naturalness" of heterosexuality and to recognize that it too is an "institution of male dominance."[51] Rich proposes a "lesbian continuum" that allows "lesbian" to define various kinds and degrees of affection among women.[52] Others prefer a definition based more narrowly on (genital) sexual preference.[53] However the word is defined, lesbian critics and theorists alike continue to challenge not only the heterosexism of sexual difference theories but the construction of the entire sex/gender system.

The universalism of sexual difference theory elides women of color and poor and working-class women as well as lesbians (obviously, these are not mutually exclusive categories). Feminist theorists in various disciplines have long realized that adequate models could not be built if they conceived only white, heterosexual, middle-class women. But the process of putting this realization into practice is still in its beginning stages. There is an increasing amount of scholarship about women marginalized by their race, class, and culture, both in feminist criticism and in social and political studies.

Using this work, some feminist theory is now trying to focus on differences among women rather than on differences between woman and man, believing, in the words of black lesbian writer Audre Lorde that difference provides the "necessary polarities between which [women's] creativity can spark like a dialectic."[55]

The point is not only that racially discriminatory models lack full explanatory power but that attention to differences among women shifts our thinking out of the binary mode to which theories of sexual difference have accustomed us. Feminist philosopher Sandra Harding, declaring "in difference we stand; united we fall," proposes a paradigm shift for feminist theory which would place the experiences of women of color at the center of an experiential model.[56] She suggests, for example, further research into the problems of women of color and sexuality, to determine how sex and power operate in relationships where both partners are already placed in a position of cultural powerlessness. One study that examines the relationship between racial domination and sexuality is Rennie Simson's "The Afro-American Female: The Historical Context of the Construction of Sexual Identity," in which she uses the work of nineteenth-century black women writers to understand how black women constructed their sexual selves based partially on societal conditioning which taught them that black men were nonproductive, weak, and unreliable.[57]

Black feminists strongly criticize exclusive academic theories, whether or not they purport to be feminist. As Lorde puts it, "The master's tools will never dismantle the master's house" (99). Women of color, oppressed not only by their sex and perhaps their sexual preference but particularly by their race, too often find themselves excluded by all discussions of cultural criticism and politics. In "Towards a Black Feminist Criticism," Barbara Smith notes, "When Black women's books are dealt with at all, it is usually in the context of Black literature which largely ignores the implications of sexual politics. When white women look at Black women's works they are of course ill-equipped to deal with the subtleties of racial politics. A Black feminist approach to literature that embodies the realization that the politics of sex as well as the politics of race and class are crucially interlocking factors in the works of Black women writers is an absolute necessity."[58] Such critiques are helping to create a growing awareness among white feminists about the intersection of race, class, and culture that will no doubt influence heavily the future shape of feminist theory.[59]

Race is the most visible otherness erased by theories that focus only on sexual difference. But class differences among women, while perhaps less visible, are no less crucial for feminist cultural criticism. The debate within feminist social and political theory over the intersections of sex, gender, and class position in determining women's oppression is well known, though the lines of argument are beginning to be woven together as we continue to work.[60] In America, feminist critical attention to class has been infrequent, but the work of Lillian Robinson, collected now in *Sex, Class, and Culture,* has long argued for attention to class issues and for a broader, less elitist, definition of "literature."[61] Feminism, postmodernism, and Marxism more frequently come together in critiques of dominant ideology, however, than in debates over class structure. "Production" in feminist criticism usually refers to the production of culture rather than to modes of production and participation in the labor force.[62]

Recent feminist criticism that situates itself in a social, historical, and economic context focuses on the ideology that shapes the atmosphere in which women write and "woman" is written. Many of these critics have chosen to discuss eighteenth- and nineteenth-century British writers, not only because this period saw a relatively rapid shift from feudalism to a capitalist economy but also because the ideology of a "woman's sphere" so dominated women's lives. Those who earlier might have catalogued "images of women" in Dickens now delineate how dominant ideology shapes the construction of character and narrative or how women writers of the period experience that ideology. There are many excellent studies focusing on women, literature, and patriarchal social contexts, particularly in the nineteenth century.[63]

Mary Poovey's *The Proper Lady and the Woman Writer* carefully combines feminist and Marxist criticism in its delineation of several women writers under the pressures of ideology.[64] She argues not only that works of literature participate in ideology but that as acts of communication they have an "occasion" as well as a speaker and an audience: "The first 'occasion' of any work is its historical situation, a situation defined not just by its position in time, in literary history, or in the history of ideas but by the dynamic interplay of collective and personal needs, priorities, ideals, and preoccupations within the society in which it was produced" (244). By placing the writers she chooses (Wollstonecraft, Mary Shelley, and Austen) in the context of a developing bourgeois society, Poovey is able to explore the strategies these writers used to help bridge the gap between the promises of an ideology of individualism and the unequal rewards it provided women in the late eighteenth and early nineteenth centuries. Her study connects women writers with an analysis of women's social condition and in so doing contributes to our reading of these particular writers and to a fuller understanding of ideological consequences for other women of the period.[65]

Toward the end of Poovey's study she notes that by choosing to discuss "literary" rather than popular women writers she is reproducing contemporary [academic] ideology (245). Other feminist critics have deliberately chosen popular writers or mass-culture media like television and video as texts for examination, perhaps in the belief that it is perverse for a criticism aimed at intervention and change to spend all its time addressing what most people don't read. Work in this area is refreshingly cross-disciplinary. Historian Mary Kelley looks at best-selling books by women in the nineteenth century to assess the conflict for previously private women living the ideology of hearth and home who are suddenly public figures as their novels become popular. In so doing she adds to a revisionist view of American literature as well as our knowledge of American social history.[66] Janice Radway joins empirical survey techniques with reader-response theory to find out more about the act of women reading popular romances.[67] Tania Modleski combines formalist reading with psychoanalytic speculation and feminist narrative theory in her study of romance, gothic, and soap operas as "mass-produced fantasies for women."[68] Studies such as these, radically different from each other in methodology but cross-disciplinary in practice and feminist in perspective, signal a move away from disciplinary boundaries which threaten to keep the most informed textual readings from their fullest cultural contexts. In treating seriously practices marginalized by academic ideology, these and other inquiries into film, television, video, performance art, and mass-market paperbacks reexamine the distinctions between high art and popular culture that have too often isolated literary criticism.

There is no question that feminist practice continues to be a significant mark of current cultural activity; one commentator says it may well turn out to be *the* most significant practice of the past decade.[69] Our critical thinking, our writing and erasing of sexual difference, provides ground for that practice by critiquing male hegemonic constructions of woman, by intervening and reimagining them, and by departing from such models to territory of our own. Such geographical metaphors recur with telling frequency in feminist criticism. We keep trying to escape the old roads while we change the social and cultural maps that have kept woman from finding herself and women from shaping the world. We use what we can, we go where we must; the master's tools may not help us dismantle his house, but they might tell us how and why it was built in the first place. More than any other critics now writing, feminists speak from a political urgency to understand how all of us, women and men, got to where we are and to draw connections between our culture and its sociopolitical base. We hope for a different, freer future, one that we are still beginning to imagine. We make our theory and act our practice to ensure the social and cultural incorporation of feminist goals, to name that future not postmodernism, but postfeminism.

NOTES

1. In Britain and in Europe feminist cultural politics has a different history. In Britain, especially, it continues to be connected with nonacademic women's groups and artists. It has still not become anything like an academic pursuit.
2. By "patriarchy" in this essay I mean the multiple cultural and socioeconomic systems that institutionalize and hence perpetuate exclusive male hegemonic power. Much social and anthropological feminist research focuses on theorizing patriarchy. To begin see Rosalind Coward, *Patriarchal Precedents* (London: Routledge and Kegan Paul, 1983), Nancy Hartsock, *Money, Sex and Power* (New York: Longman, 1983), and Peggy Sanday, *Female Power and Male Dominance: On the Origins of Sexual Equality* (New York: Cambridge University Press, 1981).

3. This essay discusses feminist cultural criticism in the United States. Obviously both feminism and cultural practices will differ in other countries, particularly in the (misnamed) Third World, where for some people day-to-day survival necessarily structures those practices differently.
4. Kaja Silverman, *The Subject of Semiotics* (New York: Oxford University Press, 1983), pp. 130–31.
5. The use of the term "ideology" in feminist criticism, especially film criticism, is influenced by that of Louis Althusser, "Ideology and Ideological State Apparatuses," in *Lenin and Philosophy and Other Essays*, trans. Ben Brewster (New York: Monthly Review, 1971), pp. 127–86. For Gayle Rubin's use of the term "sex/gender system" see "The Traffic in Women: Notes on the 'Political Economy of Sex,'" in *Toward an Anthropology of Women*, ed. Rayna Reiter (New York: Monthly Review, 1978), p. 159.
6. Julia Kristeva, "Woman Can Never Be Defined," in *New French Feminisms*, ed. Elaine Marks and Isabelle de Courtivron (Amherst: University of Massachusetts Press, 1980), p. 137.
7. Mary Jacobus, review of Sandra Gilbert and Susan Gubar, *The Madwoman in the Attic, Signs*, 6 (Spring 1981), 520.
8. For the distinction between speaking and spoken subject, see Emile Benveniste, *Problems in General Linguistics*, trans. Mary Elizabeth Meek (Coral Gables: University of Miami Press, 1971).
9. Teresa de Lauretis, *Alice Doesn't: Feminism, Semiotics, Cinema* (Bloomington: Indiana University Press, 1984).
10. For a now-classic exposition of this position, see Catherine MacKinnon, "Feminism, Marxism, Method and the State: An Agenda for Theory," in *Feminist Theory: A Critique of Ideology*, ed. N. Keohane et al. (Chicago: University of Chicago Press, 1981), pp. 1–30. See also *Powers of Desire: The Politics of Sexuality*, ed. Ann Snitow, Christine Stansell, and Sharon Thompson (New York: Monthly Review, 1983), and *Pleasure and Danger*, ed. Carole Vance (Boston and London: Routledge and Kegan Paul, 1984).
11. Jane Gallop, *The Daughter's Seduction* (Ithaca: Cornell University Press, 1982), p. 15.
12. Juliet Mitchell, Introduction to *Feminine Sexuality: Jacques Lacan and the Ecole Freudienne*, ed. Juliet Mitchell and Jacqueline Rose (New York: Norton, 1982), p. 23. For discussions of Freud from a feminist perspective see especially Juliet Mitchell, *Psychoanalysis and Feminism* (New York: Vintage, 1973), and Nancy Chodorow, *The Reproduction of Mothering* (Berkeley: University of California Press, 1978).

13. Jane Gallop, "Psychoanalysis and Feminism in France," in *The Future of Difference,* ed. Hester Eisenstein and Alice Jardine (Boston: G. K. Hall, 1980), p. 106.
14. Silverman, *The Subject of Semiology,* p. 183.
15. See Jacqueline Rose, Introduction to *Feminine Sexuality*; Gallop, *The Daughter's Seduction;* and Ellie Ragland-Sullivan, *Jacques Lacan and the Philosophy of Psychoanalysis* (Urbana: University of Illinois Press, 1986) for detailed explanations and critiques of woman in Lacan's model.
16. Carolyn Burke, "Irigaray Through the Looking Glass," *Feminist Studies,* 7, no. 2 (Summer 1981), 288. Burke is quoting from an interview, "Women's Exile," *Ideology and Consciousness,* 1 (1977), which is a helpful restatement of some important directions in Irigaray's work. Translations of Irigaray in English include *Speculum of the Other Woman,* trans. Gillian Gill, and *The Sex Which Is Not One,* trans. Catherine Porter with Carolyn Burke, both (Ithaca: Cornell University Press, 1985), and "Veiled Lips," *Mississippi Review,* 11, no. 3 (Winter/Spring 1983), 93–131. For additional commentary on Irigaray see Gallop, *The Daughter's Seduction;* Josette Feral, "Antigone, or *The Irony of the Tribe,*" *Diacritics* (Fall 1978), 2–14; and Elizabeth Berg, "The Third Woman," *Diacritics* (Summer 1982), 11–20.
17. Burke, "Irigarary Through the Looking Glass," 289.
18. Hélène Cixous, "The Laugh of the Medusa," in Marks and de Courtivron, *New French Feminisms,* pp. 245–64. See also "Castration or Decapitation," *Signs,* 7 (Fall 1981), 41–55; and Verena Conley's critical study, *Writing the Feminine* (Lincoln: University of Nebraska Press, 1984).
19. Christiane Makward, "Interview with Hélène Cixous," *Sub-Stance,* 13 (1976), 28, quoted in Helene Wenzel, "The Text as Body/Politics: An Appreciation of Monique Wittig's Writings in Context," *Feminist Studies,* 7, no. 2 (Summer 1981), 267.
20. For representative critiques see in addition to Wenzel cited above, Christiane Makward, "To Be or Not to Be . . . A Feminist Speaker," in *The Future of Difference,* ed. Eisenstein and Jardine, and Rachel Bowlby, "The Feminine Female," *Social Text* (Spring/Summer 1983), 54–65.
21. Catherine Stimpson, "What Lies Beyond 'The Woman as Victim' Construct," *MS,* October 1984, p. 84.
22. Dudley Andrews, *Concepts in Film Theory* (Oxford: Oxford University Press, 1984), p. 134.
23. Laura Mulvey, "Visual Pleasure and Narrative Cinema," *Screen,* 16, no. 3 (Autumn 1975), 6–18.

24. Mary Ann Doane, "Film and the Masquerade: Theorizing the Female Spectator," *Screen,* 23 (September/October 1982), 74–87. Mulvey does comment on the female spectator in "Afterthoughts on 'Visual Pleasure and Narrative Cinema,'" *Framework,* nos. 15/16/17 (1981), 6–18.
25. Annette Kuhn, *Women's Pictures: Feminism and Cinema* (London: Routledge and Kegan Paul, 1982), p. 197.
26. For example see Molly Haskell, *From Reverence to Rape* (New York: Holt, Rinehart and Winston, 1977); and Marjorie Rosen, *Popcorn Venus: Women, Movies, and the American Dream* (New York: Coward, McCann and Geoghegan, 1973).
27. Ann Kaplan, *Women and Film: Both Sides of the Camera* (New York: Methuen, 1983). The book is especially helpful for those teaching film courses because it has a good glossary of terms, a filmography, and an appendix with syllabi and suggestions for course design.
28. Kuhn, *Women's Pictures.* Though it is specifically focused on cinema, *Women's Pictures* is a basic book for anyone interested in feminist cultural politics.
29. There have always been exceptions of course. See, for example, the work of Margaret Homans, Mary Jacobus, and Christine Froula. I believe the revisionist spirit of feminist literary criticism will move increasingly in this direction, though there is certainly resistance on both theoretical and political grounds.
30. A survey of review articles in feminist literary criticism clearly indicates the shift in direction from male to female writers. See Elaine Showalter, "Literary Criticism," *Signs,* 1 (Winter 1975), 435–60; Cheri Register, "American Feminist Literary Criticism: A Bibliographic Introduction," in *Feminist Literary Criticism,* ed. Josephine Donovan (Lexington: The University Press of Kentucky, 1975), pp. 1–28, and "Literary Criticism," *Signs,* 6 (Winter 1980), 268–82; Sydney Janet Kaplan, "Literary Criticism," *Signs,* 4 (Spring 1979), 514–27 and "Varieties of Feminist Criticism," in *Making a Difference,* ed. Gayle Greene and Coppélia Kahn (London: Methuen, 1985).
31. The term is Mary Ellman's in *Thinking about Women* (New York: Harcourt, Brace and Jovanovich, 1968).
32. Kate Millett, *Sexual Politics* (Garden City, N.Y.: Doubleday, 1970).
33. Annette Kolodny, *The Lay of the Land* (Chapel Hill: University of North Carolina Press, 1975); Judith Fetterley, *The Resisting Reader* (Bloomington: Indiana University Press, 1978).
34. This is not to say, however, that there are no recent "images of women" studies being written. There are literally hundreds of such books and articles, some quite recent. For virtually every male writer

in the traditional canon, there are one or more studies of his women characters and there is now a growing body of feminist work about his place in social and literary contexts as well. We are simply past the point in time when nonfeminist scholars can plead lack of available materials, either primary or secondary in any literary period or genre.

35. Ellen Moers, *Literary Women* (New York: Anchor, 1977); Elaine Showalter, *A Literature of Their Own* (Princeton: Princeton University Press, 1977); Barbara Christian, *Black Women Novelists: The Development of a Tradition, 1892–1976* (Westport, Conn.: Greenwood, 1980); Sandra Gilbert and Susan Gubar, *The Madwoman in the Attic* (New Haven: Yale University Press, 1979).

36. Annette Kolodny outlines her position in a series of articles: "Some Notes on Defining a 'Feminist Literary Criticism,'" *Critical Inquiry*, 2 (Autumn 1975), 75–92, "A Map for Misreading: On Gender and the Interpretation of Literary Texts," *New Literary History,* 11 (1980), 451–67, "Dancing through the Minefield: Some Observations on the Theory, Practice and Politics of a Feminist Literary Criticism," *Feminist Studies,* 6, no 1 (Spring 1980), 1–25. See also Judith Kegan Gardiner, Elly Bulkin, Rena Grasso Patterson, and Annette Kolodny, "An Interchange on 'Dancing through the Minefields,'" *Feminist Studies,* 8, no. 3 (Fall 1982), 629–75; Sandra Gilbert, "Life Studies; or, Speech after Long Silence: Feminist Critics Today," *College English,* 40 (April 1979), 849–63; Elaine Showalter, "Feminist Criticism in the Wilderness," in *Writing and Sexual Difference,* ed. Elizabeth Abel (Chicago: University of Chicago Press, 1982), pp. 9–37; Myra Jehlen, "Archimedes and the Paradox of Feminist Criticism," *Signs,* 6 (Summer 1981), 575–601. The following appear in a special issue of *Diacritics* (Summer 1982) on feminist criticism: Peggy Kamuf, "Replacing Feminist Criticism," 42–47; Nancy Miller, "The Text's Heroine: A Feminist Critic and Her Fictions," 48–53; Alice Jardine, "Gynesis," 54–65. See also Catherine Stimpson, "Feminism and Feminist Criticism," *Massachusetts Review,* 24 (Summer 1983), 272–88.

37. For a delineation of feminist criticism by a critic working in other areas of postmodern discussion, see Jonathan Culler, *On Deconstruction: Theory and Criticism after Structuralism* (Ithaca: Cornell University Press, 1982), pp. 42–64. Culler focuses on woman as reader rather than on woman as writer. Though he does not address the gynocritical direction of much Anglo-American feminist criticism, and though I disagree with his mapping of the territory, his focus on the woman as reader is useful, if incomplete. For a feminist response, see Elaine Showalter, "Critical Cross-Dressing: Male Feminists and the Woman of the Year," *Raritan* (Fall 1983), 130–49.

38. Biddy Martin, "Feminism, Criticism, and Foucault," *New German Critique*, 27 (Fall 1982), 17.
39. Gayatri Spivak, "Displacement and the Discourse of Women," in *Displacement: Derrida and After*, ed. Mark Krupnick (Bloomington: Indiana University Press, 1983), pp. 169–95, and "Love Me, Love My Ombre, Elle," *Diacritics* (Winter 1984), 19–36.
40. Gayatri Spivak, "French Feminism in an International Frame," *Yale French Studies*, 62 (1981), 154–84.
41. Ibid., p. 170.
42. Spivak, "Love Me," p. 25. For an interview with Derrida in the context of feminist discussion, see Derrida and Christie V. McDonald, "Choreographies," *Diacritics* (Summer 1982), 66–76.
43. See, for example, critiques of Foucault in Martin, "Feminism, Criticism, and Foucault"; the introduction to *Powers of Desire: The Politics of Sexuality*, ed. Ann Snitow and Christine Stansell (New York: Monthly Review, 1982); and Mary Lydon, "Foucault and Feminism, A Romance of Many Dimensions," *Humanities in Society* (Summer/Fall 1982), 245–56.
44. Sarah Kofman, "The Narcissistic Woman: Freud and Girard," *Diacritics* (Fall 1980), 36–45. The essay is from *L'enigme de la femme: La femme dans les textes de Freud* (Paris: Galilee, 1980). For a helpful introduction to Kofman that poses her work against that of Irigaray, see Berg, "The Third Woman."
45. Toril Moi, "The Missing Mother: The Oedipal Rivalries of René Girard," *Diacritics* (Summer 1982), 21–31.
46. Mary Jacobus, "Is There a Woman in This Text?" *New Literary History*, 14 (Autumn 1982), 136.
47. For some of these dissenting voices in film theory see, for example, "Women and Film: A Discussion of Feminist Aesthetics" by several well-known feminist critics in *New German Critique*, 13 (1978), 83–107, and Ruby Rich, "Cinefeminism and Its Discontents," *American Book Review*, 6 (July-August, September-October 1984), 12–13.
48. Of course, feminism has already produced a number of theorists who have no interest in working with dominant models, even to refute them. See especially the work of Mary Daly and Marilyn Frye. Feminist reviewers are often critical of work done in a masculinist framework while ignoring feminist models. See, for example, Helen Longino's review of Ruth Bleier's *Science and Gender* in the *Women's Review of Books*, 1, no. 12 (1984), asking why Bleier uses Foucault while overlooking Daly. The entire topic is highly charged and deserves more space than I can give it here.
49. Judith Kegan Gardiner, "Power, Desire, and Difference: Comment on

Essays from the *Signs* Special Issues on Feminist Theory," *Signs,* 8 (1983), 733–37.

50. Monique Wittig, "One Is Not Born a Woman," *Feminist Issues,* 3 (Winter 1981), 47–54.
51. Adrienne Rich, "Compulsory Heterosexuality and Lesbian Existence," *Signs,* 5 (Summer 1980), 633.
52. For a book-length study of lesbian relationships with a similar definitional point of view, see Lillian Faderman, *Surpassing the Love of Men* (New York: William Morrow, 1981).
53. See, for example, Elizabeth Wilson, "Forbidden Love," *Feminist Studies,* 10, no. 2 (Summer 1984), 213–26. There is now a large body of lesbian-feminist criticism. For an overview and references, see Jane Rule, *Lesbian Images* (Garden City, N.Y.: Doubleday, 1975); Bonnie Zimmerman, "What Has Never Been: An Overview of Lesbian Feminist Literary Criticism, *Feminist Studies,* 7, no. 3 (Fall 1981), 451–76; J. R. Roberts, *Black Lesbians* (Tallahassee, Fl.: Naiad Press, 1981); Margaret Cruikshank, ed., *Lesbian Studies* (Old Westbury, N.Y.: Feminist Press, 1982); Catherine Stimpson, "Zero Degree Deviancy: The Lesbian Novel in English," in Abel, *Writing and Sexual Difference,* pp. 243–60. See also a recent study of lesbian readers, Jean Kennard, "Ourself Behind Ourself: A Theory for Lesbian Readers," *Signs,* 9 (Summer 1984), 647–62.
55. Audre Lorde, "The Master's Tools Will Never Dismantle the Master's House," in *This Bridge Called My Back: Writings by Radical Women of Color*, ed. Cherríe Moraga and Gloria Anzaldúa (Watertown, Mass.: Persephone Press, 1981), p. 99. This collection is unusual in that women of color speak of their own racism as well as recounting their experiences in a racist culture. For another book examining relationships among white, black, and Jewish women, see Elly Bulkin, Minnie Bruce Pratt, and Barbara Smith, *Yours in Struggle* (New York: Long Haul, 1984).
56. Sandra Harding, "Building Feminist Theory," paper read at the National Women's Studies Association conference, 1984, Douglass College.
57. Rennie Simson, "The Afro-American Female: The Historical Context of the Construction of Sexual Identity," in Snitow and Stansell, *The Powers of Desire,* pp. 229–35.
58. Barbara Smith, "Towards a Black Feminist Criticism," in *But Some of Us Are Brave: Black Women's Studies,* ed. Gloria T. Hull, Patricia Bell Scott, and Barbara Smith (Old Westbury, N.Y.: Feminist Press, 1982), p. 159. This anthology provides an excellent introduction to the topic. See also *Home Girls: A Black Feminist Anthology,* ed. Barbara Smith

(New York: Kitchen Table, 1983). This press is run by women of color and is a good source for studies in the area. See also for literary criticism, *Sturdy Black Bridges,* ed. Roseann Bell, Bettye Parker, and Beverly Guy-Sheftall (Garden City, N.Y.: Anchor, 1979); Erlene Stetson, "Black Women In and Out of Print," in *Women in Print I,* ed. Joan Hartman and Ellen Messer-Davidow (New York: Modern Language Association, 1982), pp. 87–107; *Black Women Writers at Work*, ed. Claudia Tate (New York: Continuum, 1983); *Black Women Writers (1950–1980): A Critical Evaluation,* ed. Mari Evans (Garden City, N.Y.: Anchor, 1984); "American Indian Women's Literature," in *Studies in American Indian Literature,* ed. Paula Gunn Allen (New York: Modern Language Association, 1983), pp. 85–144; *Woman of Her Word: Hispanic Women Write*, ed. Evangelina Vigil (Houston: Revista Chicano-Riquena, 1983).

59. See, for example, two books: Paula Giddings, *When and Where I Enter: The Impact of Black Women on Race and Sex in America* (New York: William Morrow, 1984), and Dorothy Sterling, *We Are Your Sisters: Black Women in Nineteenth-Century America* (New York: Norton, 1984).

60. This debate—with its resulting tendency to categorize feminist thought into versions such as liberal, radical, Marxist, socialist—has innumerable variants. Readers looking for a place to begin or for a sense of the weave should consult the following overviews: *Women and Revolution,* ed. Lydia Sargent (Boston: South End, 1981); Alison Jaggar, *Feminist Politics and Human Nature* (Totowa, N.J.: Rowman and Allanheld, 1983); and Hester Eisenstein, *Contemporary Feminist Thought* (Boston, G. K. Hall, 1984).

61. Lillian Robinson, *Sex, Class, and Culture* (Bloomington: Indiana University Press, 1978). For further work on women and class in American feminist criticism see Rena Grasso Patterson's response to Annette Kolodny, *Feminist Studies,* 8, no. 3 (Fall 1982), 654–65; and Paul Lauter, "Working-Class Women's Literature: An Introduction to Study," in Hartman and Messer-Davidow, *Women in Print I*, 109–34.

62. In film theory, critics who argue against feminist semiotics (and who often cite Althusser, but seldom Marx) frequently include in their work a focus on actual film production and the position of women in the industry. See, for example, *Heresies 16* on film and video, and feminist film criticism in *Jump Cut,* especially that of Julia Lesage and Ruby Rich.

63. See, for example, Judith Lowder Newton, *Women, Power, and Subversion: Social Strategies in British Fiction, 1778–1860* (Athens: Uni-

versity of Georgia Press, 1981); Kathleen Blake, *Love and the Woman Question in Victorian Literature* (New York: Barnes and Noble, 1983). A useful anthology with a variety of approaches most often informed by a historical ideological critique is *Women Writing and Writing about Women,* ed. Mary Jacobus (London: Croom Helm, 1979). For an earlier, more strictly Marxist, view see Marxist-Feminist Literature Collective, "Women's Writing: *Jane Eyre, Shirley, Villette, Aurora Leigh,*" *Ideology and Consciousness,* 3 (Spring 1978), 27–48.

64. Mary Poovey, *The Proper Lady and the Woman Writer* (Chicago: University of Chicago Press, 1984).

65. For two other postmodern studies involving ideology and the eighteenth century, see Terry Castle, *Clarissa's Ciphers* (Ithaca: Cornell University Press, 1982), and Terry Eagleton, *The Rape of Clarissa* (Oxford: Basil Blackwell, 1982). Castle's study draws on a feminist hermeneutic, Eagleton's primarily on a psychoanalytic and Marxist one, though he makes feminist claims. For a disparaging of those claims see Showalter, "Critical Cross-dressing."

66. Mary Kelley, *Private Woman, Public Stage* (New York: Oxford University Press, 1984). For a related study using domestic fiction to provide a women's view of the American frontier see Annette Kolodny, *The Land before Her* (Chapel Hill: University of North Carolina Press, 1984). For a critique of male bias in critical thinking about American literature see Nina Baym "Melodramas of Beset Manhood: How Theories of American Fiction Exclude Women Authors," *American Quarterly* (Summer 1981), 123–39.

67. Janice Radway, "Women Read the Romance: The Interaction of Text and Context," *Feminist Studies,* 9, no. 1 (Spring 1983), 53–78.

68. Tania Modleski, *Loving with a Vengeance* (Hamden, Conn.: Archon, 1982).

69. Craig Owens, "The Discourse of Others: Feminists and Postmodernism," in *The Anti-Aesthetic: Essays on Postmodern Culture,* ed. Hal Foster (Port Townsend, Wash.: Bay, 1983), p. 61.

GREGORY COLOMB

The Semiotic Study of Literary Works

SEMIOTIC STUDY OF LITERARY WORKS BEGAN, some say, with Aristotle. If we think of semiotic studies in terms of broadly defined methodological features, any formal poetics is a form of semiotics and Aristotle's formal analysis of such formally conceived entities as epic, tragedy, and comedy is indistinguishable in its essentials from even the most elaborate of recent "high tech" semiotic studies. Curiously, so long a perspective on semiotics attracts apologists and debunkers alike. A more contextualized, historicist view ties semiotics to its roots in modern linguistics and yields a more manageable canvas. The relevant lineage begins with the Swiss linguist Ferdinand de Saussure, and literary semiotics dawns early in this century, when East European linguists and literary critics begin to explore the possibilities of a formal criticism grounded in Saussurean principles of linguistic analysis. In this light the figure that stands above the rest is Roman Jakobson, whose work in linguistics and poetics (culminated in his landmark essay of that name) has spanned this century and influenced every major school and scholar.[1] But even in this more modest portrait, semiotics would encompass a good portion of the literary criticism of this century, especially that of continental scholars, and would include much of the criticism discussed in this collection.

Since semiotics still struggles to define itself and its place, the choice of origins is not self-evident. An origin near the beginning of this century is a popular choice, while the French historian, Michel Foucault, sees the whole of the modern, post-Renaissance era as the time of semiotic man.[2] So does the American philosopher Charles Sanders Peirce, who at the turn of this century credited Locke for the first modern use of the term "semiotics" and for inspiring Peirce's influential conception of "the essential nature and fundamental varieties" of signs.[3] Here, I adopt a consciously narrow view, one that gives prominence to the experience of Anglo-American critics and that takes into account such matters as common interests and goals, shared models and vocabularies, and the various signs, often tacit, that announce professional and intellectual affiliation. This accounting does acknowledge a relatively long perspective. It must recognize the substantial American tradition represented in the work of Peirce and, later, of Charles Morris. It must recognize the central, though relatively silent, presence of semiotics in what we think of as traditional criticism—in, for example, René Wellek's advocacy of positions developed by the Prague school or in I. A. Richards's use of Peirce's work. And it must acknowledge other traditional forms of criticism: philology, rhetorical analysis, and to some extent intellectual history (seen as the reconstruction of the conditions of meaning governing the production of texts) are all necessary parts, albeit only parts, of an adequate semiotic explanation of literary works. But the definitive fact in this accounting is our authors' sense that they have engaged a new enterprise, one whose origin is somewhat more recent.

In 1975 there appeared in the usual booksellers' shopping lists at the back of the convention program issue of *PMLA* a small advertisement of Umberto Eco's *A Theory of Semiotics*. The lists in that issue offered for sale only one other book concerning semiotics—a translation of Pierre Guirard's brief, structuralist-oriented, and comparatively primitive *La Semiologie* of 1971.[4] While not comprehensive, these lists do reliably indicate which books are, if not necessarily influential, then at least popular. The program for that year's MLA convention offers additional evidence: only two of the almost 350 seminars and other meetings indicate a relationship to semiotics in their titles and descriptions—and then only as a minor feature; and of the many hundreds of papers whose titles are listed only two mention semiotics. It would be a mistake to make too much of such a small and arbitrary sample of the profession's activities; structuralism had, for example, made many aware of its "semiology." But even so casual a survey can show how little Anglo-American critics then knew of semiotics and how well Eco's *A Theory* can serve not as an origin but as a landmark in the development of American literary semiotics.[5]

A Theory of Semiotics was not aimed chiefly at students of literature (although that had been Eco's own interest), but it did address the situation in which many critics then found themselves. Massively learned, delightfully eclectic, and always intelligent, *A Theory* brought between two covers work from many disciplines, work whose latest developments had seemed to promise at least some avenues of convergence and whose relation to recent formal strains in literary criticism proved tantalizing. Most of this work bore strong relations to linguistics; indeed, significant portions of it were direct off-shoots of linguistics. In a sense, Eco's range of reference merely recorded the fragmentation of contemporary linguistics. And therein lay much of its appeal. Criticism with a formalistic bent had been largely dominated by linguistics, often falling into rather simple applications of transformational grammar and its immediate offspring. By the mid seventies, that criticism had run its course and was increasingly seen to have lost its claim to serious attention.[6] Thus, Eco's eclectic, wide-ranging semiotics appealed because it opened new vistas on formal criticism by opening a new vista on linguistics.

In offering its intelligent, critical, and concise accounts of this new work in semiotics, *A Theory* cast these accounts in a quasi-systematic frame that, while not entirely coherent, did chart the correlations and trace the family resemblances among the various fields and so made their interrelation as a theory seem almost possible. As Eco bravely put it: "The aim of this book is to explore the theoretical possibility and the social function of a unified approach to every phenomenon of signification and/or communication. Such an approach should take the form of a general semiotic theory, able to explain every case of sign-function in terms of underlying systems of elements mutually correlated by one or more codes." It is hard not to have doubts about so general a semiotic theory, doubts such as those that at times surface in *A Theory* and are expressed more forcefully in Eco's later work.[7] Its grander ambitions aside, what *A Theory* finally offered was in fact not a theory of semiotics but a rich and suggestive collection of theories and snippets of theories which seek to explain particular domains of semiotic activity. None of those theories is yet definitive, and a few have proved less than promising. But together they made Eco's project, the project of semiotics, credible. This credibility came in part from the prospect of so much novel, interesting work. But it also came from familiarity. Most critics had known only that distinctly parochial, peculiarly French, and in many ways uncharacteristic brand of semiotics redefined as "semiology" by the structuralists. Because his view of semiotics was so international, Eco put structuralism's alien presence in its place in the larger community of semiotic studies. By the same token, that internationalism made semiotics seem more domestic because it tied semiotics to major Anglo-American strains in linguistics and philosophy of language, strains that had already left their mark on the practice of many critics. So, Eco offered literary critics a glimpse of a general scholarly project that was relatively coherent in the articulation of its parts and seemed quite coherent in its basic conceptions and goals, a project in which the formal study of literary works seemed to have a natural place and a new life. And perhaps most importantly, Eco also offered, in his cogent accounts of many different such semiotic studies, a way into the project of a literary semiotics, a map of the territory within which a literary semiotics would have to make its place.

As I use the term, semiotics cannot be considered a strongly unified field of study; indeed it is not yet clear exactly what kind of unity semiotics might have—as a school, method, theory, or discipline. But however that field is circumscribed, all varieties of semiotics are grounded in the study of sign functions and their typologies. The most useful general definition of the sign is still Peirce's reformulation of the classical *aliquid stat pro aliquo*: "something which stands to somebody for something in some respects or capacity" (2:228). To the classical version Peirce adds two specifications: the sign counts as a sign only insofar as it is taken to be a sign by a receiver, and the sign is always taken as "standing for" in some particular way, which Peirce calls its "ground." Here I will distinguish three hierarchically related fields of semiotic study, fields which are best differentiated by how they delimit the relevant range of signs, sign users, and sign types or grounds. *General semiotics* is the most inclusive field; it takes each item in Peirce's definition as entirely variable. *Anthroposemiotics* is a branch of general semiotics differentiated by its specifications of sign users. *Literary semiotics* is a branch of anthroposemiotics differentiated by its specification of particular kinds of signs.

The most comprehensive fields of semiotics allow the widest ranges of signs, users, and grounds. In all versions of general semiotics, only the specification of the receivers is at issue.[8] Any general semiotics must presume that all sign types fall within its purview, and there is widespread agreement that the class of sign sources is unlimited, indeed, that the source of a sign need not be semiotic in any way, as, for example, the fire of which we take smoke to be the sign is extra-semiotic. But there is considerable debate over who are possible sign receivers: does a smoke detector take smoke to be a sign of fire? Although smoke detectors have few champions,[9] many theorists argue that the class of sign receivers must not include only humans, but all life forms. Another, related area of debate concerns the standing-for relationship. Theorists disagree whether a fully deterministic standing-for (as with certain biochemical processes) can constitute a sign: do our cells use signs when they communicate with each other? Although there is significant controversy over the proper limits to the concept of the sign, most theorists take a narrow view. Eco, for example, excludes from semiotics any sign that cannot be used to lie (*Theory*, 6–7). In fact, these debates involve no genuine theoretical questions. Any theoretical difficulties can be easily overcome by introducing intermediate distinctions (such as the possibility of degenerate or partial sign functions). What is really at stake in these debates is the question of with whom and what humanity will share its jealously guarded signifying capacities, and that is a question that will hear no purely theoretical evidence.

The next, more directly relevant, and far less controversial field of semiotics is anthroposemiotics, the study of all those signs in which the source and the receiver of the sign are human and the standing-for is governed by convention. This is of course the study of culture, the so-called "human sciences." With anthroposemiotics we are comfortably back within the confines of the traditional distinction between the human and the natural. But this field is not without its own boundary disputes: the nature of conventionality is not itself particularly well understood, and not all signs produced by humans are anthroposemiotic—only those which are conventional. The burning martyr produces at least two clearly different kinds of signs—one because he is a martyr and is taken to have died for a cause, and one because he is a combustible object and emits smoke. There are harder cases. We have, for example, reason to believe that certain gestural signs, such as smiling, are humanly universal and have instinctual bases similar to those that underlie animal communication systems. What then do we make of the politician's smile? How does his smile affect our understanding of the infant's?

The inclusiveness of general and anthroposemiotics indicates the range and explanatory power claimed by many semioticians. No major scholar goes so far as to claim that all our explanations of ourselves or our world must be semiotic ones or even that semiotic accounts are always to be preferred, but it is routinely argued that semiotic explanations are always available; nothing of interest to man is not a sign in some respects or capacity. When Eco introduces the idea of semiotics, his list of "areas of contemporary research" properly within the domain of semiotics would touch all but a few departments in the largest university (*Theory*, 9–14). And it has been the enduring project of Thomas Sebeok, America's most active and for some years its lone semiotician, to efface the outer bounds of the semiotic enterprise. But such generality has its price. It may be that the price is the very existence of such a field of study. Eco has recently come to wonder whether general semiotics is distinguishable from philosophy of language (*Philosophy*, 7–8). Even if we can find a coherent ground for a general semiotics, we may purchase its explanatory power at the cost of the kind of detailed attention thought essential within the disciplines it would include.

Nevertheless, the context of the more general field is indispensable. By keeping before us the kinds of explanations with which semiotic accounts of literary works must be compatible, we remind ourselves what is implied in the logic of any semiotic account. This is a corrective especially important in a hybrid area such as literary studies. The promise of semiotics is the promise of a common language and a common ground of analysis. When literary critics with a formalist bent go wrong, they most often do so by forgetting how much literature participates in the general semiotic of our lives. Without the context of the more general fields of semiotics, it is too easy to make semiotic studies only one more way of looking at literature and to fail to recognize what is entailed by such a way of looking. To take an old but still relevant example, while there is no theoretical reason why a semiotic account cannot focus on the individual text, the norm of semiotic accounts of literature—their "center of gravity"—is at a higher level of generalization. The individual text is valuable to a semiotic analysis chiefly as an instance of, a demonstration of, or evidence for something else—some pattern, feature, or process shared by a number of texts. Any other sense in which the text is valued is just one more matter to be analyzed. Because the warrant and tools for semiotic analysis come from this higher level of generalization, the semiotic study of literature places itself as one aspect in the study of cultural behavior and artifacts, as one branch of a broadly defined cultural anthropology. To ignore this generalizing impulse in literary semiotics is to fail to understand what it is good for and what it is not.

Defining literary semiotics in terms of the more general fields is not easy. Because literary study, semiotic or not, is defined by its object, the success of any definition of literary semiotics will depend on an adequate semiotic understanding of the literary object. This object has, from earliest times, no doubt from its original times, been taken to be crucially different both from the general mass of cultural objects and from the group of verbal texts it so much resembles. Most who have studied literature as a semiotic phenomenon have also taken the literary object to be special, even unique, among cultural objects and so have set about to find in the semiotic structures of the object itself those distinctive features that mark literature's special character. Yet all such attempts have met only failure: no designation of a particular class of sign users, or of a particular kind of sign, or of a particular kind of standing-for can adequately delimit the class of literary texts. For what separates the literary work from others is not the nature of the object but its location in the field of culture: it has inhabited a different and special cultural position, one it has shared with the sacred and the demonic. It is our attitude, not the object, that makes the crucial difference.

Semiotic attempts to discover the principles of inclusion in the class of literary texts have been presented as investigations of "literariness," usually said to be analogous to grammaticality in language. Such analogies drawn from linguistics are dangerous: they have, since Saussure, been frequently misused as patterns or blueprints for semiotics. But this particular analogy can, rightly seen, shed light on the problem of what is to count as literature and why. Only in this century did linguists overcome the problem of naïve, value-based preselections of the object of study: it is now accepted that the English language is what its speakers speak and that differences among speakers and speech communities are a function of familially related dialects. A similarly self-conscious attitude toward literary values is apparently harder to maintain. John Ellis has argued persuasively against naïve preselections of the object of literary study: literature is what a community of readers is willing to count as literature.[10] But most critics are inextricably wedded to their own reading community, beginning their studies with a canon whose membership, categories, and valuations they seem unable to question. Of course the features of literary objects uncovered by the investigations of literariness have been important, interesting, useful—*and* nondistinctive. So long as the concept of the object of study remains inadequately historicized in terms of specific reading communities at specific times—that is, so long as it is inadequately semiotic—so long will searchers for literariness miss the point.

When considered not as a branch of general semiotics but as a way of looking at literature, literary semiotics is more easily defined, although somewhat at the cost of obscuring crucial issues. From this angle, literary semiotics has two diagnostic features: the analysis places the text as the focal object in a communicative or transactional model of the literary event, and it explains that event in terms of code or systems theory. Although it is often thought that a mad formalism is the sole distinguishing feature of semiotics, the value of highly formalized code or systems descriptions has yet to be demonstrated. In some branches of semiotics—textgrammar, for example—something approaching complete formalism does appear to be useful; but it seems likely that fully systematic formal accounts of literary texts and transactions will prove inefficient. Without some additional reasons for complete formal specification—as, for example, the sort of benefits provided by calculation in the physical sciences—accounts which are code-based but not fully formal will be preferred (See Eco, *Theory,* 11–13).

The transactional model of literary semiotics is a specialized version of the general sign model, one that specifies a human source and a particular range of intentions on the part of receivers and, perhaps, producers. Eco's version of the transactional model, developed from Jakobson and distantly from Saussure, can serve as an example.[11]

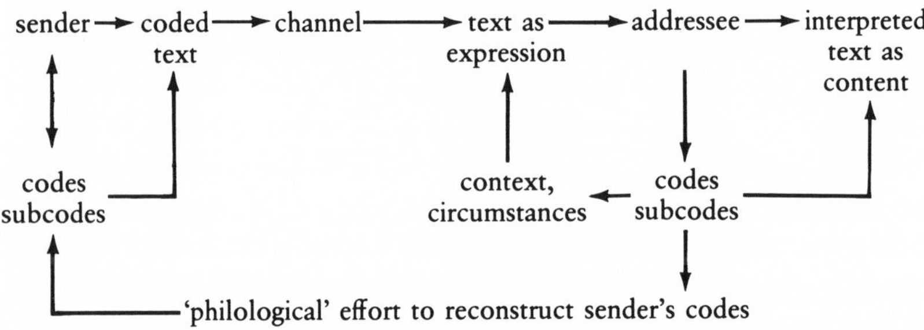

The model is both semantic and pragmatic in design: it demands investigation both into the structure of texts as semiotic objects and into the activities of readers, writers, and their intermediaries (editors, publishers, booksellers, critics, librarians et al.) as semiotic participants. Because this is a general model of text structure rather than a specifically literary model and is designed to analyze rather than to produce interpretations, it can account for a variety of quite different ways of reading, including those whose assumptions and claims are incompatible with semiotics. While the model and its theory might thus appear suspiciously imperialistic, it has the important advantage of placing most debates about ways of reading at the level on which they belong—that of values. Semiotics' promise of a common language is the promise not of a common understanding but of a vigorous debate informed by reliable analyses. The transactional model assumes that to practice a particular way of reading is to adopt a specific, though not necessarily well-defined, set of reading codes and that to adopt this or that way of reading is a matter not of literary necessity but of value-governed choice.

Eco's comprehensive and sometimes difficult *Theory of Semiotics* aside, anyone seeking a basic, reliable introduction to general semiotics will be largely disappointed.[12] Somewhat dated, but still useful are three essays in Cesare Segre's *Semiotics and Literary Criticism* of 1973. In these essays, Segre takes stock of the state of semiotic studies in the face of the overwhelming popular fascination with French structuralism. Theoretically and, what was then more rare, historically informed, Segre's eminently sensible account recognizes very well the place of the more popular brands of semiotics and charts with some precision the path along which semiotics would retreat from the ground staked out by structuralism. Segre carefully analyzes what he takes to be the defining issues of literary semiotics, including what was then the best account of what it would take to explain adequately the relationship between the poetic and the "ordinary." Not only does Segre correctly assess the relationship between poetic and ordinary language, but he recognizes that that matter is correlative to and fully implicated in another: the relationship (in his Jakobsonian terminology) between the poetic and the ordinary "message," an issue that opens crucial questions about other relationships—between the poetic text and the world, the poetic text and its author, and the poetic text and its readers. This statement of the state of semiotic theory is paired with a review of then-current work in semiotics, including a very useful review of semiotics in film studies and an interesting discussion of Eco's *La Struttura Assente* (Milano, 1968), the work that after several transformations became *A Theory of Semiotics*.

The next most useful path into the general field is found in the many heterogeneous collections of work in semiotics. Among the most appealing of these are the two companion volumes of the late seventies edited by Thomas Sebeok: *A Perfusion of Signs,* the transactions of the First North American Semiotics Colloquium of 1975; and *Sight, Sound, and Sense,* a selection of papers given in Indiana University's Semiotics in the Humanities program of 1975–1976.[13] These volumes offer a useful picture of the range of anthroposemiotic studies now under way as well as some preliminary but interesting suggestions concerning the place of zoosemiotics in the study of man. These reports of specific findings in a number of disciplines nicely characterize the semiotic enterprise in action, an enterprise which has a common goal and theory but which these volumes show to be quite various in its specific deployments. Only a few of the essays in these collections deal directly with literature, and those that do are not particularly strong; but the context of these essays provides a helpful standard for evaluating specifically literary semiotic studies.

The best single account of the position that argues the widest possible domain for semiotics can be found in Sebeok's *The Sign & Its Masters*.[14] In this typically polemical, yet genial collection of essays, Sebeok attempts to trace the range of semiotics' reach across disciplines as well as the depth of the semiotic account of the nature of life itself. One of the most prolific figures in modern semiotic studies and by far its most tireless promoter, Sebeok's is the major voice advancing so far-reaching a definition of semiotics, primarily by advancing the case for zoosemiotics—a case which argues that semiosis is grounded in biology. Championing, as always, the work of Jakob von Uexküll in ethology and of René Thom in the mathematical foundations of biology, Sebeok equates semiosis with life and explores the "parallelisms between the semiotic mechanisms of the Mind and the evolutionary processes of Nature" (xi). "The profound problem of signification" is, for Sebeok, not the nature of the thing which stands-for (so often the focus of the semiotics of the past) but the nature of the thing signified, which only the naïve anthropomorphically identify with thought or idea. "The ultimate solution," he argues, "had to be anchored in the biological make-up of organisms": (*Sign*, x). Although Sebeok's examples are rather too few and well-worn to be fully convincing, they are suggestive and do demand serious consideration by those whose interest is focused on semiosis of so high an order as literature.

More recently, Sebeok has teamed with Eco to edit a delightful, off-beat collection, *The Sign of Three: Dupin, Holmes, Peirce*, which though not strictly a work of literary criticism may prove the most pleasant of all first avenues into semiotics for the literary critic.[15] This collection of essays which seek out the philosophic and semiotic lessons to be learned from its trinity of detectives is hardly a systematic account of semiotics itself and offers not a single exemplary work of literary analysis, but what it does offer is a wealth of engaging, sophisticated, but in no sense technical, conversation with the common theme of how things semiotic shape what in life we know and how we know it. The collections opens with Thomas Sebeok and Jean Umiker-Sebeok's superb piece, "'You Know My Method': A Juxtaposition of Charles S. Peirce and Sherlock Holmes" as entertaining an account of what semiotic study can be as any that I know. Along the way, the reader encounters first-rate semiotics, learns a bit about the history of semiotics, a bit more about our detectives, and ends with an English translation of an essay sure to interest those who enjoyed *The Name of the Rose*. If nothing else, here is sure proof that semiotics need not be difficult and a sure proving ground for whether one has a taste for semiotics.

For those seeking an introduction to a strictly literary semiotics, there are several explicitly introductory works, many of them admirably basic.[16] These introductions often conflate semiotic studies with structuralist or poststructuralist work, and they are more than anything else guides to further reading. Perhaps the best text for a more serious initial venture into the semiotic study of literature is Maria Corti's *An Introduction to Literary Semiotics*.[17] Without assuming too much familiarity with semiotics or too little knowledge of literary criticism, Corti guides the reader slowly and effectively to a semiotic conception of the literary work by means of a comprehensive and judiciously arranged survey of the field. The presentation is general yet well informed, critical yet not dominated by her own judgments, theoretical yet sensitive to the pragmatic concerns of the working critic. Corti's is a view of the critical enterprise which opens possibilities, both to the reader new to semiotics and to the scholars whose work she reports. Nowhere in the texts cited here is there a better example of how the ecumenicalism of the semiotic transactional model can ground an integrated yet diverse discipline of literary studies. Corti's discussion of how semiotics allows the critic to use the tools of sociology is a model of what would otherwise be called interdisciplinary study. Moreover, Corti is admirably cognizant that the question of the historical and cultural distance between authors and readers is central to any adequate literary semiotics. There is a bibliography included, but it is incomplete and strongly reflects Corti's personal interest in the sociological aspects of semiotics.

Another work that is in some sense a primer is Seymour Chatman's *Story and Discourse: Narrative Structure in Fiction and Film*, a synthetic survey of recent work in the theory of narrative.[18]

Narrative has been perhaps the most productive (and, significantly, the most traditional) area of semiotic research. But, with the exception of structuralist work,[19] this research has been conducted almost exclusively in the journals; the few book-length studies tend to be themselves collections of essays with perhaps a theoretical introduction—as, for example, Cesare Segre's fine, but limited, *Structure and Time*.[20] Thus, those in search of ongoing work on narrative structure will have to scan the journals, though collections such as the three special issues on narrative in *PTL* (1980–1981) can make that job easier.[21] For a more basic review, Chatman's survey will do nicely.

Chatman characterizes his work in *Story and Discourse* as "dualist and structuralist in the Aristotelian tradition" (9); it is by present criteria fully semiotic. His arguments "are contributions to a theory of narrative, not the theory itself" (11). Like other professedly preliminary contributions to semiotics, *Story and Discourse* has a large measure of taking stock. There is accordingly relatively little in Chatman's discussion that cannot be found elsewhere; he is more likely to suggest than to pursue new lines of inquiry. Yet within the limits of his broad synthesis, Chatman performs a valuable service.

Chatman's professed alliances leave him with a sharply circumscribed model: his interest extends no wider than the inscribed participants—the implied author and the implied reader—which are the outer limits of the text itself. Within this compass, Chatman's concern is further limited primarily to questions of form. Thus all narrative is said to consist of a signifier or expression, the *discourse,* and a signified or content, the *story*. Story is constituted by events and existents—actions, happenings, characters, and settings. The chief features of discourse are plot, space/time framing, and the narrative participants (implied author, narrator, narratee, implied reader). Chatman further analyzes story and discourse by distinguishing, in the manner of the Danish linguist Louis Hjemslev,[22] between form and substance at each level: "We must distinguish between the discourse and its material manifestation—in words, drawings, or whatever. The latter is clearly the *substance* of narrative expression, even where the manifestation is independently a semiotic code. . . . The substance of events and existents [story] is the whole universe, or better, the set of possible objects, events, abstractions, and so on that can be "imitated" by an author (film director, etc.)" (23–24). Within this framework Chatman focuses on the formal, rather than the substantial, level and elaborates a theory of the structure of narrative based on a number of different, and in some cases incompatible, positions. He does this with tact and without failing to note the obstacles to a full synthesis.

Given the care with which Chatman states and executes his purpose and given the usefulness of this work as a primer, it would be inappropriate to charge the book with superficiality. As a collection of many different and differently motivated studies, *Story and Discourse* is valuable work. But it is also work that confuses its theoretical foundations. Consider Chatman's preliminary demarcation of his subject, which leads to "a reasonable and modern answer to the question" of "what narrative is *in itself*. Literary critics tend to think too exclusively of the verbal medium, even though they consume stories daily through films, comic strips, paintings, sculptures, dance movements, and music. Common to these artifacts must be some substratum; otherwise we could not explain the transformation of "Sleeping Beauty" into a movie, a ballet, a mime show" (9). Even if we give Chatman the assumption that those things we call by a single name must have some one common "substratum," we have to wonder what by this formulation is not narrative. If we make Chatman stand by these criteria (and he offers no better ones), then he must hold that we consume stories in recipes, in expense account reports, in flow charts, in "expository" texts of all kinds, in any number of forms of discourse that are neither narrative nor (very often) literary. This is undoubtedly the fact of the matter, and it is a conclusion that the theory, which is premised on the discovery of literariness (17), cannot absorb.

Presumably Chatman did not have available soon enough Mary Louise Pratt's convincing use of the work of William Labov to demonstrate that narrative is not a specifically aesthetic category and that narrative in literature is not different in kind from "ordinary" spontaneous narrative speech.[23] Perhaps Chatman was also unaware of the substantial body of work on narrative structure published in journals devoted to textlinguistics, psycholinguistics, and cognitive psychology and in a few cases reflected in essays found in journals devoted to literary theory—though this omission is more troubling. No semiotics can afford to be parochial, especially not a semiotics of literature, where the temptation is especially powerful. An informed survey of what we know about narrative makes it clear that narrative is not a literary category but one of two major forms of discourse structuring.[24] Thus narrative is not to be explained in terms of literariness, and narrative discourse is not coincident with pictoral narrative, film, drama, or any number of other story vehicles. Chatman is certainly right that there is a stratum of semiotic structuring which stories in different media share, and we can only welcome attempts to describe what that stratum might be. But that is certainly not a discursive stratum, and it is likely to be only poorly described by analytical categories specifically designed for narrative discourse.

Most semiotics practiced in English is dominated by stylistics, now dormant, or by works attempting to isolate the distinctive features of literary discourse. The latter tend to be fragmentary, openly professing to be preliminary to any coherent formulation. They are often theoretically primitive. Typical is Barbara Herrnstein Smith's *On the Margins of Discourse: The Relation of Literature to Language*, a collection of pieces which are said to be unified by a common concern and are offered as a part of "the general study of social and symbolic behavior."[25] At the center of Smith's project and basic to the definition of marginal discourse is her distinction between natural and fictive discourse. Fictive discourse is discourse represented or displayed; it belongs to the general category of fictive objects and events, the creation of which "reflects our impatience with nature, with that which merely *happens* to exist, happens to happen, or happens to 'appear.' They are the products of our impulse and ability to fabricate, by acts of hand, eye, or mind, *representations* (simulacra, images, quasi-instances) of natural 'phenomena': that is, to construct or to *make appear* either counterforms of phenomena or counter-feit instantiations of *types* of phenomena which, 'in nature,' exist or occur independent of our own designs or desires" (xi). Natural discourse, natural objects are everything else. But it is hard to know what this everything else might be like. Although there is surely much that is independent of human desires, where might we find in our world anything not touched by humanity's myriad designs? Where, in the realm of phenomena relevant to literature, is this natural existence that just "happens to happen"?

Smith's definition of the fictive/natural distinction rests on two more familiar ones: the "traditional opposition of 'art' and 'nature'" (x) and the more recent distinction between culture and nature. The latter is closer to what the definition requires, as is shown by her observation that fictive objects include "mask, costume, effigy, and illustration" as well as "play, sport, or simply manufacture" and that they are analogous to "the fashioning of tools, the cultivation of plants, or the domestication of animals" (xi). Again, one can only wonder what aspects of culture are not included in such a category. Unwilling to argue the patent absurdity of a noncultural form of discourse, Smith continues: "While discourse itself is certainly the supreme instrument and product of human designs and desires and may therefore seem to be naturally artificial, nevertheless utterances, like other objects and events, can be regarded as 'natural' *relative* to such representations of them (that is, 'fictive utterances') as we may produce for special ends, aesthetic and other, and which thus serve novel or distinctive functions" (xi–xii). Now there are three categories: natural objects, fictive objects (which include discourse), and especially fictive objects (such as fictive utterances) which serve "special ends" and are thereby "novel."

The title chapter provides the best example of the confusions that plague this kind of endeavor. It begins well, with an argument that no natural category of verbal objects will correspond to the class of literary or poetic texts. Smith offers an alternative procedure: she will account for poetry in terms of our behavior with poems—another good start. Then she finds in that behavior two "covert functional categories"—natural and fictive discourse (45). Natural discourse consists of "all utterances, spoken or inscribed, that can be taken as someone's saying something, sometime, somewhere, that is, that are understood to be verbal acts of particular persons on, and in response to, particular occasions" (47). Fictive discourse is, accordingly, discourse that is somehow "not said," whose production is not an event. Smith analyzes various kinds of fictive utterances: verbal illustrations, advertisements, greeting cards, quotations, proverbs, found poems, and poetry. Remarkably enough, poetry invites (requires) a response that is unique among fictive utterances: it alone demands interpretation, the act of "construing—imagining, projecting, elaborating—a particular plausible but not actual context" (75) which is "unfixable, unlocatable, in the natural universe" (55). No explanation of this response is offered; it is just what we do: "With respect to what we take to be poetry, interpretation is understood to *be* the purpose" (75). Despite the apparatus of the "covert functional categories," poetry is once again inexplicably special—and special in a distinctly contemporary, highly parochial way. Smith's kind of interpretation has not always or even usually been taken to be the purpose of poetry; indeed, many readers do not now take it in that way.[26] In the course of only ten pages, Smith moves from the claim that the study of fictive discourse will allow us to "abandon the thankless enterprise of stalking definitions" for poetry (45) to a "description" of the only correct response to poetry (55), where, moreover, the response defines the object. In between she generously allows the "option of behaving *inappropriately* in response to a given verbal structure" (49).

The best antidote to all such attempts to advance one or another semiotic feature as defining literariness is Mary Louise Pratt's *Toward a Speech Act Theory of Literary Discourse*.[27] Pratt's study includes a definitive argument against what she calls the " 'Poetic Language' Fallacy" and an excellent analysis of how ordinary literary narrative really is. And when Pratt turns to her own sketch of a theory of literary discourse, it falls out that literary discourse is marked only by a particular (and not unique) concatenation of "ordinary" linguistic and pragmatic features. Using speech-act linguistics, sociolinguistics, and the philosophical analysis of conversation associated with Paul Grice, Pratt offers an unusually comprehensive account of the "literary speech situation." That this account seems not to reveal astonishing new facts or to lead to major reevaluations of what there is to say about literary discourse is a considerable virtue in a work that looks to "a unified theory of discourse which allows us to talk about literature in the same terms we use to talk about all the other things people do with language" (vii). That the analysis is incomplete and professedly preliminary is, alas, par for the course.

There are at present relatively few substantial and refined bodies of semiotic scholarship. For the most part, semiotic accounts of literature proceed with an ad-hoc group of theoretical principles, each time constructing anew a proto-theory useful to some particular end. One body of semiotic scholarship that is indeed substantial and refined—and anything but ad-hoc—is that produced by the Soviet scholars in the Moscow-Tartu Group. These scholars have developed a highly suggestive, wide-ranging version of semiotics that focuses primarily on the study of culture as an information-bearing system governing behavior and that studies literary systems as only one aspect, albeit a major aspect, of cultural information. Heir to such distinguished scholars as the folklorist Vladimir Propp and the cognitive psychologist Lev Vygotsky, to the linguists and literary critics now called the Russian formalists and their Czech successors, the Prague Circle (both of which groups included Roman Jakobson), and more recently to the group of linguist-critics centered around Mikhail Bakhtin, Soviet semioticians have a sense of tradition unique in contemporary semiotics. Their works begin as though engaged in a conversation already under way, with terms and goals already defined and a body of research already in motion—something that can be said of little of the semiotic work produced in English, which seems always to suffer from a state of permanent preliminariness. First gathered in the early 1960s to share their work in mathematical linguistics (including machine translation), artificial languages, and the "poetics" of a variety of cultural communication systems, the Moscow-Tartu Group remains acutely aware of its ties to information theory and cybernetics; in this way, too, its work is more fully developed and more sophisticated than any to be found in the West.

Together, the sense of a strong traditional base and of their ties to highly developed and highly technical forms of analysis give the writings of Soviet semioticians a character somewhat out of step with prevailing practice in the West. For the most part these writers first appeared in English in collections of essays,[28] and the essay is in fact their dominant genre—as one would expect for researchers working together in what they take to be a collective enterprise. But it is easy to be misled by those collections. Here, we tend to hold a view of critical and even theoretical discourse that supposes a relatively general audience: even the most narrow specialist or the most recondite theorist holds to standards of explanation that make sense only if one assumes an audience of more than just other workers in the same specialized fields. This is not so in all disciplines, and it is not so of these Soviet theorists. Their works are, by our standards, remarkably dense and remarkably short—short on explanation, short on supporting detail, short on discussion of the claims they make. Indeed, some of their essays seem to be all claim, more pronouncements than arguments. In part, this is a tradition that can be traced to the Russian formalists and the critics of the Prague Circle, whose works sometimes have a like character. But more important is that these texts are chiefly memorials of conversations held elsewhere. In that context explanations, details, and other gestures toward an unknowing or skeptical audience are, quite precisely, beside the point. For these writers, the grounds of the conversation—explanation, detail, argument, all that we would most care about—are not in the text but in their common experience.

The two literary scholars in the group whose works are most widely available are Boris Uspenski and Yuri Lotman. They produced the first two volumes, both quickly translated into English, in a series more recognizable by our standards, entitled "Semiotic Studies in the Theory of Art." Uspenski's contribution, *A Poetics of Composition*, is a study of the structures by which authors create "point of view."[29] Uspenski investigates point of view on four "planes"—the ideological, the phraseological, the spatial-temporal, and the psychological; in each case, Uspenski explores specific semiotic structures which signal point of view, finding on each plane various kinds of signs (themselves at levels ranging from diction and sentence structure through global plot structures). This is traditional formalist criticism, known to us in many exemplars, Slavic and American. What is distinctive here is chiefly the range of analytical tools which Uspenski brings to bear on his subject, a range much expanded by Uspenski's wide knowledge of recent work in the semiotics of language. If nothing else, Uspenski greatly enhances our ability to describe our impressions of point of view in terms of what we find on the pages we read.

Although Uspenski's is an exemplary work of formalist criticism and an example of how a good critic can integrate the many tools semiotics puts at our disposal, there is little definitively "semiotic" about *A Poetics of Composition* (for many readers a positive virtue). More to the point of our present interest is Yuri Lotman's contribution, *The Structure of the Artistic Text,* which sketches the state of the art in Soviet literary semiotics.[30] Now fifteen years old, *Structure* only imperfectly represents his and his colleagues' current position. Nevertheless, *Structure* remains the best statement of Soviet literary semiotics yet available in English. Art is, for Lotman, a "secondary modeling system" which is "constructed *on the model of a language*" (9); that is, the aesthetic structure of the literary text is a second-order structure coexisting with the primary structure of the natural language. Such modeling systems, which include most of culture, are secondary both in the sense of "second order" and in the sense of "derivative": "Inasmuch as man's consciousness is a linguistic consciousness, all types of models erected as superstructures on that consciousness—and art among them—can be defined as secondary modeling systems" (9–10). From his bi-planar structural model of the text and from the well-known evidence of the inadequacy of any paraphrase of the artistic text, Lotman concludes that the secondary modeling structure of the artistic text, its aesthetic component, conveys information (what is lost in the paraphrase) and that the artistic text is to be studied as a communication.

Lotman professes to be concerned only with the structure of artistic texts, "the system of their internal organization" (69), but such a claim must be taken in the context of Soviet academic practice, where various kinds of "extrinsic" criticism are the norm. Thus Lotman presupposes an expansive, rather than exclusive, conception of "internal organization." Because it is a complex sign necessarily constructed in at least two modeling systems, the artistic text is never only aesthetic but routinely incorporates a number of other primary and secondary modeling systems. As Lotman had earlier argued, "there is no conclusion more important" than that "the historical-cultural reality which we call 'the literary work' is not confined to the text. The text is only one element of a relation. The real body of the literary work consists of a text (a system of internal relations) in its relation to extra-textual realities—life, literary norms, traditions, ideas. It is impossible to conceive of a text cut off from its extra-textual background."[31]

Because of this dualistic character, artistic texts are said to be closely related to two other kinds of secondary models: "Scientific models are a means of cognition—they organize man's intellect in a certain manner. Game models are a school of activity—they arrange man's behavior. . . . An artistic model is a unique combination of scientific and game models, organizing the intellect and behavior simultaneously. Play in comparison to art is *without content*; science in comparison to art is *inert*" (69). If the artistic text is a sign which "organizes man's intellect," it must be a sign of something. Using Peirce's concept of the iconic sign,[32] Lotman argues that the artistic text models or reproduces some individual part of "the universe": "The artistic message creates an artistic model of some concrete phenomenon" (18). To describe the text as a semiotic entity is to describe both the "individual norm of aesthetic communication" by which that phenomenon is organized and a more general "language of art" (the aesthetic modeling system, the conventions that distinguish aesthetic texts from other kinds), which models the structures by which a culture or community organizes and understands the universe: "Artistic language models the universe in its most general categories which, being the most general content of the universe, are the form of existence for concrete things and phenomena. Thus the study of the artistic language of works of art provides us not only with a certain individual norm of aesthetic communication, but also reproduces a model of the universe in its most general outlines. From many standpoints, the most important information is that which arises when a type of artistic language is selected" (18).

Lotman's account of the semiotics of literature is far too extensive to be surveyed in detail here. Though introductory, his text is still quite dense, its implied audience already well-versed in semiotic theory. He often fails to provide anything like a full argument for his positions, nor does he always confront the implications of those positions. Although Lotman is a learned literary historian, he can be alarmingly casual, even cavalier, in assuming that the results of the particular investigations he envisions are readily available. Discovering codes or norms seems to him a rather simple procedure: one merely compares "functionally similar texts" and isolates the invariant features (15), as though even the preliminary selection of "functionally similar" texts were not fraught with difficulty. That he thinks Vladimir Propp's classic, but primitive, study of narrative structure in folktales an exemplary use of this technique also suggests a great oversimplification of the task facing literary criticism.[33]

One of the few substantial, cohesive bodies of semiotic scholarship produced in the West is the work of Michael Riffaterre, who started early on the periphery of structuralism and has in recent years developed a unique semiotic theory of literature, one that reflects a familiar view of the nature of the poetic text but that is startling in its austere allegiance to positions others hold more often than not in the breach. Riffaterre also assumes that the task of a literary semiotics is to describe the internal structure of the poetic text, but with a crucial difference in intellectual, institutional, and social context. Whereas the Soviet focus on the internal structure of the text presupposes the dominance of a highly developed "extrinsic" criticism, Riffaterre pursues the most extensive, the most refined, and the most narrow of recent studies of "literariness." In his *Semiotics of Poetry* and in his later, less theoretical *Text Production*, Riffaterre has developed a semiotics designed to account for poetic texts that come to their readers shorn of all ties to author, context, or even language.[34] For Riffaterre, the poetic text is simply, purely a "closed entity" (*Semiotics*, 2). Although Riffaterre has, since 1966, also argued that the literary text is part of a communicative exchange, this communication is of a very special sort: only those aspects of the communicative process which are explicitly signaled in the text and which are independent of writers' and readers' cultural and personal situations count as features of poetic communication.[35] Moreover, this communication is impoverished in still other ways: "Whereas a normal communication act involves the presence of five elements [encoder, message, decoder, code, context (reality)] . . . literary communication has only two components physically present as things—the message and the reader" (*Production*, 3). Assumptions like these ground the necessary closure of the poetic text, which in turn grounds the most striking of Riffaterre's theoretical claims, the perfect singularity of the literary sign function. Such assumptions also explain Riffaterre's exceedingly narrow range of reference. It might seem strange that theoretical works that maintain such wide-ranging, universalist claims should employ "only French examples, primarily from nineteenth-

and twentieth-century writers" (*Semiotics,* ix), but if the "poeticity" of all poems is the same, then any poems will do for a working corpus. Not only is this *the* semiotics of poetry, but that semiotic is itself singular: there is only one thing that any poem, as a poem, can do.

The lineaments of this theory are laid down in *Semiotics of Poetry*. Riffaterre argues that because a poetic text is composed of language, it appears to invite the reader to consider it as an instance of mimesis; such experience is characteristic of first readings and generates the *meaning* of the text (4–5). But poetic texts by their nature "threaten" mimesis: subsequent readings reveal a number of "ungrammaticalities" or deviations from the norm of mimesis (4). The deviations are, he argues, always systematic variant readings of a "matrix"—an abstract semiotic structure realized only in its variants. Thus in a proper, poetic reading of the text, one that causes the reader to recognize the matrix, the poetic text becomes a single complex sign whose signified is a *hypogram,* a word or sentence that generates all the ungrammatical variants. Such a reading discovers the *significance* of the text and actualizes the process of *semiosis.*[36] The poetic text is thus overdetermined (because all the variants have the same signified) and intertextual (because it is grounded in the hypogram, which is another text). This established, the majority of *Semiotics of Poetry* argues for and demonstrates the process of semiosis. Riffaterre suggests a number of rules for the relationship between hypogram and text, providing along the way some remarkable readings of individual poems.

The theory of *Semiotics of Poetry* has both simplicity and great explanatory power. Riffaterre claims universal status for some of the rules delineated in *Semiotics of Poetry*, and in *Text Production* he shows that the poetic encompasses more than just verse: literary prose narrative is equally closed and hypogrammatic. Any interpretive method so simple and so powerful threatens to be banal, reductionist, or both. Riffaterre confronts the charge of reductionism by arguing that the process of reading for significance is not the reduction of the text to its hypogram but "the reader's praxis of transformation, a realization that is akin to playing, to acting out the liturgy of a ritual" (*Semiotics,* 12). While certainly more interesting than mere hypogram-hunting, Riffaterre's transformations from mimesis to semiosis can have—like ritual but unlike play-acting—only one authorized realization. And Riffaterre's startling, sometimes brilliantly inventive readings can make one despair that in this praxis very many readers will get it right. This reductionism is anything but naïve. Nor is it simply banal—Riffaterre is far too ingenious and interesting a reader of poetry. But however exciting some of the readings may be, it becomes disturbing when poem after poem, even a Balzac novella, come to be elaborations on clichés.

When we turn from the consequences to the constitution of the theory, the problems are no less serious. Much of Riffaterre's argument, especially in *Text Production*, rests on very precise claims about what poetry is (and does)—claims for which Riffaterre offers no argument, supporting one unargued claim with another. So Riffaterre banishes the historical author as "outside the literary phenomenon": "If, however, we amend the rationalized author's image [the author as inscribed in the text] with the help of the historical author, we destroy the text. We cannot, therefore, invoke the former to explain other texts written by the same person" (*Production,* 5). One would think that such a surprising conclusion might merit more substantial support than an unspecified claim about the destruction (surely a metaphorical destruction) of the text. But this is a very common pattern: "The [literary] text is always one of a kind, unique, and it seems to me that this *uniqueness* is the simplest definition of literariness that we can find. This definition can be quickly confirmed if we can remember that the literary experience is characteristically disorienting, an exercise in alienation, a complete disruption of our usual thoughts, perceptions, and expressions" (*Production,* 1). Riffaterre finds this claim about the essential alienating function of all literary texts especially useful. There seems to be no end to what it can "prove" (see *Production,* 6, 42). Although worse in *Text Production,* all of Riffaterre's accounts share the habit, far too common in all areas of semiotics, of building into the initial conception of the object of study so rich a set of prejudices that the analysis merely redescribes the consequences of those prejudices. It is impossible not to recognize in the central positions that generate Riffaterre's theory—in the autonomy (closure) of the poetic text, its alienating function, its necessary unity, its necessary uniqueness, the necessary absence of the historical author, the necessary presence of deviations from nonpoetic norms (ungrammaticality), and the self-referential (nonmimetic) character of poetic language—the configurations of a limiting (and dated) modernist aesthetic.

In the more systematic exposition in *Semiotics of Poetry* the problem is less often what Riffaterre assumes is true of poetry than what he takes as self-evidently true of the nonpoetic. Riffaterre's argument rests on his claim that poetic texts are ungrammatical because they violate "mimesis," the norms of language's referential function. Riffaterre begins solidly in the Jakobsonian line of literary semiotics, with his own version of the projection of "the principle of equivalence from the axis of selection into the axis of combination":[37] "In the semantics of the poem *the axis of significations is horizontal.* The referential function in poetry is carried out from signifier to signifier: reference consists in the reader's perceiving certain signifiers to be variants of a single structure [the hypogram]" (*Production,* 35). For Riffaterre, this signifier-to-signifier reference necessarily produces ungrammatical results, and it is only by this deviation from the norm of mimesis that a reader comes to recognize the poetic: "*A word or phrase is poeticized when it refers to (and, if a phrase, patterns itself upon) a preexistent word group*" (*Semiotics,* 23).

> The semiotic process really takes place in the reader's mind, and it results from a second reading. If we are to understand the semiotics of poetry, we must carefully distinguish *two levels or stages of reading,* since before reaching the significance the reader has to hurdle the mimesis. . . . But this reader input [the second reading] occurs only because the text is ungrammatical. To put it otherwise, his linguistic competence enables him to perceive ungrammaticalities; but he is not free to bypass them, for it is precisely this perception over which the text's control is absolute. (*Semiotics,* 4–5)

Riffaterre's version of a Jakobsonian poetics is but the latest in a long history of deviationist definitions of poetry. In its present form, the theory bears a strong resemblance to the deviationist account of poetic language developed early in this century by the Czech linguist and colleague of Jakobson, Jan Mukařovský, who included in his theory a deviation matrix called the "dominant."[38] As with all other such attempts to delimit the uniqueness of poetic discourse, Riffaterre's deviation argument rests on a wholly inadequate caricature of nonpoetic discourse, his ungrammaticality on a travesty of grammaticality. We can hardly dispute that poetic language will deviate from mimesis conceived in terms of pure, transparent, fully adequate references—but then so will all representational language. And it should hardly surprise us that we can discover in these "deviations" a logic of self-reference or that this logic will be particularly consistent in some kinds of poetry. What is, however, a genuine puzzle is why readers so sensitive to the nuances of language in literary texts should so blithely retail so gross a caricature of all other language. Another, related puzzle is the distinction Riffaterre suggests in the opening pages of *Text Production* between "text analysis" and poetics: "The difference between poetics and textual analysis is that poetics generalizes and dissolves a work's uniqueness into poetic language, but analysis, as I see it, attempts to explain the unique" (1–2). Riffaterre gives little more detail, but given that the analyses in *Text Production* are indistinguishable from the discussion of examples in *Semiotics of Poetry,* it would be intriguing to see what a coherent explanation of their difference might be like. For if this is a theory of such a text analysis, then the *Semiotics of Poetry* is no semiotics at all.

Most literary critics know Saussure's definition of the sign as a dyadic structure (signifier-signified), the conception which has dominated semiotic studies for most of this century.[39] But as the limitations of the Saussurean dyad have been increasingly felt, Peirce's more puzzling and more cumbersome account of sign structure has become increasingly important in contemporary studies. Unlike Saussure's sign, Peirce's is irreducibly triadic: "A sign, or *representamen,* is something which stands to somebody for something in some respect or capacity. It addresses somebody, that is, creates in the mind of that person an equivalent sign, or perhaps a more developed sign. That sign which it creates I call the *interpretant* of the first sign. The sign stands for something, its *object.* It stands for that object, not in all respects, but in reference to a sort of idea, which I have sometimes called the *ground* of the representamen" (*Papers,* 2.228). Peirce's definition of the sign differs from Saussure's chiefly in the necessary presence of an addressee, represented in the structure of the sign by the interpretant—"an equivalent sign, or perhaps a more developed sign" created in the mind of the addressee.[40] Because Peirce's sign is irreducible and must include the interpretant, any Peircean semiotics must be a pragmatics.[41] In this way, Peirce's account makes impossible Saussure's abstraction from *langage* to *langue,* from language as it is used to language as a pure system—the fundamental position which has made Saussurean theory such a powerful tool in the development of most branches of modern semiotics. In Saussure's linguistics, explanatory power and systematic coherence are gained at the cost of persons and the semiotic choices they make. Yet even Peirce's account of the sign is ultimately too static. As we now move to consider more closely the transactional nature of reader's relations with literary works, a still more complex and less stable sign becomes necessary. So long as semiotics is grounded in the sign-as-entity, we cannot account fully for the nature of semiotic transactions. A fully pragmatized semiotics will be based not on the sign-as-entity but on the sign-as-event.

As early as 1943 the Saussurean linguist Louis Hjemslev argued that the basis for semiotic studies must be shifted from the sign to what he called the sign function. Using the Saussurean framework, Hjemslev argued that the sign-as-entity is inappropriately one-directional and content-oriented: we come to think that "the sign [expression] is a sign for something [content]" (Prologomena, 57). That traditional formulation mistakenly privileges the signified and neglects the mutually determining character of the signifier-signified relationship—what Hjemslev calls its "solidarity." Privileging the signified can only lead us to misrepresent and undermine the chief value of the modern concept of the sign: "In the interest of clarity, despite the time-honored concepts whose shortcomings now become increasingly evident, we feel a desire to invert the sign-orientation: actually we should be able to say with precisely the same right that a sign is a sign for an expression-substance" (57).

Hjemslev brings us closer to an account of the sign compatible with a transactional theory. Yet the solidarity of the sign function is still too static, too firmly set. Hjemslev's analysis of the sign function in many ways just elaborates the consequences of Saussure's insistence on the arbitrariness of the signifier-signified relationship: we are still left with the problem of the nature and force of the associative bond Saussure found to hold between them. That bond, the solidarity, is not such a strong candidate as a foundation for the stability of signs once we recognize that the bond of expression and content in the sign function occurs only in texts, in uses, not as Saussure thought in preestablished, definitive codes—after all, even the dictionary is only a canonical text. If, as Hjemslev saw, signs are the concrete result of particular correlations of expression and content elements in the sign function, and if the expression form (the signifier) and content form (the signified) thus related are themselves complex entities constituted for that particular occasion, then the solidarity of the sign function must itself be occasional. As Eco puts it, "signs are the provisional result of coding rules which establish *transitory* correlations of elements" (*Theory*, p. 49). A semiotics of the sign thus becomes wholly inadequate: "One can maintain that it is not true that a code organizes signs; it is more correct to say that codes provide the rules which *generate* signs as concrete occurrences in communicative intercourse. Therefore the classical notion of 'sign' *dissolves* itself into a highly complex network of changing relationships" (49). The concern of a pragmatic semiotics is not primarily signs and their typologies or syntax but sign users' codes, the choices they make within them, and their reasons for making those choices.

In this way, the sign has become subject to a number of challenges from within semiotics, all leading to a suspicious regard of the associative bond Saussure presumed to hold between the signifier and the signified. If this bond can only be regarded as the "*transitory* correlation of elements," we are left with no guarantee—indeed, in many situations we have no reason to expect—that sign producers and sign receivers will envision the same or even closely similar correlations. It is, to be sure, undeniable that most semiotic transactions result in something we call understanding and that understanding is largely protected—by the overdeterminedness of most texts, by the redundancy afforded by the multiple codes that bear on most social exchanges, by the common interests of the participants, by the opportunity to obtain further clarification (that is, roughly synonymous messages), and so on. Yet for a number of cases, in ways that are only exacerbated by the use of written or otherwise recorded texts, the protection afforded to understanding dissolves, like the sign, into a complex network of choices. The traditional, stabilizing privilege of content seems to be not only undermined, but reversed. As Eco says in *The Role of the*

Reader, "The existence of various codes and sub-codes, the variety of socio-cultural circumstances in which message is emitted (where the codes of the addressee can be different from those of the sender), and the rate of initiative displayed by the addressee in making presuppositions and abductions—all result in making a message (insofar as it is received and transformed into the *content* of an *expression*) an empty form to which various possible senses can be attributed."[42] (*Role*, 5).

Saussure had warned against privileging the expression plane, for he knew full well that to do so would be to threaten the associative bond of signifier and signified which was the ground of his semiotics. The danger, he saw, is particularly acute when we, like his philological predecessors, regard only writing: "The graphic form of words strikes us as being something permanent and stable, better suited than sound to constitute the unity of language throughout time. Though it creates a purely fictitious unity, the superficial bond of writing is much easier to grasp than the natural bond, the only true bond, the bond of sound" (*Course*, 25). Unlike the bond of writing, which as the sign of the signifier brings us no closer to content and threatens to give the signifier a life of its own, the bond of sound (the associative bond) guarantees the stability of our semiotic forms. In our own times the temptation to privilege the signifier has proved great. Witness Derrida:

> In all senses of the word, writing thus *comprehends* language. Not that the word "writing" has ceased to designate the signifier of the signifier, but it appears, strange as it may seem, that "signifier of the signifier" describes on the contrary the movement of language . . . the signified always already functions as a signifier. . . . There is not a single signifier that escapes, even if recaptured, the play of signifying references that constitute language. The advent of writing is the advent of this play; today such a play is coming into its own, effacing the limit starting from which one had thought to regulate the circulation of signs, drawing along with it all the reassuring signifieds, reducing all the strong-holds, all the out-of-bounds shelters that watched over the field of language. This, strictly speaking, amounts to destroying the concept of "sign" and its entire logic.[43]

This is not the place to trace the threads of Derrida's rich and confusing tapestry or to sort out the relations between the present concern and Derrida's performances as fool and seer to the court of philosophy (were anti-foundationalist arguments relevant here, we might do as well with the rather less histrionic strains of Quine).[44] But semiotics must take seriously the instability of the sign. There is something akin to the "signifier of the signifier" in Peirce's triad, in which every object is associated with two "signifiers"—the representamen and the interpretant (which is always also a representamen). Peirce, no less than Derrida, took pleasure in the bound- and bond-shattering infinity of his "unlimited semiosis": "Lo, another infinite series" (*Papers,* 1.339). But most semioticians, no less than Peirce, also take seriously that we regard most of our semiotic transactions as more or less successful (as they would have to be to merit such a place in our behavior and physiology). Of those scholars who have produced major semiotic accounts of literature, only two seriously attempt to account for the criteria, the mechanisms, and the limits of successful literary *transactions,* those transactions to which readers give the name understanding. More than any others, these scholars, Eco and the German critic Wolfgang Iser, mark the direction that a future semiotics must find.

Umberto Eco's *The Role of the Reader* collects nine essays written over a period of twenty years, each concerned with the reader's interpretive labor in response to literary texts and with the text's influence on that response. Though the collection attests to Eco's long-standing recognition that an adequate semiotics must also be a pragmatics, it does not itself offer anything like a complete account of what such a pragmatics might be like. Six essays were written before Eco formulated his general theory and have interest primarily as a record of that theory. The remaining three present a preliminary glance at a theory yet to be formed. One essay, "Peirce and the Semiotic Foundations of Openness," suggests the theoretical grounds for the other two more practical essays. Another quickly sketches an account of the textual strategies which influence readers' "interpretive cooperation"—a sketch in which Eco once again demonstrates his remarkable ability to synthesize disparate materials but which is very brief. The last essay, "*Lector in Fabula*: Pragmatic Strategy in a Metanarrative Text," uses possible world analysis to produce an impressive account of the reader's options in response to Alphonse Allais's "*Un drame bien parisien.*" This too suffers a little from preliminariness, in that it is an exemplary analysis of a short text which presents its problems in a relatively explicit and simple form: we care about the analysis more for what it shows us might be done—or might be too difficult to be done—with other, more complex works than for what we learn about this one. As was the case with *A Theory*, the chief achievement of *The Role of the Reader* lies in Eco's powers of synthesis. Thus much of the interest is to be found in the texts which stand behind Eco's—in this case the many recent works in text semiotics, which, Eco tells us, "has reached a dreadful level of sophistication" (*Role*, viii) and which continues to develop in scope and difficulty. But if this *Reader* owes much to the work of others, what it brings to a literary semiotics is recompense enough.

Whatever the importance of pragmatics in semiotic theory, the fact remains that literary semiotics is inseparably attached to the analysis of texts. The six essays written before 1976 are more concerned with texts than with readers; the three more recent essays consider the reader chiefly as inscribed in the text as the "model reader" projected in textual features and strategies.[45] Eco devotes his most theoretical chapter to the task of establishing a Peircean distinction "between a theory of signification and a theory of communication" (*Role*, 180) which will in turn make it possible to describe a model reader in terms of textual features without denying it pragmatic force.[46] A good part of this work was accomplished in *A Theory*. Here, Eco calls attention to Peirce's suggestion that although all *signs* must be concrete occurrences with definite objects and interpretants, some *representamen* must exist only as potential signs; these representamen are already endowed with significance (in virtue of the configuration of those signs which have occurred for a speaker or a group of speakers) but have not yet occurred in fact. That is, once we take a class of signs as configured by a code, the code will generate the possiblity of further signs which never have or never will occur.[47] Moreover insofar as they are configured by a code, *all* representamen, concrete occurrence or not, can be thought of as having that same virtual character. The result, Eco argues, is a separation of our way of talking about codes (a theory of signification) and our way of talking about sign production (a theory of communication); but the separation is never more than partial, and signification must always find its ground in communication: "A *semiotics of the code* is an operational device in the service of a *semiotics of sign production*" (*Theory*, 128).

One consequence of separating signification and communication is a correlative separation between intensional and extensional semantics—a distinction that will prove necessary for Eco's analysis of the model reader in terms of possible worlds. Signs enable us to construct "a fictitious state of the world" only because of the "self-sufficiency of the universe of content": a sign "does not require the presence of the referred object as an element of its definition" (*Role,* 179). The argument for this familiar position focuses on Peirce's distinction between two kinds of objects of signs, dynamic objects and immediate objects. By restricting our attention to immediate objects, Eco argues, we have the basis for a purely intensional semantics.[48] This leads, of course, to another infinite series: "the meaning of a representation can be nothing but a representation" (*Papers,* 1.339); "meaning is, in its primary acceptation, the translation of a sign into another system of signs" (*Papers,* 4.127); "the meaning of a sign is the sign it has to be translated into" (*Papers,* 4.132). Again we engage the network of unlimited semiosis, although we should not conclude that unlimited semiosis leads us either to the domain of free play or to a prison-house of language. In practice, the infinite chain of interpretants is broken by the demands of particular situations and the interests of the participants, and the multiplication of interpretants is precisely what makes meaning public, accessible, and so richly connected to our world: "The analysis of content becomes a cultural operation which works only on physically testable cultural products, that is, other signs and their reciprocal correlations. . . . Thus one is never obliged to replace a cultural unit by means of something which is not a semiotic entity, and no cultural unit has to be explained by some platonic, psychic, or objectal entity. Semiosis explains itself by itself; this continual circularity is the normal condition of signification and even allows communicational processes to use signs in order to mention things and states of the world" (*Role,* 198).

The centerpiece of Eco's intensional analysis is the model reader. For the author, the model reader is a projection, "a model of the possible reader . . . supposedly able to deal interpretively with the expressions in the same way as the author deals generatively with them" (*Role,* 7). For the reader, the model reader is an invitation, or even a demand, to participate in the transaction in a particular way. Texts can be typed by the relative coerciveness of their model readers. Some texts, clearly only the lesser ones, have little or no force, primarily because their invitations are too crass: "Those texts that obsessively aim at arousing a precise response on the part of more or less precise empirical readers . . . are in fact open to any possible 'aberrant' decoding. A text so immoderately 'open' to every possible interpretation will be called a *closed* one" (8). Open texts, on the other hand, call for more varied and flexible responses, although, Eco warns, "you cannot use the text as you want." An open text "outlines a 'closed' project of its Model Reader as a component of its structural strategy" (9). Eco has no arguments to support this typology, only rather bluff versions of familiar metaphors of the fullness of good readings of open texts and of the self-interested consumerism of bad ones. Open texts "work at their peak revolutions per minute only when each interpretation is re-echoed by the others, and vice versa"; also, "it is possible to be stupid enough to read Kafka's *Trial* as a trivial criminal novel, but at this point the text collapses—it has been burned out, just as a 'joint' is burned out to produce a private euphoric state" (9–10).[49]

For the reader as critic, the model reader is the focal point of the text's organization as a semiotic object. "The text is nothing else but the semantic-pragmatic production of its own Model Reader" (10). The model reader is thus a group of "felicity conditions" that must "be met in order to have a macro-speech act(such as a text is) fully actualized" (11). From this point of view, the model reader enables a quite sophisticated analysis of texts, one which can deal with all levels of structuring in a text and which can account for both intensional and extensional interpretive elaborations. Despite the brevity of Eco's account of such an analytical system, he makes its power evident throughout. This discussion should benefit readers of any degree of familiarity with the materials reported.

I will not summarize Eco's already dangerously brief account of the textual structure of the model reader. Nor will I detail the analysis of Alphonse Allais's "*Un drame bien parisien*" in terms of its model reader. Eco's chief interest in this analysis lies in the interrelations among discourse structures, narrative structures, and world structures and in how the model reader constructs the latter. His chief tool is possible world analysis, a method of analyzing intensional structures as hypothetical extensional structures. Although the status of possible world analysis in philosophy is somewhat uncertain, in the study of texts it proves to be of considerable value.[50] It should be easy to see how a "fictional world" can be analyzed as a possible world—after all, that's where philosophy found the concept of a possible world; but what may not be evident is the utility of using possible world analysis in discussing such matters as the doxastic world of characters within a fiction or the projections of readers as they draw inferences and hold expectations in the course of reading. Among the successes here is Eco's account of the relationship between possible and actual worlds. Because it is impossible for any text to fully elaborate a world, every possible world must rely on a prior actual world. But the relationship does not rest on the "reality" of actual worlds; in this case, "actual" is the name we give to our own semiotic encyclopedia, to the constructed world we accept as our privileged field of reference. Actual worlds are different from possible worlds but only because they are cultural, not personal, constructions and because they are more fully elaborated—but never completely so: a "Global Encyclopedia is a mere regulative hypothesis" (*Role,* 222; cf. *Theory,* 129). This mode of analyzing fictional texts opens the possibility of powerful and suggestive answers to questions that are currently much discussed, such as the diagnostic features of fictional texts, the status of actual persons and events in fictional texts, the relationship between fictional and nonfictional narrative, and the necessity of fictionality in literature. Some of these questions Eco discusses at some length; others he only mentions; still others follow from the logic of his account.

Although Eco's discussion of "*Un drame*" can be impressive, it is subject to some of the criticism I brought against his discussion of the model reader. Eco is far too complacent about the integrity and force of his model reader. He carefully sets limits to the range of his interest: "to say that it is possible to recognize the type of reader postulated by the text does not mean to assume that it is possible to completely foresee his final and definitive interpretation"; "the adventures of [Allias's] readers [are] spurious data borrowed from a psychological or sociological enquiry about the empirical fate of a textual object" (257, 205). Despite such warnings, it is evident that at many points Eco can only be referring to real, not model, readers (see 254–255). And yet for any number of competent readers, the program Eco outlines cannot be followed as he presents it. Consider, for example, one kind of reader we would expect to come to Allais's text through Eco's presentation of it. That reader, probably a professional critic and presumably a highly practiced reader, encounters the story only after Eco has warned him to expect a "metanarrative text." Surely such a reader will anticipate Allais's disruption of the narrative pattern. If so, how likely is it that such a reader will be fooled into producing the naïve reading in anything like the form Eco argues for? The naïve model reader would still have a function in that case, but its function would be much more as a character within the fiction than as the model for the reader's activities that Eco envisions. Although a powerful analytical tool, Eco's model reader will nevertheless always remain a part of the text—that is, a complex sign that like all other signs depends on persons for its existence and will thus always be ready to accommodate itself to a personal universe of content.

Eco's model reader is only one of the many kinds of readers recently discovered. By now, many of my readers must have recognized the quite strong similarity between Eco's model reader and Wolfgang Iser's implied reader—a similarity that, as far as I can tell, Eco fails to acknowledge (Iser is not mentioned in Eco's bibliography; there is no index). This similarity is sufficiently great, and Iser's work so suggestive, that the omission is not a little surprising. Here is Iser's description of the implied reader in *The Act of Reading: A Theory of Aesthetic Response*:

> If, then, we are to try and understand the effects caused and the responses elicited by literary works, we must allow for the reader's presence without in any way predetermining his character or his historical situation. . . . The concept of the implied reader is therefore a textual structure anticipating the presence of a recipient without necessarily defining him: this concept prestructures the role to be assumed by each recipient, and this holds true even when texts deliberately appear to ignore their possible recipient or actively exclude him. Thus the concept of the implied reader designates a network of response-inviting structures which impel the reader to grasp the text.[51]

Iser develops the implied reader and his theory of reading in the context of the phenomenological tradition, especially the work of Roman Ingarden: "The phenomenological theory of art lays full stress on the idea that, in considering a literary work, one must take into account not only the actual text but also, and in equal measure, the actions involved in responding to that text . . . the ways in which it can be *konkretisiert* (realized)."[52] Although the differences between the semiotic and the phenomenological contexts are material, there are crucial similarities between a (transactional) semiotic approach to literary texts and Iser's phenomenological one. Roman Ingarden was a most semiotic phenomenologist, and in this as in so much else Iser has followed his lead, as evidenced by Iser's frequent references in the early parts of *The Act of Reading* to works in semiotics, linguistics, systems theory, information theory, and game theory. Conversely, the growing role of pragmatics in semiotic theory can be seen as an attempt to accommodate within semiotics some of the questions central to phenomenology.

Like Eco, Iser begins *The Act of Reading* with an aesthetic manifesto, "Partial Art—Total Interpretation," which uses the example of post modernist poetics to argue that "the traditional expository style of interpretation has clearly had its day" (10). In place of the "classical" concept of a meaning to be discovered or uncovered, Iser offers "the interaction between the text and, on the one hand, the social and historical norms of its environment, and, on the other, the potential disposition of the reader" (14). The textual component of that interaction consists primarily of the "repertoire" of codes and conventions and the "strategies" which organize them. Iser defines the repertoire by positing a basic difference between ordinary and literary uses of language. Whereas in most speech acts "the success of a linguistic action depends on the resolution of indeterminacies by means of conventions, procedures, and guarantees of sincerity," in literature "there can be no such given frames of reference. On the contrary, the reader must first discover for himself the code underlying the text. . . . The fictional text makes a selection from a variety of conventions to be found in the real world, and it puts them together as if they were interrelated. . . . As a result these conventions are taken out of their social contexts, deprived of their regulating function, and so become subjects of scrutiny in themselves. And this is where fictional language begins to take effect; it depragmatizes the conventions it has selected, and herein lies its pragmatic function" (60–61). This repertoire of depragmatized conventions is reorganized by the text into a structure of themes and horizons. Iser explains this structure in terms of perspectives: "As perspectives are continually interweaving and interacting, it is not possible for the reader to embrace all perspectives at once, and so the view he is involved with at any one particular time is what constitutes for him the 'theme'" (97). The horizon, then, is "made up of all those segments which had supplied the themes of previous phases of reading" (97).

For the reader, this theme and horizon structure becomes what Iser calls the "wandering viewpoint"; the reader must engage the text through a process of constant synthesis: "It is clear, then, that throughout the reading process there is a continual interplay between modified expectation and transformed memories . . . thus every moment of reading is a dialectic of protension and retention, conveying a future horizon already filled; the wandering viewpoint carves its passage through both at the same time and leaves them to merge together in its wake" (112). From the wandering viewpoint emerge images, the reader's mental constructions which are neither objects of experience nor ideas but something between the two. These images are the final point of the reader's interaction with the text: images are realized by virtue of the "schematized aspects"[53] provided by the text, but only within the context of the reader's own experience and mental habits. Iser concludes: "Meaning is the referential totality which is implied by the aspects contained in the text and which must be assembled in the course of reading. Significance is the reader's absorption of the meaning into his own existence. Only the two together can guarantee the effectiveness of an experience which entails the reader constituting himself by constituting a reality hitherto unfamiliar to himself" (151).

There is much to be gained from the juxtaposition of Eco's model reader and Iser's implied reader. Iser's analysis of the textual component of the interaction between reader and text—in which he relies heavily on Eco's early work—would be much improved by the contact with Eco's analysis of discourse, narrative, and world structures. The analytical work done by repertoire-theme-horizon is accomplished with greater subtlety and delicacy by Eco's possible-world analysis. Moreover, Eco's version has the additional advantage of not committing us to the two assumptions Iser needs to make his system go: because Iser's analysis can only work on fictional texts whose conventions have been "depragmatized," he must assume, first, an identity between literature and fiction and, second, an absolute (and caricatured) distinction between literary and ordinary discourse (59–63). And yet there is no genuine incompatibility between Eco's textual analysis—which gives a more appropriate account of fictionality, has superior explanatory power, and does not require additional assumptions about the nature of literary texts—and the real strength of Iser's work, his analysis of the reader's assimilation of the text.

Iser's analysis of response in *The Act of Reading* represents, in turn, a challenge to Eco's account from which it can only benefit. Iser's argument that any implied or model reader must be assimilated to exist and that any such assimilation must also be a transformation severely undermines any easy confidence that a reader will, or even will be able to, enact the program of a model reader. I do not think it necessary to take the whole of Iser's strong phenomenological orientation in order to take seriously his account of the process of interaction. Nor do I think it will do to dismiss, as Eco would, such inquiries as psychological or sociological and therefore outside semiotics (*Role,* 205). Thus, if semiotics is to give literary response the theoretical place it demands, Iser's *Act of Reading* is the best place to begin such a task. And taken together, these two works represent the most sophisticated and most promising account of readers and reading yet available.

It would take someone wiser or braver or more foolhardy than I to predict the course of so unformed an enterprise as semiotics. Some predictions seem safe enough: semiotics in the broadest sense will almost certainly continue as a force in literary studies. Critics have, at least since Aristotle, sought to describe literary works in relatively rigorous, usually formal ways, chiefly so that their judgments about those works could be correlated with recognizable textual features. Though such practices have fallen, and no doubt will again, into desuetude, it seems most likely that as we pursue our disagreements we will continue to appeal to what we take to be separately grounded descriptions of what we find on the page. Other predictions have only a short horizon: since very little in contemporary theory (or in this volume) does not involve semiotics—either directly, or indirectly by employing largely semiotic means, or inversely by defining itself against some semiotics—it seems likely that the literary theory of the immediate future will continue to bear the stamp of semiotics. Other predictions seem more like hopes: now that literary critics have recognized how semiotic investigations into the significance we make and find in the world bear on its inquiries and how, in turn, its inquiries bear on those investigations, one would like to think that criticism will not fall back into a ghetto of self-imposed isolation. But, ignorance and folly being what they are, that is a dicier proposition. At the same time, I see no signs, nor have there ever been signs, that semiotics will coalesce into a discipline, into a school transcending disciplines, or even into major schools within disciplines. That is all to the good, for the best fate for a general semiotics is that it dissolve itself under the pressures of use—not because a general semiotics can find no intelligible standing apart from the specific inquiries of specific disciplines (though that does indeed seem to be the case), but because the real good of a general semiotics can be known only by those who feel the press of the boundaries of specific disciplines. Then the dream of a general semiotics, like the dream of a universal language, will have had its day.

NOTES

1. Roman Jakobson, "Linguistics and Poetics," in *Style in Language*, ed. Thomas A. Sebeok (Cambridge: Technology Press of the Massachusetts Institute of Technology, 1960).
2. Michel Foucault, *The Order of Things: An Archaeology of the Human Sciences* (New York: Pantheon, 1970), pp. 42–44. Jacques Derrida sees ours as the century of semiotics, the century that by foregrounding semiosis generated the rupture that brought us into the domain of (free or [play]full) signification; "Structure, Sign, Play in the Discourse of the Human Sciences," in *The Structuralist Controversy: The Languages of Criticism and the Sciences of Man*, ed. Richard Macksey and Eugenio Donato (Baltimore: Johns Hopkins University Press, 1970), pp. 247–65.
3. Charles Sanders Peirce, *Collected Papers*, ed. Charles Hartshorne and Paul Weiss (1931–58; rpt. Cambridge, Mass.: Belknap, 1960), 4.214.
4. Umberto Eco, *A Theory of Semiotics* (Bloomington: Indiana University Press, 1976); Pierre Guirard, *Semiology*, trans. George Gross (London: Routledge and Kegan Paul, 1975).
5. Another indication of the importance of the mid-seventies in the

growing awareness of literary semiotics among Anglo-American critics can be found in the fact that, in this age of proliferating professional societies, the first North American Semiotics Colloquium was held in 1975; the Semiotic Society of America was not founded until 1976.

6. For a useful survey with an extensive bibliography, see Morton W. Bloomfield, "Stylistics and the Theory of Literature," *NLH,* 7 (1976), 271–311.
7. See Umberto Eco, *Semiotics and the Philosophy of Language* (Bloomington: Indiana University Press, 1984), pp. 6–8.
8. Some theorists question the specification of producers. Cesare Segre, for example, argues that to include "symptoms" (what Peirce calls "indexical signs") in the category of signs is to risk excluding intention (and thus producers) from semiotics [*Semiotics and Literary Criticism,* trans. John Meddeman (The Hague: Mouton, 1973), pp. 54–58]. There is here a genuine issue in the philosophy of mind [see John Searle, *Intentionality* (Cambridge: Cambridge University Press, 1983), pp. 1–36], but not, I think, in semiotics.
9. Remember, however, that in this respect there may be no relevant distinction between smoke detectors and the computers that some philosophers of mind do think are sign users.
10. John Ellis, *The Theory of Literary Criticism: A Logical Approach* (Berkeley: University of California Press, 1974), pp. 24–53. Although I endorse Ellis's argument concerning the definition of literature, I cannot accept the conclusions he draws from that premise.
11. For other versions of a transactional model, see Mary Louise Pratt, *Toward a Speech Act Theory of Literary Discourse* (Bloomington: Indiana University Press, 1977), and Siegfried Schmidt, "On a Theoretical Basis for a Rational Science of Literature," *PTL,* 1 (1976), 239–64.
12. One partially useful introduction is Sandor G. J. Hervey, *Semiotic Perspectives* (London: Allen & Unwin, 1982), which includes helpful introductions to Saussure, Peirce, and Charles Morris and an informative discussion of Roland Barthes but which veers off into a specialized, highly technical, and not very useful account of peripheral matters. Also see John Deely, *Introducing Semiotic: Its History and Doctrine* (Bloomington: Indiana University Press, 1982). See also note 3.
13. Thomas Sebeok, ed., *A Perfusion of Signs* (Bloomington: Indiana University Press, 1977), and *Sight, Sound, and Sense* (Bloomington: Indiana University Press, 1978). Also see the two collections edited by Wendy Steiner, *Image and Code,* Michigan Studies in the Humanities

(Ann Arbor: Michigan Slavic Publications, 1981), and *The Sign in Music and Literature* (Austin: University of Texas Press, 1981).

14. Thomas Sebeok, *The Sign and Its Masters* (Austin: University of Texas Press, 1979).
15. Thomas Sebeok, *The Sign of Three: Dupin, Holmes, Peirce* (Bloomington: Indiana University Press, 1983).
16. Among the most useful and widely available are Robert Scholes, *Semiotics and Interpretation* (New Haven: Yale University Press, 1982), and Terence Hawkes, *Structuralism and Semiotics* (Berkeley: University of California Press, 1977).
17. Maria Corti, *Introduction to Literary Semiotics,* Advances in Semiotics, trans. Margherita Bogat and Allen Mandelbaum (Bloomington: Indiana University Press, 1978).
18. Seymour Chatman, *Story and Discourse: Narrative Structure in Fiction and Film* (Ithaca: Cornell University Press, 1978).
19. See Gérard Genette, *Narrative Discourse: An Essay in Method,* trans. Jane E. Lewin (Ithaca: Cornell University Press, 1980); Algirdas J. Greimas, *Semantique Structurale* (Paris: Larousse, 1966); Tzvetan Todorov, *The Poetics of Prose* (Ithaca: Cornell University Press, 1979). Another notable exception is Ann Banfield's *Unspeakable Sentences: Narration and Representation in the Language of Fiction* (Boston: Routledge and Kegan Paul, 1982). Banfield's is a highly technical linguistic analysis of the syntax of certain forms of narrative utterance. Though the linguistics is interesting, Banfield is unable to argue coherently *that* her syntactic evidence bears on the question of how narrative structures are to be described, much less *how* it does so.
20. Cesare Segre, *Structure and Time: Narrative, Poetry, Models,* trans. John Meddeman (Chicago: University of Chicago Press, 1979). A similar book-length study is Christine Brooke-Rose, *A Rhetoric of the Unreal: Studies in Narrative and Structure, Especially of the Fantastic* (Cambridge: Cambridge University Press, 1981).
21. A useful survey of earlier work in "narratology" can be found in Thomas G. Pavel, "Some Remarks on Narrative Grammars," *Poetics,* 8 (1973), 5–30.
22. Louis Hjemslev, *Prologomena to a Theory of Language,* trans. Francis J. Whitfield (Madison: University of Wisconsin Press, 1961), pp. 47–60.
23. Mary Louise Pratt, *Toward a Speech Act Theory of Literary Discourse* (Bloomington: Indiana University Press, 1977), pp. 38–78. See also William Labov, *Language in the Inner City: Studies in the Black English Vernacular* (Philadelphia: University of Pennsylvania Press, 1972), pp. 354–96; Labov and Joshua Waletzky, "Narrative Anal-

ysis: Oral Versions of Personal Experience," in *Essays in Verbal and Visual Arts* (Seattle: University of Washington Press, 1967), pp. 12–45.

24. For a preliminary account of the distinction, see Jerome Bruner, "Narrative and Paradigmatic Modes of Thought," in *Learning and Teaching: The Ways of Knowing,* ed. E. Eisner (Chicago: University of Chicago Press, 1985). For a very limited account of the other major form, which for present purposes we can loosely call expository, see Gregory G. Colomb and Joseph M. Williams, "Perceiving Structure in Professional Prose," in *Writing in Non-Academic Settings,* ed. Lee Odell and Dixie Goswami (New York: Guilford, 1986). For a fuller account see Colomb and Williams, *Discourse Structures* (forthcoming).
25. Barbara Herrnstein Smith, *On the Margins of Discourse: The Relation of Literature to Language* (Chicago: University of Chicago Press, 1978), p. xv.
26. In her sixth chapter, "The Ethics of Interpretation," Smith argues against the position adopted by E. D. Hirsch in *The Aims of Interpretation* (Chicago: University of Chicago Press, 1976). Hirsch argues that readers ought to interpret literary texts precisely as specific and specifiable speech acts. If, as Smith argues, fictiveness and the response to it are purely conventional, what warrant can she have, in a book that includes this debate with a member of her own culture who reads differently (*and* conventionally), for her indefinite, imperialistic "we"?
27. Pratt, *Toward a Speech Act Theory of Literary Discourse* (see note 20).
28. See, for example, Daniel Lucid, ed. and trans., *Soviet Semiotics* (Baltimore: Johns Hopkins University Press, 1977), and "Soviet Semiotics and Criticism: An Anthology," *New Literary History,* 9, no. 2 (1978), 189–411.
29. Boris Uspenski, *A Poetics of Composition: The Structure of the Artistic Text and Typology of a Compositional Form,* trans. Valentina Zavarin and Susan Wittig (Berkeley: University of California Press, 1973).
30. Yuri Lotman, *The Structure of the Artistic Text,* trans. Ronald Vroon (Ann Arbor: University of Michigan Press, 1977). For more recent examples of Uspenski's and Lotman's work, see *The Semiotics of Russian Culture,* ed. Ann Shukman (Ann Arbor: University of Michigan Press, 1984).
31. Yuri Lotman, *Leksii Po Struktural'noi Poetike: Vvedenie Teoriia Stikha* (Providence: Brown University Press, 1968), p. 163.
32. Loosely speaking, an iconic sign is a sign that represents its object by

virtue of its similarity to that object, a sign that represents by reproducing.

33. Vladimir Propp, *Morphology of the Folktale,* 2nd ed., trans. Laurence Scott (Austin: University of Texas Press, 1968).
34. Michael Riffaterre, *Semiotics of Poetry* (Bloomington: Indiana University Press, 1978), and *Text Production [La Production du texte* (1979)], trans. Terese Lyons (New York: Columbia University Press, 1983).
35. Michael Riffaterre, "Describing Poetic Structures: Two Approaches to Baudelaire's '*Les Chats,*'" *Yale French Studies,* 36–37 (1966), 200–242.
36. Riffaterre refers the reader to Peirce, *Papers,* 5.484; but Riffaterre's use of "semiosis" much distorts Peirce's conception.
37. Jakobson," Linguistics and Poetics," p. 95.
38. Jan Mukařovský, "Standard Language and Poetic Language," in *A Prague School Reader*, ed. Paul Garvin (Washington: Georgetown University Press, 1964), pp. 17–30.
39. See Ferdinand de Saussure, *Course in General Linguistics,* trans. Wade Baskin (New York: Philosophical Library, 1959), pp. 65–70.
40. In some, though not all, of his later writings Peirce was less clear about the relationship between interpretants and minds. For a contrast to this statement (of 1897) see the fragment of his third Lowell Lecture of 1903, printed under the title "Degenerate Cases" (*Papers,* 1.521–44). Also see J. Jay Zeman, "Peirce's Theory of Signs" in Sebeok, *A Perfusion of Signs,* pp. 24–28.
41. See Peirce, *Papers,* 1.345–47. A pragmatic semiotics is one that concerns the uses and interpretations of signs. The pragmatics of Peirce's semiotics has no direct connection to his pragmatism.
42. Umberto Eco, *The Role of the Reader* (Bloomington: Indiana University Press, 1979), p. 5.
43. Jacques Derrida, *Of Grammatology,* trans. Gayatri Chakravorty Spivak (Baltimore: Johns Hopkins University Press, 1974), p. 5.
44. W. V. Quine, *Word and Object* (Cambridge: Technology Press of the Massachusetts Institute of Technology, 1960).
45. Until very recently, model readers and other such critical constructs were inevitably male. Whether a model reader inscribed in a text is marked for gender is clearly a relevant consideration, as is the question how that gender differentiation affects actual readers' willingness to accept the invitation that the model reader represents.
46. For a somewhat different attempt to establish a Peircean distinction between signification and communication, see Alain Rey, "Communi-

cation vs. Semiosis: Two Categories of Semiotics," in Sebeok, *Sight, Sound, and Sense,* pp. 98–110.

47. Writing of the triadic relation that serves to determine the representamen, Peirce says: "It follows at once that this relation cannot consist in any actual event that ever can have occurred; for in that case there would be . . . an endless series of events which could actually have occurred, which is absurd. For the same reason the interpretant cannot be a *definite* individual object. The relation must therefore consist in a *power* of the representamen to determine *some* interpretant to bring a representamen of the same object (*Papers,* 1.542).

48. Eco's argument for an intensional semantics is a standard one in that Peirce's dynamic and immediate object are analogous to Frege's reference and sense (see Michael Dummett, *Frege: Philosophy of Language* [Cambridge: Harvard University Press, 1981]). The dynamic object is relatively external to the general network of signs: it "by some means contrives to determine the sign to its representation." The immediate object is wholly internal to the semiotic network: it is "the object as the sign itself represents it, and whose Being is thus dependent upon the Representation of it in the Sign" (Peirce, *Papers,* 4.536).

49. It is worth noting that Eco's only examples of open texts in this discussion are Joyce's *Ulysses* and *Finnegans Wake* and Kafka's *The Trial.*

50. For a very useful sampling of recent work in possible world analysis, see John Woods and Thomas G. Pavel, *Formal Semantics and Literary Theory,* a special issue of *Poetics,* 8 (1979).

51. Wolfgang Iser, *The Act of Reading: A Theory of Aesthetic Response* (Baltimore: Johns Hopkins University Press, 1978), p. 34.

52. Wolfgang Iser, *Implied Reader: Patterns of Communication in Prose Fiction from Bunyan to Beckett* (Baltimore: Johns Hopkins University Press, 1974), p. 274.

53. Iser borrows the term from Roman Ingarden (*The Literary Work of Art: An Investigation on the Borderlines of Ontology, Logic, and Theory of Literature,* trans. George G. Grabowicz [Evanston, Ill.: Northwestern University Press, 1973]), but for Iser's purposes "views" or "perspectives" would be more appropriate (*Act,* 170n).

Notes on Contributors

CAROLYN J. ALLEN is Associate Professor and Chair of Graduate Studies in English at the University of Washington, where she teaches courses in feminist critical theory and twentieth-century writers. She has published on a number of modern writers, including Adrienne Rich, William Gass, John Hawkes, and Djuna Barnes, and on feminist criticism and pedagogy.

RICHARD A. BARNEY is completing his doctoral work at the University of Virginia. He has published a bibliography on deconstructive criticism in a supplement of *Society for Critical Exchange Reports* (1980) and essays in *Genre* and the *James Joyce Quarterly*. He is presently writing on the political and social basis for the emergence of the novel of education in eighteenth-century Britain.

TEMMA F. BERG is Assistant Professor of English at Gettysburg College. She has guest-edited an issue of *Reader: Essays in Reader-Oriented Theory, Criticism, and Pedagogy* on the interrelationship between reader-response and deconstruction, and published essays on the subject of reading in *Studies in the Novel* and *Canadian Review of Comparative Literature*. She is currently editing an anthology of essays about sexual difference, reading, and writing entitled *Engendering the Word: Feminist Essays in Psychosexual Poetics*.

GREGORY COLOMB is Associate Professor of English at the University of Chicago, where he works in eighteenth-century literature, linguistics, and semiotics. He is presently completing a book on the Augustan mock epic and has published articles on textlinguistics and literary theory.

EVA CORREDOR wrote her Ph.D. dissertation on György Lukács (Columbia University, 1975) and has since read numerous papers on sociocritical and contemporary French theory, both in the U.S. and abroad. Some of her work has appeared in *Diacritics, The French Review, The University of Ottawa Quarterly, Philosophy and Literature, Comparative Literature,* and *Sub-Stance*. Her book on the philosophical development of György Lukács's literary criticism will be published in 1987. Another manuscript on the uses of Lukács's theories in contemporary literary analysis is nearing completion. She has taught at Barnard College, Douglass College, and Mills College, and has held visiting professor positions at Reed College and the University of Washington. Since 1983, she has been teaching French and German at the U.S. Naval Academy in Annapolis.

ALBERT DIVVER is Associate Professor of English at the University of Massachusetts, Boston. A specialist in seventeenth-century French and English poetry, he is presently engaged in a study of hermeneutics' confrontation with Marxism and Freudianism.

A. C. GOODSON works on romantic poets, English and German, and is currently completing a book treating Coleridge on language and the formation of Cambridge English. In addition to essays, he has recently published a volume of translations from the French of Robert Marteau, *The Universal Eros of the Alchemists*. He teaches poetry and criticism at Michigan State University.

IRENE HARVEY is Assistant Professor of Philosophy at the Pennsylvania State University. She is the author of numerous articles on contemporary French philosophy, deconstruction, and textual studies, has recently published *Derrida and the Economy of Différance,* and is the founder and director of the Center for Psychoanalytic Studies at the Pennsylvania State University.

JOSEPH NATOLI is English and American Literature Bibliographer at Michigan State University. Besides articles and chapters on textual criticism and literature and psychology, he has published *Twentieth-Century Blake Criticism,* co-authored *Psycho-criticism,* and edited *Psychological Perspectives on Literature.* He is currently editing *Tracing Literary Theory: A Present/Future Dialogic.*

HERMAN RAPAPORT is Associate Professor in English and Comparative Literature at the University of Iowa and specializes in critical theory. He is the author of *Milton and the Postmodern* and has recently published an article on Laurie Anderson in *Theater Journal* and a piece on video art in *The Kremlin Mole.* His work has appeared in several anthologies and he has published in *Diacritics, MLN, Enclitic, Social Text, L'Esprit Createur,* and *Genre.*

DANIEL STEMPEL is Professor Emeritus of English, University of Hawaii, and has published articles on topics ranging from Shakespeare to Beckett in scholarly journals. He is now working on several projects, including further research on William Blake.

BARRIE RUTH STRAUS is an Associate Professor of English at the University of Florida, where she teaches medieval and modern literature, critical theory, and women's studies. She has published on Old and Middle English literature. Her current projects include work on Chaucer and phallocentric discourse, as well as speech act and feminist theory.

Index